1985

WHY
POE DRANK LIQUOR

The Prophetic Poet and the Spirit of the Age

WHY
POE DRANK LIQUOR

Volume II of a Trilogy
by

Marion Montgomery

Sherwood Sugden & Company
PUBLISHERS

1117 Eighth Street, La Salle, Illinois 61301

ISBN 0-89385-026-8

First Edition
Printed in the United States of America. All rights reserved.

Copyright © 1983, Marion Montgomery.

Sherwood Sugden & Company, Publishers
1117 Eighth Street
La Salle, Illinois 61301

This is for

James B. Graves, Jr., and Robert Longshore

ACKNOWLEDGMENTS

This work has been encouraged and supported by many people, some of whom I here name. Through the generosity of the Earhart Foundation I was able to take a year's leave from teaching to write the first version of these volumes, and I especially thank Dr. Anthony Sullivan, Program Officer, and the Directors of that Foundation for their support and for their continuing interest in the work. Professor John C. Stephens, then Dean of the Franklin College of Arts and Sciences, and Professor James Colvert, then Head of the Department of English of the University of Georgia made my leave possible, and my Department has generously continued support of my work. For their early interest in my project, I remember Caroline Gordon, Lewis Simpson, Russell Kirk, and Henry Regnery. Mrs. Elizabeth Crabtree not only typed and retyped the manuscript; she read it with the considerate attention of an editor.

I wish especially to thank Professor Harold McCurdy, who read each volume with a generous, critical interest; I am deeply in his debt. Professors Thomas Stritch of the University of Notre Dame, Robert Hunter West and James Colvert of the University of Georgia have read large sections closely and with the same generous critical concern, and I am more confident of the work in consequence. I express appreciation to many friends at Milledgeville, Georgia, several of them old friends of Flannery O'Connor, all of whom serve her memory with felicity: to the editors of the *Flannery O'Connor Bulletin*, Sarah Gordon and Mary Barbara Tate, to Rosa Lee Walton; to Charles Beard and to the curator of the Flannery O'Connor holdings in the Ina Dillard Russell Library at Georgia College, Gerald Beacham. Mrs. Regina O'Connor has always been gracious in her encouragement, and I also owe particular debt to Mr. James Tate. Many long time friends, students, and colleagues have provided intellectual and spiritual support beyond their knowing, and very often explicit help with the work in hand: Edward Krickel, Warren and Patsy Leamon, Robert and Conn West, Calvin Brown, Steve Maloney, George Martin, Randy Loney, William Provost, Victor and Priscilla Gallerano, John and Miriam Talmadge, Walter Gordon, Simone Vauthier, Kenneth Cribb, James Graves, Bruce Fingerhut, Aileen Parks, Betty Sargent, and many more.

The Kemper Educational and Charitable Fund has given timely assistance in the closing stages of this long labor, and I thank the Directors of that Fund, and especially the Reverend Bruce W. Coggin, for their aid.

I wish also to acknowledge publication of parts of this first volume, often in considerably different form, to the following periodicals: *Critique: Studies in Modern Fiction*; *Denver Quarterly*; *Flannery O'Connor Bulletin*; *Georgia Review*; *Intercollegiate Review*; *Mississippi Quarterly*; *Modern Age*; *Recherches Anglaises et Américaines* (Strasbourg); *Renaissance: A Critical Journal of Letters*; *Southern Review*; *Studies in the Twentieth Century*.

Finally, and above all, I here remember my good wife, Dorothy, who both made possible and tolerated my absence during the project, at the same time having me always in her keeping and nearly always underfoot. She and several of my children may perhaps welcome me back from my retreat under the north eaves of our home in Crawford.

C O N T E N T S

CHAPTER I

MAKING DARKNESS VISIBLE

Through the hundred and thirty years since his death, that homeless spirit, Edgar Allan Poe, has wandered through our literature, tempting poets and novelists and critics to restlessness. The peace of oblivion, which his writings conjure, has not often settled upon those who read him seriously. He stirs response as various as Yvor Winters' angry excommunication and Baudelaire's devoted homage. He inspires work greater than his own, and yet he does not seem superseded. When we critics have had our say, there seems yet more to say on the Question of Poe. Mallarmé's prayer is at least answered—so far. If poets of his generation have failed to honor the dark-spirited American, Poe's granite slab still attracts *poètes maudites*, those "black flights of Blasphemy scattered in the future." And what a variety of bright and dark spirits have been drawn to him. Of course Baudelaire and Mallarmé. But Dostoevsky and Henry James, D. H. Lawrence and T. S. Eliot, Walt Whitman and Allen Tate, Nathanael West and Flannery O'Connor.

But Miss O'Connor acknowledges an unusual attraction she found in Poe, one hardly the center of interest for the French poets, or for any of the selected few I name, except possibly Nathanael West. "Many years ago," she says in an interview in 1962, "I read a volume of 'The Humorous Stories of Edgar Allan Poe,' and I think that started me thinking of a writing career." (In the ten-volume Commemorative Edition of *The Works of Edgar Allan Poe* in the farm home at Andalusia in Milledgeville, the eighth volume is entitled *Tales—Humor*.) She mentions Poe three times in passing in those collected talks, *Mystery and Manners*. Yet the role he plays in her fiction is, I believe, more considerable than the scant mention suggests, and it lies at a deeper level than that of humor. Constance Rourke long ago called our attention to Poe's humor, pointing out that it is a dark humor indeed. "His laughter was of a single order: it was inhuman, and mixed with hysteria. His purpose in the hoaxes was to make his readers absurd, to reduce them to an involuntary imbecility. . . . To this end, in his burlesques and extravaganzas, he showed human traits or lineaments in unbelievable distortion, using the grotesquerie which lies midway between the comic and the terrible." Poe is given to the leg-pull, a bent which he shares with the frontier humorist; but as Rourke suggests, he seems to wish to pull his reader's leg off. There have been few writers with more contempt for the reader than Poe, a point some readers would find correspondence to in Miss O'Connor, though mistakenly. For Poe's spirit is sardonic. There is a strong undercurrent of self-destruction running through his most shocking outrages against the unwary reader.

There is such a marked difference, finally, between his humor and Miss O'Connor's that it will be worth our while to pursue its causes, not only since that pursuit will reflect Miss O'Connor's accomplishment more fully, but because Poe will be seen to stand at a particular remove in English and American letters from those with whom he is usually associated. His is a peculiar vision, and a prophetic one as well. With chilling foresight, it reflects upon one kind of modern mind very much in our critical attention. In that story which was Baudelaire's first encounter with Poe, "The Black Cat," Poe's narrator remarks "the spirit of PERVERSENESS" as one of "the primitive impulses of the human heart—one of the indivisible primary faculties or sentiments which give direction to the character of Man." What is one to make of this "unfathomable longing of the soul *to vex itself*—to offer violence to its own nature." Of this spirit in us "philosophy gives no account." There is, of course, a vast body of philosophical literature addressing itself to the problem of evil, which is what Poe is concerned with; but his strategy here and at other points is to refuse an engagement with the problem on any grounds other than the primitive and psychological. To do otherwise would require an address to man's place in nature such as Poe is unwilling to make, preferring to limit his concern to an appeal to his own heart, as he urges in "The Imp of the Perverse."

One can readily imagine that Miss O'Connor would be much attracted to Poe's wild, if not hysterical, fascination with the perverse, and to the effects in his tales achieved by exaggeration. Of her references to Poe in *Mystery and Manners*, one of them simply numbers Poe among Southern writers of reputation. Another is really aimed at the facile critic who reduces the complexities of such a "Southern" writer as herself to formulae: "Most of us are considered . . . to be unhappy combinations of Poe and Erskine Caldwell." The final comment occurs in a speech to high school English teachers, in which she urges that students first be taught to read rather than have their untrained curiosity entertained by questions that are seemingly peripheral. "Why was Hawthorne melancholy and what made Poe drink liquor and why did Henry James like England better than America?" Her questions suggest antithetic ones applied to her, in each instance, but the questions and the suggested antithetic ones are hardly peripheral to critical concerns unless too early or inordinately pursued. Her references to Poe assumed him so well established as not to require her direct evaluation. She does mention him directly, but there is a neutral politeness in her words. She would certainly recognize in him both a metaphysical and aesthetic position sharply antagonistic to her own. I suggest that her manner of dealing with that opposition lies in her dramatizing Poe's position, one which is more general in our world than any limited restriction to Poe alone, though he is a principal. We may note as well that she is seldom given to extended analytical remarks about any writer such as one finds James and Tate making about Poe. She is cryptic; but, as we discover, her remarks have extensive and profound reflection behind them.

In his *Hawthorne*, Henry James says of Poe that he "had the advantage of being a genius," that "his intelligence was frequently great," but that as a literary critic he rattled the critical scales loudest and "pretended, more than any one else, to conduct the weighing-process on scientific principles." The result is that Poe's criticism "is probably the most complete and exquisite specimen of *provincialism* ever prepared for the edification of man." The passage occurs in the context of his discussion of Hawthorne's allegory, James quoting with approval Poe's judgment in his famous review of *Twice-Told Tales.* Flannery O'Connor marks this passage in her copy of James's book, particularly the quotations from Poe, in such a way as to suggest that she is in agreement with James and with Poe. They share a reservation about "allegory *as* allegory," in Poe's phrase. Given the depths of Hawthorne's concern, the New Englander seems to Miss O'Connor ill-advised to elect allegorical paraphernalia. But it is at this point that she diverges from Poe, since Hawthorne's spiritual concerns are her own.

We shall consider Hawthorne in relation to Miss O'Connor at some length in our final volume. Here, the problem we must explore in Poe is precisely that mode of his art which he rejects as suitable to art, the allegorical. Yvor Winters makes the caustic remark that Poe is himself allegorist, selecting "The City in the Sea" to demonstrate his charge. He concludes from his analysis that the poem has "all the paraphernalia of allegory except the significance"; Poe is "a poet devoid of moral intelligence." (Winters' phrase, incidentally, Miss O'Connor puts into Mr. Shiftlet's mouth at a high point of that shifty character's discourse on the general wickedness of the world; Shiftlet declares himself possessed of "a moral intelligence" with such conviction that he seems "astonished himself at this impossible truth.")

We may add to these objections by James and Winters those of Allen Tate, particularly those found in his "Our Cousin, Mr. Poe," an essay which brings us closer home, closer to the problem of Poe as Southerner, and hence closer to Miss O'Connor's interest in him. Mr. Tate tells us that he too read Poe very early in life, and he testifies to having been deeply and lastingly affected. But he was drawn, not by the humorous Poe as was Miss O'Connor, but by Poe's romantic music—that, plus the bogus intellectualism of *Eureka.* The older Tate winnows Poe's poems down to a precious few. And he sets *Eureka* in a much lower place than his youthful enthusiasm had accorded it. For Tate at last agrees with James: "An enthusiasm for Poe is the mark of a decidedly primitive stage of reflection." James makes his remark in a review of Baudelaire's *Les Fleurs du Mal*, in which he wonders at Baudelaire's enthusiasm, Baudelaire having been hardly primitive at the time of his captivity.

One keeps running into Baudelaire when he attempts to come to terms with Poe, as in James's puzzling over why Baudelaire, the greater poet, sets Poe so high in esteem. Baudelaire, we remember, discovers Poe at the time he is discovering himself an exile in the world. For Baudelaire becomes a poet of that unreal city, Paris, a city inhabited by homeless ghosts, himself the principal among them.[1] Poe, too, he realizes, had hit upon that modern malady, which is not modern of course, though we tend to cling to it as our own, setting ourselves as different from our predecessors. By that act we would rescue the particularity of our age, though we cannot rescue our private individuality. For one may cling to lostness as the Misfit clings to his perverseness—as some evidence at least of one's existence. To conclude one's own age lost is to enjoy in some degree at least the ghost of community that still haunts Western civilization. Since Poe seems such a particular sacrifice to that disease, he readily becomes the dark angel Baudelaire needs. The myth of the *poète maudit* has a necessity about it in a world where the poet can find neither his true Penèlope nor any Beatrice. Still, Baudelaire is concerned with alienation at a spiritual level which is somewhat difficult for the pragmatic mind to understand, that mind more common in English and American circles. Quite possibly that is why we tend to be puzzled by Baudelaire's adulation of Poe.

It is true nevertheless that there is a gap in Baudelaire's understanding of Poe at exactly this point of their similarity, for the darkness each engages is not quite the same darkness. Baudelaire is less content with his alienation than Poe. He finally places a less high value on his own existence than Poe. The anemic, lost soul in that new world dreamed into being since the Enlightenment seems indispensable to Poe. This is to say that Baudelaire does

---

1. "France," he says in a tentative preface to his famous volume, "is passing through a period of vulgarity. Paris, a center radiating universal stupidity. . . . no one would ever have believed France would take to the road of progress at such a rate."

not value himself as the first cause of his own spiritual estate in the degree Poe does. We may see the difference by an indirect suggestion. Eliot is drawn more to Baudelaire than to Poe, but it is not simply because Baudelaire enlarges prosody beyond Poe's advances. It is in part because he finds Baudelaire's exile accompanied by a longing for a home larger and more inclusive of the world than Poe's contentment with the enclosed mind. "Baudeliare," Eliot says, "is essentially Christian." And he goes on to say, "Genuine blasphemy, genuine in spirit and not purely verbal, is the product of a partial belief." Poe's attempted revolt lacks an object against which to revolt, except in so far as he revolts against his own material being and the material being of the world. His revolt is not through the world toward something beyond, then, as with Baudeliare, but is rather a flight inward away from the world, borne by a music he considers of his own making. Thereby Poe expects "to attain to . . . brief and indeterminate glympses" of Beauty, as he says in his "Philosophy of Composition," in that "wild effort" that eschews "that evil genius of mere matter-of-fact" which the intellect must perforce feed upon.[2]

We may see this difference between Poe and Baudelaire more concretely in Baudelaire's theory of correspondences. Poe remarks, in *Marginalia*, that "odours have an altogether peculiar force, in affecting us through association." It is an idea Baudelaire seizes upon. But we notice that, if Baudelaire finds "perfumes as cool as children's flesh, / sweet as oboes, as meadows green and fresh," the recognition thrills him with the promise of their filling "infinite expanses" that are in nature, not in the poet's skull. The association he perceives is through experiences in a nature understood as external to the perception. The fresh green meadows are hardly those we find in Poe's artificial world, "The Island of the Fay." Thus Baudelaire is closer to Wordsworth in a poem like his "Correspondences" than to Poe, though he undoubtedly thought himself closer to Poe. His sense of correspondences implies a relation between the world outside the poet's mind and some higher

---

2. We may recall Saint Thomas's insistence cited in our first volume and hold it as a counter to this Manichean inclination: "A perfect judgment of the mind obtains through turning to sense-objects which are the first principles of our knowledge . . . ." (*Summa Theologiae*, 2a2ae. 173, 3).

region of existence, in which the poet's powers are those of a mediator, so that he seeks the causes of estrangement in more orthodox spiritual realms than does Poe. The very title of *Les Fleurs du Mal* suggests as much, and it is in a preface to that work that he remarks, with more than metaphorical intent, that Satan's cleverest wile in the modern world has been to convince us that he doesn't exist.

Miss O'Connor quotes Baudelaire on the point. And she makes use of it in her fiction. In *The Violent Bear It Away*, for instance, Tarwater engages his friendly enemy, that stranger whom he has such difficulty identifying. In resisting Old Tarwater's pull to Christ, the boy at one point sees the struggle as between Christ and the Devil. "No no no, the stranger said, there ain't no such thing as a devil. I can tell you that from my own self-experience. I know that for a fact. It ain't Jesus or the devil. It's Jesus or *you*." But we dwell in territory held largely by the Devil, Miss O'Connor says, and "we need a sense of evil which sees the devil as a real spirit who must be made to name himself, and not simply name himself as vague evil, but to name himself with his specific personality for every occasion." (This, Miss O'Connor knew, is a necessity the exorcist comes to in formal exorcism.) To talk of perversity as an instinct, as one of "the primitive impulses" or an "unfathomable longing," as Poe has done, is to traffic in vague evil such as one may think to reconcile to the other impulses of one's being by the strategy of leaving it vaguely named. Evil is to Poe something in the human heart which one expects to be explained by the advance of science, as if it might yield finally to the advances of biochemistry, for instance.

Nevertheless, there is in Poe's territory a Devil of which he is aware and against which he on occasion hurls his inkpot. Poe wants to call it Reason, rather than an inclination of the will to malignancy. He sets his own will against it, but the very frustration of his engagement suggests that he is aware of how dependent he is upon that particular Devil. His scathing remarks on the Benthamites and their utilitarianism which flourishes under the auspices of Reason are such that he seems faintly Voegelinean on the point. But one should proceed with caution here. For Poe's objection is not simply to the distortions made by Bentham in his extension of Lockean ideas about the body and its senses, Bentham's perversion of our physical being in the world. It is out of a discomfort with physical being *per se*, however one might name it. This is the point in Poe that D. H. Lawrence recognizes and attacks scathingly, in Poe's own manner. Lawrence finds Poe "rather a scientist than an artist," one who "set up his will against the whole of nature."[3] In part, Poe's dilemma is one Kierkegaard points out when he says that "the poet purchases the power of words . . . at the price of a little secret he is unable to utter . . . a poet is not an apostle, he casts out devils only by the power of the devil." The *rational* is for Poe at times the devil's very country, and he shows us that he can play the devil—as a sort of belittling of the more innocent reader who is the devil's thrall. But he would reject the attempt to categorize him as "romantic" in contrast to "realist." His is a "higher reason." The realist from his own point of view is he who makes the most of the given by his own light. To call Poe's light darkness would elicit his scorn, but it would not therefore be inaccurate.

It may be well at this point to recall something of the perspective we established in our first volume in regard to the problem of "realism" as it becomes a critical term in our literature, and especially in relation to Miss O'Connor's self-characterization as "a realist of distances." That the concern is still an active one at this late date is indicated by a recent interview in the *Times Literary Supplement* with the author of *In the Shadow of Gogol*, Andrei Donatoviet Sinyavsky. (Recalling Poe's "humorous" short stories as influencing her toward a writing career, Miss O'Connor adds, "I'm sure Gogol influenced me.") Sinyavsky distinguishes two stylistic traditions in Russian literature: "One is the realistic tradition which depicted

---

3. G. K. Chesterton, from a perspective quite different from Lawrence's, comes to a similar conclusion. Poe "really was morbid; not because he was poetical, but because he was specially analytical. Even chess was too poetical for him; he disliked chess because it was full of knights and castles, like a poem. He avowedly preferred the black discs of draughts, because they were more like the mere black discs on a diagram. . . . Poetry is sane because it floats easily in an infinite sea; reason seeks to cross the infinite sea, and so make it finite. . . . The poet only asks to get his head into the heavens. It is the logician who seeks to get the heavens into his head." *Orthodoxy*, 17-19. However, one is not a poet or a logician in any pure sense, but some of each, the conscious mind often struggling to emphasize the one propensity over the other.

the world in life size—let us say the tradition of Turgenev, Chekhov, Tolstoy. . . . It is the other category which I find more important—namely Gogol, Leskov, Dostoyevsky and the evolution of their tradition into certain modern manifestations. . . . I call it 'the art of exaggeration' in contrast to the art which presents a life-sized portrayal of reality." One may generalize without violence that the first tradition affects our literature through James; in it he finds Flaubert comfortably associated and to a lesser degree Balzac. But the second tradition of which Sinyavsky speaks is the one most attractive to the "Southern" writer such as Miss O'Connor or Faulkner. In so far as they are interested in the first, their interest is largely technical, as in their dependence upon James in the interest of craftsmanship. In matter, however, they are drawn to the writers of the second tradition, as they are drawn to Hawthorne and Melville for similar reason.

Sinyavsky, in giving an account of his own attraction to the writers of the second tradition, sheds considerable light upon the Southern grotesque. In that writing also (to borrow his words) "people are exaggerated, are caricatures—are unnatural, if you like," but such writing "provides an access to reality from another side . . . in contrast to the direct representation of the world as it is. . . . If realism penetrates far enough into certain ultimate and fundamental matters, it inevitably approaches a condition which in modern terminology is called 'borderline' or 'extreme' situation." That argument is comfortably parallel to Miss O'Connor's words in "Some Aspects of the Grotesque in Southern Literature" and in other places. She, too, sees the "borderline" character. He is man seen as a freak by the realist of the first tradition but seen by Miss O'Connor as not primarily grotesque, for that figure's "fanaticism is a reproach, not merely an eccentricity." He is a figure the writer projects, having first descended "into himself" and into his "region." The beginning of vision lies in that descent, whereby the writer learns "how far he can distort without destroying." The descent is "through the darkness of the familiar into a world where . . . he sees men as if they were trees, but walking." It is from this risking of the writer himself toward vision that Sinyavsky's "borderline" agent of such fiction is derived. Miss O'Connor says in an interview, "The prophet-freaks of Southern literature are not images of the man in the street. They are images of man forced out to meet the extremes of his own nature." The final phrase anchors that character in the reality of the world, through a penetration that (in Sinyavsky's words) goes "far enough into certain ultimate and fundamental matters." In that push against "realism" we have a counter to a push from the other side of realism, as it were, that push which we call *naturalism*, the emphasis of which is the extremity of literalness, naturalism giving rise to another species of the grotesque. The pressure upon "realism" such as one finds in Turgenev, the younger Tolstoy, Flaubert, James—a pressure brought to bear by Dostoevsky, Gogol, Faulkner, O'Connor and similar writers—forces realism to redefine itself in such a way that it takes into account the spiritual dimension of reality. Sinyavsky sees this necessity as a recovery from a perversion of reality in the modern mind which grew as a reaction to medieval thought. He observes in the interview cited that the Middle Ages saw realism as "that current of thought which recognized the reality of the spiritual world, as opposed to nominalism, which limited itself to 'names' (*nomina*). A philosopher or writer who perceived the spiritual nature of things and penetrated to it was regarded as a 'realist.' " Those statements are self-evidently within the climate of thought we see in Richard Weaver's attack upon William of Ockham's Nominalism; they are in Voegelin's attack upon the rise of gnostic thought since the Renaissance, as they are akin to Miss O'Connor's repeated argument that the "realist of distances" is forced to penetrate the surface of reality to spiritual depths in things. A pervasive nominalism is called "realism" in the nineteenth and early twentieth century, leading to the two sharp reactions to the posture of timidity about the nature of reality which settles about "realism": naturalism—an angry realism—and the penetration of surface reality to spiritual dimensions such as we witness in Eliot's tortured journey and in Miss O'Connor. What we are concerned to demonstrate, however, in relation to Poe and his mind, is that Poe's figures, his grotesques that he establishes at a "borderline," are exaggerations out of a vision radically different from Miss O'Connor's conception of the grotesque, since her vision of reality is radically different from Poe's. It is a difference she asserts, through her consideration of the perversion of reason in nominalist thought out of the late Middle Ages and her refocusing of the role of reason in relation to the imagination. For hers is a view of intellectual decay very like Eric Voegelin's. It is significant that Voegelin contributes an essay called "The Gospel and Culture," published in a collection under the title *Jesus and Man's Hope.* A passage early in Voegelin's essay says much about the intellectual world Poe found himself inhabiting and casts that world in a perspective such as we wish to establish, especially as it shows the difficulty of the modern mind in finding a place to stand so that it may raise a world with the Archemedean lever of the Ego. The general influence of Descartes, through Hegel, we have mentioned as developed by Voegelin in its political and social effects in our first volume. Here Voegelin says, in "The Gospel and Culture":

> From the reality of the search [which "moves in the metaxy, as Plato calls it, in the In-Between of poverty and wealth, of human and divine," which is "the life of reason"] as it disintegrates in [Descartes'] *Meditations,* there are set free the three specters which haunt the Western scene to this day. There is, first, the God who has been thrown out of the search and is no longer permitted to answer questions. Living in retirement from the life of reason he has shrivelled into an object of unreasoned faith; and at appropriate intervals he is declared to be dead. There is, second, the *Cogitare* of the Archimedian observer outside the movement [of the life of reason in the In-Between]. It has swollen into the monster of Hegel's Consciousness which has brought forth a God, man, and history of its own; this monster is still engaged in the desperate fight to have its dialectical movement accepted as real in place of the real movement[4] of the search in the In-Between. And finally, there is the man of the *cogito ergo sum:* He has sadly come down in the world, being reduced as he is to the fact and figure of the Sartrean *sum ergo cogito*; the man who could demonstrate not only himself but even the existence of God, has become the man who is condemned to be free and urgently wants to be arrested for editing a Maoist journal.

In suggesting it appropriate to call Poe's vision darkness rather than light, we have in mind most particularly his rejection of the external world and the consequent necessity of his rejecting the

---

4. The conditions of this "real movement" we have seen Voegelin describing in its tensional aspects in a passage quoted in the "Editor's Preface" to *From Enlightenment to Revolution,* page viii, a passage several times used in our first volume. One finds an interesting and helpful parallel to Voegelin's examination of Descartes from a Thomist position in Jacques Maritain's *3 Reformers: Luther, Descartes, Rousseau.* Maritain's examination of Descartes' "sin of angelism" is of importance to our concerns, especially as he shows its culmination in Kant.

spiritual depth in things of that external world. But our experience within the "In-Between" teaches us that the imagination has no choice but to accept the presence of reason, as trying as that necessity may be; for a primal state of innocence such as one dreams might obviate reason is not available to the poet. And the reason draws us again and again to the question of externality, to the inadequacy of "the monster of Hegel's Consciousness" to occupy infinity with the new God, the popular deity which is a disguised figure of man.[5] Poe, willynilly, finds himself numbering an unholy member in his trinity; the will, the imagination, and reason. But reason uses as it is used, and it is this very member in which Poe takes most delight as he turns it upon his reader in that inhuman and hysteric comic mixture that mocks absurdity with the Absurd. An elaborate hoax is a manipulation of reason itself no less than of the reader, though a very temporary manipulation. For trickery must at last yield; it must at last stand revealed as a *seemingly* "reasonable use of the unreasonable," to borrow a phrase from Miss O'Connor.

If Poe takes the rational element of one's awareness as of doubtful aid, it is because he sees in it and with it a hated tie with that world he would deny; for one's reason anchors the mind in the world of nature and in other minds, and so prevents the absolute freedom for which he longs. Thus he has his alienated Orpheus of "The Assignation" protest that the "Proprieties of place, and especially of time, are the bugbears which terrify mankind from the contemplation of the magnificent." This tale, one of Poe's earliest, is supposed to be based on Lord Byron's affair with the Countess Guiccioli and to be deliberately a mockery of the tale of passion currently popular. But one can not escape Poe's inclusion of ideas and arguments with which he is in sympathy and which become dominant in later work. There is no reason to suppose that Poe intends merely satire, though the general frame of the projected

5. There is an ironic suggestiveness of Poe's entrapment in this dilemma evidenced in his precise catalogues of food and drink in the midst of his most fantastic tales, contrasting to the deliberately vague generalities of other details. Such catalogues emphasize quantity and specialty, as if the reflections of a hungry gourmet or thirsty connoisseur. The body, Socrates argued, holds one to the external world, however persuasively one argue that world a shadow of the true reality.

stories for the "Tales of the Folio Club" does seem intended for satiric purposes. As exaggerated as the encounter between the lady love and the narrator's confidant appears in that interview in the "bower of dreams," a reader recognizes an allegorical relationship expanded beyond satiric effect. The narrator is awed by a gathering of the "incongrous" that makes the apartment a studied rebuke of Poe's constant enemies: time and place. In this tale one notes as well the discourse on laughter as a response to what we have come to call the Absurd. For Flannery O'Connor, dangers do not lie in reason *per se*, but in limited human reason which so easily forgets its limit through self-seductions of pride and envy. (Arrogance, let us suggest, suspends the soul in its quest for the object of quest. It is the shadow of pride and envy cast upon reality, so that one looking into the eyes of the arrogant may see the two—pride and envy— shifting the focus, as Dante sees their perfect opposites in Beatrice's eyes on Mount Purgatory. Such dark suspense, while it may be the delight of the dramatist, is the despair of the hopeful soul.) Those bugbears time and space, as dangerous as they may be, are for Miss O'Connor the very bounds within which reason operates to find its limits. On the outer limits one touches upon an encompassing and sustaining mystery, at which point one recognizes that the whole of existence is permeated by that mystery.[6]

And here one travels into that mysterious country which Tarwater tries desperately to avoid; one is set on a journey radical- ly different from Poe's pursuit of deracinated magnificence. Hence, as is revealed by the concreteness of her fiction in contrast to Poe's, O'Connor seeks to locate a point in time and place which defines her protagonist at his outer limits. "The writer," she says, "operates at a peculiar crossroads where time and place and eter-

---

6. The "Archemedian" problem of a "place" to stand in hoisting the world, to which Voegelin speaks in his "The Gospel and Culture" and in a more uneasy vein in *The Ecumenic Age*, is a modern problem not peculiar to the philosopher alone. One sees it disturbing the erstwhile calm waters of modern physics. *Science News* (April 19, 1975) reports on "General Relativity's Catch 22," the subtitle reading, "We need determinism to do physics, but when we get determinism, we find we can't do physics." In a lengthy report on "Weak Interaction in the Universe," (May 31, 1975) the news story reports physics' growing problem with the necessity of a "place" to stand in dealing with the universe more immediately than through Archemedian speculations.

nity somehow meet. His problem is to find that location." And
again, "Fiction is about everything human and we are made of
dust, and if you scorn getting yourself dusty, then you shouldn't
write fiction." It is evident from such remarks that her studied concern for the world adjacent to the senses is not simply in the interest
of an aesthetic concreteness learned of Flaubert and Joyce.

Poe feels particularly cursed by the necessity to operate at the
crossroads where time and space intersect, since that necessity confounds the inner country of his mind. One sees him from the
earliest point in his writing resisting the rational. It is in his images
of passageways, walls, rooms, windows through which imagery he
distorts to vagueness.

He gives the architecture and furniture of his fictional worlds
"a visionary remoteness from the physical," as Richard Wilbur
suggests.[7] Poe's constant struggle then is to establish a province of
the mind, in consequence of which he is conspicuously provincial.
This is the point Lawrence makes when he speaks of "Eleonora" as
a "fantasy," a description of the life of introspection and of the love
"which is begotten by the self in the self, the self-made love." And
similarly Lawrence comments on "William Wilson" as a story in
which "The lustful ego lives on, gradually reducing itself towards
the dust of the infinite." At best, truth is for Poe a secondary concern, its province being "the satisfaction of the intellect." Truth depends upon "precision," which is "absolutely antagonistic to that
Beauty which . . . is the excitement . . . of the soul." One sees Poe at
a mid-station between Donne and the early Eliot: between Donne's
passionate protest against God for the burden of intellect, in Holy
Sonnet 9 ("If Poisonous Minerals"), with its reconciliation through
mercy, and Prufrock's spiritual stagnation, with Prufrocks's choice
of revolt being through a violent displacement of the signification in
language. Poe would bear away the heaven of Beauty by the force of
his imagination, but only as heaven's absolute creator; and even in
his tales he attempts to escape, through visionary poems, that

---

7. Richard Wilbur's analysis of Poe's use of architecture and furniture is very helpful in pursuit of our point. See his "The House of Poe," the Library of Congress Anniversary Lecture,
May 4, 1959, reprinted in *The Recognition of Edgar Allan Poe*, pp. 255-78, and especially pp.
270-72.

entrapment by the world which prose seems to force upon him.
Such one notices is the case in "The Assignation," "The Fall of the
House of Usher," and "Ligeia,"—stories in which poetry figures as
an escape.

Poe's is a provincial mind, then, but not quite that mind as
defined by Allen Tate at about the same time Tate was writing his
"Our Cousin, Mr. Poe." In "The New Provincialism," Tate sets
his term against the regional mind, in a definition which will be
useful to us in discovering both Poe's differences from Tate's conception of provincialism and Poe's peculiar kinship to a particular
kind of modern mind, a mind very much in our literature and
criticism these past fifty years. Tate says:

> Regionalism is . . . limited in space but not in time. The provincial at-
> titude is limited in time but not in space . . . provincialism is that state of
> mind in which regional men lose their origin in the past and its con-
> tinuity into the present, and begin every day as if there had been no
> yesterday. . . . what a difference—and it is a difference between two
> worlds: the provincial world of the present, which sees in material
> welfare and legal justice the whole solution to the human problem: and
> the classical-Christian world, based upon regional consciousness, which
> held that honor, truth, imagination, human dignity, and limited ac-
> quisitiveness, could alone justify a social order however rich and efficient
> it may be . . . . From now on we are committed to seeing *with*, not *through*
> the eye: we, as provincials who do not live anywhere.

Poe's provincialism is more stringent than Tate's characterization of our own, for he maintains the present moment of the mind
not only against place and the past, but against a present moment
of materialist concern as well. He seeks a spot of time, a still point,
a moment of grace, but such a point of awareness as differs widely
from Wordsworth's or Eliot's or Flannery O'Connor's. That point
requires his severing all roots. Whatever he rescues for use from the
world is ultimately in the interest of denying that world. The stage
direction appropriate to his most intense work reads *no time, no place*,
or alternately, *darkness, the void*. But his pursuit only heightens his
dilemma by calling attention to his entrapment by existence, even
the existence of the very awareness itself which pursues its own
obliteration. Though rejecting any concern with "material welfare
and social justice," he is yet trapped by material effects. It is that
entrapment that leads Dostoevski to say of him, in a mixture of

praise and reservation, that Poe "merely supposes the outward possibility of an unnatural event, . . . and this premise once granted, he in all the rest proceeds quite realistically. . . . Not fantastic should he be called but capricious." In contrast to Poe, with whom he is wrongly compared, E. T. A. Hoffman possesses (says Dostoevski) "an ideal full of purity and of inherent human beauty. . . . Poe's fantasticalness, as compared with that, seems strangely 'material'." (Dostoevski seems to be speaking here of psychological realism, of a literalness about the mind's actions.)

Poe's difficulty as the poet of a disembodied world lies in the necessity of using sensation for his emotional effects. He is caught in the contradiction of using pen and paper to bear his denial of the world to the world. The compromise he makes is the use of the particular, but with particularity removed.[8] He is left then with only the vague counters of an abstract universal: *death, beautiful, young, girl, winding, drifting, rising.* In championing "pure poetry," he asserts that a poem's beauty gives one a spiritual experience, and at the same time he is scathing in denouncing the didactic. The poem represents, it would seem, inspired scripture, its effect mesmeric. It is purest when vaguest. "I know that indefiniteness is an element of the true music. . . . Give it an undue decision—imbue it with any

8. William Carlos Williams makes a very curious excursion into Poe in his *In the American Grain.* Poe's "feeling" gives him "the firmness of INSIGHT into the conditions upon which our literature must rest, always the same, a local one . . . but not of sentiment or mood, as not of trees and Indians, but of original fibre . . . ."(229) Again, "Disarmed in his poetry the place itself comes through. This is the New World. . . . surrounded as he was by that world of unreality, a formless 'population'—drifting and feeling—a huge terror possessed him." (233) "The language of his essays is a remarkable HISTORY of the locality he springs from. . . . Unwilling to concede the necessity for any prop to his logical constructions, save the locality upon which originality is rested, he is the diametric opposite of Longfellow—" One begins to see that the "local" and "place" as Williams uses the terms are proved by their absence. Place is a sterile spot in the mind, and hence it has no "aroma" in Poe's words. In a passage which is intended to reflect the originality and nobility in Poe, Williams paraphrases Poe's position in words that remind one inescapably of Haze Motes: "Either the New World must be mine as I will have it, or it is a worthless bog. There can be no concession. His attack was *from the center out.* Either I exist or I do not exist and no amount of pap . . . can dull me to the loss. It was a doctrine anti-American. . . . [Poe's criticism] was a gesture to BE CLEAN." (219-20) "And so one has in Poe 'new locality': it is America, the first great burst through to expression of a re-awakened genius of place." (216) That the position is a very old one needs only those citations from Voegelin or Niemeyer we make in our first volume, or perhaps our recalling Miss O'Connor's Bible salesman who asserts dramatically what Voegelin calls "the Sartrean *sum ergo cogito.*" As for Williams' emphasis upon the primary concern of "originality," we shall find a point for disquisition presently.

very determinate tone—and you deprive it, at once, of its ethereal, its ideal, its intrinsic and essential character." Mallarmé, Poe's purest disciple, speaks of the poet's responsibility in giving "a purer meaning to the words of the tribe" in his "The Tomb of Poe," but it is a task to be accomplished through such vagueness as Poe argues for. It is a concern the opposite of Eliot's in *Little Gidding*, where the poet's task is defined as being "To purify the dialect of the tribe." For Eliot is to be concerned with that decay of words in their signification to which Poe so largely contributed. Dostoevski comments on Poe's "material" dimension, to which he adds that his "unbounded imagination betrays the true American." The remark suggests that there is a very private strain of the pragmatic in Poe, practiced in the service of his private vision. Nevertheless that practice does not make him unique as he wished; the same attitude toward language has been raised to a pragmatic science in advertising and propaganda, of which in this respect Poe is one of the fathers. The pure poetry of the typical television ad aims at an emotional effect, reason being studiously set aside, even though a product is set in Beauty's place.

Miss O'Connor affirms herself repeatedly as that regional mind such as Tate defined, committed to sensation through the particulars of the existing world. She recognizes a graver danger in such provincialism as Poe's than in the temptation to worldliness through sensation, for his error is of that intellectual mode she speaks of as Manichean, the "spirit of the times" which suffers "the much-discussed disjunction between sensibility and belief." The Manichean separation of spirit and matter, which holds material things evil, tried, she says, "to approach the infinite directly without the mediation of matter." It is pretty much the modern spirit in spite of an accompanying lust for the material world, in which lust there is some hope of rescue from gnostic inclination. For the "infinity" to which the modern spirit is given is indeed the gnostic desire for power over being. And sin is reduced in that spirit to the guilt we enjoy so hugely in our lamentations over our affluence, as if the ends of gnostic power have been perverted. *Power over being* is spirit willfully divorced from creation, isolated from the metaxy of reality, the In-Between, so that it may be focused by concentration, like a laser beam, upon the remnant of reality supposed to remain after the divorcement. That remnant is to be transposed by force. But when the act of transposition ceases to be the central attraction of the will (and there are ascetic gnostics out of Enlightenment thought), when the thing transposed becomes the principal object of the will, one has the principal sin to modern gnostic thought. Against that sin the gnostic is as capable of sermonizing as any. He, too, may fulminate against our world's "materialistic" obsession, as the neo-Thomist might preach against excessive love of the world. The central difference, however, is that the gnostic may not allow re-entering the metaxy; that is, he must not allow an attempt at ordinate love of creation, the reincarnation of the particular spirit and the world. For that would be to abandon power over being. That would be to become what Voegelin says the true philosopher must, a lover of being in all its manifestations, not its "director."

"Fiction," says Miss O'Connor, "is so very much an incarnational art." Its affinity is to our spiritual being, which properly seen is also incarnational. A proof of that affinity lies in language itself, a point which the regional writer is less likely to overlook. For "We carry our history and our beliefs and customs and vices and virtues around in our idiom." Idiom echoes an irreducible presence of time and place, to ignore which is to forfeit not only aesthetic control if one is a writer, but spiritual being in any event. It is a point made rather forcefully through Haze Motes's use of his automobile, the Essex serving as his "place to be," which he wishes at once to be no place. It is a world separate from the world which includes it, insofar as his will can make it so. And it is kept separate by constant motion toward something Haze can never quite name, but which is a "place" nevertheless though not to be measured in time by space.

As we have already remarked, Haze too is in pursuit of a nameless perfectibility, and his elevation of the automobile as its symbol reveals the confused state of his quest in a confused world. The popular spirit of the times has rather simplified the quest; Lawrence makes the point in seeing Ben Franklin as the father of this "American" simplification: "The Perfectibility of Man! Ah

heaven, what a dreary theme! The perfectibility of the Ford car!
The perfectibility of which man? I am many men. . . . I am not a
mechanical contrivance." In protesting his freedom from the
mechanistic, Lawrence says pretty much what Miss O'Connor
does in her statement, which she applied to Haze, that "free will
does not mean one will, but many wills conflicting in one man."
Franklin simplifies that thorny problem, as Lawrence says. To
Franklin, "God is the supreme servant of men who want to get on,
to *produce*. Providence. The provider. The heavenly storekeeper.
The everlasting Wanamaker." It is in a world of which Franklin
would approve that Haze must find his way, but he is as restless a
spirit as Lawrence. Nor is he content with a companion version of
Franklin's God, characterized by C. S. Lewis in *The Problem of Pain*:
"We want . . . not so much a Father in Heaven as a grandfather in
heaven—a senile benevolence who, as they say, 'liked to see the
young people enjoying themselves' and whose plan for the universe
was simply that it might be truly said at the end of each day, 'a
good time was had by all.' " It is against such conceptions of God,
among others, that Haze directs his blasphemy, while caught up by
them.

Poe, no less than Haze, is offended by the emerging gods of his
nation, but while Haze chooses to stalk them in the jungle city, Poe
chooses to retreat from encounter into his own version of the
Absolute—into a Disney-land *Fantasia* such as the "Domain of
Arnheim" or into a spiritual masochism, the ego's self-cannibalism
which Lawrence spots in "William Wilson." Poe, of course, is
everywhere aware that his most powerful antagonist is the very
language he must use. We see him struggling with the problem:
truth requires a satisfaction of the intellect through "precision,"
but passion, the "excitement of the heart," requires "a homeliness." And both "homeliness" and "precision" are "absolutely antagonistic to . . . Beauty," the province of poetry. Here he is attempting to remove from language its regional anchors that it may
serve what he calls "the circumscribed Eden of . . . dreams." Spurred on by that "immortal instinct" Beauty, he declares poetry "the
Rhythmical Creation of Beauty," a ritual of sound through which

signification is escaped; such prose poems as "The Island of the Fay" and "The Domain of Arnheim" are attempts to purify the language in this direction. Their manner is the one celebrated by Mallarmé. Friend Ellison, in "The Domain of Arnheim," holds that "the extent of attainable happiness was in proportion to the spirituality of this object," the object being one of "unceasing pursuit," presumably never to be obtained.

The problem is that Poe's object can be rendered in words only from the world's side, a burden particularly heavy upon the medium of prose, so that he can only hint at what he is attempting, namely a conjuring within his inverted vision. He must depend upon a negative allegory and a negative metaphor. For it is not so much that his allegory lacks significance from Poe's point of view, as Winters declares of it, as that his terms attempt to signify something for which no sign will stand. Richard Wilbur's reading of Poe's allegory comes to the border of making just this point without quite completing the argument. Wilbur shows rather convincingly that the common pattern in Poe is to set up an enclosed world in which the awareness, "the dreamer within," is in that "unstable threshold condition called the hypnagogic state." A Roderick Usher for instance "has very nearly dreamt himself free of his physical body." The movement is an inward journey, at the end of which the mind is plunged into "sleep." What I now suggest is that even sleep in Poe is allegorical, that the consummation Poe pursues is, finally, a nonexistence such as Socrates also attempts to characterize in his famous analogy of death to sleep—that one possibility of death's being the nonstate of dreamless sleep. Poe pursues that state with an imagination firmly in the service of a burning will, a point Mallarmé sees far more clearly than does Baudelaire. Darkness and vacuity are Poe's themes also, with the poem understood as performing a kind of alchemy "successful only when death takes place."

How often Poe casts his protagonist, in poem and tale alike, as the sacrificial hero of the imagination, destroyed by a malignant world. That is the closest he can come to witnessing that negative vision he pursues. The opening sentence of "The Assignation" is not only an epitaph for that tale's Orpheus, descended into the world of time and place to rescue his Eurydice; it is as well an epitaph for that "forlorn demon" Poe (as Tate calls him): "Ill-fated and mysterious man!—bewildered in the brilliancy of thine own imagination, and fallen in the flame of thine own youth!" And in this tale, Poe is even so bold as to describe his character with imagistic details that fit his own appearance. As the narrator makes his lament from the world's side, he cautions his listener against any presumption in calling the strange hero's "conduct into question," as if we were justified in deciding that those "visionary hours" he spends locked away from the world in the heart of rich Venice is an occupation which wastes life away. The hero of the imagination, the story suggests, has saved his life beyond physical death, escaping into the region of Beauty's magnificence. We are left puzzling the meaning of life, but Poe seems rather confident that he has found a good man, the evidence of which is that he has just departed, leaving his body as his crumbling victim.

CHAPTER II

THE REASON AS MAKER

To call Poe a provincial does not make him go away, any more than characterizing modern provincialism dispels it from our minds or protects us from its encroachments. And so Tate suggests that we must properly see Poe as cousin and with good grace make room for him at our table. We do so, he says, in "recognition of a relationship, almost of blood, which we must in honor acknowledge: what destroyed him is potentially destructive of us." While I do not suppose that Poe, given the choice, would accept our invitation, it is equally evident that we are hesitant to make it, since it would be to acknowledge the threatening aberrant in our own potential being. One imagines Poe might be shocked to find himself so comfortably placed as a Romantic "loner," below or above the salt according to whether we consider ourselves Classicist or Romantic, those labels we have such difficulty growing beyond. He was certainly scornful of some poets we call Romantic. "I have . . . for the metaphysical poets, *as* poets, the most sovereign contempt," he says in his "Letter to B—." It is a statement rather early in his critical career, and though he is more cautious in subsequent evaluations, the early outburst is inevitable and enduring. He says he means specifically by "metaphysical" Wordsworth and the Lake Poets. One notes in passing a caution necessary in evaluating Poe's superlatives. He is inclined to elevate a poet or cast one into outer darkness according to the enthusiasm of the moment. In "perfect sincerity" he regards Tennyson "as the noblest poet that ever lived," and finds Keats "the sole British poet who has never erred in his themes," since "Beauty is always his aim." But there are reasons fundamental to Poe's developing metaphysics that prevent his adulation of Wordsworth. As late as *Eureka*, he is still careful to set Wordsworth aside.[1]

Coleridge he accepts as he will not Wordsworth. "The wise must bow to the wisdom of such men," he says in his "Letter." And elsewhere he finds Coleridge "the man who, of all writers living or dead, has been most successful in writing the purest of all poems." One can easily see what it is in Coleridge that draws Poe. "Causality and Comparison were most singularly developed" in him, Causality meaning for Poe the use of such reason as builds the parts of a poem into a logical whole. It is significant that Poe does not pick up and use Coleridge's metaphor of the poem as organic, for it is the analytic faculty that Poe elevates, the dominance of which faculty in his thinking leads Lawrence to call Poe "rather a scientist than an artist." Poe is of such a mind as to find Wordsworth's complaint that we "murder to dissect" hardly pleasing. But the author of *The Narrative of Arthur Gordon Pym* and "The City in the Sea" is inevitably drawn to "The Rime of the Ancient Mariner" and to "Kubla Khan," the one a calculated poem, the other drawing on the resources of the subconscious in which Poe is acutely interested before that region is given its modern name. Coleridge's division of that labor with Wordsworth in the composition of *Lyrical Ballads* suits Poe's principles; Wordsworth's do not. By choosing to write on "persons and characters supernatural, or at least romantic," Coleridge is committed to no question of belief in the actual existence of the supernatural realm, though in fact he is more largely committed to that realm than Poe acknowledges. The anchoring of the primary imagination in the "infinite I AM" was not to Coleridge what Poe would understand it to be, the infinite I AM for Poe being rather a commitment to the infinity within his own head.

---

1. Setting Poe in an intellectual milieu reveals many ironies. Wordsworth, for instance, anticipates Poe's "Philosophy of Composition" in the following: "When I compose a poem I generally begin with the most striking and prominent part; and if I feel pleased with my execution of that, I then proceed to fill up the other parts." (Wordsworth, recollected by the Reverend Alexander Dyce, quoted in the *Times Literary Supplement*, January 22, 1971, 102.)

What seems to impress Poe about Coleridge is his intention, in such a poem as "The Rime of the Ancient Mariner," to "transfer from our outward nature a human interest and a semblance of truth, sufficient to procure for these shadows of imagination that willing suspension of disbelief for the moment, which constitutes poetic faith." In other words, the concern is an experimental one, to see whether the poet may deliberately embody psychological states in such a way as to affect the reader's emotion. That is a concern separate from the question of whether any reality is to be ascribed to the furniture of the psychological mind—the images borne by music—or to the relation of those images to a world separate from the awareness in which the poem is held for the moment in solution as the chemist's metaphor might have it—the state of "suspended disbelief." It is that accomplishment in Poe's estimate which makes Coleridge the creator of the "purest of all poems," an accomplishment through calculation, not through inspiration. "For a poem is not the Poetic faculty," says Poe, "but the *means* of exciting it in mankind. Now this means that the metaphysician may discover by analysis of their effects in other cases than his own, without ever conceiving the nature of these effects—thus arriving at a result which the unaided Ideality of his competitor would be utterly unable, except by accident, to attain."[2]

The "Ideality," the "Poetic Sentiment" of a Wordsworth, must depend for its highest effect upon accident, in Poe's reading of it—one supposes primarily the accident of what Miss O'Connor would call the poet's peculiar gift. But to call it a gift commits one to the problem of the *giver*, which Poe avoids. If the analytic control of the poem under construction appeals to Poe, then "The Rime of the Ancient Mariner" is a more conspicuous exemplum of the best poem than is "Tintern Abbey." For Wordsworth is very much concerned with the complexity of the *given*, out of which the poet creates. He is deeply concerned in this poem in particular with the intimate relation between form in the mind and the origin of form in natural objects. He pursues truth about the human situation no

---

2. Eliot, in "Tradition and the Individual Talent," is still heavily under Poe's influence; the principal antagonist there on the question of "feelings" and "emotion" is also William Wordsworth, though named only by allusion.

less than beauty, and he argues the mind firmly and properly anchored in nature through the senses so that mind becomes a "mansion for all lovely form." Thus if we make even a cursory comparison of "The Haunted Palace" or "The City in the Sea" to "Tintern Abbey," we discover the abiding antipathy between Wordsworth and Poe.

In his review of Hawthorne's *Twice-Told Tales* we may see Poe's own position on the creative process as approximating his simplified version of Coleridge. For Poe's argument against allegory is not simply that it is a mode unacceptable as mode, "*as* allegory." Allegory by its very nature must have a significance, and the significance Hawthorne tries to give his work relates to a mystery Poe will have nothing of. Hawthorne can say, with good humor, that he does not himself understand what allegorical meaning attaches to certain of his own stories, which is a way of acknowledging that he depends on "Ideality" more than "Causality" in Poe's terms. Yet it cannot be simply that Poe objects to the mode called allegory, as he insists, since he is so obviously committed to precisely that mode in both his poems and tales. What he rejects in Hawthorne is the absence of the absolute control by the poet's mind of the terms of allegory. "The Minister's Black Veil" is weakened by its "mysticism." To resolve the mystery Poe asserts: "that a crime of dark dye (having reference to the 'young lady'), has been committed, is a point which only minds congenial with that of the author will perceive." Hawthorne's concern in this story, which he subtitles "A Parable," is with the effect upon a self-satisfied congregation of their minister's presumed specific sin, a point that goes unmentioned by Poe. For Poe is not interested in Father Hooper's refusal to reveal his inner heart as an object lesson to a smug complacent congregation. Clearly, Hawthorne is more interested in the ironic consequences of the salvation of many sinners, deliberately making the minister's particular sin ambiguous.

Mystery means for Poe *puzzle* in his evaluation of Hawthorne's "Parable," and the specific crime lacks sufficient clues to allow it to be entered on the register by the rational faculty. Thus his objections are actually more to Hawthorne's conception than to his execution, a conception intrinsically fraught with the dangers of diffusion in its execution. But it is not simply upon aesthetic grounds that Poe objects; the very meaning of "mystery" differs essentially between him and Hawthorne. We may see Poe wrestling with this same difference in his review of Fouqué's *Undine*. He finds "beneath all, . . . a mystic or under current of meaning, of the simplest and most intelligible . . . character." He would deny that it is an allegorical meaning, since he is impressed by how "elaborately managed" an "objectionable under current of meaning" is. But he nevertheless gives us an allegorical reading of circumstance and event as his praise of the work. The work implies the "natural troubles of love." And Undine's disappearance into the river, in consequence of her abuse by her husband, signifies the truth that quarrels between man and wife are seldom or never irremediable unless when taking place in the presence of third parties," the third party here being for Poe the river and not the Lady Bertalda, who is also present in the scene.

Poe's "City in the Sea" or "The Haunted Palace," in spite of objections by such critics as Winters, is surely meant to bear a solvable mystery, though such a dark one as might alarm the innocently complacent. Poe's fallen capital, veiled as a literal head or as a city buried deeper than Homer's Hades, reveals at the moment of its collapse a chaotic disintegration, not a glimpse of Hawthorne's hope of Heaven. In death "No rays from the holy heaven come down" to the city of dissolving images. With such a message, it is perhaps better transferred to a reader through the strictness of the poet's rational "Causality," through which control it may be transmitted directly into the emotions rather than through the reader's own analytic operation upon the details. The deepest meaning is thus reserved to that rarer reader whose mind is "most congenial with that of the author." In his review of Hawthorne, Poe says:

> If wise, the maker of tales has not fashioned his thoughts to accommodate his incidents; but having conceived, with deliberate care, a certain unique or single *effect* to be wrought out, he then invents such incidents—he then combines such events as may best aid him in establishing this preconceived effect.

The effect is primary, calculated, and not one brought about by the poet's emotion out of an experience recollected in tranquility, recollection being Wordsworth's poetic engine rather than Poe's Causality. Reason alone cannot excite imaginative effect for Wordsworth as it can for Poe, and incident is not a matter of invention for him but of actual experience in nature. One sees from this premise in Poe that he very early enunciates the ideal championed by the strictest among the New Critics, though he does not often please them by his poems. He strives to make the tale or poem a self-contained world, being less interested than a John Donne in the work as a macrocosm echoing the large world in such a way as might emphasize unity through correspondences and thus be recognized by a community of minds and reconcile a community mind in the poem. In "The Poetic Principle," Poe insists, against the "heresy of the Didactic," that one must "write a poem simply for the poem's sake," poetry and truth mixing "like oil and water."

The poem as a willed world is an independent creation whose truth is simply itself. That is the position Poe will maintain when pressed, but the truth is, as we have said, that the act of creating the world of the poem is never so potent as to cancel the larger world that in turn contains it, that world in which, in spite of himself, the creator lives and breathes and has his being and from which of necessity he must draw the materials of his poem, including the very words he uses. The phrase in Coleridge's statement about the willing suspension of disbelief to which Poe pays insufficient attention is "for the moment." When he is forced to deal with the problems implicit in that limitation, he must attempt a more systematic metaphysics, of which *Eureka* is the conspicuous document.

CHAPTER III

PROBING
MISERABLE EXISTENCE

We have suggested that it is a Poe-like mind that Miss O'Connor dramatizes as central to her fiction. Let us then consider for a moment Poe's imputed cousin, Hazel Motes. Haze, too, is the "artist-type," an epithet Hoover Shoates appropriates to himself while he charges Haze with being one of those "innerleckchuls." Haze, like Poe, insists upon the powers of his own mind to build a world through which he may deny the world that exists in nature and history and which contains him in the present moment of history by its constant confrontation of his mind through his senses. As with Poe, Haze is tormented by that larger world which is not of his own making, tormented to the point that (as John Crowe Ransom might say) his "capital" threatens to crumble. But there is no suggestion in the resolution of *Wise Blood* that he achieves the realm of the "magnificent" as Poe would have his hero do. The mummy's glass case (mirroring the mummy in himself), his mother's lensless spectacles (through which he observes his image reflected in the mirror in a desolate, decaying rooming house), his encounter with that walking mimic Silas Layfield—all these mock Haze's attempt to deny the larger world by constructing one of his own, a detached world in which he dreams of being self-contained. Such a dream is echoed ironically in Haze's several nightmares of entombment, showing him less in love with easeful death than Poe apparently was. The mockery of the exterior world not only threatens Haze with the terrors of the Absurd world he would make, a world focused inward upon the abyss, but it also threatens with a mercy which is destructive of pride. For Haze is forced toward the realization that, as Jacques Maritain puts it, "all our perishable treasures of being and beauty are besieged on all sides by the immensity and eternity of the One Who Is."

Still, in the beginning it is the Absurd world Haze pursues, and we recall Poe's words, "All that we see or seem/Is but a dream within a dream." Both the self-made world and the larger world dissolve at the edge of madness, which we as auditors are presumed, even by Poe, to see from the "sane" side. It is from a position assuming sanity in the auditor that we see Poe's "red-litten windows" of the eyes which reveal in the swamp of the soul "Vast forms, that move fantastically / To a discordant melody." Haze, we are to understand, gets beyond such nightmare entrapment, though he too goes to the edge of madness, his nightmare dreams of entombment very like tales of horror as they might be written by Poe. His landlady at the end thinks she sees in his darkened eyes a pinpoint of light at the end of a dark tunnel, the dark tunnel being the world as it has formerly been seen by Haze and as it now begins to appear to her. Haze's changed bearing in the world as he moves toward death is meant to suggest that Mrs. Flood is not at this brief moment of light simply a victim of illusion. We have been shown, up to this point, a country of thought not far removed from Poe's, for the *poète maudit* and Miss O'Connor's epithet for Haze, a "Christian *malgre lui*," are blood relations, issuing out of those ideas progressively consuming Western thought since the Renaissance and settling into our thought with the new authority of the Enlightenment. The temple Poe erects in *Eureka* and Haze's Church Without Christ are out of the same intellectual mold, given meaning in the same tradition of thought that feeds Comte, Nietzsche, and the prophets of that recent tradition who still command honor and obedience from the popular spirit of our age.

In order to see Poe's kinship to Haze more fully, it is necessary to "Go high," to "Go deep," as Donald Davidson advises us in "Sanctuary," a poem whose theme crosses ours here. Both Tate and Davidson, we remark, commanded Miss O'Connor's respect, for both they and she look for an accommodation of time and place with the abiding, to discover again our "fathers' paths" as Davidson's poem puts it, paths lost to us by our losing our "origins in the past," in Tate's phrase. Their quest, and the conclusions of the quest, are not Poe's, though each sees in Poe an end possible to them, except for a right will aided by grace. It is with Poe that Davidson begins one of his portraits of modern man, that truly grotesque figure whom Miss O'Connor remarks as unfortunately appearing normal to the modern eye—the man in the gray-flannel suit. "The Nervous Man" borrows its title from Poe and begins with an epigraph from "The Tell-Tale Heart": "True! Nervous—very, very dreadfully nervous I have been and am! But why *will* you say that I am mad?" The poem's first lines:

> He cannot sin, and so cannot betray. Therefore his desk is clean.
> Bloodless the rugs.

There is in Davidson's modern man nothing of Hawthorne's Adam, sin being for Hawthorne and the Puritan New Englander as James says (in a sentence underlined by Miss O'Connor) "the most importunate fact of life." Still, as Davidson argues through most of his work, secularized Puritanism, that grimly intense concern for a world from which sin is removed by denying its existence, leads frighteningly to Poe's nervous man, that provincial mind which reduces human life to the dimensions of "material welfare and legal justice" which must then be escaped by withdrawing into the self. Tate responds to Davidson's poem: "I am struggling with a book on Poe. . . . I am very pleased to see as epigraph to your poem Poe's words. Poe's Nervous Man is our ancestor, however clumsily he creates him." But both men recognize in Hawthorne's concern for the tell-tale heart, in Conrad's look into the heart of darkness, and in the depths of the human heart as Eliot addresses it in the concluding section of *The Waste Land*, a vengeful destruction by spirit when its existence is denied. Both insist upon the necessity of dealing with human failure at a level beyond the naturalistic.

These Fugitive-Agrarians seek to understand Poe as our ancestor, but they are also concerned with the ancestors of Poe, as their essays and poems reveal. Davidson's *Long Street*, Tate's Mediterranean Sonnets and his novel *The Fathers* explore the disjunctions with our past which cause our present wasteland.[1] They resist that encroaching thought which rises with Hulme and Hobbes, a thought that dictates centralization of power. But they also resist that late counter movement of which Poe is harbinger, the refuge of alienation. Both are concerned with the individual's integration in community which makes him an organic part of the body of mankind as it grows into the present moment; they reject the mechanistic reading of man that makes him a machine and an element of a larger machine called society. They resist as well the assumption by the individual that he is necessarily a cancerous cell in the body of the world. That is, they resist both a misreading of Western history in the name of a faceless progress and the rejection of that history—that source of the present world—through an inordinate interest of the private being with itself such as we see in Poe. For Poe is our first "existentialist," as Tate would have it. They resist both these inclinations because these are not the only alternatives, though the growing anxiety of the past hundred years has tended to make it appear so, leading us too easily into false choices. For the choice is not simply to use history in the interest of worldly power as is done in the totalitarian exploitation of egalitarian sentimentality; nor in reaction to such uses to choose that individual randomness which Sartre champions. Sartre is "still running" he says in his *Words*. "For me, speed is measured not so much by the distance covered in a given time as by the power of uprooting." What Tate and Davidson argue for is our regaining a community of spirit, in which the sense of rootedness is restored.

If the chaos in our secular world seemed late in arriving on the American scene, becoming of general concern only since World War II, it was not so in Europe, nor was it really late in our own country. Those Fugitive-Agrarian investigations of the causes of our being uprooted in the twentieth century led them to argue a convergence of antithetic ideas in a war, the first "modern war," whose principles have been perfected in our own century to the verge of annihilation.[2] That war was the one "Between the States,"

1. I have explored this interest at some length in "Bells for John Stewart's Burden," *Georgia Review*, XX, 2 (Summer, 1966), 145-81.
2. See Lytle's *Nathan Bedford Forrest and His Critter Company*, particularly the introduction, and his "A Hero and the Doctrinaires of Defeat," *Georgia Review*, X, 4 (Winter 1956), 453-67.

but the conflict of ideas behind it was not homegrown, but transplanted. Nurtured by victory and grown by intellectual neglect, the triumphant ideas entangle and strangle almost decisively today. Hawthorne found himself divided by that conflict, reflecting "upon a kind of treason in insulating one's self from the universal fear and sorrow." He remarks upon the displaced persons he encounters, recalling the irony that the *Mayflower's* second voyage to the new world brought slaves. Though his piece in the *Atlantic Monthly* in 1862 echoes with patriotism, and protests too much the righteousness of the Union cause, his nationalism rings hollow. We know now some of his private thought in the prelude to the war and as it was getting under way: "We have no country—at least, none in the sense in which an Englishman has a country. . . . The States are too various and too extended to form really one country. New England is quite as large a lump of earth as my heart can really take in." And he will write again at the beginning of the war, "Whatever happens next, I must say that I rejoice that the old Union is smashed. We never were one people, and never really had a country since the Constitution was formed." He, then, must qualify in his own mind for that epithet "traitor" which he ascribes to those Northerners who would choose to set the South adrift. And as if that were not enough, he was faced with pressure from his publisher to drop the dedication of *Our Old Home* to ex-president Pierce, a Southern sympathizer. Hawthorne's concern for "country," for place which the "heart can really take in," suggests that his reading of that bloody struggle was more complex than to take the issue of slavery as the principal cause. One could wish that Hawthorne had himself anticipated Donald Davidson's *Still Yankee, Still Rebel* or *Attack on Leviathan*. But then, surely he does in some important respects, as we shall see when we turn directly to him.

Meanwhile, it is worth our remarking that Hawthorne sees some of the European sources of that conflict, a considerable element of which lies in the shifting of spiritual concerns. Kierkegaard sees them too, in the recent history of Europe, and characterizes the age to come as a "reflective" one, an age in which, with the masses emerging as tyrant, journalism becomes the great enemy. In a world turning to the "intensive development of the state itself" out of the masses, the masses will become the "only tyrant." It is against the masses that Kierkegaard sets himself. "From now on the human race will no longer be led on by prophets and judges but forced back by martyrs, who will run headlong against that human discovery, progress." What Kierkegaard opposes is a false conception of community, exploited for worldly ends, in which conception the individual loses his identity and thereby has no ground in which identity may survive more largely in the world than in contemplation of itself alone. Kierkegaard knew some of Poe's work, a work symptomatic of a new disease of mind in nature. At about the time Poe was conceiving and writing such tales as "The Assignation," "Ligeia" and "The Fall of the House of Usher," Kierkegaard was writing of this new world, in his *Journal*:

> Oct. 7 [1837]. How dreadful it is when everything historical vanishes before a diseased probing of one's own miserable history! Who is to show the middle course between being devoured by one's own reflections, as though one were the only man who ever had existed or ever would exist, and—seeking a worthless consolation in the *commune naufragium* of mankind? That is really what the doctrine of an *ecclesia* should do.

It is what Miss O'Connor finds an intellectual *ecclesia* in fact doing. In the light of history, that coincidence of event and idea upon the moment, she discovers what is revealed of the eternal, and it is this common interest which draws her sympathetically to the Fugitive-Agrarian movement. With the advantage they and like-minded thinkers afforded her, plus the advantage she enjoyed from her own mind's being settled confidently in the Church, she developed as an artist more rapidly than she might otherwise have done had she been forced to their discoveries through her own intellectual wandering. This is not to say, of course, that she did not examine with her own close reason the position she inherited. But it has been often remarked that she began writing seriously at the University of Iowa Writers Workshop under Paul Engle. What is perhaps less well known is that one of her teachers there was Andrew Lytle; or that Caroline Gordon was a significant mentor; or that John Crowe Ransom was attentive and helpful to her. Such help from such minds proved an economy in her discovery of subject and mode, but most importantly it helped assure her of the validity of her particular culture in particularizing and making concrete her vision. In an age so largely moved by vague humanitarian emotions, she discovered that a fiction writer "has to realize that he can't create compassion with compassion, or emotion with emotion, or thought with thought. He has to provide all these things with a body; he has to create a world with weight and extension."

One notices about her prose other than the fiction itself, in contrast to Poe, a confident reading of her place in creation such as allowed her to value herself and creation in general with a steady, direct eye, and hence with a disturbing eye. It is a confidence in her from the beginning, but it is purged of arrogance and pride, though not thereby of forcefulness. Her directness may strike one as haughtiness, especially if one overlooks her concern as a fiction writer with possibilities rather than probabilities, as she says. There is a strong element of certainty in her hope, and a joyfulness, with which she addresses our despair with a certain audacity. It is Sartre and Camus she has particularly in mind when she says that "Alienation was once a diagnosis, but in much of the fiction of our time it has become an ideal." But the remark applies to Poe as well. She completes that remark, in an essay called "The Catholic Writer in the Protestant South," with a characterization of the hero as he has developed in our fiction since the agonies of Poe and Kierkegaard:

> The modern hero is the outsider. His experience is rootless. He can go anywhere. He belongs nowhere. Being alien to nothing, he ends up being alienated from any kind of community based on common tastes and interests. The borders of his country are the sides of his skull.

And in words that speak directly to Poe's rejection of time and place, in defense of the necessity of their use by the poet or story writer, she says "Somewhere is better than nowhere. And traditional manners, however unbalanced, are better than no manners at all."

A concluding note of some importance. Miss O'Connor is interested in Aristotle's *Poetics*, especially as that work affects St. Thomas's view of aesthetics and as she finds Maritain and Gilson among others reflecting on Aristotle in relation to St. Thomas. Her remarks on *possibility* and *probability* in several places in *Mystery and*

Manners signal her awareness. But she is also particularly attracted to a passage in Kierkegaard's *The Sickness unto Death*. In the section called "The Despair of Necessity is Due to the Lack of Possibility," Kierkegaard distinguishes the terms in relation to the writer's new difficulty with an audience born of the Enlightenment:

> Philistinism is spiritlessness . . .; but such spiritlessness is also despair. Philistinism lacks every determinant of spirit and terminates in probability, within which the possible finds its insignificant place. Thus it lacks sufficient possibility to take notice of God. Devoid of imagination, . . . he lives in a certain trivial province of experience as to how things go, what is possible, what usually occurs. Thus the Philistine has lost himself and God. For in order to be aware of oneself and God imagination must enable a man to soar higher than the misty precinct of the probable . . . and, by making possible that which transcends the *quantum satis* of every experience, it must teach him to hope and fear, or to fear and hope. But imagination the Philistine does not possess, he does not want to have it, he abhors it. So here there is no help. And if sometimes reality helps by terrors which transcend the parrot-wisdom of trivial experience, then philistinism despairs—that is, it becomes manifest that it was in despair. It lacks the possibility of faith in order by God's help to be able to deliver itself from certain destruction.

CHAPTER IV

LOOKING FOR THE CHILD IN THE GARDEN

For Miss O'Connor as a Southerner, no less than for Davidson or Tate or Lytle or Gordon, the question is: who are the outsiders' fathers—the fathers of a Camus or Sartre or Poe. For Poe is conspicuously an outsider, one of that tribe of our importunate kin multiplied in the modern world by provincial desires, particularly that desire to border one's country with an outer boundary of the skull. She pursues our question back in time, declaring herself a Thomist in dealing with history, and particularly as she deals with the outsider, of whose tribe Hazel Motes is conspicuous member. The Thomist clue is one we must follow if we are to see the world with her eyes, whatever eyes we choose to see with subsequently. We will discover that Miss O'Connor is, in an important respect, also an outsider, being not only a Southern Catholic but even a close student of Saint Thomas. Just what she means precisely by her Thomism in respect to her vision and its aesthetic demands we defer for the moment. At this point we need only introduce the historical ground upon which Saint Thomas stood at the threshold of the modern world. We may then reflect upon the consequences to our world of that interval of thought about man's place in the world between Thomas's day and our own. In so doing, we shall see as well an affinity of thought between Saint Thomas and the Fugitive-Agrarians. It might be added, we shall see a distinction between the modern world's perversion of creation and the vision which makes Miss O'Connor judge it a perversion. For judge she is, and a severe one. Having already visited in our first volume the development of Western philosophy and science since Thomas, with the aid of such scholars as Voegelin, we shall now look to the effect of that thought on the imaginative writer.

It is a commonplace of literary history that imaginative writers, particularly since the nineteenth century, have attempted to go back to those abandoned grounds in the twelfth and thirteenth centuries and start over, though that journey has been more largely through literary sources than theological ones. It is a journey which has usually stopped short of the medieval world, for Shakespeare and Spenser lie in the poet's path, and just behind them Chaucer. It has been largely through the work of those giants that the poet has looked at the anterior world. The literary critics who follow the poets have tended to do the same, particularly the literary critic in his role as academic teacher. He has done so in the name of his specific discipline, far less inclined than the poet in this respect to range among ideas and disciplines. No lecture summary of Tennyson or Browning or Keats or Wordsworth is complete that does not comment upon their interest in the medieval world, but that interest is commonly simplified as a "Romantic" interest in the long ago and far away, with some reference perhaps to the impact of the Industrial Revolution upon sensibilities. That is, the approach is simplified by confining the concern rather strictly to history's dimensions, however colored by the reflective imagination, so that the spiritual import of their journey is overlooked or underestimated. That is why this particular impulse is so easily burdened with Romanticism as a pejorative term. The rhetorical charge that such an interest wishes to "turn back the clock" is more or less lurking somewhere in the analysis, depending upon the degree to which the critic is infected by the doctrine of Progress.

There is another way to look at our "romantic" inclination to journey into the past: it may be out of a longing for a lost country which is not ultimately to be found in time. That is, it may be a journey more subtle in its promptings than its cultural or social manifestations—the clothings of history—reveal. This is not to say that the impulse to such travel into the past is free of error, that the desire to "turn back the clock" does not for some become a false end out of a valid concern. We know too well our literature's emphasis upon arrested development, the longing for childhood's happy days of simplistic response to the world. And the most significant philosophical development of the past hundred years and principal support of that escape—phenomenology—is devoted to that very pursuit, to a discovery of the child in the garden of the mind, and here we may make a preliminary foray into that philosophical development.

Leo Strauss, in his "Philosophy as Rigorous Science and Political Philosophy" (*Interpretation: A Journal of Political Philosophy*, II, 3) analyzes Husserl's position in opposition to the "reigning naturalism" of the day, that positivistic naturalism seen as necessarily destroying all "objectivity." The analysis shows Husserl's attempt to find a position from which to wield his own Archimedean lever outside the restrictions of naturalism. For, as Strauss says, this naturalism holds that "everything that is is either itself 'physical' or if it is 'psychic' it is a mere dependent variable of the physical, 'in the best case a secondary parallel accompaniment.' As a consequence, naturalism 'naturalizes' both the consciousness and all norms (logical, ethical and so on)." The difficulty lies in giving a full account of existence which will account as well for the accountant. Consequently, Husserl declares, an "adequate theory of knowledge must be based on scientific knowledge of the consciousness as such, for which nature and being are correlates or intended objects that constitute themselves in and through consciousness alone, in pure 'immanence'," so that a "radical clarification of every possible object of consciousness can be the task only of a phenomenology of the consciousness in contradistinction to the naturalistic science of psychic phenomena." Naturalism's psychology is inadequate because it is built on experiences unexamined objectively from the phenomenological position. To the contrary of naturalism's psychology, Husserl asserts that phenomena appear in an "absolute flux," an "eternal flux," but that nature is eternal. Thus it follows the phenomena have no natures, only essences. Therefore phenomenology is the "study of essences and in no way of existence."

For this reason, Strauss argues as he adumbrates Husserl's position, "the study of the life of the mind as practised by the thoughtful historians offers to the philosopher a more original and therefore more fundamental material of inquiry than the study of nature." Yet this pursuit of some system whereby we may recover wisdom, an "exaltation and consolation" (Husserl's words), only delays the final crucial moment. We have seen that moment arrive for Voegelin, in his study of the life of the mind called *Order and History.* It is the moment when objective rational analysis is forced at last to raise questions about itself, as for instance the question why the truth is so tortured by such objectivity as to be forced to "go through the historical torment of imperfect articulation, evasion, skepticism, disbelief, rejection, deformation, and of renaissances, renovations, rediscoveries, rearticulations, and further differentiations?" (*The Ecumenic Age*, 316) Philosophy as a rigorous science, even at its best, is able to account for questions about existence and essence only up to the point at which the wielder of that philosophy must give a self-account, at which point rationality is baffled and forced to bow to the ineffable. Husserl's own position from which he posits an immanent, whole world, is an extrinsic one, to which questions swarm at last in attack. That is the point C. S. Lewis makes in another context when he remarks that Freudianism can account for everything but Freud.

In this line of thought, we may introduce Gabriel Marcel, who confronts the problem intrinsic to knowing reality. We observe that to assert, as Husserl does, that phenomena is "absolute flux" or "eternal flux" and that nature is "eternal" is to have thereby occupied an extrinsic position, from which to categorize; by categorizing, we "denature" that "something" about which we wish to express comprehension, thereby making that "something" (phenomena, flux, nature) an object. Interposed terms defeat the attempt, language itself appearing perverse to the attempt, as Brice Parain argues in *A Metaphysics of Language.* Marcel, following as he does the philosophical developments of Husserl and then Heideg-

ger, encounters this difficulty, his solution resting upon a faith in
our memory and in intimations alive in the mind. Husserl's objection to "naturalism" has led him to a species of supernaturalism
which is such only by its attention to its extrinsic position of comprehension; it does not differ in kind from the position opposed,
since its own concern for "objectivity" is still anchored in the knowing mind. In relation to this self-defeating attempt, we may compare Marcel's position, expressed in his introduction to the English
edition of his *Metaphysical Journal*. In his remarks "empiricism" appears rather closely allied to Husserl's "naturalism," but it also
comes close to including phenomenology. Not only does "pure empiricism" exclude any "idea of direction; under pain of giving the
lie to the definition, it can only drift." Yet "From the standpoint of
immediate existence nothing can be explained or even understood.
Empiricism, in that it is a philosophy of the immediate, is self-
destructive. The immediate is the very reverse of the prinicple of intelligibility." Hence the problem, which is most immediate in
language itself, since by intelligibility *being* is distanced. But
Marcel senses and believes in a calling in being which will not let
the mind rest. How then may mind approach *being*, which Husserl
would exclude from intelligibility by asserting essence as the object
of intelligibility, resident in phenomena, the eternal flux? ". . . to
say 'this is reality' is to *indicate* something; the designation can only
bear on objects. Now the central theme of the *Metaphysical Journal*
and . . . of subsequent works, is precisely the impossibility of thinking of being as object. . . . Being cannot be indicated, it cannot be
shown; it can only be alluded to, a little as some third person now
disappeared is alluded to amongst friends who . . . keep his memory
green. . . . The being in question, who has become active subject,
must magnetise a certain silence charged with memory and affec-
tivity." The solution proposed to the apparently insoluble dilemma
is to bear an *almost* silent witness to reality in so far as the mind
engages the problem—a continuous allusion which by that tactic
keeps the mind engaged in some degree *in* reality and so prevents its
absolute defeat by the extricating act which makes reality an object
and no longer reality. The *Metaphysical Journal* is singular in its title
and continuous, Marcel holding resolutely to an incompleteness of

his witness. All his work is, in this respect, metaphysical journal. If this seems a strategy of trickery practiced on being, it would seem to appear to Marcel as the only way mind may engage reality without violating the relationship.

In the world of getting and spending, as well as in the philosopher's world, or the poet's, there is the same temptation to arrest the moment to our comfortable experience. Consider for instance the products sold us for our leisure, even our children's toys, and we see that a whole panorama of the busy business world is predicated upon our desire for an Eden Regained, rather than for Paradise. A study of the devices and rhetoric of advertising shows our general restlessness conclusively. Even science, a significant segment of it, has taken Bacon's argument that the cultivation of science has as its end the "merit and emolument of life," so that the meritorious life one must protect is the one he may lose in a traffic accident, in those mobile capsules of comfort out of Detroit in which we hide ourselves to gain a sense of immortality. In the latest automobile or aeroplane, we defy both place and time, a dislocation such as Poe ironically anticipates in his "Mellonta Tauta."

Thus our emphasis upon comfort and prosperity, so characteristically American in its centering upon the good things in life. From beer to color television and vitamin-added frozen foods, we pursue a still point whose spiritual ground is largely obscured. We are disturbed in our pursuit, not by a sense of lost spirit, but by fears of carcinogens. And thus the arrested development in the spiritual dimension of being, with water not an element of sacramental dimensions; water is held in a dream of chemical purity against a polluted reality. The pursuit of the country of the self, whether seen as the comfort and prosperity of our material being or that interior journey of alienation within the borders of the skull, is an action of compromise with our "romantic" longings. The one emphasizes the material dimension, the other the dimension of self-awareness; but both are forms of refuge from a deeper call to a lost country in which the world and time are reconciled to each other through a higher reconciliation. Certainly this is so in Miss O'Connor's view of our age. It is a conspicuous characteristic of American life at this moment of our history that *place* is of little significance and that time is an enemy to be avoided, whether by travel at the speed of sound, and perhaps of light, or through longevity out of medical science. And so as a people we have something over two hundred million Displaced Persons drifting from ocean to ocean, in a vague country called the United States of America. In the light of such a view then, Poe appears more nearly American than Southern, an aspect we reflect in calling him an outsider.

An apologist for Miss O'Connor's position, and one whom she read with respect, speaks in a number of places of this "desire for our far-off country." It is a secret desire, C. S. Lewis says, "upon which we take revenge by calling it names—Nostalgia, Romanticism, Adolescence. . . . Our commonest expedient is to call it beauty and behave as if that settled the matter." Thus the journey in history—of the self or of the race. "These things—the beauty, the memory of our own past—are good images of what we really desire; but if they are mistaken for the thing itself they turn into dumb idols, breaking the hearts of their worshippers. For they are not the thing itself." "What is universal," Lewis says of this longing for a lost country, "is not the particular picture, but the arrival of some message, not perfectly intelligible, which wakes this desire and sets men longing for something East or West of the world; something possessed if at all, only in the act of desiring it, and lost so quickly that the craving itself becomes craved." Thus the danger in that journey we undertake to satisfy our longing, for one is tempted to suppose that a half-remembered state of being is what one really wants—that is, to be once more as we were as children. In reality our true but obscured longing is to experience once more that old desire for the lost country which made us believe it existed. This error in our thought we hear Pascal commenting on when he says that "we never are in search of things, but always in search of the search."

Thus at the threshold of the Enlightenment, Pascal engaged the terrors of the void in his agonized spiritual quest, attempting to rescue spirit from those terrors through Christianity even as the new rationalist thought (to which he significantly contributed) was opening the modern mind to the void and reducing Christianity to the status of superstition. In seeing man suspended between the infinitely small (the void) and the infinitely great (the Divine), he found himself divided. Through his own mathematical and scientific work, he contributed to the mechanical theory of nature. He, too, stood opposed to Aristotelianism with his age. The year civil war began in England, he invented the calculating machine, at the age of nineteen. Five years later, he advanced an argument for the existence of the vacuum against received scientific opinion, insisting that "nature has no abhorrence of a vacuum" and "that all the effects that are ascribed to this horror are due to the weight and pressure of air; and that . . . people have deliberately invented the imaginary horror of a vacuum in order to account for them." But the soul's vacuum was altogether another horror, against which reason unaided proved insufficient. Like his successor Kierkegaard, he found the closed system of propositions erected by man's reason insufficient to account for the world. Suspicious of philosophy, he chose skepticism as the most congenial mode because it revealed man's misery in his separation and heightened the threat of the void, thus preparing him through a dark night of the soul for the act of faith and the hope of grace. Like Hawthorne, he insists that "we know truth not only by reason but more so by the heart." (*Pensées*) And so he comes to the spiritual gamble to solve the riddle of the spiritual void. In doing so, he continues to hold our attention as the spiritual Oedipus of the modern world.

To come to rest in history is to come to rest in time, but to magnify the present moment or some future moment in our pursuit of Progress is also to be limited by an alternate version of the same error. What Miss O'Connor finds satisfying in St. Thomas is a vision in which the past, present, and future are reconciled to the timeless. In her journey into history she does not rest on reaching Thomas; she then looks at our own world through his eyes, and with his eyes abides her own present moment joyfully, reconciled to time as ancient as the Greeks or as future as millennium. It is that position, arrived at through a journey in time, that can allow her to say shocking things to those trapped in the world, and in respect to a variety of entrapments. She does so most effectively in her fiction, but elsewhere also. Of a friend's correspondence course in fiction writing, through a text with chapters called "The Story Formula for Writers," "How to Create Characters," "Let's Plot," she remarks, "This form of corruption is costing her twenty-seven dollars." Of Cardinal Spellman's novel, *The Foundling*: "You do have the satisfaction of knowing that if you buy a copy . . . you are helping the orphans to whom the proceeds go; and afterwards you can always use the book as a doorstop. But what you owe yourself here is to know that what you are helping are the orphans and not the standards of Catholic letters in this country." Of that sentimental concern for her physical condition, the intrusion of disseminated lupus: "The disease is of no consequence to my writing, since for that I use my head and not my feet."

If our significant American writers in general seem less inclined to pursue their fathers' paths back in history than their Southern cousins, it is only an appearance, for the myth of lost Eden bears directly upon our general history, America being that new-found land, a potential *New Atlantis* at least. The journey is of acute concern to Hawthorne. It is in James's address to manners as gestures echoing a lost estate. In their writings one finds the concern for some still point in which history is reconciled in a vision larger than that simplified historical perspective out of the eighteenth century which has come to pass as vision rather than history in the current of ideas.[1] The emergence of determinism as a new faith, with its postulate of the god of Progress leading us to the promised land of a future world has left many of our writers uncomfortably reactionary, neither their faith nor reason allowing a commitment in that direction.

A clue to whether a given writer—Hawthorne or James or Poe—goes back to start over as it were or chooses to go forward or inward—more or less on his own—lies in his comfort or discomfort in the presence of that most decisive schism in Western thought which Thomas tried to prevent. We notice often enough some of the spectacular evidence of that schism, without always appreciating the division that lies beneath the dramatic surface. We speak much,

---

1. We have seen something of the evolution of that "vision" through the assistance of Eric Voegelin. One may see a comparable address to the problem in the work of Leo Strauss, particularly in his *Natural Right and History*, in spite of divergences between Voegelin and Strauss.

for instance, of such historical processes as the Reformation or the rise of nationalism in the modern world. The deeper split I mean is that willful separation of faith and reason in Western thought, occurring before the consequences of such a split are forced upon our attention by historical events. Josef Pieper, Jacques Maritain, Etienne Gilson among others have examined the circumstances of that separation, the climax of which each agrees occurred at a particular time in a particular place—at the University of Paris in the late thirteenth century. It is of ironic interest, given the general crisis in higher education in our own day, to note that the opposing forces at Paris came to be centered in the Faculty of Theology on the one hand and the Faculty of Arts on the other. Thomas Aquinas stood between those factions, in a position his own faith and reason brought him to, receiving the fire of either side. For from the point of view of each faction, he seemed aligned with the enemy. It is on that battleground that he writes what he considered a textbook for beginners in theology, the *Summa Theologiae*, intending to prevent a stagnation of mind in the one faction through its tendency to exaggerate faith to the exclusion of reason, and the excesses in the other faction of a reason liberated from faith. A faint echo of Thomas's difficult position we may hear in Miss O'Connor's words from time to time, caught as she is between the faction in her Church which would set art as the handmaid of evangelism (thus misjudging Cardinal Spellman's novel as art), and a faction of the secular world which sees her professed Catholicism as an inevitable limitation of her art, since her religious position is considered an unreasonable one.

One might argue, as Maritain does, that the cause of the modernist malady reflected in the *angst* of our letters lies here in the thirteenth century, where faith and reason stand starkly and openly opposed. Pieper in his reading of that segment of our intellectual past, the Scholastic period, sees it properly concerned from the beginning with establishing a mutual support of the intellect by faith and reason. With the execution of Boethius, he points out, reason took refuge from the secular world in the cloister. With William of Ockham's desertion of the Minorite cloister for the German imperial court, reason turned its back on faith and rejoined the secular world. The tenor of Miss O'Connor's reading of history is that a new secular scholasticism has become progressively pervasive, appropriating to itself that formerly generous term "science." (One remembers that Richard Weaver, independent of Pieper and Maritain, finds in Ockham the beginnings of the modernist thought; he explores the proposition incisively in *Ideas Have Consequences*, a book familiar to Miss O'Connor.)

Such in brief is the ground we may keep profitably in mind in discovering one line of our intellectual descent, so that we may establish degree of kinship between such various minds as Poe's and Miss O'Connor's. That fundamental separation has been rather obscured to us in the interval since St. Thomas, with reason finding antithesis in many places other than faith—in intuition, imagination, instinct. And faith under pressure has rather often taken the position of declaring itself sufficient reason, thinking itself possessed thereby of a knowledge not kindly disposed to questioning. The discomfort between the scientific and poetic mind has a principal cause in that very separation, for with the decline of Faculties of Theology the old battle has been continued within what is generally called Faculties of Arts and Sciences, a vestigial naming of an ideal to be pursued: complete intellectual being. (We remarked earlier that poets have for a long while assumed the role of theologians.) The antipathy between C. P. Snow's "Two Cultures," then, is of considerably more ancient origin than the mid-twentieth century, being so deep-rooted and long-grown as to lead a Nobel Laureate in transplantation biology, Peter B. Medawar, to declare that "The way things are at present, it is simply no good pretending that science and literature represent complementary and mutually sustaining endeavors to reach a common goal," an excessively pessimistic conclusion. One may parade minds in the centuries between Thomas Aquinas and Flannery O'Connor and see them torn within by this schism or see them engaging factions without from a partial position that most poets and most scientists of our own day still find themselves occupying: Kepler, Galileo, Hegel, Descartes, Pascal, Hume, Kant, Kierkegaard, Nietzsche, Heidegger, Sartre. Such minds as these Miss O'Connor reflects upon with the light she finds in Thomism and from the evidence she discovers in her own sharp observation of the world about her. It is such reflection that leads her to preface many of her evaluations of the modern mind with such phrases as "Since the eighteenth century" or "Since the beginning of the Renaissance."

We might, to suggest the combat between science and literature by example, recall two events in the life of scientists, important in their effects upon our world. The one occurs on July 10, 1600, when Kepler set up a *camera obscura* of his own construction in the market place in Gratz "with the twofold result," says Arthur Koestler, "that a thief stole his purse containing thirty florins, while Kepler himself discovered an important new optical law." The other is the experience of Fourier, eating an apple in a city restaurant and being suddenly struck by the disparity in its cost to him and its cost at the orchard, a thought whose researches he says "led to the discovery of the theory of industrial groups in series," and subsequently of the law of universal movement that Newton had missed. But what a poet sees in the two events is an inclusion of the events in larger circumstances, the conjunction of which breeds metaphors of relationship; out of such metaphors come questions about being which the discoveries themselves do not incorporate. The science of the refraction by lenses, proceeding from Kepler's *Dioptrice*, has to do with seeing, but not with sight such as includes the thief and the thirty florins. And in the more signal achievement of Kepler—those laws through which astronomy was divorced from theology and married to physics, as Koestler says—it is of more than casual interest to the poet that the instrument which served witness in the divorce, the telescope, made its first public appearance as an attraction at the Frankfurt fair in 1608. The poet may also be given pause by the fact the Kepler copies erroneous figures for three longitudes of Mars, but later makes errors in simple arithmetic which precisely compensate for the first errors.

Fourier, having eaten his apple, declares: "one may speak of four famous apples: two which have caused disasters—that of Adam and that of Paris,—and two that have rendered service to science,—that of Newton and mine. These four famous apples—do they not deserve a page in history?" Indeed so, replies the poet, and more than a page. And noticing Fourier's pride in his ignorance of history, which he expresses as an accomplishment (he declares his being unread a virtue), the poet feels compelled to add comment on the two apples "that have rendered service to science." For the poet observes the awkwardness of the machine in the garden of the modern world, all the spawn of technocracy. Borrowing whatever aid the philosopher affords in such observations, the poet observes the effects upon science of a narrowing provincialism following Kepler and Newton.

Modern science, and particularly physics, says Jacques Maritain in "God and Science," has come a long way since Newton. It has, "in the realm of the mind, entered a period of deep and fecund trouble and self-examination." If Kepler freed astronomy from theology and wed it to physics, thanks to mathematics, modern science has also "freed itself from philosophy." That action, in Maritain's view, is a principal cause of the new period of troubled thought to the scientific mind. For, "consequently the science of phenomena (particularly physics) became able to pick out among various possible mathematical languages or conceptualizations, which make sense only to the mathematician, and deal with entities existing only within the mind, the one most appropriate to a given set of phenomena." Because the ground of its reason is "in the realm of merely logical or ideal being (*ens rationis*)," says Maritain, modern physics "has its head in a mathematical heaven, populated with various crowds of signs and merely ideal, even not intuitively thinkable entities."

Thus, the Thomist philosopher suggests, the scientist is in that peculiar position once ascribed by science as unacceptable, such as was to be found only (it was thought) in the visionary. For through mathematics, in order that science may come to grips with nature's intelligibility, it must "reach for [nature] in an oblique fashion." The wonder in that necessity is that science begins to restore as a necessity a Prime Being, the realization of which necessity increases among the scientists. Physics finds itself substantiating by that necessity a variant of Aquinas' fifth proof of the existence of God, the proof from order and purposeful governance of the world. For the presumption necessary is of "the intelligibility of nature . . . the very ground of those relational constancies which are the 'laws'. . . . to which science sees phenomena submitted." That the position has implicit in it Thomas Aquinas' fifth proof is reflected by Einstein's remark that "God does not play dice," even if one assume Einstein's *God* merely figurative. Furthermore, says Maritain, there is an additional variant of Thomas's fourth proof in the position taken by modern science. The activity of intellect in the perception and refinement of the laws of nature demonstrates that the intellect itself is "a spiritual activity which can neither proceed from matter nor be self-subsisting, and therefore limitless and all-knowing . . . . it necessarily requires the existence of a Prime, transcendent, and absolutely perfect Intelligence, which is pure Intellection in act and whose being is its very Intellection."

One might conclude from our past four centuries, during which astronomy, physics and companion phenomenal sciences have been increasingly divorced from theology and married to science, that those new relationships are not true marriages but sinful relationships which ignore or flaut a higher law. And one remembers of those earlier witnesses in the divorce that they did not *intend* a separation. Kepler, in being larger than his scientific gifts, intended those gifts to be used to demonstrate the glory of God. In attempting to riddle the secret of the spheres, he introduces the *ideas* of the five regular solids in conjunction with concentric circles to reveal the framework of creation, his own "chain of being." His inspired vision, taken over by his intellect, requires the sun as the center of our immediate universe, requires the postulation of a force in the sun and one in the planet locked in combat (gravity and inertia). Thereby he turned the world inside out, the Prime Mover at the center rather than "beyond" the periphery. The apparent effect of the discoveries he made, built upon by Newton, was to destroy the relation of the transcendent to creation in the thinking of smaller minds. Creation became immanent, an idea upon which subsequent rationalists of the Enlightenment build those intramundane worlds that Pieper, Maritain, Voegelin, Strauss, Niemeyer, Parain, Weaver, and others examine, and show to be distortions of reality.

But it was an apparent effect only. The picture of the world which is emerging now from science, says Maritain, "constitutes a kind of framework or imagery more suited to many positions of a sound philosophy of nature than that which was provided by Newton's science." He lists some of the images in that picture to which the philosopher may address himself in rescuing science from its troubled mind:

> unification of matter and energy, physical indeterminism, a space-time continuum which implies that space and time are not empty pre-existing forms but come into existence with things and through things; gravitational fields which by reason of the curvature of space exempt gravitation from requiring any particular force, and outwit ether and attraction; a cosmos of electrons and stars in which the stars are the heavenly laboratories of elements, a universe which is finite but whose limits cannot be attained, and which dynamically evolves toward higher forms of individuation and concentration.

Such is the prospect increasingly revealed by science, whose composure and implicit meaning require the aid to science not only of the philosopher, but of the poet as well.

Science does not foster an optimistic view of nature, Maritain says. But in the very powers of destruction and death, the violence inherent in matter, there is argument for hope, not only in the accompanying element of nature, its "generosity and progression," but in the very law of degradation that is nature's. It is that law which casts a dark shadow across the future such as leads Robert Heilbroner, in *An Inquiry into the Human Prospect* to a very pessimistic expectation:

> This is a danger that can be glimpsed in our deep consciousness when we take stock of things as they now are: the wish that the drama run its full tragic course, bringing man, like a Greek hero, to the fearful end that he has, however unwittingly, arranged for himself. For it is not only with dismay that Promethean man regards the future. It is also with a kind of anger. . . . let mankind suffer the end it deserves.

In his initial characterization of our desperate moment in history, Heilbroner finds in us a "civilizational malaise [which] reflects the inability of a civilization directed to material improvement . . . to satisfy the human spirit." From that hopeful beginning, however, one is progressively disappointed by the argument, since in it is revealed a very limited and unsatisfactory conception of the "human spirit," a problem prominent in the current spiritual crises in the West. One begins to realize that the pessimism reflected in the conclusion, as desperate as is humanity's situation, is unfounded, resting too simply upon a taking "stock in things" which sees existence only in an intramundane, closed perspective such as Newton's discoveries seemed to force upon the world. What one fears is that in reflections such as Heilbroner's, which very rightly see the dangers of the machine in nature, the reflections are themselves limited by the very antagonistic forces that he would confront. One sees evidence of that limitation in Heilbroner's hope for the future, the possibility of a return to myth:

> Myths have their magic power because they cast on the screen of our imagination, like the figures of heavenly constellations, immense projections of our own hopes and capabilities. We do not know with certainty that humanity will survive, but it is a comfort to know that there exist within us the elements of fortitude and will from which the image of Atlas springs.

If Heilbroner's observations upon the state of mankind's affairs are cause for alarm—and they are—the understanding reflected in his conception of the possibility of hope is even more alarming. For in them he reveals himself much closer to the popular spirit of the times, which is cut off from hope, than to those minds who are preparing the grounds for restoration. Maritain speaks of that popular spirit:

> The impact of the habits of thinking prevalent in an industrial civilization, in which manipulation of the world through science and technique plays the chief part, results in a loss of the sense of being in the minds of a large number of people, who are not scientists but grant rational value to facts and figures only. . . . the people of whom I am speaking have no experience of science, and they believe all the more naively that science is the only valid rational approach to reality, nay more, that science has all the rational answers which human life can need.

In Heilbroner one detects a very limited understanding of the nature of myth as it may be seen from Maritain's, Voegelin's, or Eliade's position. If the Prometheus or Atlas in us has meaning only in its capacity to please us by our will's magic power in projecting a high starry romance, if the world is only that which man makes of his own will in the face of nature, the most tempting and perhaps heroic response to being is its annihilation; not simply out of anger, but with that Odyssean curiosity of testing being to a final end. Man's use of myth, in Heilbroner's version of it, is simply an additional datum of that closed world of nature developed out of Renaissance science through the philosophy of the Enlightenment. The humanity which seems to Heilbroner to be threatened seems a humanity conceived by Comte and subsequently raised to the authority of a secular religion. That this is an apt reading is underlined by his prediction of one of the possibilities lying ahead for industrial man:

> It is possible that a post-industrial society would . . . turn in the direction of many pre-industrial societies—toward the exploration of inner states of experience rather than the outer world of fact and material accomplishment. Tradition and ritual, the pillars of life in virtually all societies other than those of an industrial character, would probably once again assert their ancient claims as the guide to and solace for life. The struggle for individual achievement . . . is likely to give way to the acceptance of communally organized and ordained roles.

These are such words as indeed tempt despair, since in attempting to lead us out of the crisis of our present civilization, they only lead us deeper into the errors that bred the crisis. For in justly attacking a materialistic world as Heilbroner does, he attacks it from its own grounds, in a range of thought limited by the naturalist-positivist dialectic which established the world as materialistic in the first place. The exploration of inner states of experience is precisely the direction taken by philosophy this past hundred years, leading us to the age of alienation. And the suggestion of an either/or ("rather than the outer world of fact") reveals an obliviousness to the necessity of reconciling the inner and outer worlds, the refusal of which task we find so heavily in Poe and which Miss O'Connor sets as the paramount necessity. The conception of *tradition, ritual, myth* as naturalistic developments out of society's condition in nature suggests the prospect of manipulation of community toward naturalistic survival—through accepting "communally organized and ordained roles" in place of the "struggle for individual achievement." The possible presence in social community of a relationship to spirit, whose anagogic level is in the Communion, the sacrificed Body and Blood, is far removed from the thinking here. Also ignored is the possibility that the significance of myth is not that it is a projection from within man out of anxiety or arrogance, but that the supposed "magic power" lies in man's touching a reality beyond the limits of reason and nature. As always, the "acceptance of communally organized and ordained roles" in the place of the "struggle for individual achievement" has lurking in it the necessity of the "director," whose office Condorcet, Robespierre, Comte and the twentieth century political activists—Lenin, Stalin, Hitler and their ilk—would gladly fill.[2]

But even the temptation to despair which one finds in Heilbroner's analysis proves not hopeless. As our philosopher Maritain remarks:

> when its vision of the world is enlightened by science, the intellect which religious faith perfects realizes still better that nature, however good in its own order, does not suffice, and that if the deepest hopes of mankind are not destined to turn to mockery, it is because a God-given energy better than nature is at work in us.

And the confidence of our poet, Miss O'Connor, in revealing the perversions of nature through perverse human nature, recovers to us "the deepest hopes of mankind" in what appears to be the darkest moment of the world. What our philosopher and poet say to the scientist such as Peter Medawar, turning his words upon him, is that, considering "the ways things are at present," it is not only irrational but sinful to pretend that science and literature are *not* complementary and mutually sustaining endeavors to reach a common goal.

---

2. Gabriel Marcel, in *Man Against Mass Society* (1951), examines our abandonment of that mystery of grace in nature which Heilbroner exemplifies. Writing just after World War II, Marcel engages a gnosticism which seems about to reach its final destructive power over nature and the human spirit through dehumanizing techniques. (See particularly the chapters "Techniques of Degradation" and "Technical Progress and Sin.") He is explicitly confronting a hostile French intellectual establishment which refuses to see Marxist reductions of man as fundamentally the same as the Nazi reductions that so recently provided spectacles of horror. He says, for instance, "in the long run all that is not done through Love and for Love must invariably end by being done against Love . . . . There is a road that could be marked out by a succession of sign posts leading from the abortionists to the death camps where torturers rage and sate themselves on a population of defenceless victims." The book, among its other values, is an analytical preface to Solzhenitsyn's *Gulag Archipelago*, Solzhenitsyn's prison experiences of systematic degradation of the human spirit occuring as Marcel writes. Marcel's analysis of the popular spirit of our age, East and West, his adumbration of our "progress" into "mass society," is strikingly pertinent to much we have been and will be arguing. There is a particularly close afinity between his arguments and those in Miss O'Connor's *Mystery and Manners*. ("I'm an old fan of G. Marcel," she writes a friend.)

CHAPTER V

SANDS UPON
THE RED SEA SHORE

We were concerned in our last chapter with that scholastically formalized separation of faith and reason in the late Middle Ages, a separation which Pieper, Maritain, and Gilson center upon as occurring at the University of Paris in the thirteenth century, with Saint Thomas Aquinas attempting to prevent that separation. Our immediate concern is with the seemingly remote effect of that separation as it is revealed in the mind and art of Edgar Allan Poe. Poe is amenable to our concern for several reasons. He is himself very much aware of a growing chaos in Western thought and sets himself in the midst of that chaos as the champion of reason who opposes reason, a partisan of the imagination who at last reduces the imagination in practice to an engine in the service of a rather desperate will. He, like Sartre, would have the imagination fill all consciousness, but he obscures thereby the entangled, embattled relationship of reason and faith in his own consciousness. He is an extraordinary prefiguring of that divided man to come—the alienated man—who threatens to fill the canvass of twentieth-century art. And so Poe is importunate of our attention as we attempt to understand the art and science of our century. Poe is prophetic, standing accusingly at the confluence of intellectual currents a hundred-and-thirty-odd years ago. However wrongheaded his thought, he stands with a courage that calls easy Enlightenment answers into question.

As for that separation of faith and reason, of course one must and does separate the two for the nonce. Or, better said, one does not so much separate as alternately suspend each, while realizing that to acquire that habit of thought in which they merge as complementary is the spiritual labor of a long lifetime, depending upon the amplitude of one's gift and one's courage in the vocation which gift implies. It is certainly a constant struggle to maintain their proper relationship; and it is impossible to separate them absolutely, no matter how strongly the will is tempted to do so. If one insist upon a separation and a choice of one to the exclusion of the other as an act of intellectual principle, he does so only to discover (or have called to his attention by someone else) that the rejected member on which thought moves in tandem with its fellow has turned subversive, even malignant. Most typically, it hides itself in the foundations of the other, when its proper function is open concert with its complement. Once buried, it undergoes a perversion through which it loses its proper object, with the consequence that it undermines its complement. One forgets that the object of faith is not reason, nor of reason faith: their object in concert is truth and goodness and a vision of the unity of truth and goodness. For the scientist or philosopher or poet to deny this end can lead him only, in Eliot's phrase, to a "paralysed force" on the one hand or to a "gesture without motion" on the other. The rejected faculty of the intellect, while it may mean to feed its complement, feeds upon it as pariah. Reason's clandestine presence, in that mind which thinks it sets reason low, reveals itself in shows of reason that are absurd, usually through the trickery of language, as when Mr. Shiftlet talks learnedly about science in "The Life You Save May Be Your Own." Faith's subservient presence in that mind which would set it aside, though it may have some comic dimensions, as in Rayber's inordinate faith in reason in *The Violent Bear It Away*, has more generally given rise to disquieting and disquieted minds that are hardly comfortably comic. Rayber is "afflicted with a peculiar chilling clarity of mind in which he saw himself divided in two—a violent and a rational self." His rational reflection is that the violent self is an inherited insanity, in the clinical sense. That is what he fears. For though his reason is assured, in respect to the idiot child Bishop, that "In a hundred years people may have learned enough to put them to sleep when they're born," his violent self is consumed by an attraction to the child which can only be designated love. His dilemma is that such violence must be declared clinical insanity or he risks being lost to the violence of Heaven's grace and mercy. The most severely rational mind, we discover if we push the point, has a burning faith in its rationality which may produce through its dogma that grotesque we are most in terror of at this juncture of history. It is a terror sprung from a glimpse of what we popularly call the "Scientific Mind," whose ends are dramatized by an Aldous Huxley or an Orwell or in our nightmares of mushroom clouds. Its purveyor may be usefully demonstrated in Peter Medawar, as his mind is exhibited in *Hope of Progress*, in much of which he sounds disconcertingly like Miss O'Connor's Rayber.

"I feel," Medawar says at one point, "that our sense of what is right and just is already beginning to be offended by the idea of taking great exertions to keep alive grossly deformed or monstrous newborn children, particularly if their deformities of body or mind arise from major defects of the genetic apparatus. There are in fact scientific reasons for changing an opinion that might have seemed just and reasonable a hundred years ago." The catch in such pronouncement, which is "addressed to all those who are interested in the history of scientific ideas and the impact of science on society," lies in the definitions of such words as *grossly*, *monstrous*, *major*. For in them Medawar plays theatrical possibilities to disguise the more complicated dimensions of such a proposal as euthanasia. Given our respect for his limited accomplishment as biologist—limited in that the biological should not be granted as the only dimension of existence—he presumes to implant a potentially consuming and subsuming idea on the authority of that limited accomplishment. His error is the one Socrates demonstrates in poets and politicians who, because they know one thing well, assume they know all things well. Who will decide that Bishop is a monstrous work of nature? Rayber does, but he at least is protected from acting upon that decision by his inexplicable love for Bishop— inexplicable to Rayber at least. Following Medawar, a progressive world will no doubt establish committees to make such decisions, thus dissipating conscience in the popular spirit.

It is rather clear that Medawar is one of those provincials Tate has characterized, one who sees evil only in the accidents of nature; history in that view may be corrected by science. It leads Medawar to the curious evaluation of scientists as a group; though his remark is intended to carry humor, it is nevertheless a serious proposal: "Scientists, on the whole, are amiable and well-meaning creatures. There must be very few wicked scientists. There are, however, plenty of wicked philosophers, wicked priests, and wicked politicians." The question is whether Medawar speaks here as scientist, or as a philosopher or a priest or a politician in the service of science. For he does on occasion speak as each. As priest he assures us that "Self-respect as human beings" is the "wider sense [in which] 'sanctity' should be construed." But it is out of such self-respect, we cautiously observe, that Rayber would do away with Bishop. One concludes that wickedness for Medawar is the absence of self-respect. So Christ concludes, but with a conception of the self more profound than Medawar sees. One loves oneself that he may love his neighbor, the proper self-love being prerequisite. Medawar's intellectual honesty does not cover the problem of action and being sufficiently. He does not consider the morally fanatical dimension accreted in some scientific minds by the astounding scientific advances of the past hundred years, an accretion which he reflects in himself when he says "I do not believe that there is any intrinsic limitation upon our ability to answer the questions that belong to the domain of natural knowledge and fall therefore within the agenda of scientific inquiry." He speaks here both for and to the popular spirit of the age, the spirit Maritain characterized in our last chapter. The solution to the population explosion is already in science's hands, Medawar tells us confidently, but "obstructed above all else by the bigotry of some of our fellow men." So, too, was it in the politicians' hands, in Stalin and Hitler, in concert with science. Medawar has just remarked that "however hard we try, we do not and sometimes cannot foresee all the distant consequences of scientific innovation," yet he is not dis-

quieted in his optimism by that admission, as many of his colleagues fortunately are, as for instance the geneticists of the present
generation.[1]

"Scientists are entitled to be proud of their accomplishments.
People who criticize the satisfaction of intellectual ownership are
confusing possessiveness with pride of possession." Not necessarily,
for one can distinguish between avarice and pride and find in both
the elements of sin. It is easy enough to say that James Watson's
failure to be generous to his predecessors in the evolution of the
theory of DNA was "not lack of generosity . . . but stark insen-
sibility." That is a nice distinction, ascribing as a defect a failure
whose possible origins are in the spiritual realm. One wonders how
gross and monstrous such defects must be to warrant correcting
nature's flaws. Defects of sensibility may be precisely the region
where some modern men have come most to suspect science, and
for reasons Medawar himself gives. "A scientist's present thoughts
. . . are the wavefront of a continuous secular process in which the
past does not have a dignified independent existence on its own."
Hence, we add, the scientist's provincialism. Not only the past

---

1. The bigotry which still lingers in the popular spirit of the present moment, despite the effort of social engineers, is no doubt the mainspring in the continuing resistance to abortion. It
is an "unscientific" attitude, we are told, to define the foetus as a *person*. The Center for
Disease Control in Atlanta, Georgia, not long since announced as the second most prevalent
sex disease: *pregnancy*. Thus the scientific approach to life abstracts life and practices what the
"bigots" insist be called murder. A bigot might be encouraged, if he have the stomach, by
Dr. Magsa Denes's *In Necessity and Sorrow: Life and Death in an Abortion Hospital* (Basic Books,
1976). Dr. Denes, a clinical psychologist and practising psychoanalyst, managed an abortion
for herself (her third attempt to commit it), and her book follows her experience with what
we might call "Mothers' Disease." On subsequent visits and interviews with hospital person-
nel, she discovers the sordid and troubling details, along with a general disease among the
minions of mercy which a bigot would call personal guilt. She inspects also the "garbage-
can-filled-graveyard" where life's unnamed refugees wait transport to an incinerator at a
"sister" hospital. There are gems of thought buried in the interviews, as in a doctor's account
of his repeated experience: "All of a sudden at the time of the saline infusion there was a lot
of activity in the uterus. That's not fluid currents. That's obviously the foetus being distressed by swallowing the concentrated salt solution and kicking violently and that's, to all in-
tents and purposes, the death trauma . . . . unfortunately, we are the executioners in this instance," because "somebody had to do it." (Milton remarks, "Necessity, the tyrant's plea.")
Dr. Denes, who insists in her preface that she is a "pro-abortionist," though one with "a bad
secular conscience," remarks also—after her visit to the garbage-can common grave of the
rejected foetuses—that "A death factory is the same everywhere. . . ." The distance between
gas chamber and saline solution begins to dissolve in her discomfort, and that is the "bigot's"
faint ray of hope against the Medawars of our age.

lacks his respect, but future consequences can be ignored. To be on the wavefront, to be the latest thing, makes one most susceptible to pride in the present moment, in a kind of blindness to time which is hardly to be confused with a mystical still point. For what is set aside is reflection upon consequences as well as upon origins of present actions of the mind. In that state of supposedly "scientific thought," one might well be recalled to a reflection upon Gabriel Marcel's insistence that "pure empiricism excludes any idea of direction; under pain of giving the lie to the definition, it can only drift." And it drifts in perilous seas of being. But Medawar's words—"to be proud of accomplishments"—do have about them a sort of future pastness, anticipating a point of arrival beyond the "wavefront" from which pride may exercise itself. In that pride of having made a mark upon the present resides a trading upon a present and future envy; it too is a substitute immortality. Thus Medawar has and eats his cake.

What is wrong here is that the questions within the domain of natural knowledge, as important as they are, are of a decidedly subordinate nature in so far as the demands of one's whole being are concerned. Why cancer? That question may mean, in the panic of the moment, why this strange deadly mutation in me. It is at that level that Flannery O'Connor found herself questioned about the effect of lupus—a form of cancer—upon her writing. But one may also see in that question, as Miss O'Connor does, the encompassing and more terrifying question: why something (even cancer) rather than nothing? One can avoid such questions only if, with Hobbes, one sees life as an endless race out of nowhere to nowhere. And that is the meaning Medawar ultimately sees in life. Strangelove and Frankenstein may be "puppets of Gothic fiction" for him, but they also represent an aspect of mind to be found among scientists who would tempt us to self-righteous crusades in the name of humanity, particularly since the sanctity of life means only personal "self-respect." Alas, these puppets of Gothic fiction are not essentially foreign but akin to Medawar's thought. For in a very disturbing way, Medawar reveals himself one of them. The fearful and dangerous aspect of his mentality, then, is its narrow atheistic base which in its rigorous, scrupulous, honest attention to the province of experimental science forgets the possibility that nature's flaws figure in the scheme of Redemption. It is a base upon which pride builds, but for which no objective measure is admitted. "Scientific reasons for changing an opinion" may be inadequate to the complexity of the questions about which opinion forms as pearls about grains of sand in an artificial culturing. The reduction of life to its biological dimension is inevitably accompanied by an indifference to the claims of life. Excessive violence becomes a way of the new life as a concomitant of the reduction. For to explain life biologically has the illusory effect of seeming to explain life away. When those tensions of mystery are erased or subdued, what is created in the general mind is that vacuum called *ennui*, especially when Promethean risks are dismissed. In that train of manipulations the general mind may be excited to actions of horrendous dimension.

Voegelin recognizes this potential in Helvetius' speculative discovery in the pursuit of the springs of power. There is an uneasiness in *ennui* which may be manipulated in the name of a possible pleasure through the passions. Voegelin says, in his analysis,

> The uneasiness of the ennui, however, is normally no more than the continuous undertone of existence. It will drive a man into activities that will procure minor pleasures, but it is not the strong passion which produces a Lycurgus, a Homer or Milton, a Caesar or Cromwell. At best it may produce a military figure like Charles XII. Nevertheless, its importance should not be underrated. Whether the ennui is the driving force of action is determined in the concrete situation to a considerable extent by the general state of society and the form of government. In times when the great passions are chained by custom or a form of government that is unfavorable to their display, as for instance despotism, the ennui has the field for itself alone and under certain social conditions it may become the *"mobile universel."*

What Voegelin describes here is the condition of the popular spirit of the age both as it is established and manipulated by Enlightenment thought in the interest of power. The culmination of that manipulation he argues persuasively: we have witnessed it in our own century in the temporary successes of totalitarianism under Stalin and his successors and under Hitler. But if *ennui* is, as Voegelin says, "the continuous undertone of existence," we may observe other uses to which we are called beyond passion and through the by-product of aimless passion, power. Poe makes an imaginative use, which dramatizes the spiritual implications of that state of *ennui*, even as he fails to understand the full implication of his drama. Baudelaire, however, recognizes something of that implication, fascinated with Poe's reflections upon his own attraction to the depths of *ennui* and spleen; Eliot later sees in Baudelaire a spiritual implication that enlightens his own intellectual arrest by *ennui*; Flannery O'Connor engages *ennui* with passion in her characters, seeing a deadly spiritual battle whose implications are spiritual life. The Enlightenment, our poets such as these tell us, is not so triumphant in its riddling of life as supposed, and the provincially scientific mind—a Rayber's or a Medawar's—is not finally so impressive in its authority as its words suggest.

Now Medawar is not shy about his intellectual parentage. He is particularly grateful to the Enlightenment for having led man out of its primitive dark age, in which old estate the individual was supposed to possess a soul, its faculty of reason understood as less than dominant and absolutely supreme. Voltaire's is the spirit most congenial to Medawar's own address to a popular audience, as Bacon is to his private address to nature in his role as scientist. Like Voltaire (in Voegelin's summary of Voltaire's position) Medawar also sees humanity as

> a general disposition in man arising out of his biological structure. Negatively, the reasonable attitude is characterized by the absence of immediate spiritual experiences. As a consequence of this deficiency, the symbolic expressions of spiritual experiences become opaque and are misunderstood as depending for their validity on their resistance to rational critique. . . . The spiritual orientation and integration of personality are ignored as a problem, the principles of ethics are severed from their spiritual roots, and the rules of conduct are determined by the standard of social utility.

To point out the deficiency here characterized in Voltaire and make it applicable to Medawar is to be automatically accused of unreason, but it is not unreasonable to be anti-rationalistic—i.e., to be anti-gnostic. In the interest of "humanity" it becomes obligatory to oppose that cultivation of a mobocracy which is practiced in the name of social utility. For utilitarianism (as Poe sees in his opposition to Bentham) unleashes a power which not only appropriates property, as in the Marxist version of the *New Atlantis*, but appropriates life itself into the hands of those Merchants of Light whom Bacon celebrates and Medawar approves. In their line Medawar sees himself standing. "That noblest foundation that ever was upon earth" which one finds in the *New Atlantis* has at its end, says Bacon's spokesman, "the knowledge of causes and the secret motion of things; and the enlarging of the bounds of human empire, to the effecting of all things possible." When gnostic thought is complemented by the power accumulated from the generality of mankind, "all things possible" come to include the solution to such a problem as Bishop represents to Rayber. It may even be raised to the ultimate solution of the gas chamber when gnostic thought consolidates its control of accumulated power in the machinery of government.

It is increasingly difficult to value life in a world we never made when our goal has become to ignore that world and build one we would inhabit, a world built upon our postulation of a divine innocence called self-respect. No wonder we find in the Theatre of the Absurd a reaction to that pretense, as in that deliberate self-binding of the new Prometheus, Ubu, in Alfred Jarry's *Ubu Enchâiné*. But most hopefully, we find in what we may call the New Scholasticism,[2] Particle Physics, an opening of larger questions out of the domain of natural science. The mystery of black holes in astronomy has healthfully disturbing effects upon our scientific complacency as well. And in 1975, 140 gene scientists met at Asilomar on the Monterey Peninsula to consider limitations of their own researches, scientific truth considered by some at least not to be the ultimate concern in the light of unpredictable consequences of such truths. But until one is convinced that the voting population is wiser than some gene scientists and most philosophers, we shall be well advised to hold reservations about the "*piecemeal genetic engineering*" which Medawar champions, rereading our *Brave New World* and *First Circle* against Medawar's beguiling promise of a New Atlantis: "When Thomas Burnet exhorted us to become Adventurers for Another World he meant the next world—but we mean this one."

2. On this point, see my "Eliot and the Particle Physicist," *Eliot's Reflective Journey to the Garden.* (Troy, N. Y.: Whitston Publishing Co., 1978.)

The terror we feel from our imaginative glimpses of such a scientific mind as Medawar's, that mind whose ends are dramatized by Solzhenitsyn or Orwell or Huxley, is a valid response to such aberrants. For scientists, alas, are men, as are poets and philosophers, and they live in the world of fallen nature where their gifts are subject to aberration no less than those of philosophers, priests, or politicians. Stephen Toulmin looks at such problems in the scientist, in his *Foresight and Understanding: an Enquiry into the Aims of Science,* and Thomas S. Kuhn examines them as well. Kuhn, in his *Structure of Scientific Revolutions,* examines a narrow scientific mind whose counterpart we discover in old New England, that Puritan mind which through analogous provincialism burned its witches. If we look at the two together, we may conclude that both minds are gnostic. (We shall examine in detail the Puritan mind as a development within the Enlightenment in our final volume on Hawthorne.) In his explanation of the role of paradigm in relation to scientific revolution, Kuhn says:

> Paradigms may be prior to, more binding, and more complete than any set of rules for research that could be unequivocally abstracted from them. . . . Scientists, it should already be clear, never learn concepts, laws, and theories in the abstract and by themselves. Instead, these intellectual tools are from the start encountered in a historically and pedagogically prior unit that displays them with and through their application.

Paradigms, one might suggest, are received gospels of the scientific mind; science too has its theologians. It has also a fair share of the partially informed among mankind. "Many scientists talk easily and well about the particular individual hypotheses that underlie a concrete piece of current research" but "are little better than laymen at characterizing the established bases of their field, its legitimate problems and methods." That is in consequence of specialization, "That professionalisation which leads, on the one hand, to an immense restriction of the scientist's vision and to a considerable resistance to paradigm change." Such specialists sometimes become the dogmatic fundamentalists of science, of which class Medawar is a more articulate spokesman than most. Current solutions to pragmatic problems are taken as proof of the validity of the current paradigm, as by analogy material success in the world is taken by the Puritan mind as evidence of election, even when one acknowledges as a loophole that one cannot, however hard he tries, "foresee all the distant consequences." It is easy enough to take the received paradigm as inspired, since it seems to work, and maintain it with the blindness of the zealot. That is why, as both Toulmin and Kuhn point out, the modern scientific mind may look with such scorn upon a remote Aristotle as hardly scientific, when what they mean is that he did not know as much as modern science knows; yet the same scornful mind may remain inflexible in the face of contradictions of its more recently received paradigms.

Both Toulmin and Kuhn supply this point with ample illustration, speaking themselves as scientists criticizing some aspects of science. But at the risk of belaboring Medawar, we may let him stand as our principal exhibit. He is, for instance, of that company who see the repudiation of Aristotle in the seventeenth century as a happy victory in the progress toward the New Atlantis. But we should observe as well that in throwing out the philosopher in order to enlarge the intellectual empire of empirical science, the responsibility of inclusiveness of mind such as Aristotle reflects was also discarded. If it could be shown with ease that the *Physics* did not fit Newton, one might not only throw it out but for good measure add the *Metaphysics* too, with its old argument of the necessity of a Prime Mover. If obsolete in his science, then obsolete in his metascience, though Bacon and later followers might use with effect the empirical element of his thought. The pursuit of the New Atlantis, as many as are its wonders visited upon mankind to his comfort and delight, bears with it less happy consequences. Industrialism for instance, and colonialism. For the enlargement of the intellectual empire of empirical science affects decisively what Maritain calls "the republic of natures which is the world," whose varied representatives to the parliament of mind include not only the scientist, but the poet, philosopher, theologian as well. These were threatened with a disenfranchisement of which the dismissal of Aristotle from the tradition of authoritative thought is a key sign. In the dismissal of Saint Thomas's chief authority on the world and on thought lies the dismissal of Thomas as well. Then who shall accompany any new Dante? The alarmed poet, coming to himself in a world whose center had been more radically shifted than by physics's simply moving Ptolemy's prime mover from periphery to center, strikes back—against Voltaire and against Rousseau, the new citizens set out, bound for the New Atlantis:

> The atoms of Democritus
> And Newton's Particles of light
> Are sands upon the Red Sea shore
> Where Israel's tents do shine so bright.

So begins a new struggle toward a metaphysics and a theology to replace those spirited away in the name of Progress, the poet feeling the necessity earlier and perhaps more acutely than philosopher or theologian.

Our concern for the social and political effects of an exhausted environment, the trauma of political confrontations between established powers and nations emerging to a consciousness of materialistic necessities in a competitive world—these underline to us the consequences of that Enlightenment address of man to the "republic of natures which is the world" in which nature became reduced to an exploitable sphere. Nationalism became a necessity in that divorce from Rome which freed many little worlds for expansion through colonialism so that each might be the Rome of some new Augustus. It is that same nationalism which haunts Western civilization in new manifestations out of Africa and South America, its roots more ancient than the nineteenth and early twentieth centuries. (It is another of history's ironies that the Roman Church currently supplies intellectual impetus to that new nationalism rising in some South American countries.) In the struggle that emerges since the Renaissance and which increasingly commands our attention, there runs one constant which we must notice: the loss of that sense of stewardship which is inimical to the dream of Progress. Stewardship is *counter*, given the reality that in the name of Progress fallen man exploits his fallen nature; the transcendent corrective of his excesses had already been ruled out of existence by reason. The gospel of that Progress we hear spoken by Miss O'Connor's prophet of the new church without Christ

> where the blind don't see and the lame don't walk and what's dead stays
> that way . . . . There was no Fall because there was nothing to fall from
> and no Redemption because there was no Fall and no Judgment because
> there wasn't the first two. Nothing matters but that Jesus was a liar. . . .
> If there's no Christ, there's no reason to have a set place. . . . Nobody
> with a good car needs to be justified. . . .

But on the other hand, if the world is the creature of a Divine
Creator, then the concept of the conservation of matter cannot be
merely a bookkeeping operation concerned with present and future
demands, whether they be demands for a good car or a good crop of
wheat or rice. For in the name of humanity, of general survival or
prosperity, we may practice sacrilege and thus content ourselves,
being self-satisfied.

In the history of our own expansion of empire by Bacon's
Merchants of Light, one with difficulty discovers any extension in
the spiritual realm. The growth out of Bacon, through Locke, of
rational humanism (which Medawar reports with a complacent
satisfaction) has grown into "an alternative or even an antidote to
religion." The attempts at a "mystical synthesis between science
and religion, like the Cambridge Neo-Platonism of the mid-
seventeenth century" is ironically amusing to Medawar, as is the
recent parallel of "the writing and cult of Teilhard de Chardin."
But the witness Medawar bears to the Enlightenment makes one
cautious of Baconian intellectual colonialism as having turned very
much into that provincialism which takes a part of the republic of
natures to be the whole.

Indeed it is not so certain that Aristotle was repudiated in the
seventeenth century as Medawar would have it. As Leo Straus
points out, from his considerable acquaintance with Aristotle and
from first-hand knowledge as a student of Husserl and Heidegger,
Heidegger's attempt to "uproot Greek philosophy, especially
Aristotle," resulted rather in "laying bare [Greek philosophy's]
roots," with the result that Aristotle and Plato alike enjoy a new
respect. Voegelin, in the third volume of his *Order and History*, makes
considerable restoration. For the careful examination of that
philosophy by such unsympathetic minds as Heidegger's led, says
Strauss, to "the laying bare of it as it was in itself and not as it had
come to appear in the light of tradition and of modern philosophy."

Not only is Aristotle rescued as philosopher, but both Toulmin and Kuhn demonstrate an Aristotle eminently scientific, when he is seen with an eye appreciative of historical circumstances in the continuity of mind through generations—as seen with the "guidance of sacred tradition," as Josef Pieper would phrase it. With that appreciative eye, one distinguishes between what Aristotle knew and discovered and what we know and discover. Only thereby may one hope to escape provincialism, for one is not necessarily exempt by an excursion into history, as Medawar's partial account of the Enlightenment shows. A provincial scorn of Aristotle after superficial journey may reveal that sophisticated mind which is very like Miss O'Connor's provincial countrywoman, Mrs. Lucynell Crater, who explains to Mr. Shiftlet that the monks of old slept in their coffins because "they wasn't as advanced as we are."

Such thinkers as Kuhn and Toulmin and Voegelin and Miss O'Connor have one important position in common: each has a respect for that continuity of mind in history which prevents our assuming history a dead hand upon the present. They know that if we do not see it as a lively influence upon the present, it will secretly and destructively invade our lives. Josef Pieper summarizes the dangers from the philosopher's position:

> . . . the very moment anyone engaged in philosophizing abandons the guidance of sacred tradition, two things happen to him. The first is that he loses sight of his true subject, the real world and its structure of meaning, and finds himself talking about something entirely different: philosophy or philosophers. The second is that he forfeits his legitimate hold on the sole binding tradition, and must therefore illegitimately and—it must be said—vainly seek support in the mere facts handed down to him, in whatever historical "material" happens to be at his disposal, following the "great thinkers" whom he has encountered more or less by chance, or occupying himself industriously with the opinions of other people.

With appropriate modification, Pieper's words fit the dangers to any mind as it attempts to deal with philosophy or science or literature. The tradition sacred to science includes Aristotle no less than Galileo, though it does not require an unreflecting acceptance of his paradigms—any more than a rigid devotion is dictated by piety to that young mind encountering, by the accident of a particular teacher for instance, the very latest thought. In losing sight of his true subject, the real world and its structure of meaning, because of a fundamentalist act of faith in the current paradigm, one may prevent himself that vision through which paradigms are shifting and modified. That closing in of the mind upon the "literal" word of God as first revealed in the King James Bible, a charge humorously leveled against the backwoods fundamentalist in ridiculing him, surely has its counterpart in that closing of the mind upon the current received paradigm in the particular science. The assumption that the fundamentalist position such as is caricatured in the Scopes Trial as a benighted position carried in that assumption another night of the mind, one which has set aside to its comfort Maritain's observation that

> evolution is less a demonstrated conclusion than a kind of primary concept which has such power in making phenomena decipherable that once expressed it becomes almost impossible for the scientific mind to do without it.

Thus Teilhard, his writing and cult, yields more convincingly to Maritain's sharply critical analysis, in *The Peasant of the Garonne*, than to Medawar's dismissal of it from his narrow perspective. It does so, just as the significance of the Scopes trial is more justly served by Richard Weaver's analysis in *The Ethics of Rhetoric* than by H. L. Mencken's reports to please an age careless of thought and hungry for spectacle, or than those appeals to inherited prejudices through sentimentality that one finds in the dramatization of the trial, *Inherit the Wind*.

Had Plato's good student failed to realize, as required of piety, that minds grow out of minds, he would have remained a little Plato rather than become Aristotle. The student of science or of literature must keep in mind that dictum of Saint Thomas, addressed to that radical activist of his day whom he feared struggling to free reason from all faith, Siger of Brabant: "The purpose of the study of philosophy is not to learn what others have thought, but to learn how the truth of things stands." The distinctions Aristotle and Thomas, Kuhn and Pieper, make may help us recover that organic community of mind which grows to us out of the past, so that we may become a part of the sacred tradition in the future. In doing so, we discover such acts of humility in those larger minds as that of Bernard of Chartres, who before Saint Thomas's day reminded us that "if we see more and further than our predecessors, it is not because of our own clear eyes or tall bodies, but because we are raised on high by their gigantic stature." Newton declares, "If I have been able to see farther, it was because I stood on the shoulders of giants." Someone said, Eliot remarks, that " 'The dead writers are remote from us because we *know* so much more than they did.' Precisely, and they are that which we know."

CHAPTER VI

INFLAMED IMAGINATION AT THE OUTER LIMITS

We have ranged widely, but with high purpose, away from our initial approach to Poe. Let us return to see Poe's mind at work in more detail, we hope with a proper historical piety. We must see in what ways he abandons the guidance of Pieper's "sacred tradition," and what the effect upon his thought. In doing so we may discover in his grotesque figuring of man in nature a parallel to the development of rational humanism such as Medawar champions, though to answer one manifestation of provincialism with another does not finally serve a wholesome purpose, a point perhaps suggested by Miss O'Connor's juxtaposing Enoch Emery's "wise blood" to Haze's.

The false postulate of the Lake School poets is, Poe says, that the end of poetry is "instruction," rather than "happiness." And that instruction has to do with reconciling oneself to the natural world in time, accepting the things of nature as instructors of the consciousness. "Is it sympathy for the sheep you wish to excite?" Poe asks. Very well, "I love sheep from the bottom of my heart." Poe's sarcasm, directed at Wordsworth (a sarcasm which will be echoed in Pound's "olde sheepe Wordsworth"), is not so much out of a repugnance he feels toward Wordsworth's inclination to "instruction" as out of an antipathy he feels for the ordinary and common. The common has no appreciable powers to agitate or inflame his imagination, the transforming energy of which would seem to increase in proportion as it is released from the anchor of nature's commonality. It is the inflamed imagination with which Poe always concerns himself, about whose powers and offices he in his turn is not reluctant to instruct us. And so one must conclude, finally, that it is not against poetry as instruction that he rails, but against the particular lessons of instruction overtly advanced by such poets as Wordsworth. One also has the gnawing suspicion that Poe, even as he expresses his awareness of Coleridge's careful distinctions between the fancy and the imagination, too often transforms that distinction in the interest of an escape through fancy. For Poe, the liberation of the imagination from its ties in nature, which liberation Coleridge characterizes as fancy, will reach the highest power of imagination, through which a supreme fiction becomes accessible.

Poe is concerned in his imaginative energies with the strange and marvelous. But he would make the distinction that his uses are not "romantic" but scientific: his is an interest in the *effect* of the strange and marvelous upon the emotions. Wordsworth is of course also interested in the reader's emotional response, but as a healing action in the reader through the ministry of the poem, so that harmony is restored between the inner and outer worlds. Miss O'Connor argues that the writer must reconcile the inner and outer world through a sense of place, whereby he transcends but does not reject the local. It is a position compatible to Wordsworth's concern, though her position is deeply anchored in Saint Thomas Aquinas, especially in his insistence that "A perfect judgment of the mind obtains through turning to sense-objects which are the first principles of our knowledge. . . ." Wordsworth is to the contrary still heavily held by the ghost of Plato, though a careful reading of "Tintern Abbey" reveals an elevation of the senses at the expense of Platonic elements in the poem. Miss O'Connor argues that, no matter what particular country is the writer's, "it is inside as well as outside. Art requires a delicate adjustment of the inner and outer worlds in such a way that, without changing their nature, they can be seen through each other. To know oneself is to know one's region. It is also to know the world, and it is also, paradoxically, a form of exile from the world." When one finds himself in such "exile," he is lifted up—"caught up," Saint Thomas or Saint

Augustine would say—beyond nature, not cast against nature. In her remarks, be it noted, Miss O'Connor is speaking specifically of the writer as prophet.

To the contrary, Poe's is a clinical interest; the relation of imagination and reason is a paramount concern, and the relation of those powers within the mind to any possible Other is strictly secondary if it can be put even that strongly. The Other is for Poe an unexamined given upon which the willful imagination and, by necessity, reason operate to demonstrate the mind's omnipotence over the Other. Allen Tate points out that the strongest theme in Poe's tales, in "Ligeia" for instance, is the subjection of the physical to the mental, in which triumph the physical is left destroyed and decaying, usually through the symbolic image of the decaying human body. Poe's interest in mesmerism is that of the eager scientist; and in mesmerism he found at least one popular concern which he could use with symbolic intention that might attract some audience to him. Given his philosophical separation from the common, particularly the common mind of the American magazine readership, he had that constant struggle of finding any grounds jointly held by his reader. For metaphor or allegory to have effect requires at least that one's audience hold in common one term or one set of terms, and the popularity of mesmerism promised that commonality. Hawthorne on the other hand sees such a popular concern as spiritually dangerous. It is an unholy tampering with the relation of body and soul, involving consort with dark satanic powers. When Sophia Peabody considers mesmerism as a possible cure for her intolerable headaches, Hawthorne writes her, deeply disturbed:

> I am unwilling that a power should be exercised on thee, of which we know neither the origin nor the consequence, and the phenomena of which seem rather calculated to bewilder us, than teach us any truth about the present or future state of being. . . . Supposing that this power arises from the transfusion of one spirit into another, it seems to me that the sacredness of an individual is violated by it; there would be an intrusion into the holy of holies. . . .

In his *American Note Books* Hawthorne reflects further on such violation, a theme most central to his own fiction:

The Unpardonable Sin might consist in a want of love and reverence for the Human Soul; in consequence of which, the investigator pried into its dark depths, not with a hope or purpose of making it better but from a cold philosophical curiosity. . . . Would not this . . . be the separation of the intellect from the heart?

Would it not, asks Miss O'Connor, be an action in consequence of Manicheanism, in that it elevates the intellect and divorces it from the world? The violations of the human heart, that holy of holies, is practiced by Chillingworth and by Ethan Brand, stark dramatic displays of Hawthorne's fears.

But just such intrusion is Poe's precise concern, he being without fear of the Devil. Whatever the danger, Poe is fascinated by the triumph of one spirit over another, or with the triumph of two spirits over their mortal worldly entanglement. The "transfusion of one spirit into another" is the theme of "The Fall of the House of Usher" and "Ligeia," but there is no sense in Poe of a profanation of the sacred, for the simple reason that the power of the individual mind is the only thing sacred in his philosophy. The power Poe worships is the one he describes, in "The Poetic Principle," as "Love . . . the true, the divine Eros—the Uranian, as distinguished from the Dionaean Venus," and that love constitutes "the purest and truest of all poetical themes." As we see that love celebrated by Poe, we may have the uncomfortable feeling that there burns in him an intense, even insane, longing for the lost country of love. D. H. Lawrence is surely right in seeing Poe's concept of power as fueled by an inordinate love, whose effect, one adds, is that of vengeance. For Poe seems unwilling to leave the vengeance of Love to the Lord, as we are cautioned by scripture to do. Thus it is that one has that insatiable vampire of love raging through the tales. As Lawrence points out, Poe's description of Liegia's eyes, elements of which description are to Lawrence "blarney," largely "sounds like an anatomist anatomizing a cat." But the vampire's hunger behind that anatomizing is for a life which escapes the operation by the very act of performing it.

The entryway for that possession is, as it must largely be in fiction as in our natural life, through the eyes. But if one look closely, one discovers in Poe only the shell of eyes, the opaqueness of the mesmerized or anaesthetized patient, not the moving depths of any variable soul. Because in his fiction the eyes are so empty, Poe must make much of them with rhetorical flourishes, the prose becoming melodramatic. Except for the weak escape into a term like "light," Ligeia's eyes are empty, like those windows as first seen on approaching the House of Usher. The external features are mechanically presented, without that intense struggle and tension Miss O'Connor manages to suggest in Old Tarwater's loving struggle of spirit with the world. The old man's "silver protruding eyes" at the moment of his death "looked like two fish straining to get out of a net of red threads." Bishop's eyes are "grey, like the old man's but clear, as if the other side of them went down and down into two pools of light." They are rather neutral in comparison to the eyes of other characters as presented to us, for Bishop functions in Miss O'Connor's novel as a medium of grace, as the "Beatrice" of that fiction in whose eyes much of the gazer is seen, and seen changing. Indeed, the eye is a principal controlling image in *The Violent Bear It Away*, presented with a range of suggested significance from the darkness of Rayber's worldly entrapment to the vision of all nature afire with God's grandeur, as Old Tarwater sees. For "the eye," says Miss O'Connor, "is an organ that eventually involves the whole personality." The decisive word here is *whole*, the conception of which in her thinking involves that growth in vision so that one's vision includes the world in its celebration.

The risk of that insatiable Uranian love in Poe is a decay in the perception of the outer world, but that very destruction seems to certify the primacy of the individual will. What is celebrated beneath the surface horror of Poe's work is an absolute supremacy of the intellect, the center in whose power it lies to exclude the outer world. Thus Poe, as Allen Tate says, "is not interested in anything that is alive. . . . The description of Ligeia's head is that of a dead woman's." By *life*, Mr. Tate means the mutual presence of body and soul. But Ligeia's head is something less even than a dead woman's; in it the fire of intellect resides, but the head is only a statue of flesh. Poe attempts to accomplish an effect through horror in his tale, and through that effect establish an idea which John Crowe Ransom attacks in his wittily contorted "Painted Head." Of body and head, heart and mind, one may say "So hardly one they terribly are two" when the artist "By dark severance [of] the apparition head" teaches it "to play truant from the body bush," thus "tickling the instinct of heads to be/Absolute." The artist, "unhousing by abstraction" performs a "capital irony," violating that first principle of Ransom's poetic creed: "Beauty is of body." It is a creed older than Kant. It is in St. Thomas's arguments on beauty as revealed in those terrible beauties of the Incarnation which require one's valuing the body of the world. Ransom's poem, though it addresses a medallion explicitly, is aimed at the sort of Manichean violation of the world that is in Poe. (Because of elements in Ransom's poem that seem to echo Wallace Stevens, one suspects Ransom of addressing the old liberty head dime as emblem; it is said to carry a portrait of Stevens's wife.)

We are struck by horror in a tale like "Ligeia" by its unhousing of being by abstraction. But we may discover that same impulse at work also in those poems that address themselves to a Beauty made sad rather than horrible. For in the poems one finds the impulse to transform the external world into an arrested and lifeless image called Helen or Annabel Lee. The image is opaque, not translucent or vital as are those of a Beatrice or Maude Gonne.

> Lo! in yon brilliant window-niche
>> How statue-like I see thee stand,
> The agate lamp within thy hand!
> Ah, Psyche, from the regions which
> Are Holy-Land!

The truth is that Poe has an obsession to reduce the outer world, including persons other than himself, to the level of statue, dead matter whose form is a projection of the transforming intellect by means of "the extravagant device of art." His advocate, P. Pendleton Cooke, praises Poe in the *Southern Literary Messenger* for his dealing "in mysteries of 'life in death'," with the "convulsions of the soul." Cooke laments that Poe is "nervously afraid of the homely," leaving "beneath and behind him the wide and happy realm of the common cheerful life of man." It could but be infuriating to a Poe to be requested to play the American Wordsworth, to be asked for "a book full of homely doings, of successful toils, of ingenious shifts and contrivances, of ruddy firesides," for such is precisely the opposite of his whole intention.

What a Wordsworth strives to see is life in the external world, with nature as a medium through which something larger than the mind of the poet speaks. He attempts to summon into presence that "something deeply interfused" in nature whose dwelling is "the light of setting suns,/ And the round ocean and the living air,/ And the blue sky" no less than "in the mind of man." If Wordsworth is right in his intimations, the individual intellect is necessarily reduced to sharing being in a brotherhood of created beings—sheep included—whose creator cannot be simply the poet's imagination. Poe's concluding words in "To Helen" leave it rather evident where his own Holy-Land lies: it is his own mind, and Psyche its high priestess. The *memory* of Helen is but the excuse for the framed portrait projected by the imagination. Helen is framed by the window, the total picture not opening upon the world but turned into a mirror in which the speaking mind reflects its own magnificence. For windows in Poe open upon no disturbing or pleasing vistas such as those that trouble Keats; neither upon fairylands forlorne nor upon some sweep of history in which one glimpses a community of the human heart continuous in time, as in Keats's figure of Ruth amid the alien corn. We see this radical difference between Keats's "Ode to Psyche" and Poe's tribute to Psyche in the poem Mr. Tate declares Poe's most perfect, "To Helen." And here we may see once more why the French symbolist poets find Poe so much to their liking. The symbol as it emerges in late nineteenth century French poetry is mirror, reflecting the projecting mind. Its properties are quite unlike the symbol as a window, as it was to Dante or as it is to Flannery O'Connor, through which the poet practices art as "a realist of distances." One finds (even if fitfully) Dante's address to images also in Keats's odes and in Wordsworth's "Tintern Abbey," and we notice how much closer these poets are to the senses than Poe will allow himself to be. We might recall that Eliot's indebtedness to the symbolist poets is attested to by himself as well as in our critical explications of his poems.[1] But one notes a movement in Eliot beyond Poe and the

---

1. Eliot wrote Michael Roberts in the 1930s that he was less influenced by "the later Symbolistes." "It is true that about 1917 at [Pound's] suggestion we both worked under

symbolists, most explicitly rendered in the section of "Ash-Wednesday" where the struggling "I" sees through the window, past Priapus to the lady between the yews. It constitutes a movement, a development, in Eliot, which one may trace in the increasing significance given to eyes and to seeing in his poetry, in "The Hollow Men," *The Waste Land*, in "Ash-Wednesday" and the *Quartets*. That is, he moves beyond the influence of Poe toward a symbolism as understood by O'Connor. His public reflection upon this change is recorded in "From Poe to Valéry."

We are upon the threshold here of a question very central to the art of Flannery O'Connor, a question which we may briefly pursue since it will clarify much of what is to follow. One recalls her insistence that, though Hawthorne is one of the fathers of her art, her hope is that she puts "less reliance on allegory" than he. At the same time she praises Hawthorne's concern for that realm touched by prophets and poets. "When Hawthorne said that he wrote romances, he was attempting, in effect, to keep for fiction some of the freedom from social determinism, and to steer it in the direction of poetry." And he was attempting to keep fiction free as well, one adds, from the determinism of abstractions such as tempt one to allegory, not only that to which Hawthorne himself succumbs, but particularly that abstractionism which Poe makes a principal end. Miss O'Connor has rather clearly in mind, in her opposition to allegory, that which attempts to reduce existence from mystery, through a mistake which C. S. Lewis characterizes as the particular danger to the writer in a reflective age: "the temptation to allegorize, to thrust into the story the conscious doctrines of the poet, there to fight it out as best they can with the inherent tendency of the fable. . . ." Both Poe and Hawthorne write allegorical "parables," such works as "The Minister's Black Veil" and "Shadow" and "Silence," each bearing "Parable" or "Fable" as a subtitle. (And even Faulkner was tempted to a *Fable*.) Fearful of this inclination to "fable," Miss O'Connor sees as a "kind of vision the fiction writer needs" for the meaning of his work an "anagogical" one. It is a vision that makes it possible "to see dif-

---

Theophile Gautier. . . . But he was not, like myself, moved in the beginning by Baudelaire, Laforgue, or Rimbaud." Quoted by Jane Adam Smith, "Mr. Eliot's Proposal: the Making of *The Faber Book of Modern Verse*," *Times Literary Supplement*, June 18, 1976, 728.

ferent levels of reality in one image or one situation." Or in one
gesture in the story, such as the one made by the grandmother to
the Misfit, which is "on the anagogical level, that is, the level which
has to do with the Divine Life and our participation in it. It would
be a gesture that transcended any neat allegory that might have
been intended or any pat moral categories a reader could make. . . .
a gesture which somehow made contact with mystery." She again
points out that it is the Manichean man who refuses to believe that
the supernatural "can be known anagogically or defined
dogmatically or received sacramentally. Spirit and matter are
separated for him," and that separation accounts for the strong
temptation to allegorize or to symbolize in the nineteenth century
manner.

In the language of her argument, one sees that she deliberately
goes beyond the more limited concern of Eliot in his famous definition of the "objective correlative," for Eliot attempts at that early
stage in his own development to limit the concern to the aesthetic
level of art as it is influenced by the psychological engagement of
the poet and reader with the art object. (Eliot at this time is writing
of Hawthorne as a "psychological" writer.) From the beginning
Miss O'Connor is concerned with the more inclusive spiritual
dimension of art, and the neglect of this dimension in our lives she
understood as the source of "dissociated sensibilities," another and
later concern in Eliot. It is in our age's spiritual malaise that "the
much-discussed disjunction of sensibility and belief" occurs, a
general spiritual confusion in which flourishes on the one hand a
Manicheanism innocent of its confusion and on the other a gross
materialism dulled by its success. There also occur strange and
grotesque crossings of the two. Miss O'Connor's formulation is an
advancement upon the complexity facing the writer as Eliot had
presented it, he being concerned that the writer find a situation, a
set of objects or actions or events through which to arouse and control an emotional response in the reader. She incorporates with
that aesthetic concern an additional problem, seeking to reconcile
"feeling and thought." But we note that her key terms are *faith* and
reason, rather than Eliot's *feeling* and *thought*. Eliot is still, at the
point of his definitions, much closer to Edgar Allan Poe in his pur-

suit of the objective correlative, though he is beginning to move beyond that position when he comes to argue that the dissociation of sensibility is an effect out of the age of Dryden and Milton. By the time of "Little Gidding," his position is at last very close to that Miss O'Connor holds from the beginning of her writing career. A summary of her position is in "The Nature and Aim of Fiction," where among other observations of historical dislocations she remarks the dissociation of grace and nature. "As grace and nature have been separated, so imagination and reason have been separated, and this always means an end to art."

The anagogical approach to art which she announces as her own was of old an approach applied (she says) "to Biblical exegesis," but more importantly "it was also an attitude toward all creation, and a way of reading nature which included most possibilities." And it is this view of existence, raised to the level of vision, "that the fiction writer has to cultivate if he is ever going to write stories that have any chance of becoming a permanent part of our literature." She remarks the paradox that "the larger and more complex the personal view, the easier it is to compress . . . into fiction." These remarks reveal the importance of the "personal view" that is her own, a view in which the whole of creation may be drawn upon to sustain the anagogical vision. Allegory, particularly in so far as it intends a moral force, is very likely to travesty the resonant vision that is her concern. (The difference is that between *The Pilgrim's Progress* and *The Divine Comedy*.) A second point revealed in her words is her conception of life as sacramental. For though she recognizes with Hazel Motes that "If there's no Christ, there's no reason to have a set place" for the formal sacraments, most particularly for that supper upon the altar of the church; if there *is* a Christ, then the whole of one's life—the whole of the *personal*, a much-repeated word in her essays—must be spent sacramentally. Fiction is an "incarnational" art, she says, and the kind of allegory she opposes as detrimental to art is anti-incarnational. Through its abstractionist inclinations, it is showing forth, once more, the Manichean spirit.

We cited a comment from C. S. Lewis very much in line with Miss O'Connor's own view of allegory's relation to art, and we may rest our generalized argument for the moment in a return to Lewis. In *The Allegory of Love*, Lewis also comments on the incarnational aspect of art:

> It is of the very nature of thought and language to represent what is immaterial in picturable terms. What is good or happy has always been high like the heavens and bright like the sun. Evil and misery were deep and dark from the first. . . . To ask how these married pairs of sensibles and insensibles first came together would be great folly; the real question is how they ever came apart.

They came apart largely, as we have been arguing, as a result of that shifting of man's perspective upon the largeness of existence to an intramundane, closed view of existence, with an authority and direction given to man's thought which seemed to drive the poet and prophet to the necessity of celebrating the *thing* as only an accident of time and matter. It was a direction which led eventually to the questioning of seeing itself, to an emptiness of eyes and to the problem of the relation of consciousness to the thing, in which relationship there was no arbiter except consciousness. In this respect, one might take it that the short-lived Imagist Movement in poetry was the dead end poetry came to in attempting to accommodate itself to the dictation of empirical and positivist thought; it is the refined extension of literary naturalism.

But at the same time one must recognize both an attempt to break out of that entrapment through image as exhibited in the poetry of the Romantics (Wordsworth and Keats have been serving us as exempla), and the development of an allegorical use of image which culminates in the French Symbolist Movement, the image becoming opaque and therefore self-reflecting. The argument for subjectivity is often a defense of such a conception of image. That is the line of development in which Poe plays an important role in his influence upon Baudelaire, but more especially upon Mallarmé. It is also the aspect in Poe which sets him apart from most of the Romantic poets with whom he is usually associated, including Coleridge.

But, says Lewis on this point, there is a kind of symbolism which differs fundamentally from these restricted developments. In that other kind of symbolism one finds another way of using equivalence, which is almost the opposite of allegory, and which I would call sacramentalism or symbolism. If our passion, being immaterial, can be copied by material inventions [as in the allegorical or in that opaque symbolist poetry in which symbol reflects the poet's passions as in a mirror—our interjection upon Lewis's argument], then it is possible that our material world in its turn is the copy of an invisible world. . . . to see the archtype in the copy is what I mean by symbolism or sacramentalism. . . . The allegorist leaves the given—his own passions—to talk of that which is confessedly less real, which is a fiction. The symbolist leaves the given to find that which is more real. To put the difference in another way, for the symbolist it is we who are the allegory.

The modification Miss O'Connor would make in Lewis's characterization of the "sacramentalist's" or "symbolist's" approach to reality is that the poet does not "leave the given" but through a community with the given sees the distant real. It is an experience of being in which the given is transformed by the grace of vision, an idea she expresses as very firm in her conviction about reality and as central to her art. For the writer, the necessary experience comes through a descent

to those underground springs that give life to his work. This descent into himself will, at the same time, be a descent into his region. It will be a descent through the darkness of the familiar into a world where, like the blind man cured in the gospels, he sees men as if they were trees, but walking. This is the beginning of vision. . . .

One must observe that it is a beginning which differs radically from Poe's descent into himself in that hers requires a return to the outer world with the writer's sight restored.

The danger to the religious writer is that he will not make that necessary descent, that "spurred on by the religious view of the world" he turns Manichean. He may attempt "to enshrine the mystery without fact," and will consequently set up an abstract symbol as the shrine, thus bypassing the incarnational, sacramental dimension to his fiction. That error is a violation of both art and reality, out of an enthusiasm ungoverned by reason. From the error "further separations . . . inimical to art" will follow. "Judgment will be separated from vision, nature from grace, and reason from imagination." But though these separations divide "our society and . . . exist in our writing," the breach may yet be healed by faith

when we realize "that faith is a 'walking in darkness' and not a
theological solution to mystery. The poet is traditionally a blind
man, but the Christian poet . . . is like the blind man whom Christ
touched, who looked then and saw men as if they were trees, but
walking." To understand what she is saying in these words is to
enter upon her particular use of the grotesque. For the words, from
"Catholic Novelists and Their Readers," are an anagogical gloss to
her work, one that may be used most obviously in reading a story
like "A View of the Woods." In that story, we observe, the denouement explicitly picks up the story from the gospels about the gift of
vision. The old man, dying at the brink of such a gift, sees the world
upside down; he sees trees as men walking. But he is at least on the
threshold of vision, and Miss O'Connor leaves the story's resolution
ambiguous and our own judgment about the old man's spiritual
rescue must be suspended, lest we presume upon the prerogative of
God's judgment. In the best of her stories, conclusion is left thus
suspended. The fiction is thereby moved into the province of a
mystery beyond both the presumptions of our reason and the distortions of our belief by enthusiasm.

Physical and spiritual vision, then, is a complex constant in
Miss O'Connor's fiction, from Haze's developing sight which leads
him to blind himself for not having seen, to Tarwater's eyes burned
clean in the final pages of *The Violent Bear It Away*. What Miss
O'Connor's protagonists attempt to avoid is vision, which always
comes to them through the physical world, though they desire an
intrusion extraneous to the already created world. That is, they
desire a special creation, a sign spectacular in its separateness from
nature, as a proof of their own importance. Tarwater, believing
himself destined to be a prophet, is hopeful of spectacle. "When the
Lord's call came, he wished it to be a voice from out of a clear and
empty sky, the trumpet of the Lord God Almighty, untouched by
any fleshly hand or breath. He expected to see wheels of fire in the
eyes of unearthly beasts." When he is at last with Rayber and
about to confront Bishop, "His eyes widened and an inner door in
them opened in preparation for some inevitable vision." But what
happens is that a "small white-haired boy" shambles into the back
of the hall. Tarwater is confronted by this mistake of nature which

he (and Rayber) are prepared to see as only subnatural. As Miss O'Connor wrote Sister Quinn, "Those who, like Tarwater, see, will see what they have no desire to see and the vision will be the purifying fire." It is a humiliating experience, in which one discovers that the meanest things of nature—the eyes of an idiot boy or water stains on a bedroom ceiling—are acceptable mediums of grace in the prophetic calling of the soul, neither the lordly sun nor the awesome prospect of one's own death being requirements of high moment in our being, as Tarwater and Asbury dreamed necessary.

The spiritual error dramatized in Tarwater is once more that Manichean one that would reject the created world which the body must inhabit and the senses come to terms with. Miss O'Connor puts the problem in relation to Tarwater as he reflects upon the old man's body and its "dead silver" eyes, the boy trying to put out of his mind the dread thought that he might have inherited the old man's hunger for the bread of life.

> He tried when possible to pass over these thoughts, to keep his vision located on an even level, to see no more than what was in front of his face and to let his eyes stop at the surface of that. It was as if he were afraid that if he let his eyes rest for an instant longer than was needed to place something—a spade, a hoe, the mule's hind quarters before his plow, the red furrow under him—that the thing would suddenly stand before him, strange and terrifying, demanding that he name it and name it justly and be judged for the name he gave it. He did all he could to avoid this threatening intimacy of creation.

This threatening intimacy of creation is not that of the Dadaist or Absurdist vision, in which objects are malignantly perverse, that *horror naturae* which Wolfgang Kayser speaks of in *The Grotesque in Art and Literature* as a development in German romanticism. In that romantic version of the grotesque as it attaches to everyday life, "the small, apparently familiar things in constant use, turn out to be strange, evil, and possessed by hostile demons who constantly swoop down on us, especially in those moments when their interference is most harmful." Rather, the vision which Tarwater (and Haze) would avoid is seeing in things the distant reality which commands, "Be still and know that I am God." That voice, that vision, repeatedly overwhelms Miss O'Connor's characters. The eyes that fail to see the sacred manifested in the profane—the hierophany of existence as Mircea Eliade calls it in *The Sacred and the Profane*, a book Miss O'Connor read—are subjected to terror in a chaos of objects. The created world stands an accuser. But when pride is sufficiently deflated, one becomes enveloped by such a terror as that which Gerard Manley Hopkins celebrates, in images of the world which Miss O'Connor echoes in the passage quoted above to reflect Tarwater's inner world. It is as if she means to rime Tarwater's terror with Hopkins's joy. For she too sees the things of the world as "charged with the grandeur of God," even a spade or a hoe. Tarwater senses with panic what Hopkins celebrates in joy. For that grandeur

> will flame out, like shining from shook foil;
> It gathers to a greatness, like the ooze of oil
> Crushed. . . .
> There lives the dearest freshness deep down things.

And again,

> sheer plod makes plough down sillion
> Shine, and blue-bleak embers, ah my dear,
> Fall, gall themselves, and gash gold-vermillion.

In that letter to Sister Quinn, Miss O'Connor prefaces the words we have quoted by saying, "I have been reading what St. Thomas has to say in the *De Veritate* on prophecy. He says prophecy depends on the imagination and not on the moral faculty. It's a matter of seeing." It is a matter of seeing with the powers of what Coleridge calls the secondary imagination, a seeing of the world as it is, the world being the steady witness to the Unnameable Cause. The lowliest of that created world demands of us, as it does of Tarwater, that we name it and be judged by our naming, an action through which the world opens in light toward the Light. That, for Miss O'Connor's characters, is the terror in the small familiar things of the world. For her it is joy which art must speak to anagogically, not allegorically.

CHAPTER VII

BLASPHEMY AS BELIEF: THE SELF AS "I's" SON

The threat of the serene grandeur *of* nature or *in* nature or *through* nature: those prepositions conjoin the reflective mind to existence from ancient days into our own, releasing all the complexities of metaphor and myth that relate to the particular vision of the particular mind. The modern mind—"the popular spirit of our age"—resists the eye's or the mind's journey beyond surfaces, Miss O'Connor keeps saying to us. Resists vision and the complex grammar of thought attendant upon vision. It is nevertheless true that the experience we see Tarwater struggling to avoid is both common and commonly threatening. And, as we talk, we reveal it so. That is an element in the comic use of language Miss O'Connor is adept at employing in revealing her characters' serious dimension; there is ironic complexity in Tarwater's having to be about his Father's "bidness" beyond the strength of his understanding. The words of our mouths as they show forth the meditations of our hearts reveal our response to the abiding threat of being, and the Calling (Eliot's word) that we hear in being as well, whether we intend our words to do so or not. And, if the eye is the body's window for the soul, it is in some degree a two-way window, revealing something of that soul that looks out upon the world, a consideration Miss O'Connor uses in her fiction with considerable effect. Poe, as we have suggested, wishes the eye to be a one-way window at best, though we suspect that it is actually a mirror reflecting inward—the self upon the self.

Now if the eye is the body's window upon the soul, words are the mind's. Prufrock complains that it is impossible for him to say just what he means, and yet he says much more than he means to. Through his own words we know him better than he knows himself, such is the perversity of words. When we "put our foot in our mouth," we find ourselves betrayed by words that reveal truths we had not intended to reveal, and in this sense it may be said that words appear an instrument of the Devil, as Kierkegaard suspects. As Miss O'Connor might well add, however, that instrument is ultimately in the service of truth, in which case it would be true that the Devil through words prepares the ground for truth, as she says the Devil prepares the arena for grace in her fiction. Our images, our metaphors, in this point of view, reveal our mind and soul more starkly than we are comfortable in realizing. With these thoughts in mind, we turn for the moment to Jean-Paul Sartre's self-revelations, since he is at once a part of that intellectual current borne to us out of Poe (and so revealing of Poe) and since Miss ·O'Connor sets herself in an explicitly revealed opposition to Sartre's position, from which we may reasonably deduce her thought on Poe.

Her reaction to Sartre is overt in such a story as "Good Country People"; it is implicit in the thought of Haze Motes and young Tarwater. Perhaps then we may consider Sartre's experience of Haze's and Tarwater's dilemma as mutually revealing.[1] In *Les Mots*, near the end of his reminiscence on his past, Sartre recalls as a final labor, necessary before he can act himself into being, the exorcism of the Holy Ghost, the Lord and Giver of Life, the Sustainer Whom Hopkins celebrates. It is a task of several years' undertaking, Sartre says. For having become a writer, he then discovers "the

---

1. It is very tempting to consider the relationship Jean-Paul presents between himself and his grandfather, Charles Schweitzer, in the opening pages of his *Words*, as analogue to Haze Motes's relationship to his grandfather. Charles, intended to be a minister by his father, fled that calling; "he preferred to take to the road in quest of a circus rider." Later he became a teacher, wishing "to devote himself to an attenuated form of spirituality, to a priesthood that would allow him circus riders." Charles's wife, a recluse, kept curtains drawn. In his grandfather's study, curtains drawn, Jean-Paul turned in upon himself through books. One thinking that strange, eccentric family relationships over several generations a particularly Southern phenomenon, because it is such rich material to so many Southern novelists, should read the opening section of Sartre's book. It is a tantalizing realization in that context that Albert Schweitzer is Jean-Paul's first cousin once removed.

penman [to be] an *ersatz* of the Christian." That is an unhappy discovery. "I thought I was devoting myself to literature, whereas I was actually taking Holy Orders." He adds:

> For a long time, to write was to ask Death and my masked Religion to preserve my life from chance. I was of the Church. As a militant, I wanted to save myself by works; as a mystic, I attempted to reveal the silence of being by a thwarted rustling of words and, what was most important, I confused things with their names: that amounts to believing.

The solution to his misery began on a morning "in 1917":

> I decided to think of the Almighty. . . . He doesn't exist, I said to myself with polite surprise . . . . never have I had the slightest temptation to bring Him back to life. But the Other One remained, the Invisible One, the Holy Ghost, the one who guaranteed my mandate and who ran my life with his great anonymous and sacred power.

Sartre is describing that entrapment which we see Tarwater attempting to avoid, his involvement in a being already existing and the necessity of naming that "silence of being" as Tarwater fears he may be commanded to do, with the penalty of being judged by the very act of naming. Sartre, who has already declared God not to exist by naming Him nonexistent, discovers that he has exorcised the threat only partially. He is not yet free. By the time he reports the experience to us,

> The retrospective illusion has been smashed to bits; martyrdom, salvation, and immortality are falling to pieces; the edifice is going to rack and ruin; I collared the Holy Ghost in the cellar and threw him out; atheism is a cruel and long-range affair; I think I've carried it through.

One notices two things of importance to our discussion: first, Tarwater is presented to us as largely having possessed himself of those powers Sartre can claim only after expelling the Holy Ghost from the cellar of his mind. Atheism is a cruel and long-range affair indeed, and in Tarwater we are shown a defeat for his attempt to establish it. The second thing we notice in Sartre's words is the metaphor he employs to describe the battle. It involves an interior violence which leaves the edifice of the self crumbling. It is, in short, a metaphor reminiscent of "The Fall of the House of Usher" and of the "Haunted Palace" of which Roderick sings in a violent and distracted way. That is, the metaphor Sartre uses suggests to us that he is indeed of the tribe of Poe.

We have only to support this suggestion with a few more words from Sartre's recollections to be surer. As a growing child, he says, he "could not grant that one received being from without. . . . The past had not made me. On the contrary, it was I, rising from my ashes, who plucked my memory from nothingness by an act of creation which was always being repeated. Each time I was reborn better, and I made better use of the inert reserves of my soul for the simple reason that death was closer each time, lit me up more brightly with its dim light."[2] It is a recollection of the action's manufacture of being out of "inert reserves," the prime matter otherwise called nothingness. One hears in Sartre's account of his anxiety a faint echo of that agony of Dante's damned souls, whose self-knowledge at Doomsday will be frozen in their own vacuity, they becoming thereby eternal inheritors of their own emptiness. Sartre intends such a daring blasphemy, of course, as showing forth the highest heroism. He concludes the history of his journey by declaring that

> my sole concern has been to save myself—nothing in my hands, nothing up my sleeve—by work and faith. . . . If I relegate impossible Salvation to the proproom, what remains? A whole man, composed of all men and as good as all of them and no better than any.

There is in Sartre, as there is in Poe, a note repeatedly struck, which in the embellishment of words presents us the sentimental rebel who never quite escapes a note of self-pity, in spite of the volume of the cry. And for both, silence is finally the greatest enemy.

We recall Poe's engagement of the problem in "Silence: A Parable," in which the ecstasy of silence lies in the "DESOLATION" of the world of the senses. But the problem for

---

2. Sartre in such passages appears a bolder Quinton Compson. That is, Quinton's attempt to reject "the South," which leads him to that deadly flirtation with a broken watch and pistol in a northern town is interestingly paralleled by Sartre's attempt to deny his family, the past which he declares not to have made him. Sartre's "pistol" is words, the suicidal act being that Nominalist separation of names and things, the necessity of unbelief, as he says in the passage quoted earlier. Haze's attempts to dissociate belief and center reality in the act of the will is again parallel, Haze rising frantically in his use of language to a point of insanity as he attempts to destroy all names, in which action things would themselves be destroyed. In his special twist of the Sartrean attempt, his success would reduce him to blood brother of Enoch Emery.

Poe and Sartre alike, in their pursuit of an ecstasy in the self, is the compulsion to bear witness to that longed-for state, and that requires the disturbing noise of words. Aside from the inherent relation of words to some species of "things"—internal or external to consciousness—there is an inevitable relation of utterance to reality. For the word uttered or written exists thereby as separate from its source and becomes an assault upon the consciousness which thinks to be its sole creator; it is by its very utterance an assault from an outer world upon the consciousness. In his essay on Camus' *The Stranger*, Sartre sees Camus as infected by the disease he is himself infected by, "the obsession with silence," which is a symptom of the dislocated consciousness as Miss O'Connor would have it. Sartre adds that "silence, as Heidegger says, is the authentic mode of speech. . . . But how is one to be silent with words?" More important to Miss O'Connor's reading of this aspect of the existentialist position is the tragic failure of spirit caused by its attempt to become its own vision, and one aspect of her comedy turns on this failure. It is revealed by conversations in which one character seems oblivious to the presence of any other character, though he speak a continuous, and confusing, flow of words.

That condition is particularly emphasized in Haze Motes's progress toward a silent country quite other than the loudly-silent one of the closed self. Haze, we notice repeatedly, hears only himself, being the "preacher and sole member" of his church. He insists to the one-eyed owl at the zoo that he is clean, words the impatient Enoch is oblivious to. When the moronic Enoch catches a glimmer of meaning in Haze's sermon and brings him the mummy, Haze seems to hear himself for the first time. Meanwhile, there are numerous comic situations such as that in which Haze blocks traffic to read the sign "Jesus Saves." Each situation by its comic twist underlines the fragmented world in the novel, emphasizing the separation between words and things. The angry truck driver is assured by Haze that there is a sin that exists before whoremongering and blasphemy and that "Jesus is a trick on niggers," to which the truckdriver responds that Haze had better get his "goddam outhouse off the middle of the road."

The comedy in such scenes results from an elevation allowed

the reader, who sees the complexity of the situation as the truck driver can't, though he sympathizes with the truck driver's suggestion that Haze must have escaped the zoo. That is, we must note that the reader is teased by the fiction into believing himself more fully possessed of Haze's world than Haze himself and therefore quite superior to Haze. But within the elevating ironic detachment afforded the reader so that he may enjoy the comic situation resides the serious, tragic theme Miss O'Connor develops. One comes at last to see that for Miss O'Connor, even a Sartre or a Haze is not so hopeless as the truck driver and even some readers, that kind of reader who expects of fiction that it lift up the heart without the reader having to pay any of the price she insists necessary. In his *Confessions,* St. Augustine remarks, in a sentence scored by Miss O'Connor in her copy: "Yet woe to those who keep silent concerning You, since even those who speak much are dumb." Those who speak much of God include not only St. Augustine or St. Thomas, but Sartre and Haze as well. In denying that silent country, to whose borders he finally comes at the end of his journey, Haze nevertheless bears witness to that country which is larger than the isolated self. He bears witness out of pride (which comes before whoremongering and blasphemy) proving—that is, testing— existence by his movement toward non-existence. Such a soul burning toward Hell, Miss O'Connor seems to suggest, is more nearly in the presence of the actions of grace than a soul caught in the slow dry rot of indecision, inaction, or obliviousness such as would better suit it to Dante's Ante-Hell. That is why a reader may well misunderstand the role of violence in her fiction. For ours is an age, she says, which "no longer has much feeling for the nature of the violences which precede and follow [the almost imperceptible intrusions of grace]. . . . I have found that violence is strangely capable of returning my characters to reality and preparing them to accept their moment of grace. . . . Violence is a force which can be used for good or evil, and among other things taken by it is the kingdom of heaven."

Now foremost among the instruments of violence (and the most powerfully destructive force in the final reckoning) are words: that ragtag army which pride most effectively marshals and sends forth against the world. In a passage in which she is talking of the violence practiced by words, Miss O'Connor quotes Pascal: "If I had not known you, I would not have found you." That is the message whispered to Sartre by his own "friend" who, so far as Sartre is concerned, is diabolical, just as we discover Tarwater's friend to be. Sartre speaks of his own evil stranger in the cellar of the mind: "The Holy Ghost whispers its staggering words in my ear: 'You would not seek me if you had not found me.' " But one might object that it is Sartre and not his friend or the words that are diabolical, for it is a perversion of Pascal's words that Sartre practices. It is his attempt at blasphemy, though Sartre too suffers Haze's dilemma. For one cannot blaspheme what does not exist. The minor pleasure of shocking the innocently superstitious, as Sartre seems bent upon in *Words*, is hardly compensation for that dream of ultimate audacity which blasphemy would be, but which requires something not the self against which to revolt. One cannot shock an audience that does not understand the language, and not many react to the violence of Sartre's throwing the Holy Ghost out of the cellar of his mind. His frustration must be at times very like Haze's in those situations where Haze is treated with indifferent curiosity by his casual street congregations. Four hundred years ago, Sartre might have been awarded the supreme satisfaction of being burned at the stake, but in the twentieth century the violence he intends us to acknowledge extends to but does not often violate our own closed worlds.

Miss O'Connor understands Sartre's language quite clearly, but she is not shocked. One might even say that she is somewhat encouraged by it, though not in the way of the philosopher's disciples. In the passage in which she quotes Pascal and looks to the problem of the violence in language as practiced by many of her contemporaries, she speaks specifically of Camus. By extension we may include Sartre, however much those two differ in their violences. She says:

> We have to look in much of the fiction of our time for a kind of sub-religion which expresses its ultimate concern in images that have not yet broken through to show any recognition of a God who has revealed himself. As great as much of this fiction is, as much as it reveals a whole-

hearted effort to find the only true ultimate concern, . . . I do not believe
that it can adequately represent in fiction the central religious experience. [For that central experience is] Pascal's . . . after his conversion
and not before.

The experience she is speaking of, and which she sets about
dramatizing, was effectively revealed in what we may call the first
great novel whose theme is alienation, a work which every day
becomes increasingly contemporary: St. Augustine's *Confessions*. In
it Augustine records his own struggle to break through the images
of the world into the same silent country that haunts Haze and
Tarwater, Camus and Sartre. In coming into that country, to rest
in the Word not his own, Augustine discovers the mystery of words
and of the world. *The Confessions* bears witness to a vision of the
silent world, recording in one instance in particular an experience
at Ostia. He recalls a conversation with St. Monica as they stand
looking over the Tiber; they "were straining with the heart's mouth
for those supernal streams flowing from your fountain." They move
toward the silent country, willingly predisposed but not in a direct
or deliberate attempt upon that country. Through "the highest
delight of fleshly senses, in the brightest corporeal light," they
proceed "step by step through all bodily things up to that heaven
whence shine the sun and the moon and the stars down upon the
earth. . . . We ascended higher yet . . . and we came up to our own
minds." And beyond that, beyond words into silence, they ascend
to an encounter of a Being beyond time. After that vision "we
turned back again to the noise of our mouths, where a word both
begins and ends. . . . What is there like to your Word . . . ?"

This experience remembered, in the *Confessions*, borne witness
to by words, is of silence louder than the world or its words: "the
tumult of the flesh fell silent, silent the images of earth, and of the
water, and of the air; silent the heavens: . . . the very soul itself."
For the experience is one allowed when one passes "beyond [the
self] by not thinking upon [the self]." And the ultimate meaning of
that vision to those in the world? "We did not make ourselves."
Such is Augustine's experience which "breaks through images," as
Miss O'Connor says, and the movement toward that vision is in a
direction opposite to that taken by Poe or Sartre as they pursue

themselves into a dark version of the silent country, the self. Augustine's is an experience, following which he is prepared to enter upon image and the world sacramentally. Miss O'Connor has marked in her *Confessions* a passage which is very revealing of her own concern for images of the world and particularly those she builds in words to reveal the mystery of reality through art. Returning to the Scriptures after his conversion, Augustine says (in the marked passage), "behold I see something within them that was neither revealed to the proud nor made plain to children, that was lowly on one's entrance but lofty on further advance, and that was veiled over in mystery. . . . My swelling pride had [earlier] turned from its humble style, and my gaze did not penetrate into its inner meaning." These words are from a brief chapter which is followed by a sharp attack upon "The Manichees," a coincidence which reminds us once more of Miss O'Connor's abiding concern for that modern problem of the spirit whose evidence is most particularly "the noise of our mouths" which attempts to separate words from things through abstractionism. In Augustine's words one detects an analogue to her own work, in which the language of banal minds is used by her vision to enter a world enlarged toward the lofty. The lowly entry through that small way of the naturalistic world as seen through images enlarges the natural and reveals the lofty as one advances, the whole "veiled over in mystery."

In this passage from the *Confessions*, Augustine remarks that the Scriptures yield neither to the proud nor to children, but only to the proud who become childlike that they may enter the lowly entrance. It is a passage whose metaphors might suggest to us the observation that neither Poe nor Sartre manages to get beyond an arrested youth, remaining proud children. That is the suggestion about Poe in Eliot's late remark that Poe's intellect is that of "a highly gifted young person before puberty." And in this respect, Poe is harbinger of a host of writers still markedly present in American letters, and particularly in our fiction, who take a more or less "gifted young person" as agent. From Huck Finn through Nick Adams to Holden Caulfield, the hero of thirteen years age is spun out of highly sophisticated minds. American letters, of course, has no exclusive claim in this development and the springs from which this writing issues are more inland in time than Poe, as we have been saying. But it is a disturbing discovery that at the heart of the most influential philosopher since World War II, Jean-Paul Sartre, there lies also this proud, sophisticated childishness which spawns adolescent heroes. His autobiography, *Words*, reveals just this, not through what he remembers of his childhood, in the manner of Twain, but through what he makes of that memory in his old age. Indeed, had Sartre been possessed of humor, that necessary assuagement of concentrated intensity and the ease of reason's canker, he might appear to us a French Mark Twain. Instead, we have only his grim conclusion: "my sole concern has been to save myself . . . by work and faith."

Miss O'Connor's version of Huck Finn—Tarwater—sets out from a position which, after many years of thoughtful pursuit, Sartre seems at last to have come to. In *Words*, he is as he was when a child in his grandfather's study. (One notes Sartre's acute awareness of the break of generations, which is a pattern dominant in Miss O'Connor's fiction.) But Sartre is like Tom Sawyer; he plays hero through words, looking through the heavy drapes to an outer world into which he is not allowed to venture. Or considering the end, Sartre in advanced years, one may shift the metaphor: Sartre remembering, in his arrested development, appears very much a bored old maid who, having refused that early suitor, the Holy Ghost, is titillated and somewhat disappointed at not finding Him under the bed, an empty consolation—though he remains fearful of finding Him beyond those heavy drapes that hang against the outer world. Or perhaps He may yet be discovered in some forgotten or secret cellar. For it is surely evident that, as with Poe's protagonist in "The Domain of Arnheim," the one overriding necessity to Sartre is to have "an object of unceasing pursuit." That object determines "the extent of attainable happiness," but "in proportion to the spirituality of this object." Of course, that object is insistently the self in Sartre's and Poe's words alike, to be pursued inward away from the world, within a country bounded by one's own decree, bounded as Miss O'Connor says "by the skull." One is never fully convinced by that insistence, since the sharp edge of desperation cuts through it.

No wonder that Allen Tate speaks of Poe as our first existentialist. But the rebellion of the self to establish its own kingdom is more ancient than Poe or Sartre and seems bound to be immortal too—or at least world-long—though the long history of contradictions of that revolt constantly refute it. As that earlier existentialist Kierkegaard remarks concerning this point, not going so far back as Lucifer and Adam as Miss O'Connor does:

> Kant held that man was his own law [autonomy], i.e., bound himself under the law which he gave himself. In a deeper sense that means to say: lawlessness or experimentation. It is no harder than the thwacks which Sancho Panza applied to his own bottom. . . . If I am not bound by anything higher than myself, and if I am to bind myself, where am I to acquire the severity as A by which, as B, I am to be bound, so long as A and B are the same?

Sartre's attempt to answer that question is that "B" is the "inert reserves of my soul," activated from its nothingness. Not asking the cause of "inert reserves," he is left practicing a masochism upon what the scholastics would have called his potential being. And that, at last, is a violence practised upon being itself such as one might, from Miss O'Connor's position, consider sacrilege. There is something more healthful and hopeful, it appears to me, in Haze Motes's final circumstance. The "unclean" Haze at the end of his adventure—Kierkegaard's "A"—acquires a severity in rebuking himself, the earlier Haze who insisted he was clean—Haze "B". The distinction between wearing a hair shirt and the extreme flagellation Haze comes to requires a nicety of distinction by reason serving faith, a nicety Haze is incapable of. For Haze is no Pascal. Penance and vengeance once confused, one transgresses upon one's own being. Yet the soul's masochism in the name of the Self, the elevation of the Self to godhead, is a more arresting if less spectacular perversion, being jealously inward. Which is not to celebrate Haze Motes's final disposition of himself; when one has only begun to see a pin point of light, one has not emerged unscathed from the darkness.

Still, Haze's is a considerable move beyond the darkness Sartre celebrates in his autobiography when he sums his memory:

> . . . each and every moment repeated the ceremony of my birth. . . . It was I, rising from my ashes, who plucked my memory from nothingness

by an act of creation which was always being repeated. Each time I was reborn better, and I made better use of the inert reserves of my soul for the simple reason that death, which was closer each time, lit me up more brightly with its dim light.

This position at the end is not advanced beyond the literal childhood stage he recalls: "I drew myself out of nothingness in a burst of altruism and assumed the disguise of childhood so as to give my parents the illusion of having a son." The difference is that, at the lag-end of his life—his parents gone as subjects for the practiced illusion—he must give himself the illusion. Declaring a numinous self-decreed out of unexplained "inert reserves," he is his own father and son.

CHAPTER VIII

JUGGLING A TRINITY: IMAGINATION, REASON, THE WORLD

The mystery Keats and Wordsworth and Eliot move toward, the mystery Hopkins celebrates and Miss O'Connor relentlessly insists upon against the resistance of her characters, enjoys the created world as a medium through which to speak to the finite mind of man. It is a mystery quite different from the one to which Poe clings. To see his version, we may take as another point of departure a comment by James Russell Lowell, meant as a tribute. "To the eye of genius," says Lowell, "the veil of the spiritual world is ever rent asunder, that it may perceive the ministers of good and evil who throng continually around it. No man of more talent ever flung his inkstand at the devil." In the passage which contains this remark Lowell is naming Poe such a genius, a conclusive sign of which he finds in those tales with their "power of influencing the mind of the reader by the impalpable shadows of mystery, and a minuteness of detail which does not leave a pin or button unnoticed." But, as Lowell must admit, "Even his mystery is mathematical to his own mind. To him X is a known quality all along. . . . to him the outline is as clear and distinct as that of a geometrical diagram. For this reason Mr. Poe has no sympathy with *Mysticism*. The Mystic dwells in the mystery, is enveloped with it; . . . it affects his optic nerve especially, and the commonest things get a rainbow edging from it. Mr. Poe . . . is a spectator *ab extra*. He analyzes, he dissects, he watches

—with an eye serene,
The very pulse of the machine,

for such it practically is to him, with wheels and cogs and piston rods all working to produce a certain end."

A very suggestive reading of Poe, particularly since it is so early in the history of Poe criticism; its burden is to praise Poe's art and his intelligence. (If Lowell had had our own excess experience of wheels and cogs and piston rods, he might have been less sanguine in his praise; his concluding lines might remind us once more of Hazel Motes, whose necessity is to be "spectator *ab extra*," with his Essex serving as a platform upon which he may stand away from the world.) Poe, by Lowell's account, has the power to rend the veil of mystery and see into the depth of existence, without being drawn into vision as is the mystic. But just as Lowell fails to examine Poe's "minuteness of detail which does not leave a pin or button unnoticed," so does he fail to look closely at those "impalpable shadows of mystery" that influence the reader. Lowell enjoys an easy residual sense of the "spiritual world," his intellect still more or less comfortable in a twilight of Christian civilization which lingers on in English and American letters until the trauma of the new science shakes that easy world in the second half of his century, leading to the announcement that ours is the "post-Christian world."[1]

Poe, we may suggest, is an early inhabitant of what has been called the "post-Christian world," and he knows it, while Lowell does not see the new world growing restive in the sobering light of its mechanistic view of existence. Whatever spiritual world there is

---

1. Lowell's comfortableness is very like that of Sir Walter Scott, as Hawthorne responds to it indignantly and as Twain makes satirical fun of it in the Grangerford section of *Adventures of Huckleberry Finn*. If Hawthorne finds a serious response to the spiritual missing from Scott (as he does in his *English Note Books*), Twain rebukes even the remnants of it from the position of his own arrested development. One cannot escape the darkness settling upon Twain in his celebration of the triumph of the modern world over the medieval, *A Connecticut Yankee at King Arthur's Court*. The triumph of wheels and cogs and pistons at the end of his novel leaves that high-spirited farce in suddenly deepening shadows. In his "Immortality: Experience and Symbol" (*Harvard Theological Review*, July 1967, especially pages 252-61) Voegelin shows the phrase "post-Christian age" an untenable one, a manufactured symbol for recent history constructed by ideologues. "For the time in which the ideologue places his construction is not the time of existence in tension toward eternity, but a symbol by which he tries to pull the timeless into identity with the time of his existence. Though the reality of the tension between the timeless and time is lost, . . . the form of the tension is preserved by the dream-act of forcing the two poles into oneness. We can characterize the ideologue's 'post-Christian age,' therefore, as a symbol engendered by his libidinous dream of self-salvation." (261)

for Poe is one in which spirit is no more than the particular intellect. Thus Poe's faith can sustain only that "mystery" in whose service the reason is paramount. He can say, in *Marginalia*, "the belief in ghosts, or in a Deity, or in a future state, or in anything else credible or incredible—that any such belief is universal, demonstrates nothing more than that which needs no demonstration . . . the identity of construction in the human brain." That identity of construction is to be explained, as Rayber will explain its variant in the idiot Bishop, as an accident of nature—that is, as a pattern of effects against the flux of phenomena of which there is no originating cause. The deep restlessness in Poe is itself ghost-like in its stirrings, drifting in an external world and by an act of the imagination attempting to subdue and exorcise that world from the mind. The theme of possession in Poe, for all its emphasis on horror, has little deliberate concern with the diabolic, that constant fear to Hawthorne. Nor is the conception of *sin* any part of Poe's thinking, beyond the use of the word as a sort of talisman from the past, its face worn away. His interest in such words lies in what he judges to be an emotional residue still available to the writer when he uses them. For the true spirit world to Poe is the mind only, at depths that fascinate him. When he "rends the veil" that Lowell speaks of, it is of an inner temple of his own soul to reveal it to the insatiable imagination. Thus those interesting modern touches in him which are of such delight to Freudian pursuits of Poe, though Poe appears to me a somewhat more innocent Jungian. He sees the dream world as somehow containing the waking world, "a dream within a dream" in his phrase, and the struggle of his imagination is to reveal that deeply interior but mysteriously inclusive world. I say *innocent*, for Jung in his explorations of the unconscious finds paths leading to a larger world than that of the individual psyche. The "identity of construction of the human brain" does not satisfy Jung's questions about our buried life, in which one encounters not only ghosts but intimations of immortality. Poe cannot go so deep. In *Marginalia* he speaks of "fancies" that come to the border between sleep and waking, "shadows of shadows," "psychal impressions." Although they are "rather psychal than intellectual," he does not presume them unique. He is more curious about

their eluding conscious articulation than with those possibilities
they suggest to Jung of affinities in separate psyches such as make
mind itself a continuum bearing a history of the race—and upon
which (we add) are attendant mysteries larger than the historical.
Poe is not interested in that Collective Unconscious to which Jung
gives our popular name and understanding.[2]

It is the uncommonness of his individual awareness that Poe
clings to, his conception of his own genius that he guards jealously.
What Flannery O'Connor calls a gift, Poe somehow thinks of as of
his own making; the traditional conception of potential being is
foreign to his thought. For the concept of the potential implies both
an ultimate cause and limitations within the gift of being as well.
Hence he concentrates on the good of the intellect under construction in himself, but with himself as the sole constructor and with no
outer limits to its reaches. In respect to those "shadows of
shadows," he conditions himself upon receiving them "to startle
myself from the point into wakefullness." He thus "*transfer[s] the
point itself into the realm of Memory.*" (Poe delights in typographical
emphasis, as if to register how startled he is by his own revelations.)
The exercise is, in his phrase for the deliberate violence, an attempt
to compel "the Heaven into the Earth." We see the result of such
exercises in the conscious artistry of his landscape studies such as
"The Island of the Fay" and "The Domain of Arnheim." Yet still
one notices that the only life in these set pieces is the life of the
speaking mind. Any necessary allusion to prior cause, to any
presence other than, or earlier than, the shaping force that spawns
the words is carefully put as supposition and is thus at the mercy of
that shaping force. Fays have had a hand, perhaps, but absent fays.
Real creation is in the mind, as in the surrealistic time-lapse images
of shadows:

> I fancied that each shadow, as the sun descended lower and lower,
> separated itself sullenly from the trunk that gave it birth, and thus
> became absorbed in the stream; while other shadows issued momently
> from the trees, taking the place of their predecessors thus entombed.

2. As there were interests in the sociological before Comte coined the name, so has there
been in the Collective Unconscious before Jung. Jung's is an attempt at a rational articulation of the idea and evidence for it. One finds the basic recognition an ancient one in our
thought, particularly in mystic thought. The idea of the continuity of the race, the idea of the

In such defoliation of images into shadows, an active decaying of the world of being by imagination, the movement is consistently toward darkness, with an occasional disruption of nature's expected correspondences, as when darkness is made to gather in the east, the traditional figurative source of light in keeping with natural phenomena. Such distortion is intended to convey "ideas of mortal sorrow and untimely death."

In the prose poem "Shadow: A Parable" a dead weight hangs on the speaker and on all objects which his mind reflects. It is the shadow of death with the epigraph lifted from Psalm XXIII, and all hope excluded by the fragmentation: "Yea! though I walk through the valley of the Shadow—" All things are depressed by isolation, "Yet we laughed and were merry in our proper way—which was hysterical; and sang the songs of Anacreon—which are madness; and drank deeply—although the purple wine reminded us of blood." The "dark and undefined shadow" steps forth into flickering light and is made to name itself ("I am SHADOW"). Its dwelling place is in the depths of an unnameable Hades, the world of Nada, toward which existence flows. The auditors react "in horror" and stand "shuddering":

> for the tones in the voice of the shadow were not the tones of any one being, but of a multitude of beings, and, varying in their cadences from syllable to syllable, fell duskily upon our ears in the well-remembered and familiar accents of many thousand departed friends.[3]

One has repeatedly in Poe that surrealist operation of the imagination upon the dead external world such as we see displayed on the canvases of Salvadore Dali. Thus his conclusions are inevitable; he must register, even in the happier attempt of "The Island of the Fay," that "darkness fell over all things."

---

history of consciousness, has implicit in it at every point such possibilities as Jung explores, some of them perhaps deeper than his: the metaphorical statement of our being members one of another by St. Paul is an instance. Miss O'Connor found Jung of considerable interest, an interest whose limitations we examined in our first volume.

3. The experience of Poe's narrator with Shadow here has interesting parallel in Sabbath Hawks's disturbed experience when she holds the mummy in her arms, and for good reason. For both our authors are attempting to dramatize the horror of emptiness. Sabbath "might have sat there for ten minutes, without a thought, held by whatever it was that was familiar about him. She had never known anyone who looked like him before, but there was something in him of everyone she had ever known, as if they had all been rolled into one person and killed and shrunk and dried." Such is Haze's "new Jesus."

Poe conceives the imagination an instrument to reconcile reason to its haunted palace; the existing empirical world he would and finally must deny, consigning it to shadow. Thus there is an uneasy triad which consciousness must juggle: reason, imagination, the dead body of the world. Imagination is at last the proffered sacrifice, by which Poe risks insanity to maintain some independence from that colder, remoter god, reason. We might, from the position we have advanced, conclude that he rather sacrifices the world. But from his point of view the risk is of that most treasured possession of all—the imagination—for the sake of an interior world thus self-made. The boldness of this risk reaches beyond the limits of reason. There is order in him; reason is not cast out, which is to emphasize once more his deep roots in the eighteenth century. For the imagination struggles at once against and on behalf of reason. His "mysticism" dissolves in an analysis of facts as he solves X, to the delight of lesser intellects—which is perhaps one cause of Henry James's cutting remark that an enthusiasm for Poe is a sign of a decidedly primitive state of reflection. Poe plunges one into "mystery," whether a murder in the Rue Morgue or the elaborate decay of an ancient house in a swamp, and attempts through a mastery of language—in the patterning of facts or through an impressionistic coloring of images—to reveal a solution to the puzzle with which he has teased our minds. Like his detective, he "glories . . . in that moral activity which disentangles. . . . He is fond of enigmas, of conundrums, of hieroglyphics; exhibiting in his solutions of each a degree of *acumen* which appears to the ordinary apprehension preternatural. His results, brought about by the very soul and essence of method, have, in truth, the whole air of intuition." But it is an *air* of intuition—to the *ordinary* apprehension. And *moral* activity is really only *intellectual* disentanglement through a *method*, whose *soul* and *essence* is solution itself. A mystic or an Aquinas would marvel at the appropriation and application of such terms. Such abuse of language in the interest of emotional response can but lead to a decay of language. Though sharing with Poe some of the fascination with the shadow world, Sartre nevertheless scores Poe's method on one occasion at least. Sartre is speaking directly of the decay of language wrought by the methods of Poe's French admirers and their followers, but his complaint applies aptly to Poe:

> If words are sick, it is up to us to cure them. . . . In many cases literature is a cancer of words. . . . There is nothing more deplorable than the literary practice which . . . is called poetic prose and which consists of using words for the obscure harmonics which resound about them and which are made up of vague meanings which are in contradiction with clear meanings. . . . If one starts deploring the inadequacy of language to reality . . . one makes oneself an accomplice of the enemy, that is, of propaganda.

One may conclude that Poe puts on a show, in part out of contempt for his audience; he is a mordant prestidigitator. "It will be found . . . that the ingenious are always fanciful," he remarks in "Murders in the Rue Morgue," "and the truly imaginative never otherwise than analytic." Thus his delight in luring a reader across the divide between the fancy and the imagination—into the region of fancy—and there solving X for him as if he were a fool, and as if imagination rather than reason is authority for his control of the show. The reader is his mouse, not only in such a hoax as "The Unparalleled Adventure of One Hans Pfaall" and *The Narrative of A. Gordon Pym*, but in the "Tell-Tale Heart," whose solution of horror comes in recognizing the mysterious sound as the speaker's literal heartbeat. But Poe's reader is left at that simple level. What a writer can do with the same material is shown us when Conrad's jungle tom-toms make concert in Marlow's throbbing ear, turning us toward terror in ourselves and a sense that the heart is considerably more complex than the physiological or simple psychological limits of Poe. But there is more than a contempt for the reader at work here. It is as if Poe, catching a glimpse of the abyss, lacks the courage to name it. He lacks even that sweet patient despair of a Kafka.

CHAPTER IX

FICTION AS MORAL ACTIVITY

Words on paper—a tale, a parable, a poem. Such is the necessary concession Poe makes to a world external to consciousness. He acknowledges that world, if for no other reason because of the necessities of the body. That old implacable inconvenience to art and thought is a special plague to Poe, given his poverty. In the light of that complication, the writer contemplates his reader, who lurks or stumbles toward or waits haughtily or indifferently or hopefully for one's offering of words somewhere in that outer world, as tempting as a god or dragon to the writer. Poe generally addresses the intruding outer world in a coldly rational manner, however much his rhetoric imitates the forces of passion. But it is when he speaks of his reader in that outer world that he appears most passionate, his lively contempt suggesting to us that the one most disturbing threat to his intellect's control of the world is that of another intellect. He often expresses a generous inclusive contempt for the anonymous reader, largely from his recognition of the dangers to his conception of literature from a popular audience.

Poe observes the sudden explosion of periodicals in America in the 1840s, upon which he is nevertheless dependent for survival, and he attempts to discount its danger to his interests. The monthly magazine will be the instrument through which that anonymous reader will be transformed to the mind's desire. The monthly magazine, he insists, has an advantage over the established quarterlies with their "ponderosity" and irrelevance to the emerging culture, lagging as they do out of time. On the other hand, the monthly has an advantage over the daily journals, committed as those are to presenting "each topic as it flits before the eye of the public." He denies the conclusion of those critics who find in the increasing influence of periodicals a "downward tendency in American taste or in American letters." It is rather a healthy "sign of the times, an indication of an era in which men are forced upon the curt, the condensed, the well-digested," as opposed to "the verbose, the detailed, the voluminous, the inaccessible." For "beyond question [men now] think with more rapidity, with more skill, with more tact, with more of method and less of excrescence in the thought." Writers and readers of the past are not so far advanced as the contemporary world, says the grandfather of Mrs. Lucynell Crater. But we are not fully convinced Poe believes his argument with an unwavering faith. At the time he is expressing this defense, Kierkegaard is arguing that the new journalism would become the medium of the mob, a threat to philosophy. Given an increasingly reflective age in which all distinctions were being reduced so that every man might be his own philosopher, Kierkegaard says, the existential realities are denied; it is inevitable therefore that the daily press become Socrates to the masses. That dyspeptic philosopher was insisting upon what Poe knew but was reluctant to admit. One cannot browse *Marginalia* or "Some Talk with a Mummy" or "Mellonta Tauta" without detecting Poe's awareness of that danger, which is why he insists that critics such as himself and the readers of *Godey's Lady's Book* and *Graham's Magazine* must "demand that [periodicals] have sufficient merit to render them noticeable in the beginning" and that they continue so.

Poe might have been writing a circular for the *Reader's Digest* or its numerous imitators in praising "the curt, the condensed, the well-digested." But what might finally have given him more discomfort is the influence of his own aesthetic principles upon the development of periodical literature since his day. His arguments about the requirements of the story or poem for instance, in respect to verbal details and their control toward a unity of effect, have a persuasiveness very attractive to one seeking an intellectual formula, a blueprint suitable to creative writing courses. Our father of the short story would no doubt feel either horror or terror—words whose implications he does not always attempt to distinguish—at the suggestion that he contributes to such a utilitarian approach to the genre, opposed as he is to social and political utilitarianism. Still, if one were so inclined he might discover a formulaic influence upon popular fiction, out of the "Philosophy of Composition" and "The Poetic Principle," wider than Poe's more obvious influence upon the murder mystery. It is to be found in that story which depends upon tricks and starts and turns, in which the game for the reader is to determine analytically a pattern which solves the story's X—the sort of expectation of the story which we find Poe asserting as unsatisfied by Hawthorne's "White Old Maid" or "The Minister's Black Veil." In Hawthorne's stories the pieces of the puzzle do not fit to Poe's satisfaction. The formulaic influence Poe has on popular fiction, more general than his detective fiction, is transmitted by mutation through writers like O. Henry. Where Poe addresses the reader's intellect in respect to the story's X, exceedingly scornful of a general audience, the O. Henry approach adapts Poe's puzzle to the service of sentiment, the irony turning pathetic. That is, the motive force of sentimentality enters upon Poe's craft of the short story. The result is the sort of story for which there are numerous How-to text books and several trade magazines, an approach to the craft of fiction that led Miss O'Connor to remark that "Unfortunately, there is a kind of writing that can be taught; it is the kind you then have to teach people not to read." And again, "Everywhere I go I'm asked if I think universities stifle writers. I think they don't stifle enough of them."

There is a second, more welcomed influence on modern fiction by Poe, though excesses born of that influence may also have contributed to the evil days upon which fiction has fallen in our time. This influence enters somewhat late, after voyaging abroad and returning to us modified and refined to the point that Poe's presence is largely unnoticed. It might strike Poe as bitterly ironic that we miss that presence largely because of the aura of romantic internationalism that speaks high art and makes it particularly attractive to the academy, given his attitude toward imported art. For his influence comes back to us through Flaubert or Joyce. In the world outside the academy, a careful reader might discover, the delayed influence enters and crosses with Poe's earlier popularizing influence, received more directly and immediately through our flourishing periodicals. One might study selected stories in the *Saturday Evening Post* over several decades up to World War II and by contrast find this later influence entering popular fiction in the late 1940s and early 1950s through the sophisticated women's magazines and somewhat later the *Post* itself, just as that magazine expires. One of the ironies of that late influence is that it helped prepare a more serious audience than Poe found available through the periodicals of his day. Miss O'Connor for instance was able to publish on occasion in *Mademoiselle, Harper's Bazaar, Tomorrow*, and perhaps with some remote credit due Poe for that possibility.

What I mean to suggest by such brief speculation on Poe's influence upon the popular spirit is that he is a considerable and continuing influence upon subsequent audiences, and most particularly through that prose literature of high seriousness which we think of as the high water marks in the stream of modern letters—Flaubert, James, Joyce. The less sophisticated reader, prepared by the first of Poe's influences, met the second influence at its higher level in the popular journals, just before fiction died out of those journals after World War II. Of course Poe's "respectable" influence on letters has been remarked by critics for a long time, though rather limited to his conspicuous effect upon Baudelaire and the symbolist poets. But as Allen Tate has pointed out, Poe's concern for the unity of effect, in the individual word's control of that effect, will illuminate the "more mature work in the naturalistic-symbolic technique of Flaubert, Joyce, and James."

Still Poe's influence upon the craft of fiction even when so credited might somewhat obscure another and more fundamental interest he holds for us in our present study. His critical arguments aside, he remains fascinating to us in his fictional practice, even when we feel somewhat embarrassed by the quality of most of it. I do not think any American writer of "major" reputation has written so much bad literature. Yet even the worst of it has an attraction, though it lead to such caustic responses as James's or Eliot's. One feels drawn to solve the problem of Poe. He attracts a swarm of critics of the psychological, those more concerned with riddling Poe's strange "personality" than with evaluating the intellectual position implicit in his work. But it was this latter dimension of Poe which drew the French writers to him immediately. It is a convenience perhaps to find him a peculiar individual, as the Freudians must inevitably do. But he is more significant than as a subject for a case study: he is of interest to our immediate concerns in his prophetic dimension, as local harbinger of gnostic maladies.

As prophet, he is a forerunner of a school of thought in our literature which has all but dominated serious letters in the middle years of this centruy, a school of thought that affects even the popular mind more generally than that mind recognizes, its very discomfort in the world distracting it from the realization. And since Flannery O'Connor is so largely concerned with that modern mind, perhaps she may be of help to us in exploring Poe's contribution to, or reflection of, the bankruptcy of reason in the popular spirit of our day. Again, we may expect his contribution to appear as somewhat remote, coming to us once more from a sojourn upon the continent, as Allen Tate suggests in calling him existentialist. But it may be also true that we were more directly influenced by Poe the Prophet than we realize. As Tate also remarks, "One reason why Americans may be a little bored with French existentialism is that we have always been existentialists, or have been since the time of Poe, who discovered it in us." Speaking of the grandmother and the Misfit in her story "A Good Man Is Hard to Find," Miss O'Connor says, "a prophet gone wrong is almost always more interesting than your grandmother." Certainly Flaubert, James, Joyce are the immediately recognizable grandmothers of much modern fiction, particularly Miss O'Connor's own. But it is the interest in prophets gone wrong that makes Poe particularly helpful in reading her fiction and in seeing the spiritual confusions in our disintegrating community. The point to consider here, therefore, is not so much whether Poe has a sense of *le mot juste*, which is part of his legacy to us, but whether his literary failures, pointed out by critics like Allen Tate and Henry James, are a consequence inherent in the vision he holds of the world. The latter is our thesis.

In examining the thesis I think we may see that Poe is more important as a subject in Miss O'Connor's fiction than as a literary influence upon her art; he is representative of the modern mind that interests her, and he is a local kinsman as well. She protests gently that most Southern writers "are considered . . . to be unhappy combinations of Poe and Erskine Caldwell." In that rebuke to the critic she surely means to dissociate herself from both writers. As we explore the grounds upon which she would establish her separation from Poe, we will see why Professor Miles Orvell, in a generally helpful book, *Invisible Parade*, is rather wide of the mark when he suggests that Flannery O'Connor's "imaginative realization of her Christian faith is strikingly close to Poe's cosmology." We shall also find, in such distinctions as may be made between them, a rebuke for those critics who think that Miss O'Connor, as Professor Martha Stephens would have it, holds a view in which "Human beings are ugly in every way; the human form itself . . . distinctly unpleasant to behold; human life . . . a sordid, almost hideous affair. The only act that is worthy of respect is the act of renouncing all worldly involvement, pleasure, and achievement." Miss O'Connor's own disengagement from her characters' views of the created world, through her fictional point of view, and Poe's virtually invariable first person point of view are important strategies out of each one's vision and not simply an election of a technical solution to an aesthetic problem. Professor Stephens's characterization of Flannery O'Connor is more nearly applicable to Poe, in spite of his verbal emphasis upon the "Beautiful." He is the poet of the renunciation of the world.

Miss O'Connor says, in words that bear obvious parallel to Poe's argument in his "Philosophy of Composition" and "Poetic Principle,"

> . . . it is from the kind of world the writer creates, from the kind of character and detail he invests it with, that a reader can find the intellectual meaning of a book . . . it cannot be drained off and used as a substitute for the book. The novelist makes his statement by selection, and if he is any good, he selects every word for a reason, every detail for a reason, every incident for a reason, and arranges them in a certain time-sequence for a reason. He demonstrates something that cannot possibly be demonstrated any other way than with a whole novel.

This could have been said by Poe—and was substantially said by him. He would not have said "novel," though he would very much like the use of "demonstrate." Where the difference lies is in the reasons behind such common fictional principles; on this point the two writers could not be further apart. The center of intellectual meaning in Poe, and it is one element of his kinship to Joyce, lies in the power of the artist as creator, a power exalted by his art "if he is any good." But to O'Connor, genius is a gift with dangerous temptations to pride. It is a gift beyond rational explanations of it, so that a certain aura of mystery beyond the reason's or the imagination's powers always remains to art. This she acknowledges repeatedly in *Mystery and Manners*.

As for the intellectual meanings of her fiction, we notice her statement that as artist she is committed to "the reasonable use of the unreasonable. In art the reason goes wherever the imagination goes. We have reduced the uses of the reason terribly. You say a thing is reasonable and people think you mean it's safe. What's reasonable is seldom safe and always exciting." One detects in such statements not only a comfortable relationship between imagination and reason in Miss O'Connor's mind, but a recognition of reason's limitations as well. For reason too is a gift of our being, its degree varying in each person. It is to be used wisely by the will, lest it also endanger one through the temptations of pride. In her memorable characters—Haze Motes, the Misfit, Tarwater, Rayber—one observes an exercise of reason within the distinctive limitation of the created characters. Haze Motes, for instance, is more limited intellectually than Rayber. But it is in the character's exercise of reason that he presses beyond the limits of reason, to a point of panic and destruction, and often to a point of partial restoration. When she says that "The prophet-freaks of Southern literature are not images of the man in the street," she is speaking of her own characters primarily, and she adds, "They are images of man forced out to meet the extremes of his own nature." They are forced out, we should notice, by their reason as well as by intuitions of transcendence; their peril increases as they discover reason's inadequacy.

The intellectual meanings of her fiction turn always toward a moment of grace, through which creation is celebrated. This is so even if that moment entails the advent of death, as it does so often in her fiction, for, like Poe, her subject is death. But what is crucial is that hers is a concern for death as addressed by St. Paul and the New Testament. Where Poe elects to believe the death of a beautiful woman the most poetic of all subjects, Miss O'Connor believes that the death of a gross, vulgar old man like old Mason Tarwater, or a seemingly cliché-ridden nonentity like Julian's mother, is the most poetic. The fictional epiphany, the moment of revelation and absolution of fictional tensions which interests Poe no less than Joyce in the structure of his fictions, bears profounder meaning for Miss O'Connor than either Poe or Joyce allow. The lowliest and most unlikely are subject to the rescue in her fiction, albeit at considerable cost to them, and rescue involves far more than a release of fictional tensions.

As with Poe, Miss O'Connor's address to death is the key to her address to the whole of creation. "I admit to . . . preoccupation with belief and with death and grace and the devil." At the bottom of a page in her copy of C. S. Lewis's *The Problem of Pain*, she copies out words from Lewis's text: "The world exists that God may love us—(on a deeper level—for our sakes)." The general enthusiasm with which she marks passage after passage in this book, and the notes she makes in its margins, show how closely its ideas correspond to her own thinking on the question of that evil in the world which is reflected by pain and death and which distorts our vision of creation most destructively, making us subject to despair.[1] On the book's half-title page she has written, "I am the mother of fair love, and of pain, and of knowledge and of holy hope. Ecclea."[2] She has written the same words, excluding their source, at the bottom

---

1. Sister Kathleen Feeley, in her survey of Miss O'Connor's library (*Flannery O'Connor: Voice of the Peacock*) very curiously omits any mention of Lewis's book; it is more heavily marked by Miss O'Connor than most books in her collection.

2. It is Wisdom who speaks the words in *Ecclesiasticus* xxiv,—the Wisdom of God: "I am the mother of fair love, and fear, and knowledge, and holy hope." (*Ancient Hebrew Literature*, volume iv, p. 166 [London: J. M. Dent, 1907]) Pascal personified God's Wisdom in the same way, and with an attention to "injustice" such as Ivan Karamazov's vision of the world flounders on, a vision Miss O'Connor explicitly attacks.

of page 97, a particularly heavily marked section in the course of
Lewis's argument justifying pain. The key words in *Ecclesiasticus* for
Miss O'Connor, in contradistinction to Poe, are love and hope, and
the position she approves here is precisely the one she takes to
refute Camus and Ivan Karamazov in her "Introduction" to the
Memoir of Mary Ann, a refutation dramatized in her reduction of
Rayber in *The Violent Bear It Away*. For Rayber does come at last to
a moment of despair.

One may easily misunderstand Miss O'Connor's emphasis
upon death as an interest in the morbid for its emotional effect
upon a reader, for she does use death as the repeated focus of her
fiction. But she does so because she believes that an insight into the
reality of human existence in the world occurs at our most
desperate moments, those moments when the alternatives seem to
be either obliteration or a rescue from obliteration. "I'm a born
Catholic and death has always been a brother to my imagination,"
she says. "I can't imagine a story that doesn't properly end in it or
in its foreshadowings." But her interest lies, not in any repulsion
she feels for the created world that might be thought to give rise to a
"death wish." It lies in the very significance of that created world,
for the world is the creature of God. She would insist that only
when one has come to terms with death is he prepared to value the
world, which—since it has a beginning—has death inherent in it.
However bizarre on the surface of its action, the conclusion of "A
Good Man Is Hard to Find" involves a rescue. There is in the old
woman, even as she is ruthlessly shot down, a change in her sight, a
movement toward vision. It is a movement from blindness in the
world itself as glimpsed in its spiritual dimension for a moment. As
the old woman lies "in a puddle of blood with her legs crossed under like a child's," her face is "smiling up at the cloudless sky." The
Misfit, on the other hand, is without his glasses, his eyes "red-
rimmed and pale and defenseless-looking," his world empty rather
than cloudless. And similarly Tarwater, at the point of his final vision just before he turns to the lost children in the city of man,
walks through young corn freshly plowed, a new beginning to his
pursuit of the Bread of Life, though it has not yet registered upon
him as such.

Planes of purpling red above the treeline stretched back like stairsteps to reach the dusk. The corn the old man has planted was up about a foot and moved in wavering lines of green across the field. . . . The boy stood there, a small rigid, hatless figure. . . .

There is in Miss O'Connor's celebration of creation a turning in her character, as these citations indicate, however slight it may seem, a turning from darkness and willful deprivation. Even a funeral, in her perspective, is a festival,[3] and her comic treatment of old Tarwater's death is possible only because she sees him as right in his violent hunger for the Bread of Life. The comedy is at Tarwater's expense. The boy will be driven through the waters of the world until truly baptized into the new life. The release she intends is one of joy for Tarwater at the end of his ordeal, a joy separate from that comic amusement which is so obvious an ingredient of her fiction, and we should notice how subdued our laughter is in the final pages of the novel. There is a release from the dramatic tensions she builds, a sense of completion, markedly different from the moment of recognition that closes "The Tell-Tale Heart" or "The Fall of the House of Usher." Death for Flannery O'Connor means a beginning, not an end as it does for Poe. It is a metaphor through which she speaks of the recovery of the whole being, whereas in Poe it is a metaphor for the dissolution of all being. Her fiction is consequently less grim than its spectacle tempts some readers to believe. That is why she feels constrained to say in an interview, "My characters are described as despairing only by superficial critics. Very few of my characters despair and those who do, don't reflect my views." Her explorations of evil in the outer world make her fiction something more than an aesthetic object which justifies the intellect that creates it. "The basis of art is truth, both in matter and in mode," she says, and truth for her touches always the transcendent cause of all existence. That is why "The writer's moral sense must coincide with his dramatic sense." In the greatest fiction, she says, this is inevitably the case, "and I see no way for it to do this unless [the writer's] moral judgment is part of the very act of seeing, and he is free to use it." Such, one might add, is an in-

---

3. On this point, see once more Josef Pieper's *In Tune with the World: A Theory of Festival.* (Chicago: Franciscan Herald Press, 1973.)

evitable dimension of art, since art is selective of the world. The artist chooses from that world for the construction of his particular world, and his judgment is implicit in his selection. This does not, of course, excuse the artist his responsibility to art as vocation; indeed it complicates his vocation. For his art is not justified by his belief or opinion; he is not a propagandist or an evangelist, but a prophet of reality. That is to say, he bears witness. "Competence" is the agent of "vision" in art. In contrast, Poe's "moral activity" of analysis is inadequate to the point at issue here. It is to his analysis of the created world that we now turn.

CHAPTER X

HUMBOLDT'S CLOTHES
AND POE'S SHADOWY EMPEROR

In *Eureka* Poe reveals a remarkable first fruits of arrested development in American letters. For he is a literary Tom Sawyer who, to borrow a phrase from Eliot, seems to have "had the experience but missed the meaning." Or, as Eliot puts it directly of Poe in his essay "From Poe to Valéry," his late farewell to one facet of Eliot's own Americanism, "That Poe had a powerful intellect is undeniable: but it seems . . . the intellect of a highly gifted young person before puberty." If the French followers of Poe are right in seeing what Eliot calls "an essential unity" in the variety of Poe's forms, we may agree, suggesting that the unity lies not in the aesthetic dimension, but in his vision. And Eliot is right in another point: it is an arrested vision. There is neither a development of vision such as is revealed in the body of Eliot's own work nor that enlarging resonance which one discovers where the vision is essentially complete from the beginning but requires a development of art suitable to the complex demands of the vision. That last was, I contend, the happy situation for Miss O'Connor.

Of *Eureka* Poe writes, in the margins of his copy of the published work: "What I here propose is true:—therefore it cannot die—or if by any means it be now trodden down so that it die, it will 'rise again to Life Everlasting'. " He adds, "Nevertheless it is as a Poem only that I wish this work to be judged after I am dead." Since Poe died the year after the work's publication, the marginal notes argue a final, emphatic commitment to the ideas. To consider the work as a poem is to conclude that Poe himself feels truth within the province of poetry, in spite of his denials elsewhere. Or at least he feels that his *own* truth is proper to the poem. Even his *nevertheless* does not succeed in removing the contradiction, unless we are prepared to say that Poe, given the revelation of truth which is the content of this work, would have us ignore the truth in the interest of the work as poem. But in that event, the work fits few of those criteria for poetry enunciated in "The Philosophy of Composition" and "The Poetic Principle."

Poe doesn't mean *Eureka* to be considered a poem of knowledge, like Lucretius' *De Rerum*, but a poem of vision, more nearly like Teilhard de Chardin's *Phenomenon of Man*. He does require us, virtually from his deathbed, to take the work seriously if we are to take him seriously as a poet. And the work does express a fundamental premise which he phrases in the margins of his copy: "The General Proposition is this—Because Nothing was, therefore All things are." His visionary poem proceeds then from a proposition diametrically opposed to Teilhard's, Teilhard's premise being that all things proceed from and depend upon perfect being, God. In the published version to which his notes are added, Poe's phrasing of his "ruling idea" is stated, with his emphasis: "*In the Original Unity of the First Thing lies the Secondary Cause of All Things, with the Germ of their Inevitable Annihilation.*" We can but observe that, though Poe uses the term God from time to time in *Eureka* and elsewhere, he is quite careful here to exclude that term from his statement of the general proposition of *Eureka*. One notices also that, wherever he uses the word *God*, it has the air of a concession to popular expectation, as if he may by that concession get on with his argument without the opposition he might encounter should he directly set aside the First Cause of more orthodox or more popularly accepted cosmologies. His use of the term *God*, indeed, is less direct in his argument than that by Descartes, against which Pascal objects: "I cannot forgive Descartes: in his whole philosophy he would like to do without God; but he could not help allowing Him a flick of the fingers to set the world in motion; after that he had no more use for God."

One nevertheless sees Poe playing Descartes's game in "The

Power of Words," published in 1845 and approximately contemporary with *Eureka*. It is a colloquy, this time between Oinos, recently dead, and Agathos, in whom resides a knowledge to be imparted to the timid, innocent Oinos as they hover above a star. The whole is "a conception I intend," says Agathos. "Deity does not create," except as Deity may be said to have created "In the beginning *only*." Agathos poses the principle of creation as follows: only motion creates, and "the source of all motion is thought." Creation is therefore out of the "physical power of words." By his act of words, Agathos is creator. The flowers of the star above which they hover are "like a fairy dream," observes Oinos, "but its fierce volcanoes like the passions of a turbulent heart." And that, confesses Agathos through his tears, is exactly what they are: "This wild star . . . I spoke it into birth." In this work is proposed "the abyss of nonentity" from which the "starry worlds . . . burst hourly forth," and from the argument here and in *Eureka's* premise (declared immortal in Poe's marginal note) we must conclude that Poe's "First Thing" to which alone unity may be ascribed is Nothingness. In so far as "nonentity" or chaos or nonbeing are terms for the cause of All Things, All Things have in them the germ of that origin which grows toward its source and home—Nothingness. One has at least an inversion of the traditional Christian view. If Baudelaire sees in Poe's negative a door to the Positive, which he pursues in his dark correspondences, Baudelaire's is a fundamental misreading of the American poet. It will take a Martin Heidegger to rescue in some degree Poe's sense of ultimate annihilation.[1] In Poe's "Material and Spiritual Universe" lies a consciousness defeated by the body, the body being Poe's immediate enemy and surrogate for the whole of that world separate from the consciousness. Such is very much Poe's position, and his poetry and tales and prose poems reveal that it is so.

1. In respect to Baudelaire's concern, the editor of the text from which we quoted "The Power of Words" introduces a remark from Professor W. LeConte Stevens in a note (287): "The author's idea is . . . the deduction of positive conclusions from negative premises, and hence utterly worthless so far as its relation to science is concerned." Poe is guilty of "neglecting the laws of scientific evidence." But on the other hand the phenomenologists, who wrestle so constantly with the problem of *intention* in relation to *reality*, might well find Agathos' "conception I intend" and the argument of the piece of interest. From this position, the empirical physicist mistakes the nature of reality, as we saw in Husserl's argument introduced in the opening pages of this volume.

As for Poe's universe, it is "*the utmost conceivable expanse of space, with all things, spiritual and material, that can be imagined to exist within the compass of that expanse.*" One must notice the passive *can be imagined*, whose agent is the speaker, and secondarily, by delegation presumably, the reader. One notices as well that this universe is *conceived* by the speaker. Indeed, the objection Poe raises at once to the cosmology of Alexander von Humboldt, to whom *Eureka* is dedicated, is that Humboldt's world does not rest on the universe's "individuality but in its generality." Now for most thinkers, generality is the way the finite mind limits the multitudinous world, considered as already existing, so that the finite mind may look at a part of it and proceed to larger assimilations. We cannot look at all of it and yet are discontent to look at only one part of it; so in spite of those risks of abstraction inherent in generalization, we attempt larger assimilations of creation by that abstracting bite in the apple of the world, *generality*. Not so for Poe; for him the conceived universe must bear the stamp of the individuality of the projecting mind, wherein it is made complete and particular at once. He quarrels with Humboldt's "theme": "the law of *each* portion of the merely physical Universe, as this law is related to the laws of *every other* portion of this merely physical Universe." To reduce Poe's objection to its base, Humboldt's theme is that an objective creation exists independent of the mind that would contain it, thus making impossible, in Poe's estimate, a satisfactory cosmology; for the universe cannot be thus contained or controlled by the individual awareness, proceeding as Humboldt does.

In this respect, one may note a difference between Poe and those activist thinkers of the Enlightenment whom Voegelin examines relentlessly. Those thinkers also assume the existence of the outer world, without which assumption their political and social actions would have no meaning at all. There is nevertheless a relation between that activist thought and Poe's, and a kinship between their minds as well, which Dostoevski sees rather effectively in his dramatization of Ivan Karamazov's dilemma. Ivan's intellectual adolescence is one explicitly nurtured by the Enlightenment's activist thinkers, as the devil points out to Ivan in that strange visitation during Ivan's delirium. The effect of his intellectual beginning is that Ivan has been brought to believe that "all things are lawful" for him because he is an intellectual. Ivan foresees the day of an absolute liberation of mankind from the superstitions that rest in a belief in God. We have seen the beginnings of this emancipation by those self-elected higher intelligences, beginning with Voltaire and developing through the fathers of the French Revolution and into our own day. Ivan's devil summarizes the course of that thought: "There is no law for God. Where God stands, the place is holy. Where I stand will be at once the foremost place[2]. . . 'all things are lawful' and that's the end of it!'" Thus Ivan's devil speaks Ivan's intellectual position mockingly, and he adds, "if you want to swindle why do you want a moral sanction for doing it?" That is the very question put to Comte by Eric Voegelin in his analysis of Comte, as we have seen.

Now from a position above the law, attained by the intellect through its act of setting itself aside from the world, wherever that intellect stands becomes the only possible holy ground. Such self-advance is also far along the road to alienation, at the end of which road lies an inevitable annihilation. This is the crucial point Dostoevski recognizes. What one may say justly of Poe is that he, like Ivan, is one of the sons of the Enlightenment, though Ivan is more passionately concerned with the external world than Poe. Ivan is offended to the point of rage and despair by the absence of justice in the external world, conceiving justice from that holy ground, his own mind. It is this passionate concern in him that prompts Miss O'Connor to call particular attention to Ivan's sentimental attachment to evil (what Ivan's devil calls "the indispensable minus") as an indictment of God. Ivan's is for her an instance of that "popular pity" which, in the interest of its own sensibility, denies reality and thereby destroys vision. It is the intellectual "sensibility" in Ivan which is offended, as his devil notes with cruel delight and humor, just as it is a pseudo-intellectual sensibility in Miss O'Connor's Asbury that is offended. Ivan's devil, who has ap-

---

2. There is a suggestion of diabolical participation in such thought, which is reflected analogically in Malachi Martin's study of exorcism, *Hostages to Satan*. The expelled spirits at the last moment become almost pathetic. They are being denied a *place*; we have the paradox of mysterious beings forced into "placelessness," and they turn to abject pleas. In one instance the spirit being displaced argues that Christ at least drove it into swine.

peared as a very ordinary old man, says: "You are really angry with me for not having appeared to you in a red glow, with thunder and lightning, with scorched wings, but have shown myself in such a modest form. . . . How could such a vulgar devil visit such a great man as you! Yes, there is that romantic strain in you . . . ." If Tarwater expects God, rather than the devil, to appear with thunder and lightning, his is but another form of the same romantic strain. And when Tarwater is visited by his own devil, we notice, it is one very much like Ivan's in manner and even in the suggestions of physical appearance and character. Asbury, a similar romantic, is reduced from his sentimentality by the Holy Spirit's descent through the medium of a water stain on his bedroom ceiling, a powerful rebuke to such "a great man" as Asbury.

One must notice of Ivan as of Poe that his is an intellectual engagement of the world, the rules of which he must be allowed to dictate. That point is made by the constant endurance of Alyosha with his spiritual commitment to the world. As Ivan's devil says, "All you care about is intelligence." That is the sort of care which rarefies one's being until the soul, stunted in its growth till reduced to a lean intellect leaning upon the weak reed of reason, finds itself so far removed from the world's reality that its only hope seems to lie in annihilation. Ivan has come to the point where, like his devil, he seems given "simply for annihilation". The devil at last defines the ground he shares with Ivan as proof of their common philosophy, and it is ground common to Poe: "*Je pense, donc je suis.*" Having accepted Descartes, Ivan's "brain fever" is assured—his separation from the world. As he tells Alyosha as prelude to his poem of the Grand Inquisitor, a belief in God is easy enough. "It's not that I don't accept God, you must understand, it's the world created by Him that I don't accept." And so it is that imagination and reason are set to battle by Ivan's will as by Poe's. Those faculties are directed largely against the outer world, though sometimes they confound each other. The "Grand Inquisitor" is a "poem" we are told by Ivan out of the imagination, in support of the reasoning that has brought Ivan to his position. In Ivan's delirium, the reason pays back a debt to the imagination through the devil's argument: "I simply ask for annihilation." For when

Ivan consults the devil on the question of God's existence, he is rebuffed by the devil's clever expression of doubt that man himself exists. Thus all being at last seems an illusion, and that is an idea that haunts Ivan to the edge of insanity, to the edge of an annihilation of intellect as the only revenge intellect has upon the chimera of existence. For Ivan, as Poe's poem says, "*All* that we see or seem / Is but a dream within a dream."

Dostoevski read Poe and understood him; Poe is of Ivan's tribe. He too can accept the existence of God: the difficulty lies in accepting the world created by Him. In the conflict which results from such aberrant thought, God becomes transformed into the poet's intellect and the world becomes an act of creation by that intellect so that it may be loved. For, as Baudelaire says, "it is more difficult to love God than to believe in Him"—on the evidence of the created world with its tangled problems of justice and mercy. "Ours," Poe says as early as *Al Aaraaf*, "is a world of words." Where the intellect stands is holy land because the ground is the intellect's own creation. Poe recognizes an inconsistency in this posture, but it is a posture he cannot resist, though he can acknowledge the inconsistency. We may see that acknowledgment, for instance, by reading his "Angel of the Odd" alongside Ivan's encounter with his devil.

Our excursion into Dostoevski is to help explain something of Poe's objection to Humboldt, whose weakness (from Poe's position) is that he put such an emphasis on the existence of a world separate from the mind that explores it. It is a consideration of some interest to us that Humboldt, in his earlier days, set out to be in one sense the Teilhard de Chardin of his day. Early in his career, he believed he detected in the actions of nature a vital power, in stone as in the vegetable and higher orders, a movement of teleological import. Had he come at the end of the century, he might have spoken of an *èlan vital*; or in our own century he might possibly have been captivated by Teilhard's vertical and radial energies, as Julian Huxley was. But his subsequent interests in natural philosophy turned him increasingly empiricist and the world became for him increasingly an object without spiritual dimension. He wanders the face of the earth, collecting material from the depths of mines and on high mountains, from jungles and arid plains, and in such volume as to occupy him and his assistants a score of years in the arranging. The aim in his work *Physique du Monde* is to catalogue Poe's "all things". His monumental work in thirty volumes, *Voyage de Humboldt et Bonpland*, prepared him for the unifying work, his imaginative *Kosmos*, which is the work Poe rejects in *Eureka*. It was to have been for Humboldt the culmination of his knowledge, a work as grandly intended as Kepler's *Harmony of the World*, though a work anchored more concretely than Kepler's attempt at a synthesis of knowledge through geometry, music, astrology, and epistemology. As Koestler says in his biography of Kepler, "After Kepler, fragmentation of experience sets in again, science is divorced from religion, religion from art, substance from form, matter from mind." Kepler's was an attempt to hold a disintegrating world together; Humboldt's to pull a world disintegrated back together. Koestler's words might be taken substantially from Voegelin or Flannery O'Connor, so closely they parallel sentences we have quoted earlier. But Koestler is not correct in saying of Kepler's Harmony that "It was the first attempt since Plato at an all-embracing synthesis, and it is the last to our day." Setting Lucretius aside, one must still acknowledge St. Thomas Aquinas at least. And we see the effect of that fragmentation in the nineteenth century as leading to innumerable attempts, Humboldt's, Comte's, Bergson's, Husserl's, Heidegger's, Poe's—all attempting to unify experience. These attempts are symptoms of that growing dis-ease which in our century found desperate expression in *The Waste Land*, that dispersal of mind among shattered images—a heap of broken mirrors. On Margate sands the mind "can connect / Nothing with nothing" in the desperate moment. And Eliot's poem was prelude to a flooding of our literature with the despair of alientation. The dead end is Sartre's philosophical attempt to establish the ultimate secret of existence upon Nothingness. That dead end of thought about being is, as we have seen, one of Miss O'Connor's principal subjects, her comedy aimed at showing that, while the Emperor of such thought has clothes enough, he has no being upon which to hang them. With that thought, we return to Humboldt's cosmological clothes and to Poe's shadowy Emperor.

Humboldt's attempt at a unified vision of existence is less abstract and esoteric than Comte's or Husserl's. It is directed against the specialization encroaching upon science and speaks in favor of a universalism such as allies Humboldt in his aim with poets like Lucretius. A biographer, Carl Theodore Trall, summarizes his significance thus: "The supreme and abiding value of his work consists in its faithful reflection of the mind of a great man." That, one realizes, is what Poe wishes his own *Kosmos* to reflect, but with his accomplishment singular in that, unlike Humboldt, he did not travel the face of the earth save imaginatively. Poe's work is deliberately a projection of his own mind as substance, its "spiritual" dimension his own consciousness which must fill the void. In this respect he is akin to Husserl or Heidegger in his attempt at a unified world. For in spite of his reservations about the rational intellect, Poe sets about projecting a rationalized image of the universe. Nevertheless, it is an image of a self-created universe whose premise undercuts its objective existence. And it is at this point that Poe's difficulties with readers begin. For the external world, which Poe cannot finally escape, is read by him as Plato's world of shadow; yet it is an inverted shadow for Poe: it is the shadow of Nonexistence rather than of perfect Idea. That difference makes the reader a particularly awkward consideration, since consistency requires a reader's creation by the poet's consciousness along with the rest of the poet's "imagined world." It makes necessary a new aesthetics, a new "Poetic Principle."

Poe's imaginative act troubles him far more than it seems to bother a latter-day cousin, Wallace Stevens, who is more comfortable with his own supreme fiction, even as he is less dogmatic in his attempt to recruit other minds to his position.[3] But to his credit,

---

3. Of Poe's truculence toward his reader and other writers, it bears remarking in passing that in his attitude he is like no other American poet so much as Ezra Pound. One is very struck by the similarity as one reads *Marginalia*. Attacking the *North American Review* and its clique, he suggests a motto from Sterne as a measure: "As we rode along the valley we saw a herd of asses on the top of one of the mountains—how they viewed and *reviewed* us!" He attacks Emerson as a "respectful imitation of Carlyle," whom he abhors. His attack upon Greek drama as inadequate reminds one of Pound's dismissal of all but a few choruses of Sophocles in Pound's early days, in his letters to Iris Barry. Poe attacks the mob, bad taste, antiquarians; he makes fun of the academy. His arguments and observations are heavy with French, Greek, Latin, even Hebrew. He comments on the order of Aristotle's works and ex-

Poe finds his universe troublesomely haunted; he is constantly disturbed by a ghost which is not his own invention. The ghost is that shadow through which Plato (and Baudelaire) make way toward a transcendent. Poe is haunted by that shadow as it intimates an objective world, and it becomes the primary and desperate task of his imagination to keep it at bay. That is one reason one finds in his fictional details an absence of those qualities we ascribe to naturalistic fiction or imagistic poetry. For there is in him the sort of discomfort that Flannery O'Connor's Rayber feels in the presence of any *thing* in the natural world, a point we may now develop.

So long as Rayber can control the mystery of being through an intellect which sees nature as scientific formulae, he is safe. The idiot son Bishop is for Rayber "part of a simple equation that required no further solution, except at the moments when with little or no warning he would feel himself overwhelmed by the horrifying love." It is this love which is Flannery O'Connor's theme, and she displays its effect upon Rayber, who cannot rationalize it away, though he is an avowed rationalist. Love is to him understandable only as a touch of insanity upon the reason, in no way to be explained by *agape*, or even by Poe's "divine Eros." He discovers that his own world, which he would maintain in safety by the mechanical hearing aid that he can shut off and the glasses that focus and so suspend the outer world, is breached. But his world is breached not only by the specific irrational love of this mistake of nature, his idiot son, Bishop: "Anything he looked at too long could bring it on. It could be a stick or a stone, the line of a shadow, the absurd old man's walk of a starling crossing the sidewalk. If, without thinking, he lent himself to it, he would feel suddenly a morbid surge of love that terrified him—powerful enough to throw

plicates a passage in Hebrew from *Ezekiel*. Hannibal's crossing of the Alps is turned to a point, and he explores current arguments concerning a suitable name for our emerging nation, settling on his own suggestion as the only reasonable one: Appalachia. In his own way he sets about overthrowing the iambic pentameter line; he praises originality of and for itself, an inclination in Pound which Pound moved beyond. Poe is not given to the celebration of local gods, of course, though William Carlos Williams would have it otherwise. In temperament Pound and Poe bear striking resemblance, their display of anger called forth by a common cause: both have a dream of what American literature might become; both assume a general stupidity of the audience at large. Except for its form, one discovers Poe's *Marginalia* serving him somewhat as the *Cantos* serve Pound. Or to put it another way, Pound raises *Marginalia* to an art of an arresting accomplishment in the *Cantos*.

him to the ground in an act of idiot praise. It was completely irrational and abnormal."[4] It is the objects of the created world
through which Rayber is brought to spiritual despair over his own
inadequacy. When he looks into his heart instead of his mind, the
insanity of love begins its descent to engulf him in its terror, so that
he must quickly retreat to the safe heights of reason lest he be lost.

One also discovers in Poe's use of details a strong suggestion of
a fear of objects as they threaten the mind, even as with Rayber; for
objects have an uncomfortable habit of either opening the heart
toward creation and its Cause or terrifying the heart till it close
upon itself. In *Marginalia*, Poe remarks, "To be thoroughly conver-
sant with Man's heart, is to take our final lesson in the iron-clasped
volume of Despair." For if the reason can find no hope of rescue
separate from its own powers, then despair is its nemesis. And
again he says, "There are moments when, even to the sober eye of
Reason, the world of our sad humanity must assume the aspect of
Hell; but the Imagination of Man is no Carathis, to explore with
impunity its every cavern. Alas! the grim legion of sepulchral terrors can*not* be regarded as altogether fanciful." Here we have an incipient Ivan Karamazov. Ivan, after that expedition into the
caverns of his own heart under the guidance of a devil he insists is
only a figment of his imagination, returns to the world with
Alyosha's knocking on the door. And he insists to Alyosha, "It was
not a dream! No, I swear it all happened just now." Poe declares
that those sleeping demons "must be suffered to slumber, or we
perish."

In such unguarded moments, we suspect that Poe recognizes
the demons that beset an Ivan or a Rayber, but he will not pursue
them too closely to discover their name, whether Lucifer or Love.

---

4. Sister Emma Therese Healy, in her Commentary on Saint Bonaventure's *De Reductione Artium ad Theologiam* examines Saint Bonaventure's conception of light in its relation to our
"seeing" the world. For him "any luminous point is capable of producing on all sides and
propagating immediately a luminous sphere centered around it with a diameter proportional
to its intensity." When one falls into that sphere of luminosity, he experiences a joy such as
Hopkins celebrates in "The Windhover." Such an attempt to yoke physics and vision, while
it may not satisfy the physicist, does cast its own light on Hopkins's "inscapes" and on Miss
O'Connor's use of the experience of vision as it strikes terror in Tarwater or Rayber. (*De
Reductione Artium ad Theologiam, Works of Saint Bonaventure*, Vol. I, Commentary on the Four
Lights", pp. 45ff. Saint Bonaventure, N. Y.; The Franciscan Institute, 1955.)

And reason is the final rescue from that danger. "Pure Diabolism is but Absolute Insanity," he says, a statement Dostoevski might well use as epigraph for Ivan's final spiritual struggle. Poe adds, simply, "Lucifer was merely unfortunate in having been created without brains." Created no doubt in Poe's thought of the moment by that failed poet, Milton. The conclusion is one we would expect Ivan to counter his Adversary with, as by implication he does in the course of their long argument. But Poe casts his retort in a form and tone more nearly the voice of another critic of Milton's Lucifer, Joyce's intellectual dandy, Stephen Dedalus. For it is a Stephen-like escape from his difficulties that Poe makes, through a distortion of the concrete by fancy, always in the name of art and of himself as artist. And though Poe's is a more substantial artistic gift for such escapes than Miss O'Connor's failed artist Asbury, one may nevertheless detect that the lines of their spiritual dimensions are parallel though not on the same scale.

We may note here that Poe's architecture is distorted from its substance and lines by the use of drapes, by fancy's obliteration of nature's designs, but not simply for fiction's purposes. His windows are described as covered or empty, sometimes to the end that through such images he may limit our response to the recesses of consciousness for dramatic effect. But sometimes Poe's windows are so limited, we suspect, lest we remember that *through* them we encounter an existence separate from consciousness. If there are "sepulchral terrors" beyond the control of "fancy," which we encounter in the caverns of the heart, there are also those wider terrors of existence, the dangers to self-consciousness of an encounter with some Other. The possibility of an existing external world presents very special terror to Poe. Thus when he is most specifically and concretely imagistic, when he is factually most precise about the senses, we must be most on our guard against the leg-pull. At such points he is often bent upon a hoax at the expense of the innocent empiricist reader.[5] That is, he is not concerned for the reader's danger in be-

---

5. The intrusion of the shadow world upon Poe is most pronounced when he is forced to concede an audience separate from his own mind. He is irritated by an indifferent world of readers. Thus his attack on that kind of American reader who is easily impressed by any book made in Paris or London. But there is a difference between Poe's attack on such provin-

ing absorbed by the world but for his own safety in this respect, being generally contemptuous of the reader. What he has to say about that world, and particularly in *Eureka* and in his dialogues and prose poems, may well be pondered in the light of his retreat from those questions raised by accepting the existence of a world exterior to consciousness. For "It is by no means an irrational fancy that, in a future existence, we shall look upon what we think our present existence, as a dream." In that remark from *Marginalia* lies the seed of that fictional strategy in Poe exemplified by his dialogues—"The Colloquy of Monos and Una," "The Power of Words," and so on. But more important to our concern, the statement carries as well a justification for turning away from the attempt to come to grips with the human heart in its dark relation to a world it never made.

cialism and Tate's: "Our antiquaries abandon time for distance; our very fops glance from the binding to the bottom of the title-page where the mystic characters which spell London, Paris, or Genoa, are precisely so many letters of recommendation." ("Letter to B," *Selected Writings*, 410) Such readers elect the known rather than dare the unknown, the objection in Poe being not simply to their disregard of the homegrown or local.

CHAPTER XI

DEMONIC CLOSURE
OF THE HEART

The dark recesses of the human heart, if one pursue them too far, confound one in the darker question of evil. But if there is no absolute good, one gets nowhere in dealing with that troublesome shadow on the world. Or perhaps we might say one gets anywhere, for there is that saving relativity of an Ivan Karamazov: whatever ground one takes, it is holy by the taking, though one go mad thereby. Good itself is relative when one, the insatiable "I," is multiplied by more than itself, leaving us in that contemporary solution to the question of evil: situation ethics. Being is always ad hoc to the will. From and through that principle, one finds himself drawn toward but lost among pragmatic and utilitarian entanglements, whether his highest good be himself, a local group, or "humanity," that surrogate of self which is created by abstraction. Yet in this line of thought, the secular escape of the self, one still discovers himself a dream within a dream. This way, too, lies madness. Neither situation ethics nor good multiplied by number is a solution for one with idealist compulsions such as Poe is possessed by. Then perhaps a solution may lie in the intellect's being made content in explaining "the machinery—the wheels and pinions—of any work of Art," as Poe proposes to do. Yet in regard to the machinery of art, "to reflect analytically upon [it] is to reflect after the fashion of the mirrors in the temple of Smyrna, which represent the fairest images as deformed." The relativist approach to man in the world, even though it posit a future perfection in man, must inevitably leave in question its own causes; the forms of the mind reflect grotesque figures where there is no measure of form except fallible mind. One is at least haunted by the spectre of the moment's necessity or expediency as a stain upon the idealist spirit in man that turns the ideal into illusion, for the moment is fleeting.

The question becomes, in what shall one anchor his idealism? In Perfect Goodness—in God? In the Soul itself? Would that it might be so, says the idealist Poe. But "All—absolutely all the argumentation which I have seen on the nature of the soul, or of the Deity seems to me nothing but worship of his unnamable idol. *Pour savoir ce qu'est Dieu,* says Bielfeld, . . . *il faut être Dieu même*—and to reason about the reason is of all things the most unreasonable." Perhaps the solution does lie in becoming God himself, and perhaps one may perform that bit of magic, not through reason or theology, with their heavy requirement of a logic which reduced God to an idol, but through art. In the attempt, the machinery of art must not be allowed to distract one from art's effect; one is able to enjoy the wheels and pinions "only just in proportion as we do *not* enjoy the legitimate effect designed by the artist." The art required, in order that one may be God, must therefore work its magic effect of transubstantiation through an indefiniteness, though presumably with sufficient definiteness that one's attention is not unduly called either to art's relation to the life of the world (and hence to life *in* the world, for there one is drawn into the caverns of the heart where the monsters sleep) or to the deliberateness of art's machinery (for then one concentrates on the causes of the mystery of effect, and the effect is vitiated). The machinery of art must be magically vague despite the necessity of wheels and pinions.

Poe praises Tennyson for his music of vagueness: "If the author did not deliberately propose to himself a suggestive indefiniteness of meaning, with the view of bringing about a definitiveness of vague and therefore spiritual effect—this, at least, arose from the silent analytical promptings of that poetic genius which embodies all orders of intellectual capacity." It were better, of course, not to examine poetic genius too closely, lest it be concluded an accident of external nature, or a gift, either discovery raising the old questions of an external Giver. In the future (these things belong to the future, Poe suggests by his title from *Antigone*, "Mellonta Tauta") one may well realize ancient axioms as blindly wrong, such axioms that raise fundamental questions of cause. One such axiom destined for history's dustbin: *Ex nihilo nihil fit*. To the contrary, something—the soul?—might indeed be created out of nothing, by the power of the imagination. Which brings us once more to the saving power of art, especially the art of words, so long as we set aside some of the questioning of causes along the way. Art, Poe is willing to say, is "the reproduction of what the Senses perceive in Nature through the veil of the soul." But lest *Nature*, *Senses*, and *soul* too quickly distract the impatient reason, it is the "veil of the soul" that requires attention. "We can, at any time, double the true beauty of the actual landscape by half closing our eyes as we look at it. The naked Senses sometimes see too little— but then *always* they see too much."

The *too much* no doubt would, under the direct assault of reason, waken sleeping monsters, and what is required for rescue is to float quietly down the stream as Afrasiab down the Oxus. *Too much* must be strained for the soul through the veil of the imagination; that is the emphasis, rather than that the soul must perceive and reproduce or imitate. One squints, lest there be too much light. If one thus proceed, all that is not the soul is transformed to soul through a refinement of that all; the soul becomes the all. That, it would seem, is the process through which one becomes God, the disturbing duality of the Self and the Other thus obliterated. Not through philosophy, but through art, Poe pursues his solution. It is his form of the answer to the "phenomenological problem" that so occupies thinking in the latter part of his century. Nor is it an accident that literature *per se* becomes a prime instrument in the general attempt to solve that problem; literature becomes prescribed as an authority as decisive as the disciplines of philosophy or theology. In evidence of the point, Heidegger depends upon the poet increasingly, celebrating solutions to the problem as reflected in Hölderlin, who through his poetry arrives upon the ground which Heidegger would occupy by argument. Eliot's own struggle with Poe's ideas leads him to abandon his formal concern for philosophy to return to poetry, the climactic strug-

gle reflected in *The Waste Land*. And Sartre's reputation as
playwright and fiction writer suggests how inextricably related to
his philosophy is the instrument of art.

David Halliburton, in his *Edgar Allan Poe: A Phenomenological
View*, suggests that each of Poe's works may be seen as a complete
creation, reflecting upon the larger, inclusive work, *Eureka*. In that
thought which accompanies his creation, Poe moves from a conception that "the lower forms of existence are contained within the
higher" to a conclusion that "the universe is God" or that "man
himself is God." But the relationship between the universe and his
works rather requires the conclusion that Poe's universe is Poe—
not "man" or "God"—though the maintenance of that universe
has required of Poe that he assume the Godhead to sustain his illusion. When we realize this necessity, we understand somewhat better why Poe, relatively young at his death, wrote such a large body
of work. For Poe's volume is not explained completely on the
grounds of economic necessity. It is through "The Power of
Words" that his universe is sustained, a necessity such as leads
Wallace Stevens to say that the poem is "The poem of the mind in
the act of finding/What will suffice." Frost puts the necessity in a
slightly different way, the poem being "a momentary stay against
confusion." As we suggested earlier, the threat of silence to a mind
such as Poe's is a threat of chaos loosed upon a world brought into
being and sustained by words. His goddess in *Al Aaraaf* invokes a
spirit which dwells where the "terrible and fair/In beauty vie," and
that spirit responds as silence. It is

> A sound of silence on the startled ear
> Which dreamy poets name "the music of the sphere."
> Ours is a world of words: Quiet we call
> "Silence"—which is the merest word of all.

Poe's *sphere* isn't chosen simply for the sake of a rhyme with *ear*, and
the emphatic final *all* fills a threatened universe. Song sustains a
world, as we see it acclaimed as doing with a less overt threat of terror in Wallace Stevens's goddess of song, the girl in "The Idea of
Order at Key West."

Poe's reduction of "the republic of natures which is the world"
(in Maritain's phrase) to one nature and one world—one

"sphere"—would seem to solve many problems. But those questions left unanswered along the way cause ruptures in that world, a tornado or whirlpool pull to annihilation. The vortex which is such a constant symbol in Poe's tales keeps breaking out of the quiet sphere of the contained world. There is a response to a drawing motion outward or downward and away from the calm center of that consciousness which is the world contained. To limit the threat of a ruptured world, Poe associates the rhythm of his world with the rhythm of the heart. In *Eureka*, pulsing is the concept central to his attempt to reconcile consciousness with what is not itself, to neutralize the force that strains an otherwise calm world. *Pulsing* is a device necessary to regularize the contending forces to prevent irruptions; it is the willed pace-setter. But the imposed metaphor leads to the illusion that the particular heart has the capacity to contain the universe. One notices in Poe's uses of the heart that the monsters in its caverns are allowed to slumber. The problem of good and evil which Milton and Dostoevski themselves wrestle with, as opposed to those rationalizations of expediency to the self used by Satan or Ivan, are foregone in the interest of speculations of a cosmological cast, as if Poe were scientist and not poet.

Poe comes thus to announce "a novel Universe swelling into existence, and then subsiding into nothingness, at every throb of the Heart Divine." The order is important. Nothingness precedes existence. And in *Marginalia* he insists to us that the " 'species of nothingness' is quite as reasonable, at all events, as any 'kind of something-ness.' " As for the "Heart Divine" in *Eureka*, Poe at once adds, anticipating our question, "*It is our own.*" The fierce affirmation of italics one feels protests too much, as if to get over a difficulty with a rhetorical flourish that seems to speak a revelation. But here one deals with Poe the Magician, not a true prophet.

On the emphasis upon rhythm in Poe's work (and one may relate Poe's metrical concerns in his poetry to this general question) Halliburton observes:

> The heart, ordinarily, is within a body, much as the occupant of a house is in a chamber and in the house itself. Indeed, *Eureka* presents a hyphenated phenomenon that is at once a wall-chamber-heart-man-universe-God. In this condition of being-within-something-larger there is no feeling of claustration, however, precisely because the hyphenated

phenomena are ultimately identical. . . . The universe can never oppress . . . because the universe is God and God is man. This climactic 'point' in the argument of *Eureka* [is experienced] by the voices of memory. . . . the message is immanent. The memories who speak are in the interpreter and in every man. In listening to the memories he is listening to himself and to Himself. . . .

Through the borrowed voices the interpreter brings to bear . . . the imperative [voice]. He becomes at the same time a prophet, a being whose access to the unity of the past reveals to him the unity of the future. . . .

Man is no longer, as in Pascal, a being of *disproportion*, caught between the *deux infinis*. If the infinite exists, says Poe, it exists humanly, in man-who-is-God. Through the power of words the interpreter thus anticipates the state he will experience once he has finished his passage through the gulf beyond. Through himself the interpreter speaks through Himself.

There is a neatness which one must grant to such a visionary attempt as Poe's, but it is a neatness at the expense of fundamental questions set aside, so that the system may not command the degree of respect afforded it by Halliburton. Halliburton sees in the early Poe, in *Tamerlane*, that "the first person stands apart from the third-person God. In *Eureka*, the last major work, there is no separation because the first-person has become the First-Person. The full design, at last, is truly full." Thus the concluding words of a helpful but not very critical reading of Poe's ideas. The objections that Voegelin brings to bear devastatingly upon Poe's contemporary, Auguste Comte, must here apply to Poe as well, though Comte's consumption of all being into the self, whereby he becomes the savior of the world, does differ in one important respect from Poe's: Poe at least does not lust after the divine power in order that he may transform that exterior world called society, as Comte would do by establishing Divine Humanity as the religion of the world and himself as that new religion's Christ.[1]

---

1. It is a sign of the intellectual times that Comte was rising to his own apotheosis at approximately the same time Poe was expressing his cosmogony, Comte's recognition of his divinity coming, by his calculation, in 1855. One notices also the crucial role played in each man's thought by an inordinate elevation of woman. To read Comte's reflections on his short-lived affair with Clotilde de Vaux is to have the uneasy feeling of being in a mind created by Poe. Comte's divinization of woman through Clotilde follows her death. In her he discovers his own annunciation as the savior, she becoming to him at once Beatrice and Mary, so that he then begins to sign himself *Fondateur de la Réligion de l'humanité*. His apartment will be the Holy See in which the relics of "Sainte Clotilde" are preserved as sacred to his New Church Without Christ But With Comte; especially important is "the red chair, enveloped in a

We have already remarked the contradiction in Poe between his conception of reality and the impulse to bear witness to a world his conception denies. When the mind is conceived as a monad whose component factors are the only forces which determine its evolution, the mind is a prison from which there is no escape. Poe's frantic, pathetic cry to a world beyond his prison, such as revealed in those marginal notes to *Eureka,* suggest that Halliburton's assertion of "no feeling of claustration" in Poe is in error. One missing the agony in Poe misses the one redeeming quality of his quest. For, unlike Comte, he is not deliberately deceptive in the matter of the monad's relation to any possible other. "We would," says Voegelin, "miss the demonic character of the construction if we forget that Comte *knows* that there is a reality outside the prison, a reality behind the 'fiction'. " Comte attempts by an act of the will to sustain an illusion of one world whose center is himself, in Voegelin's charge, primarily for the purpose of recruitment. The attempt requires that he declare "as illegitimate all questions that cannot be answered by the sciences of the phenomena." The core of his attempt, Voegelin concludes, "is the murder of God," whereby he prepares the stage for the entry of Nietzsche, who "neither planned [the death of God] nor committed it."

There is no such deliberate intellectual deceit in Poe. The excited voice of the prophet chanting its imperatives, reminds one more (as we have said) of the prestidigitator than prophet, and it is himself more than any other that he would fascinate. For Poe is deeply committed to finding a way to reconcile himself to the world. Even so, good intentions do not rescue one from fundamental errors, and it remains true that Poe's course like Comte's is the demonic one, whose principal victim is himself. In summoning the voices of memory out of the desire of a spirit in desperate straits, Poe constructed a world apart, a "demonic closure of the monad,"

green cover and marked on its front board with my initials in red wax." It is the chair Clotilde sat in on her Wednesday visits. That such bizarre thinking is of central relevance to the elevation of "sociology" as the new testament is sufficiently demonstrated by Voegelin. See particularly pp. 151-59, 161-66 of Voegelin's *From Enlightenment to Revolution.* And one might also compare Comte's red chair to Enoch Emery's "tabernacle-like cabinet" in his washstand, "meant to contain a slop jar" but which Enoch prepares with chintz curtains and gilt paint to be a temporary ark for his symbol of the covenant he makes with spiritual death, the mummy.

to borrow Voegelin's phrase. Poe's phenomenological quest is one characterized by Pascal's remark about the modernist displacement of the self, that "we never are in search of things, but always in search of the search." Such is the principle most necessary to the protagonist's happiness in Poe's "The Domain of Arnheim": the necessity of a goal unattainable. For the goal attained, as Cass Mc-Caslin tries to explain to young Ike who is baffled by the mystery of Faulkner's fabulous bear, admits a resolution which is destructive of the quest for the quest. Old Ben dead empties existence by arresting the quest. For Poe, most particularly, to posit an attainable goal, let alone arrive at it, is to admit a something separate from the questing self. Nothing so concrete as a three-toed bear, or even a white whale, will serve him, but only the cold white maëlstrom issuing upon the void. The pursuit, in other words, must occur within the vacuum of existence denied. What Poe's character requires, in Pascal's words, is "the hunt and not the capture." For capture ruptures in a terrifying way the closed monad, introducing by collision some Other that is death to the self-sustaining monad. The quest for the quest is Poe's psychological response to "a secret instinct driving [men] to seek external diversion and occupation . . . the result of their constant sense of wretchedness." It is an instinct counter to a second one in man "left over from the greatness of our original nature, telling [us] that the only true happiness lies in rest and not excitement." In that first instinct lies a cause of the Manichean error which comes to dominate in Heidegger and Sartre, the pursuit of pursuit in which an illusion of an object is necessarily projected, like a carrot before a donkey. Pascal is characterizing the motive force which we recognize as reaching traumatic proportion in Western life in the nineteenth century and the twentieth; its effect we describe as alienation.

Concerning this terror of an encounter with a *something* beyond the self, a fear which stirs us to a pursuit of the self leading ironically into *nothingness*, let us recall an earlier point. In Chapter 22 of our first volume, we said that, as if it were a law of our spiritual existence within the In-between, the centripetal force of egocentricity weakens our power to respond to any presence in the world other than man's mind itself. Thus the self, feeding upon itself, becomes a

strange parasite, an existence which one might represent in a
bestiary of the spirit with the emblem of the serpent swallowing its
tail. The irony springs from a larger truth ignored by the self only
through willful illusion: the destruction is not limited to the self-
isolated (and thus self-devouring) self, because no part of existence
can be absolutely separated from creation as a whole by the will
alone. Thus one hears that modernist illusion stirring in Tennyson's words, put in Odysseus' mouth: "I am a part of all that I
have met." I have put my stamp upon what is, as only an independent, separate creature may. But that truth deeper than arrogance, the truth restoring piety as governor of will, requires: "I
am a part of all that is." (The Devil's agony, a theologian or a poet
might suggest, is eternally present through this aspect of the
Creator's gift—particular, but shared existence.) Creation is the
thorn which self-isolation never quite expunges. Thus in self-
destruction there is necessarily a diminishment of creation, but
never an obliteration. (And thus, Miss O'Connor would no doubt
argue in defense of the existence of the Devil, the Devil can never
not exist, though he can manipulate the circumstances to please
our will to illusion.)

In isolation from creation, there is primarily a diminishment of
the self, but it finds at least an analogical display concretely insistent to us and requiring no doctor's subtlety to read, though there
are many subtle readings: those ravagements of nature and of man
that had become so much a general concern in the 1970s. Collec-
tively, we express that concern in the desperate attempts to raise a
secular ecology of nature to the status of a metaphysical system
with an often amusing and sometimes impressive neo-
scholasticism, such as the recent elevation of sociobiology. But
those systems are reluctant to address teleological questions
beyond the vagueness of a concern for abstract "generations of the
future."

In an age much troubled by its metaphysical poverties, in
which it is difficult to discover any cause of hope for a spiritual
recovery and scant hope even for the survival of the
species, it is well to return to the irony that accompanies self-
alienation, to the serpent swallowing its tail. This emblem gives us

a hint, perhaps, of the implicit defeat in the modern gnostic's approach to creation. It lies in this: gnostic power is haunted in the created world by the very marks it leaves upon creation. But the scars speak less of an absence of existence, of the diminishment of creation, than they speak a threat of Presence. The lords of gnostic power who would diminish the self—the person—whether for an individual or collective use of creation have constant reminder of a power beyond their diminishments. Though generations may tread the earth till, as Hopkins says, "all is seared with trade; bleared, smeared with toil," that world nevertheless continues "charged with the grandeur of God." And among the signs of that grandeur, as Hopkins joyfully recognizes, are those very scars on the world made by man, scars heavy with the pathos of self-diminishment. They constitute, then, not only a record of loss, but prophecies of restoration, a promise that the lords of gnostic power over man and nature must repeatedly fail.

We need but note a recent event to our point, the workers' strikes in Poland in 1980. Gnostic power, we have argued, must concentrate itself inexorably upon the material dimension of existence, though usually with elaborate extensions of materialism in the sophistications of psychology. That very concentration undermines the presumption of man's absolute power over material existence. The individuals of any collective, when directed to an intense address to the material world, become caught up in a personal address as well, to the hazard of any over-riding gnostic dream. It would seem an inevitable effect that in such concentrated attention, the spiritual dimension of existence will be increasingly encountered. For there is a mystery beyond the finite mind's reductions in the intimate relation between materialistic and spiritual hungers in that mind. It is a mystery which makes the figurative yoking of those hungers deeper in reality than fanciful metaphor, as the prophetic poet knows. That is Miss O'Connor's point, for instance, in *The Violent Bear It Away*, in her elaborate metaphor of Tarwater's hunger. The same message is dramatized in Solzhenitsyn's *One Day in the Life of Ivan Denisovich*, in which story the struggle for biological survival becomes transformed out of naturalism. But those are fictions. What we set out to say is that the

Polish worker's demands for pork is accompanied by their demands
for free access to the Mass, those seemingly disparate hungers
yoked by their violence together in such a way that the violence
speaks to the world of human hungers so forcefully that gnostic
lords are helpless to answer except by temporal force. What happened in Poland in 1980 casts an ironic light upon Joseph Stalin's
sarcastic question at the outset of World War II: "How many divisions has the Pope?"[2]

There is danger, then, in a collective movement or an individual's movement upon the material world which presumes to
project as a final goal a material gain. When acquisition of *things*
becomes the fundamental justification of man's restless pursuit, one
is already well along on that road to a dangerous encounter which
Hebrews 10:31 speaks of in a language which brings together in an
arresting way the material and spiritual dimensions of our existence in the In-between: "It is a fearful thing to fall into the hands
of the living God." Better restless pursuit than its consummation,
says the modern spirit. Thus, as through words one avoids a pregnant silence, through restlessness one avoids the rest in spiritual
surrender. Indeed, lest such a rest be victorious, our world has
chosen to characterize it as ennui, the subterfuge depending upon
our residual antipathy to sloth which has long since lost its rational
purchase in Christian theology. The restlessness of which we speak
is conspicuous in the Puritan address to the world, the approach to
existence which gives rise to the much-discussed "Puritan work-
ethic." Puritan unrest we shall examine in detail in our final
volume in relation to Hawthorne's discomfort with it, but we must
anticipate here because Poe's own discomfort is not so far removed
from the Puritan as he supposed. Indeed, Josef Pieper shows us a
very similar restlessness in Immanuel Kant, who is suspicious of

2. The poet might see as one of the signs to us of gnostic man's destructive limits the eruption
of Mt. St. Helens in May of 1980. The destruction of Washington state's bluegreen world
dwarfed our nuclear pretensions, not only in the force of its destruction but by the elevation of
such destruction beyond willful malevolence in its serene indifference. Viewing the volcano's
devestation, a commentator for *Science News* (July 26, 1980) says: "This is fashioned from no
such malevolence [as that of nuclear holocaust]; it is even less than impersonal." And yet
beyond the awesome natural violence, the event may be more than personal, for the miracle
that succeeds the terror of the erruption is the surprising return of life to the wasteland,
generated almost at once in the polluted waters of Spirit Lake.

any intellectual gain which is not the product of intellectual labor. As Kant says in *Die Lebenslehre* (1796), "the law is that reason acquires its possessions through work."

The source of this restlessness is more ancient than its manifestation in the Puritan fathers, as it is more general in Western thought than our attempts to restrict it to sectarian diaspora. It is heavily present in the Western intellectual community in a range as wide as from Kant to Jean-Paul Sartre, in whom the necessity of action as a cause of being makes necessary an action-ethic as grimly colored as any Puritanism. Pascal, a writer to whom Poe is drawn, looks at that restlessness in its more ancient ground. The fear which attempts to make restlessness a virtue, Pascal argues, settles upon us because we have lost the proper ground of rest; in rest, the object pursued is at last recognized. But if one makes the mistake of supposing that the ultimate object one pursues is the self, he begins to wake those sleeping monsters of the heart feared by Poe. Poe, though he quotes Pascal on occasion, cannot bring himself to dwell upon Pascal's cry, "How hollow and foul is the heart of man!"[3]

I suggest here once more a cause of that modern form of Manicheanism to which Miss O'Connor refers often and which she treats as a constant in her fiction, for alienation is the effect of abstracting oneself from the world. Not that the outer sign of self-distraction is a withdrawal into the desert. Indeed the signs given are more often in a direction opposite, often a surface appearance of materialistic devotions; Mrs. May in "Greenleaf" is an instance from Miss O'Connor to the point. The spirit longing for "Distraction" (Pascal's general title for discussing alienation in the *Pensées*), suspends *things* in the future as the object of pursuit, like a carrot. The donkey is that second instinct in us, according to Pascal's naming of it, "left over from our former greatness" and considered anti-

---

3. There is, in Poe's "Mellonta Tauta," a prophetic note struck by the narrator, assumed speaking a hundred years after Poe—that is, in our post-World War II world. Far beyond the "primitive" world of a hundred years ago, the narrator writes a letter to a friend while aboard an aircraft travelling at (to Poe's world) incredible speed. All sense of place is lost; time is reduced; intellect is so far advanced as to make the old axioms irrelevant, as for instance the ancient belief (c. 1840) that "darkness cannot come out of light." But the narrator is nevertheless "almost devoured by *ennui*."

quated, vestigial by the progressivist instinct. Thus that first instinct signals a movement toward rest in *things* to disguise its real
addiction to distraction, the quest of the quest. And so it is that one
may appear a materialist (as do Mrs. May and Mrs. Cope) when
he is quite the opposite, the materialistic show allowing an indulgence in that addiction which Eliot speaks of as a being
"distracted from distraction by distraction." Such spiritual opiate
prevents a looking into the heart.

Consider the restlessness that permeates the most materialistic
society of the West—to hear other societies tell it: that is, American
society. Clusters of restless souls devote themselves to a variety of
causes, each seeking common cause against a fragmentation that
threatens a dark age. The absence of communication exacerbates
the frustration. What *grounds* are common to what causes? The
grounds are missing, W. H. Auden suggests of American society,
because we are really a people given to abstraction despite our
materialistic pretension. In the restless chaos of post-World War II
America we have reached at least a penultimate consummation
(our scattered prophets speak various ultimate catastrophies) of an
old quest Hawthorne observes in Puritanism. For it is Hawthorne
who as an artist first deals acutely with that conflict in which a
materialistic surface disguises the distortions of our spiritual quest.
A particular instance of Hawthorne's treatment of the theme is
"Young Goodman Brown." It is Miss O'Connor who treats the
penultimate consummation of that distortion, reflecting in her fiction the displaced persons who, because of restlessness in the world,
abuse that world in a blind revenge upon being. The Misfit is what
Young Goodman Brown becomes; for him there is only the
pleasure left of doing meanness to *being* by "killing somebody or
burning down his house." From the days of Young Goodman
Brown, on whose tombstone there was carved "no hopeful verse,"
to the days of the Misfit, a good man becomes increasingly hard to
find.

Between these two points that measure an accelerated decline
of a possible good lies Poe, struggling to establish "what will suffice" to keep the sleeping dragon undisturbed in the dark chambers
of the human heart. But, the Misfit insists by his actions, better the

dragon aroused than such palid existence as an ultimate isolation from existence. It is a point made rather quietly by Donald Davidson in his poem "The Nervous Man," the poem's epigraph taken from Poe's "Tell-Tale Heart." The poem gives a portrait of a final reduction to anonymous alienation, protected by a lifeless material world. The portrait begins:

> He cannot sin, and so cannot betray.
> Therefore his desk is clean. Bloodless the rugs.

CHAPTER XII

THE QUESTOR OF THE QUEST
IN PURSUIT OF PURSUIT

The alienation of which we speak develops from our sense of a disproportion between man's being and God's, once we have lost faith and thereby lost vision of any reality beyond the self. That is why Miss O'Connor finds particular assurance in St. Thomas Aquinas in this disoriented age. The year she died, one of her favorite philosophers, Gilson, published a series of lectures under the title *The Spirit of Thomism,* in which he presents succinctly that heart of Thomism to which Miss O'Connor responded so confidently. We may lean here on Gilson to benefit our understanding of Miss O'Connor's position and to see more clearly the radically different position we find in Poe. In St. Thomas she found that emphasis upon the outer world which she was to find in Teilhard, an emphasis upon nature as the proper point from which reason must move if it is to become a healthy complement to faith. As for Poe's dilemma in the presence of an external world that seems to threaten consciousness, we might apply Gilson's remark that

> Even in our irreligious and unmetaphysical times, great minds sometimes wonder at the two-fold fact that there is intellectual knowledge and that the world of nature is intelligible to mind. What is eternally incomprehensible about the world, Einstein says, is its comprehensibility.

Concerning this unintelligible intelligibility Gilson adds in his note, "Thomas Aquinas simply refuses to consider that unintelligibility is final; but the possibility of intelligibility in physics is accountable in terms of metaphysics and theology only." That is so, because there is no possibility of passing from the natural to supernatural "naturally," that is, by reason unaided. What one recognizes through faith is that the supernatural comes down to inform and perfect the natural. "Revelation does precisely that with respect to man's natural cognition of God."

In respect to that "natural cognition," Thomas argues (speaking, says Gilson, of "the philosophizing reason of baptized men") that the relation of intellect to an intelligible universe is precisely the clue the mind must follow if it is to be given to right reason. For "since man is an intelligent being in an intelligible universe, everything proceeds as though the reason for the existence of both was to make possible the cognition of God by some intellects." There follows from this supposition an insight of the relation of faith to reason, both of which are sustained by revelation:

> . . . the human reason finds itself conducted through a series of hierarchically ordered causes up to a supreme cause, which we call God.
> . . . the reason metaphysical knowledge is almost totally ordered to the cognition of God is that, in fact, the end of nature is to make God knowable to man and the end of man is, through knowing nature, to know Him.
> The relationship of reason and faith is therefore conditioned by that of nature and grace. The philosopher ascends from the knowledge of nature to the knowledge of God, the theologian descends from the perfections of God to those of His effects, but since the twofold movement takes place within one and the same mind, the philosopher and the theologian are bound to meet.

The reality of the world requires our slow participation in it; the ineffable is approached through the senses. The awe-inspiring beauty of absolute perfection is approached through the peacock with his feet on the ground of being; nature, dust, matter. That is, Gilson's words immediately remind us of Miss O'Connor's repeated concern for our modern disorientation, her words echoed by Gilson. "Today's reader," she says, "if he believes in grace at all, sees it as something which can be separated from nature and served to him raw as Instant Uplift." In that separation, one type of modern man, having separated spirit and matter, "wanders about, caught in a maze of guilt he can't identify, trying to reach a God he can't approach, a God powerless to approach him." "The beginning of human knowledge is through the senses," St. Thomas says, but in our world, Miss O'Connor adds, "As grace and nature have been separated, so imagination and reason have been separated," leaving reason helpless in the presence of the unintelligible intelligibility. "Faith," she writes on a slip of paper, "breeds faith but faith in this age appears as dead as Sara's womb. When we believe today, we believe like Abraham."

That rather desperate intellectual wrestling with our special angel which Einstein characterizes as comprehension's incomprehensibility is the heart of *Eureka*. But in that work, the significant point is that Poe has shifted the mind's twofold journeying to an end which is our origin: the self. As Gilson says in his exposition of Thomism, "although philosophy ascends to the knowledge of God through creatures while sacred doctrine grounded in faith descends from God by the divine revelation, *the way up and the way down are the same.*" That echo of Heraclitus which Gilson uses to dramatize the twofold journey of mind toward the transcendent (that passage from Heraclitus, we recall, is used by Eliot as epigraph to *Burnt Norton*, his *Eureka* returned to its Christian perspective) is conspicuously present in Poe's philosophical poem. It is most evident in its presence in those metaphors of pulsing, of expansion and contraction of the human heart, which is the divine heart. We must emphasize, however, that what is central to *Eureka*—and central to our concern—is the *self*. For St. Thomas, the mystery of man's being created in the image of God, as revealed through his natural theology (the reason's pursuit of intelligible nature) is man's capacity "as a rational creature," in which capacity he "somehow achieves a representation of God at the level of the species." But for Poe, the supernatural theology of the self consumes all sense of species; all *creatura* are reduced to vague projections of consciousness, within the constructing—if pulsing—sphere of the self. His argument that detail in art must be vague has this origin, out of the necessity of his "metaphysics" of the self, a fundamental necessity which the French Symbolists are haunted by and which turns them toward Poe as godfather. It is a necessity inherited from gnosticism and transposed from the transcendent to the intramundane self.

In the metamorphoses of being by modern gnostic thought which Voegelin exposes to us, St. Thomas's argument itself becomes transposed. That man as rational creature "somehow achieves a representation of God at the level of the species," and so gains rationally some insight into the mystery of man's having been created in God's image, falls too easily into the process of transposition from God as the cause of existence to man as the cause of existence. For with the centering upon the self as god, Thomas's idea is shifted so that it not only serves to displace God as a reality but in doing so also serves to further elevate man as creator: he is capable of such a supreme fiction as that of creating God in man's image. The most immediate evidence for that argument has been traditionally the human dimension of those images through which man attempts to speak of the otherworldly, an evidence adduced more anciently than the Enlightenment of course, as Eliade points out in *Myth and Reality*. The rationalization of Greek myth to fiction, the "demystification" of that deepest experience of the *metaxy*, the In-between which Voegelin recalls us to, is already under way by secularizing rationalism in a strikingly "modern" manner by Xenophanes in the sixth centruy B.C., with anthropomorphism the reasoned explanation of the gods. To that "modern" spirit C. S. Lewis speaks in his essay "Transposition," with a cogency that clarifies Thomas's argument and speaks to the differences between Miss O'Connor's uses of the natural world as a source of images toward the transcendent and Poe's restrictions upon imagistic detail to vagueness. The argument brought against the Christian, says Lewis, is "the obvious continuity between things which are admittedly natural and things which, it is claimed, are spiritual; the reappearance in what professes to be our supernatural life of all the same old elements which make up our natural life and . . . no others. If we have really been visited by a revelation from beyond Nature, is it not very strange that an Apocalypse can furnish heaven with nothing more than selections from terrestrial experience (crowns, thrones, and music), that devotion can find no language but that of human lovers, and that the rite whereby Christians enact a mystical union should turn out to be only the old familiar act of eating and drinking?" What Lewis points to in this skeptical argument is its presumption of man's adequacy to mystery through reason, a failure to acknowledge finiteness. For "if the spiritual is richer than the natural . . . then this is exactly what we should expect. And the skeptic's conclusion that the so-called spiritual is really derived from the natural, that it is a mirage or projection or imaginary extension of the natural is also exactly what we should expect. . . . The brutal man never can find anything but lust in love; the Flatlander never can find anything but flat shapes in a picture; physiology never can find anything in thought except twitchings of grey matter."

To make his argument of the ascent toward knowledge of God through creatures and the descent of revelation through doctrine grounded in faith, a parallel to St. Thomas, Lewis turns to his own experience of the In-between. "Introspection can discover no difference at all between my neural response to very bad news and my neural response to the overture of *The Magic Flute*. If I were to judge simply by sensations I should come to the absurd conclusion that joy and anguish are the same thing." But one may reflect that the nerves' resources "are far more limited, the possible variations of sense far fewer, than those of emotion." Thus the senses must compensate "by using the *same* sensation to express more than one emotion." For if the "richer system is to be represented in the poorer at all, this can only be by giving each element in the poorer system more than one meaning." For otherwise we could never be reconciled to such obvious anomalies in the lower system, sight, as that the "very same shape which [one] must draw to give the illusion of a straight road reaching from the spectator is also the shape [one must] draw for a dunce's cap." In regard to images, through which consciousness reconciles itself to being other than the self, we discover that "In varying degrees the lower reality can actually be drawn into the higher and become part of it. The sensation which accompanies joy becomes itself joy: we can hardly choose but say 'incarnate joy'. " And in the light of our experiences, "It is of some importance to notice that the word *symbolism* is not adequate in all cases to cover the relation between the higher medium and its transposition in the lower. . . . I should call it not symbolical but sacramental," for in that experience the emotion "descends bodily, as it were, into the sensation and digests, transforms, transubstantiates it, so that the same thrill along the nerves *is* delight or *is* agony.

Symbolism is not adequate in all cases, Lewis suggests; yet the rationalist position Lewis and O'Connor and Gilson and Thomas are answering requires that it be so. Thus we discover cogent reason for Poe's appeal to the Symbolist Movement. For symbol in this sense must function as a projected satellite for intraself communication; against symbol the closed self bounces its emotional unrest and receives it back as sensual response, maintaining thereby its closed world as inviolate against threats of revelation. The "poem" becomes a moment's solace to the alienated man, performed through images dissociated from any response other than a subjective reaction to the existence of the self. The two-fold journey, the way up and the way down, are thus contained in a bubble such as that which Miss O'Connor's Julian attempts to maintain, a bubble pricked at the end by a reality larger than the self in her story "Everything that Rises Must Converge"—not "Must Redound."

The alienation of modern man, we were saying earlier, develops from our sense of a disproportion between man's being and God's when faith is lost. The unrest which follows leads us to attempt a rationale for consciousness which soothes the sense of disproportion—the sense of an inordinate relation of the outer and inner, the disturbing incomprehensibility of the world's comprehensibility. And so that desire for rest turns inward to a dream of the self as self-contained monad. Halliburton in his study of Poe as Phenomenologist holds Poe to have solved his problem. But one must notice that Pascal's statement—that we are given to the quest for the quest—holds true only so long as we are able to put from us that other instinct for rest. When the "thing" for which we search is detected, even vaguely, beyond the distractions of the search for its own sake, a restlessness of a new kind begins. The "thing" we would rest in, says St. Thomas (and Flannery O'Connor), is God, but the redefinition of God as the sole self, whether in the manner of Comte or of Poe, is a betrayal of the self. Until one undertakes the naming of the true God, one is committed to the necessity of endless distraction, as in the poem as a momentary stay against confusion momently repeated. But how and with what shall we name the true

God, without reducing Him to the idol such as Poe finds in every attempt at the naming?

In our pursuit of distraction, we are in danger of becoming consumed by abstraction from the world, and our language tends toward the purely abstract. Symbol is refined of all stains of the world, so that through it we may attempt a levitation by thought into that mathematician's heaven of which Maritain speaks in "God and Science." ("The *highest* order of the imaginative intellect," says Poe in "Mr. Griswald and the Poets," "is always preeminently mathematical.") Until that hopeless point, however, we may not escape the dominant power of metaphor in the language which pulls us, in open or in secret ways, back to the world. The poet or philosopher of the Ideal (a Keats or Plato) may regret the necessity of analogy, but he never quite escapes it except by silence. The difficulty of naming the unknown lies in the necessity of using names of the known, and that naming draws one again and again back into the shadows of a world where he wakes to his sole self forlorn—having been denied rest in that country toward which his unnamed, vague impetus draws him. What is stirring one is a wisdom in the blood, like that in Haze Motes. That is precisely the sort of metaphor which denies one his escape. Death, says Socrates, is *like* a sleep in which. . . . But it is *only* something *like* this, he must remind his auditors. Night, the poet says, is death's second self.

Though poet and philosopher struggle to overcome a language born of the body and the body's world, and hence suspected of being stained by time and space, that struggle to disengage language from the world must be in the end destructive of our desire to see the fullness of being so that we may come to rest in it. Here is graver limitation than that of talent or intellect upon the mind. For the limits of discursiveness upon the finite mind, whose order and direction are dependent upon the mystery of language, may finally profit by that pull of mind toward the world as the necessary prelude to freedom and rest. That is an idea Dante suggests at the outset of his famous journey when his hero is prevented direct passage to the sun itself, that constant character in Miss O'Connor's fiction. Dante as pilgrim is turned back and forced to descend into the caverns of the human heart before the world may be truly seen as more than a dark wood. The magnetic attraction of language to the world has as one of its gifts to our mind a corrective to that hasty desire of intellect for abstractionism, and the anchor of some vision of the transcendent in Thomas's "level of the species" is an anchor in the created world itself.

Of course one often feels in language a presence of the diabolic. Kierkegaard is quite explicit on the matter. And Brice Parain remarks, in *A Metaphysics of Language*, that "Freedom is only won by a fight with language." The act of speech is the act of taking sides; yet in our own words we see ourselves taking a side that is not the one we would take. "There is a gap between our words and us. We go out to meet them as if they came from somewhere else," says Parain. In the engagement which follows, we discover that through an apparent treachery in words we have been led "to put our foot in our mouths," as we say. What we may here suggest is that, in this aspect of their nature, words are the soldiers of the tyrant thought in us which nevertheless retain a substantive relation to reality. (The downfall of the tyrant is invariably brought on by his losing sight of reality.) Of that old divorce of thought from knowledge with which Aquinas contends, Parain too remarks the victory of immanence over transcendence since the Renaissance, a point we reiterate. Descartes requires a reversal. I think; therefore I am. Not so, says Parain, "For to think is not to be, it is to wish to be." Kierkegaard also attacks Descartes' proof of the existence of the self in his *Concluding Unscientific Postscript*. The *cogito*, he says, already contains 'I am.' "What then does the ergo mean? There is no conclusion here, for the proposition is a tautology." Ivan Karamazov's devil is more subtle: "*Je pense, donc je suis*, I know that for a fact." What Dostoevski's devil is not sure of is the existence of "all these worlds, God and even Satan." And particularly, which brings the argument's circle to rest in doubt of Descartes's proposition, he is unconvinced that man exists. The sum is zero, at best Poe's "dream within a dream."

That way lies despair if we discuss such matters too much with ourselves. But a poet like Miss O'Connor rescues us from the diabolic enlistment of our thought and words against being. Even the devil is turned to good use by the largeness of Providence, for what he does and what he intends are separate questions when placed in those larger dimensions of reality which relate the finite and infinite. It is this confounding of Satan's intension that makes him the restless wanderer to and fro who confronts Job. Ivan Karamazov's devil complains, "I am X in an indeterminate equation. I am a sort of phantom in life who has lost all beginning and all end, and who has even forgotten his own name." He is an apotheosis of the Quester of the Quest, and out of the pathos of his condition longs "simply to be transformed into the soul of a merchant's wife weighing eighteen stone and set candles at God's shrine." His, then, is the longing of the Manichean spirit doomed by his intellect to a separation from the good of the world, of grace in conjunction with nature; thus his insatiable, sentimental lust for the world. For there is no one formed substance sufficient to his hunger. His is the dark image of that devouring hunger Tarwater experiences in his final vision of the loaves and fishes when his hunger is "so great that he could have eaten all the loaves and fishes after they were multiplied."

We need, says Miss O'Connor, "a sense of evil which sees the devil as a real spirit who must be made to name himself, and not simply to name himself as vague evil, but to name himself with his specific personality for every occasion." Parain, reflecting on the necessity of our thought to do such naming remarks, "When we name something we in fact kill it." There is a limited truth in the remark which it is well to understand rather than deny. One naming a tree by that act separates his own being from the tree in proportion as he believes the name absolute. The name cannot contain, but in so far as one has confidence that it does, he is reducing "the republic of natures" among which the tree exists to the tyranny of the name he imposes. Still, the act of naming does not so much "kill" the object named as it controls and limits and denatures the act of naming itself, the difficulty which Husserl's phenomenology attempts to circumvent. Miss O'Connor says we are not required to name the devil, but that the devil must name himself—that (in the case of Ivan's devil) he be required to *remember* his name. In that species of action lies a destruction of pride, for such high intellect is forced to recall the limitation of his being under the one Being. It is simultaneously a turning to an inner reality and a placing of that reality in the proper context of a larger, outer reality. The wily spirit will avoid this necessity in proportion to its reluctance to surrender the freedom of alienation. When Mrs. Crater asks of the wandering stranger at her door, "Where you come from, Mr. Shiftlet?" he replies: "I can tell you my name is Tom T. Shiftlet and I come from Tarwater, Tennessee. . . . How you know my name ain't Aaron Sparks . . . and I come from Singleberry, Georgia, or how you know it's not George Speeds and I come from Lucy, Alabama, or how you know I ain't Thompson Bright from Toolafalls, Mississippi." In an earlier draft of the story, Miss O'Connor explicitly made those names pseudonyms which the stranger had used in those places. The shift from that explicit factual information to ambiguity calls special attention to Shiftlet's evasiveness under the pious pretense of serving truth in a corrupt world. What Shiftlet concludes as answer to the question is, "the best I can tell you is, I'm a man."

The devil's "specific personality for the occasion" is an interesting phrase. As Miss O'Connor's repeated use of *personality* in *Mystery and Manners* indicates, she means the term to designate being, realized and potential, which resides in the particular creature of God's special creation. (The Devil's assumptions of form are a parody of divine creation.) Naming has a sacramental relevance to the personality. Naming is an act, not simply reflective thought, through which one pays proper homage to both the creature and its creator. Naming was Adam's first test, we recall. Through naming one recognizes the source of "personality," a term far deeper in Miss O'Connor's use than in its more popular meaning. Such is the central reality recognized through the sacrament of baptism, a sacrament upon which some of her fiction turns, as does "The River" and *The Violent Bear It Away*. To give a suggestion of the importance of her "sacramental view of life . . . that sustains and supports at every turn the vision," she must use exaggeration, distortion as the instrument needed to make apparent that the fiction "has been made what it is because of belief." If the central action is baptism, she recognizes that it is a meaningless rite to most of her

readers, so that "I have to see that this baptism carries enough awe
and mystery to jar the reader into some kind of emotional recognition of its significance." The mystery which establishes a relation of
the named child "in the Name of the Father, Son, and Holy
Ghost," as the rite says, leads to a new "personality," the beginnings of the new man in whose interest the old Adam is put off. Particularity is certified sacramentally.

Poe deliberately shuns particularity, but for Miss O'Connor it
is the anchor of being in the world, in creation, in the Name of its
Creator. And language in so far as it may be made to participate in
that anchoring cannot be diabolic. For her it is through metaphor
that one approaches the nameless. The sacraments are an action
out of metaphor, through the mystery of which the things of the
world—and most particularly ourselves—become reconciled to the
Thing man seeks. That is why for Miss O'Connor the sacrament of
the Lord's Supper is so crucial, for it is in that celebration that we
become reconciled to all creation through Christ's abiding reconciliation of creation to the Father. "When Emerson decided, in
1832, that he could no longer celebrate the Lord's Supper unless
the bread and wine were removed, an important step in the
vaporization of religion in America was taken, and the spirit of that
step has continued apace." One consequence of Emerson's position
is the sentimentalizing of religion, through which the vaporousness
of abstraction is allowed to confuse the abstracted self with the
abstracted Creator. "When the physical fact is separated from the
spiritual reality, the dissolution of belief is eventually inevitable,"
she says. And the quest for the quest will then have stifled the instinct for rest. In Emersonian "Deism," Poe saw a truth: it reduced
the Creator to an idol; in reaction he asserts, with Bielfeld, "*Pour
savoir ce qu'est Dieu, il faut être Dieu même.*" But despite Poe's angry rejection of Deism (he is particularly scornful of New England
Transcendentalism), his shunning concrete particularity in images
in favor of a vaporized impressionism is itself a species of gnosticism
parallel to Emerson's.

CHAPTER XIII

ON SPIRITUAL LEUKEMIA: THE SELF DEVOURING

It is through the metaphor of the world, nature and human nature, seen as a multiple creature of the Creator, that one comes to understand the relation of *seeing* to *vision*. Through the physical fact one sees the spiritual reality in that "transposition" C. S. Lewis argues. That is why, for Miss O'Connor, art must be anagogically and not allegorically conceived. Her relation to so-called symbol, then, her understanding of the function of language in its relation to reality, is complex. Michael Polanyi, in *The Study of Man*, speaks of the nature of common symbols such as maps, graphs, words: "They are never objects of our attention in themselves, but pointers towards the things they mean. If you shift your attention from the meaning of a symbol to the symbol as an object viewed in itself, you destroy its meaning. Repeat the word 'table' twenty times over and it becomes a mere empty sound. Symbols can serve as instruments of meaning only by being known subsidiarily while fixing our focal attention on their meaning." In naturalistic fiction, we may say, images are symbols that point one to the physical facts, to be verified by our senses. But Miss O'Connor holds that the naturalist's is only a partial perspective upon existence. She speaks often of a limited validity in literary naturalism, but always emphasizes that it is limited. If a writer is concerned "with an accurate reproduction of the things that most immediately concern man, with the natural forces that he feels control his destiny," he "may produce a great tragic naturalism, for by his responsibility to the things he sees, he may transcend the limitations of his narrow vision."

Even thus limited, however, the naturalist's vision may reveal a second dimension in his images, in so far as he has been artistically responsive to the things he sees. For in those things he points toward lie the avenues to the transcendent, openings unaffected by whether the individual sees them or not. The image as a mirror of a thing may become a window opening upon the mystery of the transcendent. Such symbols, even though they may function at the naturalistic level as arrows "pointing towards the things they mean" may also point *through* those things toward the Cause of things. To discover a larger vision in symbol than the naturalist enjoys is to see double as it were. That seeing, under the gentle guidance of reason, prevents appetite on the one hand or spiritual ennui or spiritual enthusiasm on the other from distorting that wholeness of the self which is necessary so that one may deport himself ordinately toward the wholeness of all being. Miss O'Connor's concern, then, is to focus her vision through symbol so that one perceives the "inscape" (Hopkins's term) of the existing world. Thus the seen is brought into its true relation to the unseen, to the "instress" of being, through the eye of the beholder. Thus one discovers himself closer and closer to the name of the unnamable. Thus the inner and outer worlds are seen in their reconciliation.

It is this focusing upon the transcendent through the "physical fact" that in turn brings into focus for us Miss O'Connor's conception of the artist: he is a "realist of distances." This conception accounts for her speaking often of the poet in relation to the prophet, naming herself with both terms, in so far as she expresses her intentions as artist. She sees that one must exercise that vague, indefinite impetus in us—the hunger in the blood—as the poet does: through an anagogical address to being. In this address to being, one is recalled "to known but forgotten things"; that is the function of prophecy which she declares her own. We may now speak once more of that impetus in us, to which prophecy speaks, as an immortal homesickness, but it is homesickness upon which rests an obscuring and confusing fear of mortality—the fear that our own "personality" is doomed to oblivion. It is out of that fear that one contrives an escape from moment to moment through the quest for the quest, whether with Poe toward annihilation or Teilhard toward the dissolution of all particularity in Point Omega.

We may observe of our attempts to reconcile the soul to its double burden that, in so far as we speak of either attempt direction, our words willy-nilly settle about familiar experiences in the world of physical fact, our experiences of the world's body such as we make particular under terms like *place, home, family, friend.* The attraction of our language to the local and familiar as if by a magnet suggests our words' validity, suggests their participation in being, even though our homesickness never quite goes away when we rest in the bosom of a community of family and friends. For one continues spiritually disturbed to some degree so long as he experiences that tension in the ground of being of which Voegelin speaks, the tension "between life and death, immortality and mortality, perfection and imperfection, time and timelessness, between order and disorder, truth and untruth, sense and senselessness of existence; between *amor Dei* and *amor sui, l'âme ouverte* and *l'âme close.*" One is also subject to a temptation either to reject the world as an evil attraction luring us from our proper journey, as the Manichean idealist is, or to give oneself over fully to the world and its uses, as the materialist is said to do. It is words finally, the noise of our mouths (as St. Augustine says) or the noise of our actions, that reveal the nature of our giving or rejecting—or of our receiving. It is, in other words, in the *art* of our being that we reveal both our own being to others and to ourselves, and the nature of our address to being other than ourselves.[1]

---

1. In regard to Voegelin's statement of the tensional grounds of being, it seems a necessity of the finite intellect that it establish two points in that ground to locate itself as well as to reconcile diversity in unity. Plato's metaphor of the egg is an instance, which the poet attempts to command. (Yeats uses it so in "Among School Children.") Then there is the ever popular *yin* and *yang*; Nietzsche's *Appolonian* and *Dionysian*; Hegel's *thesis* and *antithesis*; Wallace Stevens's *green* and *blue*; the multitudinous uses of *heart* and *head*. It is as if we believe that in naming our experience of the dividing tension within our intellect, the halves may then be reunited by intellect in some sense of the lost wholeness. The difficulty is to turn or return to a vision of the whole, the first experience of which—faint in our memory, and so disturbing—is followed by division, of which we sense ourselves the unthinking agent. That first division, however, comes before the reason's naming of points to describe the division; it is that separation of (and by) the irreducible "I"—the observer—from the "Thou" whereby *Thou* becomes *It,* to borrow Buber's terms to our purpose. That is the separation which the un-

And that is why the art of person—"personality"—is crucial; it is why finally one's critical concern must be enlarged beyond the aesthetic level. For art is an act of bearing witness, whatever the mode of its language. In that witnessing, Miss O'Connor says, the moral sense necessarily coincides with the dramatic. If art's language is words, and the artist is Flannery O'Connor, the burning necessity is always to use words in the name of and in the light of the Word. And thus it is that, while tract is to be shunned as the plague of art, the word—the symbolic action of art—requires of the poet a concern which is more soul searching than his fascination with the machinery, the wheels and pinions that tempt Poe. Even so, it is a noticeable characteristic of the modern artist that he tends to worship his art, the form of rest his "search for the search" takes. "Nobody with a good car needs to be justified," Haze says at the height of his defiance. One can name for himself (especially since the eighteenth century, Miss O'Connor would say) poets who take Pegasus as superior to Haze's Essex for purposes of self-justification. But for Flannery O'Connor art is not the instrument whereby the imagination calls one's being into existence; it is an act of homage which by its proper nature requires that it be what it is and no more. Art neither proves the existence of God, as tractarian art attempts to do, nor is it properly served when commandeered to carry one away from the world and its spiritual problems. Art is, finally, a celebration of being whereby the artist pays tribute to the creative Cause of all creation and all creating.

What the Quester for the Quest must admit to finally is that the quest is really for a fullness of his own being. And it is here that the danger of Manichean error emerges in the press of battle. It is in this press also that Poe's desperateness forces him into the hope

---

aided "I" cannot anneal for all its dreams of doing so. Its attempt to do so leads to a sequential recession of the "I" such as one finds dramatized in the poetry of Walt Whitman, for instance—a positing of the "I" in words from which one's "self" is already discovered withdrawn. The problem is a spiritual one, not simply philosophical or aesthetic, so that philosophical or poetic solution proves insufficient. Thus Eliot, pursuing with his own powers the phenomenologists' attempt to solve the problem through his own philosophical and poetic thought, at last reaches a point from which he must make a departure radically different from poetry or philosophy. We have already cited the key passage, the surrender of the self, in *The Waste Land*, pointing particularly to the note in which Eliot juxtaposes Bradley's comment on the closed "World" of the self to a passage from Dante which points to the prospects of openness of the self through grace.

of annihilation. For if one seems incapable, through his own will, of realizing pure being, then annihilation—pure unbeing—seems the second best bed to lie in. The confusion in the choice is out of a distortion of being, in which the world of matter becomes enemy, to which confusion Plato is a continuing contributor through our readings of him, erroneous readings Voegelin argues. Certainly Augustine sees that danger in Plato and the Neo-Platonist: a rejection of the world of matter, in which act there is also a rejection of the Creator of that world. The difficulty with heresy, says Eliot (in *After Strange Gods*) is not that heresy is wrong, but that it is partly right. And the heresy of Manicheanism is not that it values the spirit but that it mis-values the body of creation. It fails to realize an ordinate vision of being and so rejects that part of existence which Miss O'Connor calls "the good under construction." In the light of the Fall, the inclusive world—all creation— is the good under construction; the creed states as an article of faith the "redemption of the world." The reasoned justification of that belief is in Augustine's and Thomas's emphasis upon the world as the creature of God, which cannot, by reason of its Agent, be declared irremediably evil. But neither is its redemption possible through that act of one's will whereby all creation is assimilated by the consciousness as the act of redemption; that is the course which phenomenology undertakes. It is also the course Poe himself takes, to a point where he teeters on the brink of annihilation. In the end, as we shall see, he chooses to turn and plunge into it.

To see the attraction to being from Miss O'Connor's orthodox position reveals that position a pole removed from Poe's, then, and from the special Manichean inclination called phenomenology. One notes that, in spite of its formal name as popularly associated with empirical science (which is in fact its avowed enemy, as Leo Strauss points out) phenomenology has as its chief accuser the created world of things. Phenomena are states of mind, to be sharply contrasted to the *noumena*, things-in-themselves. That world of multitudinous *creatura* tends to become to the phenomenological approach either dead instruments of, or illusions in, the consciousness through the killing power of thought. *Things* must be transcended by or dissolved by consciousness. But as Pieper says of the

Thomistic position, "Existence . . . does not 'adjoin' the realm of Eternity; it is entirely permeated by it." That is the revelation Gilson speaks of as coming down to man through nature. To treat the things of the world otherwise is a form of sacrilege, precisely the charge one must ultimately bring against Poe from Miss O'Connor's perspective. For as we have emphasized, though he does not, as Comte does, elevate humanity to the divine as a stratagem for the manipulation of the world, Poe nevertheless does elevate his own consciousness to the divine. Comte's effects in the world, through such disciples as Marx, Lenin, Stalin, Hitler, hardly find comparable effects out of Poe, but it is nevertheless true that in Poe one has what Voegelin characterizes as "The satanic Apocalypse of Man." Comte promulgates a program; Poe sees and pursues an enticing idea through which he would exorcise that homesickness for Eternity.

Eternity in Poe (and in Heidegger and Sartre as extensions of Husserl) is consumed by consciousness, in the process of which *things* themselves are exorcised from their impingement upon consciousness, or they are dissolved into it. That is the cause of the pathos of loneliness that permeates existentialism, haunted as it is by the ghosts of the world it has murdered in its intellectual panic. But in another act of faith and through the reasoning that supports it—that of Voegelin or Pieper or O'Connor—one sees that *things in places not the self* allows us an acceptance of separateness and finitude, while at the same time compensating for that finitude and separateness through our realization of multiple presences in a community of being. In seeing with a Hopkins the multiplicity of being as the shining forth of God's grandeur, one recognizes particularity in separateness, and thence the substantial being of others and of other things, but without that terror of Otherness engendered by the phenomenological inclination. (It is a recognition correlative to the mystery of the resurrection of the body.) Home, family, community in their lowly presences are anagogic here. Discourse, response to other beings, while not free of that disturbing suggestion of separateness which existentialism has thought necessary to exploit, bears in it as well that solution to the larger terror of being: the consciousness reduced to talking only to itself.

That is the central consequence in *Eureka* when Poe, "Through himself speaks Himself": he is condemned to that inevitable interior schizophrenia of the isolated monad.

That self-ventriloquism which Poe practices, named *himself, interpreter, God, Heart,* does not finally satisfy him for the loss of self in the annihilation of "individual identity" with which he wrestles in *Eureka.* His final marginal note still gnaws at the problem: "The pain of the consideration that we shall lose our individual identity, ceases at once when we reflect that the process, as above described, is neither more nor less than that of the absorption, by each individual intelligence, of all other intelligences (that is, of the Universe) into its own. That God may be all in all, each must become God." Thus Poe's system proves to be that sort of spiritual leukemia called Manicheanism, in which multitudinous "monads" of the world's body, gone awry, devour each other toward annihilation. And Poe's tales are a true revelation of the nature of Poe's metaphysics, for the struggle toward such absorption in those tales yields horror, as in "The Fall of the House of Usher" and "Ligeia." The last minute marginal note to *Eureka* is hardly reassuring, either to the reader or (one strongly suspects) to that writer for whom the first person personal pronoun was of such commanding importance.

Poe's work does reveal the "interpreter" of whom Halliburton speaks, the absolute voice which is necessary to self-communion. For that interpreter is the self-created daemon through whom the vehicle of the sole consciousness is not only ratified but transubstantiated into the whole of existence, to which the borrowed term God is applied. The infinte becomes "man-who-is-God" and through "himself" he talks to "Himself" and talks "Himself." There is a sleight of mind, through which the homelessness crying in the blood is stilled by thought, or that other fear that consciousness itself may be an illusion is kept partially at bay: the *himself* has created the *Himself.* It is a consequence, as Pegis says in defense of St. Thomas, of Western man's ceasing to be *knower* by becoming *thinker,* of our moving "from man knowing the world of sensible things to man thinking abstract thoughts in separation from existence. What is thinking but dis-existentialized knowing?"

Voegelin describes the spectacular appearance of such "thinking" in the outer world, that confused state in which man has condemned himself "to be free and urgently wants to be arrested for editing a Maoist journal."

The "voices of Poe's interpreter" are not borrowed then, as Halliburton says. Or rather, they are borrowed, but in a way separate from what Halliburton seems to mean or Poe to suggest. For to "borrow" requires going outside oneself; there is implicit a "loaned," a "given" such as flaws the unified construction of the particular consciousness as autonomous. Those passive verbs have in them as always the ghost of an agent. Such is the splinter language drives into the consciousness as a token of the denied world, and the pain is such as to make imperative a reaction to things, even if it is a denial of things by our acts of thought which Pascal describes as the quest for the quest, an escape into the most abstract country of the mind. The *anxiety* (in Heidegger's sense, which we shall presently examine), is precisely out of a feeling of claustration, a sign of which in Poe is his insistence upon the imperative voice. That voice of command is evidence of a necessity of the consciousness to a loud prophecy lest it be devoured by doubt. It is a self-calling to prophecy, but a prophecy whose necessity is questionable if the consciousness is conceded to be self-contained. For in that concession the question rises: to whom must prophecy be given? Only to self it would appear, so that it may still its fear that its own existence is an illusion. Thus doubt has already raised the possibility either of *being as illusion* or of *being as other*, the possibilities Ivan Karamazov's devil advances to feed Ivan's wild discomfort. The phenomenal world is thus shaken to its center.

And pouring through the fissures in that shaken world comes the problem of time. For it signifies nothing to say that in Poe's prophet in *Eureka* one has a being "whose access to the unity of the past reveals to him the unity of the future," as Halliburton says. Time is a concept of no logical validity to the closed monad. Yet in naming it *closed monad* one has already decisively violated the timeless universe of its pretense. The words (and all depends on words) must be logically exterior to the monad, and hence it is not all-inclusive, for it does not include the words. Something stands outside it and speaks of it. Such was the dilemma T. S. Eliot engaged in his own examination of Leibnitz' monads and the subsequent extensions of that concept in phenomenology. In *The Waste Land*, Eliot breaks out at last from the feeling of alienation, from the desperate terror in the consciousness's isolation, through the recognition that in speaking of the dilemma of time and the closed universe of the consciousness, he was already necessarily outside that closed world. One should observe that in this period of his thought Eliot is repeatedly drawn to comment on Poe in his prose, and a passage discarded from *The Waste Land* bears striking parallel to the conclusion of Poe's *Narrative of Arthur Gordon Pym*, the segment of 72 lines from which Part IV, "Death by Water," derives, including its present title. Eliot goes on from *The Waste Land* to a new conception of the relation of time past, present, and future in *Burnt Norton*, and to an insight into the mystery of the Word within the word, the Word within the world. In that opening of the closed self, he was able to lay the ghosts of memory, those "voices of memory" out of which Poe builds the chimera of an interpreter, his own several "voices singing out of empty cisterns and exhausted wells." Reconciling memory to desire, Eliot, unlike Poe, goes on to the larger problem of the spiritual wanderer in a world he never made, the problem of hope's burden of despair.

The dilemma in phenomenological existentialism, subsequently represented exhaustively by Heidegger and Sartre, is precisely Poe's. And it is the dilemma of Miss O'Connor's Misfit as well, for whom the world is "thown off balance" by the Advent. The Misfit protests he cannot witness that event in time and place. The Misfit's confusion is the one general to our age, the confusion of the literal *historical* presentness of the past with the continuous witness in time of that Presence. "I wisht I had of been there," the Misfit says. "It ain't right I wasn't there because if I had of been there I would of known."

It is the relation of the created to creation in respect to history, in respect to time and place, that distinguishes the Christian's Advent from moments of reconciliation of time to eternity in other religions. Thus Eliade is led to say in *The Sacred and the Profane*, that "Christianity radically changed the experience and concept of liturgical time" because it "affirms the historicity of the person of Christ. The Christian liturgy unfolds in *a historical time sanctified by the incarnation of the Son of God."* And again, in *Rites and Symbols of Initiation,* "The *newness* of Christianity is constituted by the historicity of Jesus. . . . the resurrection of Jesus *could not be* identified with the periodic death and resurrection of the God of the mysteries." While other myths strive to escape history, "Christianity strives *to save* history," an aberration Eliade calls special attention to in *Image and Symbol.* In what sense Christianity attempts to rescue history is perhaps more clearly put by Voegelin, who says that "in the encounter with Incarnation the individual human existence has come into view as the point of transcendental irruptions which constitute history . . . . in the Israelite experience of the covenant type the ruler and empire receded and society existed in immediacy under the kingship of God; in the encounter with Incarnation, we may say, history has become articulated down to individual man, who through his faith participates in the constitution of history." ("History and Gnosis") The leap in being (Voegelin's term) of the Israelite experience prepares for that leap in being in the encounter with Incarnation, a consummation in which history is redeemed through (not *by*) the individual man. Thus time is "sanctified," in Eliade's word. In *Image and Symbol,* looking at the Judaeo-Christian experience from the outside, Eliade says of it: "Judaeo-Christianity presents us with the supreme hierophany: the *transfiguration of the historical event into hierophany . . . .* it is the *historical* event as such which displays the maximum of trans-historicity: God not only intervenes in history, as in the case of Judaism; He is incarnated in a historical being. . . . in reality, this 'historical event' constituted by the existence of Jesus is a total theophany; what it presents is like an audacious effort to *save the historical event* in itself, by endowing it with the maximum of being."[2] One may observe that the inclination in Poe is in an opposite direc-

2. I must here emphasize Eliade's standing aside from Christianity as an aberration in the world's religions. For though I have cited Eliade in support of my arguments a number of times and shall subsequently do so, a note of caution to the reader seems in order: it is one thing to accept gratefully the researches and observations of so thorough a historian of religions as Eliade, but quite another to accept the conclusions he draws from them, or the position from which he makes his researches and observations. In these later concerns I find in him dangers requiring my own observations and a conclusion. A close student, Wendell C. Beane, gives a summary evaluation of Eliade's position in a postscript to the two-volume anthology, *Myths, Rites, Symbols: A Mircea Eliade Reader.* It seems to me an accurate summary and one to which Eliade speaks no disclaimer in his own "Preface" to the work, in which he

tion. If Voegelin sees in the Incarnation that "the individual human existence" is the point in time of "transcendental irruptions which constitute history," Poe by an audacious effort would cancel that history. In effect he attempts a self-induced amnesia whereby any Other separate from the Self (most particularly the created world and its inevitable entanglement of consciousness with the problem of time) ceases to be. Consciousness by an act of will becomes a vortex into (but never out of) which creation is drawn toward annihilation. The bright star of the full person, individual human existence, as the point of transcendental irruption in creation

once more reiterates his hope of the "History of Religions opening doors toward 'a new humanism.' "

Beane remarks Eliade's vision as that of a "remarkable religious naturalism," in which one returns to the conditions of earliest man and his myth. Such intellectual analysis reveals that archaic men through myth had an "inherent religious tendency to be themselves creators of meaningful solitary and social situations that they would come to regard as sacred." Through myths, rites, symbols their "recourse to the sacred past meant . . . the affirmation of faith in humankind's own potential to *make* history, to *remake* human nature, indeed to *revaluate* the relation between nature and humankind at the level of religious contemplation." Thus do we arrive at a conclusion to Eliade's "remarkable religious naturalism," one which "invites the paradoxical realization that man, indeed, 'makes himself' (i.e., people create culture) *and* that man himself 'is made' (i.e., in the myths of the Supernatural)." There is then an "ineradicable role" played by religion "in the evolution of the human mind." To recognize this is to be confronted by a challenge: "humankind *can* save itself, if it would *be* saved."

What we observe is that such a position as ascribed here to Eliade reveals him as a nineteenth-century child of the Enlightenment. Man is seen as his own saviour, although we must observe that Eliade says incisively critical things of that elitist rationalism of the Enlightenment, whose principal corruption he describes as the desacralization of Western thought. But here is precisely where one must be most cautious as to Eliade's own conception of the sacred. For his argument finds the sacred most blossoming in archaic man in his sense of himself as the center of existence. Man, by his ritual enactment of a return to chaos, becomes the creator of reality. The question here avoided by this comparativistic approach is whether human religiosity is an instinct, within the naturalistic limits of existence. If so, the nostalgic hunger for old timeless time, upon which Eliade dwells, speaks only a timeless time crested by man himself at the ritualistic self-centeredness of his acts—his creation of a supreme fiction. Or, alternately, we may ask whether we have in Eliade's position a dualistic trap with no exit. He sees as indisputable a division between two times which he calls Historical Time and Liturgical Time. But what is the position from which we see the two and not one and how are they to be reconciled? Which is the reality and which fiction or illusion? In *Patterns in Comparative Religion*, Eliade is aware of the difficulty: "man, whatever else he may be free of, is forever prisoner of his own archetypal intuitions, formed at the moment when he first perceived his position in the cosmos. . . . Man's concept of the absolute can never be completely uprooted: it can only be debased."

As appealing as that promise is, it still leaves one with a strange conception of intuition as a byproduct of self awareness, as if man comes into being in all his complexity out of nothing anterior to his own perception of "his position in the cosmos." The religious inclina-

becomes instead a black hole, for even consciousness becomes victim of the vortex which draws all to annihilation.

As for the rescue of time by the Incarnation, and the possibility of a "person's" participation, Josef Pieper puts the problem more soundly and more hopefully. The celebration of festival, he quotes someone as saying, is the act whereby we enter into the presence of deity in time. That Presence does not, in the world, destroy time. As Eliot among many others has said, that Presence redeems time. It is only the finite, incomplete thought (i.e., an action by the partial being of the soul) which would destroy time, a usurpation of and judgment upon God's office through pride. Milton perceives its satanic nature; it divorces mind from the rest of creation, the mind thus becoming its own timeless place. The closed monad attempts

---

tion in man, it begins to appear, is only a mode of a naturalistic dimension of reality. From primitive spirituality we proceed into culture, with culture itself being the full being of man, whereby he "makes himself." As he says in *Patterns in Comparative Religion*, primitive spirituality is not "a thing man can effectively accomplish" as primitive man could, but is for us rather "a *nostalgia* which creates things that become values in themselves: art, the sciences, social theory." Spirituality, while not an opiate of the people as formulated by religion, is nevertheless thus reduced to a naturalistic inclination in man. Through that inclination, with the aid of the historian of religions, a culture may be engineered that would be far superior to those attempted by social or economic directors. But in such argument one hears loud echoes of Comte. The religious director (and I echo here Voegelin's term *director* as he uses it in *From Enlightenment to Revolution*) has as his intent to establish "a universal type of culture" Eliade says in *The Quest: History and Meaning in Religion*.

Anticipating the Christian reaction to such a position, Eliade remarks that theologians are "suspicious of historical-religious hermeneutics that might encourage syncretism or religious dilettantism or, worse yet, raise doubt about the uniqueness of the Judeo-Christian revelation. On the other hand, the history of religions envisages, in the end, cultural *creation* and the *modification* of man. The humanist culture poses an embarrassing problem for theologians and for Christians in general: What do Athens and Jerusalem have in common?"

There is a considerable body of argument which rather puts humanism in the position of embarrassment, some of which we have introduced in our pages and will subsequently in volume three. Here let us observe that, aside from the rather persuasive answer to the question Eliade poses which is made by Voegelin in his *Order and History*, not only does Eliade's humanistic position leave fundamental questions unasked: the end he envisages also reveals itself as another instance of the millenialist dreams that proliferated out of the Enlightenment, each requiring its own director, in this instance the historian of religions. That is, the end he envisages for the historian of religion is a gnostic manipulation of being. What Eliade argues for in the end is a pantheon of "Supernatural Beings" accommodated in an ecumenical syncretism, a United Heaven of those Ambiguous Gods that are created by man through ritualistic myth, in whose several names a fundamentally secular humanism calls itself sacred. One must, therefore, take cautious access to Eliade. For while he is incisive and helpful in his speculations, his ends are suspect. For his vision of man as the maker of reality through ritual does not satisfy the problems of reality experienced in the *metaxy*, the problems of our experience of the In-Between on which Voegelin speaks far more persuasively.

to make, as Satan says, a heaven of Hell, a hell of Heaven—as it wishes. Such is the final divorce from reality which means the death of the soul.

CHAPTER XIV

CATCHING EARTH ANGELS
IN CLEARED ARENAS

Allen Tate, in his "Poetry of Edgar Allan Poe," wonders "why the modern proponents of the Big Bang hypothesis of creation have not condescended to acknowledge Poe as a forerunner," citing *Eureka*'s cosmology to his point. But the question seems rather why Poe critics have not seen him more particularly as the forerunner of Martin Heidegger, our contemporary existentialist whose arguments repeatedly call Poe to mind. Both Poe and Heidegger have reservations about the propriety and capability of science to explain the human situation, though Poe enjoys those analytic functions of the mind upon which science depends. We have heard Poe say that "The *highest* order of the imaginative intellect is always preeminently mathematical." As we have suggested, Poe seems more interested in the act of solving problems than in the solution—more interested in the game the mind plays with an analytic question than with any answer derived from the game. Perhaps he is so since, when the answer becomes paramount to the analytic mind, it seems thereby wooed either toward St. Thomas's prudence or Jeremy Bentham's utilitarianism, both being directions Poe resists. Having rejected St. Thomas, our world prefers to enter upon that race toward collective utopianism which Poe finds extremely dangerous and which he scathingly attacks. For he will not have the poet's role subsumed to the uses of social utopias nor explained away on deterministic grounds, any more than he will submit to the higher demand upon the poet's gift from the regions of the transcendent. "Because we are not all Homers in the beginning, it has been somewhat rashly taken that we shall be all Jeremy Benthams to the end." Poe comments on the propensity of the analytic mind to a distortion of the world in "The Colloquy of Monos and Una," a discourse spoken from beyond Death and to be supposed as spoken a hundred years after the death of the principals, a hundred years being Poe's favorite outer limit of prophecy, as also in "Mellonta Tauta." Imagined by Poe as spoken in our own day, the colloquy's indictment of "Progress" indeed sounds very like editorials written in 1979 by an ecologist or a second-generation Vanderbilt Agrarian.

Poe does not wrestle with the niceties of time and eternity at this point, his hundred years a stock phrase like the balladeer's "a year and a day." His principal intent is to criticize those "rough pedants," the "utilitarians," those enemies of the "poetic intellect." We are to imagine ourselves as readers at a point in the literal world where there is a "fiery overthrow" of civilization even as the words are spoken, but they are nevertheless supposed to be spoken in a timeless dimension, though thus contradictorily fettered by time. The old prophecy of holocaust is now fulfilled. But the significant record in the colloquy is of a transposition of the five senses into a sixth sense, "the first and obvious step of the intemporal soul upon the threshold of the temporal Eternity." "Intemporal," not immortal. What Poe says here seems interestingly paralleled by Heidegger's conception of time argued in the second section of Part I of his *Existence and Being*. James Collins remarks of that conception its concern for "the future as the primary phenomenon of temporality, as that kind of anticipation of self and death whereby human reality exists finitely." I die; therefore I am. Ontological ease is approached, not by moving thought back or out from the present moment of self-awareness toward the past or future, but by moving from the future back to the present. The procedure is a form of philosophical utopianism which posits death as the condition necessary to the realization of the self, a move which would seem to transfer the grounds of particular being from the old grounds of the potential inherent in the actual living present. And though Heidegger complains that Sartre as disciple abuses him, one detects glimmers here of a conclusion that being necessarily follows action, since action is inextricably consumed by the future, out of which fire Being rises.[1]

Poe's fictional structure in his colloquy makes use of cosmological analogy, in an attempt to express the idea of a coming to be of "the intemporal soul upon the threshold of the temporal Eternity." But it is a cosmology of the self which he pursues, a point from which we may be distracted by the pretense that the discourse is a satiric commentary upon a span of time in the history of the world. Heidegger sets aside the possibility of cosmology's aid in developing his ontological argument, a point seemingly divergent from Poe, if we give only a casual reading to the colloquy or to a work like *Eureka*. As I think we have seen from our exploration so far, however, Poe's work is a pseudo-cosmology, a necessary fiction to the expression of ideas that are at once terrifying and difficult to articulate. As Monas says, "Words are vague things," and especially when one must talk of Nothingness as Poe is attempting to do. As for the terror, it lies not only in the prospect of confronting Nothingness but in Poe's belief in the awesome power of words. For words force being, as that dialogue the "Power of Words" argues; yet the originator of that force lacks absolute control of the force he looses. Hence at the last his narrator weeps over the world his words have created. (By analogy, Poe's fear of the consequences of words is like the geneticist's fear of the effect of his experimentation, a fear that leads Medawar to settle for "piecemeal genetic engineering".) Heidegger too is cautious in respect to the limitation

---

1. Voegelin, in "Immortality: Experience and Symbol," also speaks of death as structuring life, but with distinctions that separate him from Heidegger. The "life structured by death is neither the life of mortals, nor the lasting of the gods, but the life experienced in the tension of existence. It is the life lived in the flow of presence." What makes Heidegger's approach unacceptable is that he shifts the grounds of being from a tensional present, the moment of experience of the In-Between, to a speculative future, death. In speaking of the "fateful confusion" within "existential virtues" to which we may succumb, and indeed to which we have increasingly succumbed since Hegel's *Begriffsspekulation*, Voegelin says, "if Nous is both the god beyond man and the divine entity within man, then the two are liable to collapse into one as soon as they are not firmly held apart by the tension of existence." Following that collapse, we have increasingly declared the "death of God," and with that assertion increasingly substituted death for God as the end toward which our being tends. Thus annihilation and nonexistence become the god of modern man, the new mystery of justification which becomes the "metaphysical" ground for endless ideologies. Voegelin's solution to the problem we saw in Volume I, particularly in his distinction of consciousness as both "the site and the sensorium of participation in the divine ground."

of the self in words, postponing release of the second part of his major work because words are recalcitrant and will not convey his intended meaning. It is this impasse with words used discursively which turns Heidegger toward word coinage and to a dependence on the poetic dimension of language rather than on conventional philosophical procedures. The reluctance of words to be commanded by logic leads him to celebrate the poet, such as Rilke or Hölderlin, as more nearly accomplishing the philosopher's task.[2]

Not, of course, that the poet's attempt to express the mystery of being in relation to Nothingness is easier than the philosopher's. Poe's own frustration with words is no doubt behind his petulant insistence that "This 'species of nothingness' is quite as reasonable, at all events, as any 'kind of somethingness.'" And if petulance doesn't solve the problem, then he is given to a longing for a condition beyond words which would allow revelation: Oh, that the poet might be gifted "with an intellect *very* far superior to that of his race" so that he may soar "above the plain of [his] race," becoming (as he says in "The Domain of Arnheim") an "earth-angel." But even assuming a vision of Being from that refined position, the task then becomes to find a way to adapt the vision to words for the sake of "the eyes which were to behold it on earth." The impossible task for the visionary poet such as Poe would be is to reveal vision to lesser souls through impossible words. We recall that the office of "earth-angel" is assumed both by Hölderlin and Rilke, in whom

---

2. On Heidegger's problem with words, see James Collins's discussion in *The Existentialists*, 190-240 passim, and the notes to this section of his book. Voegelin is critical of Heidegger's confusions in terminology as it avoids complexities through neologisms and figurative adaptations. In "History and Gnosis" he says in a note, "*Das Dasein übernimmt sich selbst* is a stock phrase of Heidegger's existentialism. . . . the phrase in German has a double meaning not intended by its author. It can be rendered either as 'existence takes charge of itself' (the meaning intended) or as 'existence overreaches itself' (what, indeed, it does when it takes charge of itself.)" We cited earlier Voegelin's remark that "German gnostics, especially, like to play with language and hide their non-thought in wordplay." (*Science, Politics & Gnosticism*) If there is any doubt as to Voegelin's evaluation of Heidegger, he makes it clear in "History and Gnosis," where Heidegger's influence on modern existentialist thought is the point of departure for evaluating Bultmann's theological inquiries. He warns that the fascination which Heidegger's work "holds for the unwary is due to the subtle blending of truth presented with conviction and untruth through omission." Deeper into his argument he adds, "one must . . . recognize that the 'philosophy' in existentialism is a façade behind which an entirely different, a nonphilosophical intention is at work," that is, a gnostic intention. He concludes that "Against the existentialist will no argument is possible. I can only say that I prefer to be troubled, in the company of St. Paul, by the mystery of history."

Heidegger sees proof of his own thought. In each poet is the feeling that God has withdrawn from creation, accompanied in each by the sense of a special burden upon the poet as divine; to the poet is committed the task of reuniting God to creation. Heidegger, with a title taken from Hölderlin ("Of what use are poets in a time of need") examines Rilke's *Duino Elegies* and *Sonnets to Orpheus* to argue that the poet must not be dissuaded by those not of the tribe of earth-angels who therefore see the poet as godless when he declares God's withdrawal. For, as Collins summarizes the argument, "this declaration [of God's withdrawal] is motivated by a strong opposition to idolatry and religious formalism, both of which seek to break down the difference . . . between things in the world and the holy." That danger of idolatry, one might recall, is Poe's reason for rejecting "all the argumentation which I have seen on the nature of the soul, or of Deity." It is "nothing but worship of his unnamable idol." But Gabriel Marcel warns us that Rilke's "angels" may be manifestations or even poets, but not messengers of the Christian God.[3] And from what we have already seen in our argument, we recognize in the position taken here by Heidegger and his poets, and in Poe, a gnostic reaction to creation, within which reaction there lingers something of the Puritan revolt against religious formalism as inevitably idolatrous. (Voegelin, in *Science, Politics & Gnosticism*, remarks that "The long history of post-classical Western gnosticism . . . appears in its continuity as the history of Western sectarianism." It is worth reminding ourselves at such a point, as St. Thomas and Voegelin would, that to see toward the holy *through* things, or to experience the presence of the holy in things, is not to obliterate the distinction between the two. Also (to anticipate our argument in the final volume) it is well to remember that a separation of *things* from the *holy*, whereby things become empty of being, is precisely the gnostic action that justifies a desecration of things— whether in the name of an absentee God, as is the tendency of the classical Gnostic, or in the name of a materialistic assumption of God's position in nature such as our world is so largely given to.

---

3. With Marcel incidentally Miss O'Connor shows affinity, which she no doubt recognized. She writes William Sessions who is abroad (September 1957): "Are you going to see Heidegger on his mountain top? . . . . What about Marcel . . . ?" *Added Dimension*, 218.

It is Marcel among others who suspects the immediate grounds from which such poets embark upon their divine calling, the assumption that God has withdrawn from His creation which they then assume necessitates the poet's calling God back to the world. One is reminded of the child who insists that the school bus left him, rather than admit that he missed the bus. What one cannot finally escape in Heidegger's poets as a sign that they are failed priests of being is an absence of joy such as might give some encouragement to those eyes that must in turn behold the world through these elected "earth-angels' " eyes. Near the end of his life, Rilke is still saying

> Is it still I that burns there all alone?
> Unrecognizable? memories denied?
> O life, O life: being outside.
> And I in flames—no one is left—unknown.

And Hölderlin's stance, bravely stoical, does not convince one of the poet as "deliverer" as he hovers suspended between the world and God:

> Alone before God, simplicity protects him,
> And no weapon needs he, and no
> Cunning, till the time when God's failure helps.

The spiritual condition described is that of the soul still calling for the bus that has left with the sad arrogance of the existentialist will, a condition in being which St. John of the Cross might speak more convincingly to as a dark night of the soul.

We have said enough now to justify our putting some of Heidegger's more specific arguments beside Poe's, in the context of our discussion of *Eureka* and of Poe's colloquies. We shall reflect upon them as they appear from Miss O'Connor's position. To do so is to bring Poe a step closer to that variegated climate of modern thought, atheistic existentialism. We here welcome the aid supplied by two minds who have labored to digest Heidegger's thought, James Collins and David E. Roberts, as we shall also depend upon recollections and analysis of Heidegger by two of his distinguished students, Leo Strauss and Eric Voegelin. (In these difficult waters, one welcomes all the help one can get.) As Robert shows us in his *Existentialism and Religious Belief*, Heidegger builds his metaphysics out of an accepted consciousness in which the active agents of being are conscience, guilt, and resolve. But, Roberts points out, he "rejects all attempts to ground them in a permanent self which transcends the world. . . . Personal identity . . . is something that has to be won through resolve which leads to isolation and independence." It is such personal identity, we notice, as Rilke expresses in the passage we quoted above. What one strives for, says Heidegger, is the "true-self," which he affirms as a point of potential consummation in time, to which one gives assent out of a sense of guilt. Once more we note that Poe's "Colloquy of Monos and Una" assumes its beginning point to be at the consummation of being in Death, from which point there is an analysis and explanation of the journey up to that point, a journey which in Poe's account involves a sense of guilt as motive power also. Monos discovers that man "must be born again," but Poe's use of the phrase is ironic, meaning to emphasize a contrast to the phrase as used by St. Paul. For Heidegger also, guilt is far removed from the Christian sense of the term. Guilt is that feeling of uneasiness, that anxiety which has no clear object, though the object is progressively discovered by the act of moving toward the "true-self." Guilt is anxiety spawned by one's not having reached the state of the "true-self."

Even so, Heidegger's "anxiety" may be seen as that condition we have spoken of already as the sense of homelessness in the world, a sense of alienation very ancient in man's history. C. S. Lewis, in "The Weight of Glory" remarks this "desire for our own far-off country, which we find in ourselves." It is "the secret which hurts so much that you take your revenge on it by calling it names like Nostalgia and Romanticism and Adolescence." It is "news from a country we have never yet visited" that stirs anxiety and restlessness in us. On this deep wound of emptiness, Heidegger builds his total argument, shifting it from its source in Original Sin as Lewis would have it. And it is precisely here in Heidegger no doubt that he holds us fascinated, prompting Voegelin to warn the unwary that the fascination is "due to the subtle blending of truth presented with conviction and untruth through omission." ("History and Gnosis") Collins remarks as the lasting value of

Nietzsche that he underlines modern man's homelessness, the "self-alienation observed by Hegel and Marx." But where the naturalist would hold that this feeling of homelessness is born of man's incomplete attachment to nature, and the Christian that it is a common wound out of Original Sin healed only by Christ's sacrifice, Heidegger suggests to the contrary that man himself may have rather failed to fulfill an indispensable condition for acquiring the sense of being at home: namely, a recognition of the presence and power of Being-itself as the foundation of all that is. Man cannot be at home in the world until he learns "to be at home with being and to domicile it in the center of that-which-is." The problem here (which is the central problem of all thought as thought) is the meaning of "being," the sense in which *being* is understood by the *thought*. Collins is somewhat kinder, one notices, in his analysis of that problem in Heidegger than Eric Voegelin is willing to be. In *Science, Politics & Gnosticism*, Voegelin speaks of Heidegger as an "ingenious gnostic," whose argument on being distorts the concept beyond thoughtful endurance. "The position of the gnostic thinker," Voegelin says, "derives its authority from the power of being. He is the herald of being, which he interprets as approaching us from the future." It is an aspect of gnostic thought in Heidegger that we have already suggested as Utopian. Its premise is an interpretation of being as presence ("the original Greek meaning of *parousia*"). The problem is how to get to that "presence." "Being is not to be understood statically, as substance, but actively, as presence, in the sense of coming into presence, as an emerging or appearing. . . . being creates for itself a world; and it creates this world through man." But man lacks the power to open himself to being or to shut himself off from its force. He is then, vis-à-vis *being*, in the relation of man to God's grace in the orthodoxy of St. Thomas or Miss O'Connor. As I think we shall see, Heidegger's reading of being in relation to individual existences is strikingly parallel to God's relation to His creation. The difficulty is that Heidegger cannot go beyond Poe's threshold of "temporal Eternity," cannot make the transcendent leap. Thus history impinges upon being in a distressing way. As Voegelin puts it, Heidegger holds that, in the historical process, "There can be times of falling away from essential being into the nonessential whence human existence can find its way back only by opening itself again to the parousia of being." Our own day is one of nonessential being, so that (in Heidegger's words) *being* is the word which holds "the spiritual fate of the West." For Heidegger, it is *being* which must be discovered at the heart of the waste land, rather than the Word—the Divine Presence.[4]

If one read Poe's "Colloquy" in the light of Heidegger's concept of being, he finds in Monos' account of his "earthly" existence an anxiety which Heidegger sets as the necessary motive force that leads man to attempt to specify the object which will dispel that anxiety. But, as Heidegger says, when anxiety is dissolved by the object specified, it turns to fear, fear being a response to a definite object. Monos "became possessed by a vague uneasiness—an anxiety such as the sleeper feels when sad real sounds fall continuously within his ear . . . commingling with melancholy dreams." Monos' early concern for the decay of civilization, he now sees, was an attempt to embody an object, to condense vague anxiety to fear. That is an error which is corrected by Death itself, which reveals the answer to that question which constitutes the first spoken words of the "Colloquy": "Born again?" "Yes," says Monos to Una, "Those were the words upon whose mystical meaning I had so long pondered, rejecting the explanations of the priesthood, until Death himself resolved for me the secret."

So, then, guilt is, for Heidegger and for Poe, that anxiety

4. Voegelin, in "Immortality: Experience and Symbol," uses the term *presence* in a sense not to be confused with Heidegger's term. "There appears to be a flow of existence that is not existence in time. Since modern philosophy has not developed a vocabulary for describing the [Platonic] metaxy, I shall use the term 'presence' to denote the point of intersection in man's existence; and the term 'flow of presence' to denote the dimensions of existence that is, and is not, time." Voegelin is engaging, it seems to me, the still point of existence in the tensional In-Between, for the question arises immediately out of his terms, he says, of the sense of *post* "if history is a flow of presence" and of *presence* "if the presence of intersection is a timelike flow." He adds that the philosopher such as himself "knows the tension of faith toward God to be not a Christian privilege but a trait of human nature." The Christian—a C. S. Lewis for instance—might respond that in so far as all men are the sons of Adam, touched by Original Sin, and that Christ's blood heals that wound in human nature, it is indeed a Christian privilege. But our main point here is that *presence* for Voegelin is a constant of experience, which we avoid by gnostic separation of the self from experience *in* the presence (*metaxy*), while for Heidegger presence is to be summoned into experience.

spawned by one's not having reached the state which Heidegger calls the "true-self." But to realize that end, one must first face the inevitability of death, not as an abstraction or a generalization about all men or about civilizations, but as it applies to the particular consciousness, which Poe in a similar train of thought absolves of "personal identity" through his otherworldly names. Or, if the names are not otherworldly, they are remote from the familiar—Monos and Una. "Death is the end whereby a man's existence becomes complete." Though Roberts thus speaks explicitly of Heidegger's argument, the statement summarizes Monos' argument as well. The realization of one's "true-self" coincides with death, which event presumably is entering Nothingness. One might say, to condense the argument in Heidegger, perhaps not too dangerously, that the future self drags the past into a present, accompanied at each point by the anticipation of its own dissolution. Life is a continuous acceptance of death in which there is a continuous attempt at the realization of one's "true-self." Poe dramatizes a moment of that process as a future consummation possible only through the individual's resolve, his courage in accepting the reality of his future existence. And in that resolve lies an experience of a consummation which one may at last report to the world, since one may face the reality of Death without being literally dead. Such at least is Poe's imaginative attempt.

One sees in Heidegger, as in Poe, a dependence upon the passive verb, in which conception the problem of *cause* is buried. It is a weakness destructive to the argument from the Christian view of a Flannery O'Connor or of a Gabriel Marcel, Miss O'Connor's modern counterpart in philosophy. The individual, says Heidegger, is "thrown into the world" and must come to terms with it, without being seduced by the world from the goal of becoming the "true-self." Empiricism is a seduction by the world, leading to utilitarianism, for both Heidegger and Poe. It is the rational empiricist who is Heidegger's principal antagonist, Collins points out. Miss O'Connor resists the pull to worldliness represented by rationalism or scientism no less than Poe or Heidegger, but we must observe here that she does so on different grounds. She would ask that necessary question of Poe or Heidegger: thrown out of where, by whom? Even statements whose expression does not require the literal passive nevertheless have that passive implied, since agency must be implied unless one refuses the basic implications of statement. The world is; man is. But thrown out of what? For the *is* in Heidegger depends upon the *being thrown*. The agency which initiates the action of being is set aside by both Heidegger and Poe. Sartre answers the question, we note in passing, to his own satisfaction. But though he proclaims himself a disciple of Heidegger, Heidegger explicitly rejects Sartre's answer as we shall see.

One notices a problem in Heidegger's formulation which disturbs Sartre: the "true-self" is a limited gift. Nor is the capacity of the individual being assumed equal among all beings.[5] The limit is not, in Heidegger certainly, created by the "resolve" in the individual existence, the approximate route Sartre takes but which Heidegger rejects. Hence the inevitable question to Heidegger's metaphysics once more: limited by what or whom? given by what or whom? Those questions not satisfactorily answered (and a satisfactory answer, as Pascal or Kierkegaard or Marcel—or St. Thomas—would insist, is possible, though not by or through reason), one has in the system another rarification of what we may call secular Platonism, though Heidegger quite specifically sets his argument against Idealism. For unless one may *posit* the "true-self," the whole argument comes to naught, and if one does posit the "true-self," at his soundest he has but assumed the position of idealistic creator of being. That is Sartre's route in answering the problem.

It is on this point that Voegelin protests against Heidegger's argument, concluding that

> Heidegger's speculation occupies a significant place in the history of Western gnosticism. The construct of the closed process of being; the shutting off of immanent from world-transcendent being; the refusal to

5. Neither is it by Poe. Monos speaks scathingly of that situation (presumably in the middle of the nineteenth century) where the odd idea of "universal equality" is rampant, "in the face of analogy and of God—in despite of the loud warning voice of the laws of *gradation* so visibly pervading all things in Earth and Heaven—wild attempts at an omni-prevalent Democracy." It is a moment of temptation to the use of a Thomistic hierarchy in Poe, the loner, such as would necessarily engage him in the hierarchical world.

acknowledge the experience of *philia, eros, pistis* [faith], and *elpis* [hope] . . . the refusal to permit the very idea of a construct of a closed process of being to be called into question—all of this was doubtless to be found in the speculative gnostics of the nineteenth century. But Heidegger has reduced the complex to its essential structure and purged it of period-bound visions of the future. Gone are the ludicrous images of positivist, socialist, and super man. In their place Heidegger puts being itself, emp-tied of all content, to whose approaching power we must submit. As a result of this refining process, the nature of gnostic speculation can now be understood as the symbolic expression of an anticipation of salvation in which the power of being replaces the power of God and the parousia of being [replaces] the Parousia of Christ.

Voegelin's naming of Heidegger's metaphysics of being as a "construct of the closed process of being" helps clarify our own description of it as a secular Platonism.

The secular gnosticism which Voegelin analyzes as the prin-cipal modern malady needs distinguishing from spiritual gnosticism, as we have attempted to do from point to point. For spiritual gnosticism does believe spirit is good, matter evil; in this thought there is an active war with matter on behalf of spirit. That older gnostic idea continues, its last significant influence upon Western thought that of the Puritans. But secular gnosticism does not declare matter evil. It is rather indifferent to matter except in so far as it can manipulate matter to the interest of abstract system, whether the manipulation be by a Comte or Marx, or by the more notable activists of secular gnosticism like Lenin, Stalin, and Hitler. Secular gnosticism separates itself by thought from being and lives in that abstract world which spawns, for instance, bureaucracies. Indeed, in bureaucracies one may observe the ironies of conflict between reality and the patterns imposed upon reality by gnostic thought; examples are a daily constant in newspaper accounts of absurdities of governmental agencies, especially those in Washington, at which geographic remove secular idealism least touches the realities of the world. But one notices its effect as more general, to be found wherever the idea dominates that *system* is *reality*, whether found in universities or state and city collectives, called committees or administrations. (My old professor, W. W. Davidson, used to suggest that Satan's first act in Hell was to form committees.) Now this secular gnosticism might be called, as we have been saying, perverted Platonism. One better understands in this light how Heidegger, a spiritual gnostic, could be tempted to the support of Adolph Hitler. The intellectual disposition which made Nazism possible is essentially the same as that of the American Left in the 1930s who were drawn to the Russian experiment. It is a condition of mind still pervasive enough to lend intellectual support to the destruction of reality which has vitiated social and educational institutions. (One notices an increasing recognition of its dangers as intellectuals of the Left like Sidney Hook and Lionel Trilling in the recent past have come to oppose it strongly. Ideas do have consequences.)

As gnostic thinker, the "herald of being," Heidegger dramatizes by his arguments a spiritual process, under the dominion of thought as opposed to wisdom, which very well symbolizes the spiritual decline of the West as one finds it at several levels in Western society, from intellectual circles downward into the social body. For that reason Heidegger's thought is of interest as a signal exemplum to one concerned with our spiritual crisis. From his thought we may fill in the general intellectual background against which Miss O'Connor casts her fiction, for even some of the details of Heidegger's arguments find interesting correspondences in her fiction. For instance, Heidegger emphasizes as the necessary prelude to an encounter with "Being-itself" a clearing of the ground in preparation for the advent of being. It is Heidegger's metaphor, but it may be seen in an ironic light by recalling how often Miss O'Connor's characters encounter, not "Being-itself" but a Presence through grace, in a clearing they have made. Mrs. May's experience is an excellent example to the point: her pastures are surrounded by woods that are intended by her to keep the sun away. One finds the clearing similarly used in "Circle of Fire." The grandmother in "A Good Man Is Hard to Find" encounters her moment of grace in a clearing, surrounded by trees, with a blue and open sky above. Even Mrs. Turpin in "Revelation" has her vision in the cleared, cleaned pig parlor. What is common to the protagonists here is their conviction that they command being. They take control of being as their province of authority within the closed world they make, from which they clear being away.

The concrete local texture of Miss O'Connor's fiction should not obscure to us our recognition of the larger intellectual arena of her fiction. That texture, through the aid of metaphor, rises above the local detail to echo in the intellectual clearing in Western thought in which one engages the spiritual crisis of our age. Heidegger's arguments reflect a disturbing conclusion to old dislocations of thought; he attempts to measure being through man emptied, rather than against God's fullness. His crucial concern for a cleared arena proves a helpful, perhaps even intentional, foil in Miss O'Connor's fiction.[6] But we notice that when Mrs. May or Mrs. Turpin or Mrs. Cope have prepared a clearing, what usually follows is that their little prepared world is shaken to its foundations by the relentless intrusion of Good News. Such an Advent is not inevitable in the fiction, nor rescue assured in every instance, as we have already shown, for that is neither in man's power to command nor forbid. The question of whether Tarwater is determined to salvation, raised against Miss O'Connor's treatment of him, overlooks the distinction to be made between the reality of the Presence and the freedom of the will in rejecting that reality. We may observe that good *reasons* not to revolt against God are presumably overwhelmingly clear to Lucifer in his deliberate encounter with God; the fullness of reality is open to Lucifer at the point of his revolt.

As Miss O'Connor has pointed out on this problem, free will in man does not mean one will, but many wills in conflict in one soul. She is talking about Haze Motes, but it is a point she refines in the drama of Tarwater. Haze or Tarwater is still open to damnation. The Church, she says, has never "encouraged us to believe that hell is not a going concern." One does not easily conclude that Rayber is rescued from that clearing in which he awaits an advent, though it is pretty evident he hungers for a rescue, which he sees as portending an unnamable agony. At the point when Tarwater is drowning Bishop (that is, doing his NO), Rayber stands at a darkening window "waiting for the raging pain, the intolerable

---

6. Heidegger's thought proves more generally applicable to our literature. It bears interesting application, for instance, to poetry as various as Frost's (his last book was *In the Clearing*, and one might read such poems as "Desert Places" and "Acquainted with the Night" in this context), Wallace Stevens's, and William Carlos Williams's.

hurt that was his due, . . . but he continued to feel nothing. He stood light-headed at the window and it was not until he realized that there would be no pain that he collapsed." Mystery, because it is beyond solution by intellect, must be kept open; Miss O'Connor avoids pat solutions as strongly as she can. What she does is dramatize some of the "possible" effects, quite carefully setting aside the *possible* from the *probable*.

What we have been seeing in Poe and Heidegger is a train of thought which comes to believe in its own power as independently capable of preparing the arena, the clearing, within which it will encounter being, presuming itself the principal agent of being. In Heidegger this position is made possible by the assumption that the soul is limited to consciousness, its potential fullness posited at a future in time. Thus soul is reduced from the older and larger assumption that it is the *substantial* form of the body, whereby one exists independent of but affected by time. The soul is, in the older conception (as in Aquinas), that whereby man *is* rather than *is to be*. The second variation Heidegger assumes is a truncation of the world by which "the power of being replaces the power of God," as Voegelin remarks. One does not proceed very far in Heidegger's discussion of "Being-itself" before one begins to suspect that Heidegger's intuition or vision has indeed revealed something to him which a Thomas Aquinas or a G. M. Hopkins or a Flannery O'Connor would recognize as the Power of the Holy Ghost, the Lord and Giver of Life. But Heidegger actively resists that intuition and names that something "Being-itself." He restricts its nature to time and the world, through which restriction his metaphysical system begins to bear affinity to eighteenth-century Deism, in that God becomes at best absentee landlord.

The idea of God's withdrawal or "death," as implied or developed by Comte and Nietzsche, has lingering about it a faint suggestion that God is not simply indifferent to creation but is the angry God one meets on occasion in the Old Testament, kept actively alive in modern thought by Puritanism. As we have already suggested, through the analysis of eighteenth-century thought and its consequences upon us, Heidegger's position is a growth out of that historical period, even as in some points it is a reaction to it.

Though he sets himself against the gnostic activists, having reduced that general complex of thought "to its essential structure and purged it of period-bound visions of the future," as Voegelin says, it is nevertheless a structure of thought whose foundations lie largely in the eighteenth century. In denying God to his attempt at a metaphysics, he is rejecting the theologians of that period who had responded with dogma to the rise of ideology in such a way as to exacerbate the increasingly virulent conflict that removed the community of man increasingly farther from the experience of reality, the grounding of man's being in the In-Between. (Voegelin speaks of this conflict, as we have seen, in "History and Gnosis," and we might remember also Pascal as trapped between dogma and ideology, fighting to recover reality in his *Pensées*.) Heidegger's reaction against the threat of dogma, then, puts him in a position which is more closely allied with the rationalist, empiricist camp than he wishes to be. It is true that he speaks of the scholastics, St. Thomas in particular, but as Collins points out persuasively, his understanding of scholastic thought is quite superficial. For his insistence upon the mystery of our encounter with Being-itself, his recognition of the limitations of language to bear witness to that encounter, his appreciation of those poets most effective in doing so, all have parallel in St. Thomas.[7] It is these aspects of Heidegger's thought that are the most objectionable to the rationalist, while for Voegelin they lack the clear focus of symbols, of precise terminology, so that one is left with "a closed process of being" shut off in an immanent world from the transcendent.

Voegelin speaks of Heidegger's attempt to rescue secular gnosticism from "period-bound visions of the future." What Heidegger is attempting is to divorce his ultimate philosophical concern from its enslavement to that concept of history upon which such existentialist activists as Comte and Marx build their systems. Five-year plans are not Heidegger's concern. But history continues a primary problem, even when he imposes the special restrictions of

7. St. Thomas's general reputation as rationalist of being distorts the considerable mystical element in him. Both Pieper and Maritain redress that imbalance, and in doing so they are countering the distortions of Thomas exercised since the Renaissance, the object of which was to discredit both Aristotle and St. Thomas. On Heidegger's understanding of scholastic thought, see Collins's *Existentialists*, pp. 180, 183, 193, 272.

history to the single consciousness. For that restriction is but a further adaptation of that eighteenth-century thought which used history as a lever for social manipulations. In Heidegger's adaptation, history is of particular significance and application to the alienated consciousness, and his uses of it are an attempt to show the way out of the anxiety that overwhelms the consciousness. If Heidegger would disallow any history larger than that of the particular consciousness to impinge upon his metaphysics of the consciousness, Voegelin would understandably object in a manner parallel to Pascal's objection to Descartes: history, like Descartes' God, is allowed to set the system going, after which its constant impingement upon the system is ignored. Leo Strauss, a student of Heidegger's at Marburg, also addresses himself to this point in "Philosophy as Rigorous Science and Political Philosophy," and he begins his analysis of Heidegger with a remark we may take as our own: "[Heidegger] is of the opinion that none of his critics and none of his followers has understood him adequately. I believe that he is right. . . . This does not dispense us, however, from taking a stand toward him, for we do this at any rate implicitly."[8]

The primary theme in Heidegger's position, says Strauss, "is not the object of perception but the full thing as experienced as part of the individual human context, the individual world to which it belongs. . . . the full phenomenon of a cow is for a Hindu constituted much more by the sacredness of the cow than by any other quality or aspect. This implies that we can no longer speak of our 'natural' understanding of the world; every understanding of the world is 'historical'." Heidegger's is a rather late argument of a very old observation: that individuals see the world with different eyes. What is of significance in it, however, is the implication that

---

8. We have used and cited examinations of this post-Renaissance background not only by Voegelin, especially his *From Enlightenment to Revolution*, but also by Gerhart Niemeyer in *Between Nothingness and Paradise*. Leo Strauss's *Thoughts on Machiavelli* has been of aid, and his *Natural Right and History* is particularly germane to our concern. A disciple of Heidegger, and a long-time correspondent of Strauss's, Hans-Georg Gadamer, recalls Strauss's antipathy to Heidegger's thought: "he listened to Heidegger in Freiburg lecture about Aristotle, and then he came to Berlin and he listened to Werner Jaeger lecture about Aristotle; and . . . since then there was no question for him which was the genius." ("Recollections of Leo Strauss: an Interview with Hans-Georg Gadamer," by Leo Paul de Alvarez, *The Newsletter*, Politics Department, University of Dallas, Spring, 1978).

those eyes that see a world are trapped by that seeing. Every world is a complete history, the *world* here being the individual Hindu. This is the circumstance which Eliot found himself in in 1909-11 when he wrote a poem which attempts to break out of that closed historical world, "Preludes," an attempt which concludes with the sardonic self-advice to

> Wipe your hand across your mouth, and laugh;
> The worlds revolve like ancient women
> Gathering fuel in vacant lots.

By the time of *The Waste Land,* as we have said, Eliot is able to move beyond that entrapment, citing in a footnote to that poem a passage from the English phenomenologist, F. H. Bradley, in contrast to a passage from Dante. The quote is from Bradley's *Appearance and Reality* and is pertinent to Heidegger's attempt to rescue the closed world:

> My external sensations are no less private to myself than are my thoughts or my feelings. In either case my experience falls within my own circle, a circle closed on the outside; and, with all its elements alike, every sphere is opaque to the others which surround it. . . . In brief, regarded as an existence which appears in a soul, the whole world for each is peculiar and private to that soul.

That is the dilemma to be solved, and Heidegger would solve it through language, the instrument that increasingly leads him to despair. He proposes that language is "grown" and not "made." But perhaps language is an instrument external to the closed world. Words enter into that closed world as some earnest of a commonality with other worlds. One recalls Brice Parain's remark in *A Metaphysics of Language* that "language only lives by feeding on the existence it speaks about." And if one reflect on that, says Parain, he comes to a disturbing conclusion:

> That which lasts best, apart from the sun, which without doubt was there before man, is words. The first words that were collected have succeeded in preserving their meaning even after the fall of the empires in which their language was spoken. What is revealed to us then in our moments of silence is that we are a kind of compost heap on which language germinates, grows, and flowers.

Parain, in his book, struggles toward an escape of our entrapment in language which seems to doom us to the immanent world and force our denial of the transcendent, though he can not quite make the leap of faith required to see the Word in the word. He does say that "Language seems transcendental to me because it is an instrument of communication." In Heidegger, language appears transcendental also, but with the idea of the transcendent severely limited, as is Being-itself. Language transcends the individual, closed world and occupies the world of time and place, but it is still restricted by the horizon of time. The individual world is frozen within an outer world, but that outer world is cut off from eternity, from the transcendent. By an act of thought, such as that imaginative one in Poe's "Colloquy of Monos and Una," one may stand on the outer threshold, but one can but look back to observe the world of consciousness within the world of time.[9] Individual being, like Being-itself, is trapped within that closure.

9. Compare Poe's alienated Orpheus in "The Assignation," who says that the "Proprieties of place, and especially of time, are the bugbears which terrify mankind from the contemplation of the magnificent." *Selected Writings*, 79. In the light of our earlier reservations about Mircea Eliade's approach to the history of religions, we might consider his remarks on Heidegger in *Myth, Dreams, and Mysteries: The Encounter Between Contemporary Faiths and Archaic Realities* (excerpted in Volume II of the *Eliade Reader*). The perspective is that upon the modern Western mind as it might be viewed by an "Indian philosopher." Such a philosopher "would say that historicism and existentialism introduce Europe to the dialectic of Maya," but be baffled that the Westerner seems arrested in the "illusory existence" that results from the encounter. For "the notion of Maya is meaningless without the notion of Brahman," the way out of the illusions of time and history. "Many centuries before Heidegger, Indian thought had identified, in temporality, the 'fated' dimension of all existence; just as it had foreseen, before Marx or Freud, the multiple conditioning of all human experience and of every judgment about the world." Western man's thought appears arrested by an anguish which "follows from his tragic discovery that man is a being destined to death, issuing from Nothingness and on his way to Nothingness." Thus Eliade prepares for his conclusion that, with the help of Asiatic or African or Oceanian thought, Western man may be rescued from "provincial formulas, creations merely of this or that fragment of History" by the evolving of "ecumenical positions." A "genuine encounter [with non-Western thought] . . . might well constitute the point of departure for a new humanism upon a world scale." We have already expressed doubt of the validity of a United Pantheon of the Ambiguous Gods evolved from man's historical encounters with Chaos or Nothingness, with man understood as the agent of their evolution through his rituals. What is most disturbing in Eliade's approach here, however, is that he avoids the fundamental antipathy between Judeo-Christian solutions to the absurdist position, in the interest, it appears, of his evolutionist dream of humanism. He has already observed in *Image and Symbol* (and he makes similar observations in *The Sacred and the Profane* and elsewhere) the uniqueness of the Judeo-Christian vision: it presents "us with supreme hierophany: the *transfiguration of the historical into hierophany*." And in the same work: "In spite of the value it accords Time, Judeo-Christianity does not lead to historicism, but to a theology of history . . . . Historicism as such is a product of the decomposition of Christianity: it could only have come about insofar as we had lost faith in the trans-historical reality of the historical event." But, then, the existentialist position in Heidegger which

If that be so, then one sees what Strauss means when he says of Heidegger's thought that the essential structure of all historical worlds must be understood as belonging to a "specific historical context, to a specific historical period." The possibility of a commonality of individual worlds must correspond to "the character of the period to which it belongs." And hence each period is sustained, with subsequent periods absorbing the past in a collective consciousness of the present moment, but moving toward an absolute moment which embodies all previous history. But in this process history bears its force inward like a funnel upon *an* individual consciousness. This is a conception of history like that which spawned the variety of Utopian dreams since Bacon's *New Atlantis,* in that it involves a redemption of time by the historicist, who has replaced Bacon's empiricist. Heidegger's concern for history is, again, very like the young Eliot's, who struggled to reconcile himself to an intellectual necessity, out of which arose his early concern for tradition. The ideas the early Eliot expresses on tradition are very like Heidegger's ideas of history and Eliot qualifies and refines them carefully in *After Strange Gods,* a book following his escape from the closed world. Eliot looks backward at his own entrapment in eighteenth-century historicism as it has been given a concentration upon individual consciousness by nineteenth-century phenomenalism and twentieth-century existentialism. He concludes that Christ, not the historicist philosopher—the phenomenologist—will redeem time. One sees his radically changed position in "Ash-Wednesday," a poem which addresses itself to the tensional problems with time and the timeless and the other poles of our experience of the In-Between.

Heidegger has a peculiar problem in his view of history, since the collective consciousness of an age, which absorbs and rescues the past, is not adequate to the rescue of the individual world into the generality of its own period or epoch. The primary "presence" is not in a people or a community, but in that individual world, in

---

engages in a dialectic with historicism is presumably also a product of that decomposition. Except that, of course, we might put the matter rather that Western man falls away from Christianity than that Christianity decays, a quite different view of the matter. For Eliade as historian of religions, Christianity is necessarily of naturalistic origins, though it articulate itself as trans-natural and trans-historical.

this instance the consciousness of Heidegger. One of the inevitable difficulties out of this confusion we have already encountered in Poe, the difficulty of an audience. Heidegger too complains that he is understood neither by his critics nor his disciples, though one might perhaps counter that he may be more considerably understood than he believes, that he says things whose full meaning he does not understand, such as Voegelin remarks of his *Das Dasein übernimmt sich selbst*. One of the particular points of mis-understanding, he feels, is on the question of nihilism; for he insists he is not a nihilist. Nihilism, he argues, has its roots in Plato's thought, Christianity being "only Platonism for the people," as Strauss puts Heidegger's position. In addressing himself to the problem of rescuing history, Heidegger observes that the great ages of the past grew out of "rootedness in the soil" (*Bodenstaendigkeit*), but Plato's "nihilism" endangers that rootedness from the beginning. There is certainly some merit in his criticism of Plato, though one might prefer a term applied to Plato other than Heidegger's. That is, one notices a similar criticism already effectively advanced against Plato by both St. Augustine and St. Thomas. The problem is that, in the Platonic pursuit of Idea, the world of matter may become disparaged as non-existence. It is at best the shadow of reality, a reading of the world which Aristotle and Thomas oppose. Here in Plato one has the incipient roots of gnosticism, as Augustine recognizes in an early chapter of *The City of God*.

Heidegger believes that at his moment of history (and it is our own) the Platonic danger is about to destroy humanity, his belief corresponding with that of his student Voegelin on this point, though Voegelin understands the root cause not Plato but a defor-mation of Plato. But it is at this very point also that student and teacher diverge widely, for Heidegger proposes as a solution a return to being as he defines being. What he proposes, says his other critical student, Strauss, is "a *Bodenstaedigkeit* beyond the most extreme *Bodenstaedigkeit*, a being at home beyond the most ex-treme homelessness." One might say that whereas Plato, feeling entrapped by the closed world of the shadow of reality, attempts to leap beyond that shadow into the Ideal—and in leaping from it re-

ject the shadow—Heidegger proposes to leap even beyond Idea. It
is this attempt in him which some of his critics (Strauss and
Voegelin) and disciples (Sartre) see as nihilism. It is out of this very
ground that Sartre derives his role as activist in the world. Sartre's
move is of course on its surface an effect coincident with World War
II and in part influenced by that war; but it is an effect out of ideas
derived from Heidegger also. Under the immediate pressure of the
war, Sartre turns to new uses of literature as instrument of reform.
An instance is his play significantly about *Baudelaire.*

As reformer, Sartre considers that literature must be didactic.
"Each character will be nothing but the choices of an issue and will
equal no more than the chosen issues. It is to be hoped that all
literature will become moral and problematic like this new
theatre." Thus the end of a Platonism turned in upon the self, to
which Heidegger in the final analysis is a contributor. For at what
point in existence lies the measure of the didactic? Such are the
questions of Heidegger's and Sartre's critics. And the answer must
be that the absolute measure lies in Sartre or Heidegger. Still, one
asks, if Orestes accepts responsibility for his actions, he does so in
whose name? For if there is no measure of one's actions,
responsibility has no meaning. Sartre's hero, in order to be, must
be in defiance. But again, in defiance of what? Accepting guilt as a
freedom-earning exile beyond "despair," sounds heroic. But—
earned from whom or what? The answers are bogus, for in the end
they cannot justify Orestes any more than they can justify Adolph
Hitler or Charles Manson. The relocation of the significant rescue
of history in the individual mind, the freeing of the modern gnostic
movement from "period-bound visions of the future" of society as a
whole, leaves thought stranded in itself, its closed world in a
random destruction of the world's body. The systematic reduction
and enslavement of the world to the comforts of man, as first
envisaged by Bacon, at least do not involve randomness, built as
they are upon a narrow consistency of impiety toward creation.

CHAPTER XV

ON SETTING STONES
TO THREAD A MAZE

James Collins defends Heidegger from the "widespread opinion that, for Heidegger, human existence, or *Dasein*, is a brief moment of light shining between two abysses of utter nothingness . . . . Nothingness has cast him up on the beach of that-which-is and has made his essence to be a care of death, leading to total extinction and return to the void." Against such a charge, Collins argues that there is "a positive significance hidden in the experience of the naught [Nothingness] and revealed by the means of a dread," though he points out that the

> . . . defect in the notion of dread, as expounded in *Being and Time* is that it remains wholly within the confines of human existence. [Still, the] total response of man to the contingency of the world . . . is not terror of annihilation but a sense of our otherness and distance from being. It is dreadful anguish before the withdrawal of being. This is not unmingled dread but dread blended with awe. For a sense of the deliberate absence of being is founded on a certain manifestation of the presence of being. Only because man is capable of responding to the call of being, is he also capable of feeling dread at the situation in which being reserves itself from that-which-is. Because it is both the foundation of that-which-is and other than the totality of particular beings, being opens itself to man as a kind of nothingness. The power of the naught over human existence is nothing other than the powerful presence of being to that which is other than itself.

It appears that the defense, however, serves mainly to underline those very weaknesses that Strauss and Voegelin have been concerned with. That the concept of dread is confined to human existence, that Being-itself is confined to a world restricted from the transcendent—those objections remain. What is called into question is the propriety of awe in the light of those restrictions, though one supposes awe a genuine enough personal response to what Heidegger chooses to speak of as the emergence of Being-itself out of Nothingness. What one begins to wonder, however, is not whether awe is absent from Heidegger's experience but whether his interpretation of it is in fundamental error. One notes the presumption that the world other than man is denied Being-itself, that Being-itself is reserved from the whole of that-which-is. What would seem more reasonable is that the individual world (Heidegger or the Hindu) withholds itself from that other, and that is what Voegelin means by charging that Heidegger refuses to acknowledge "*philia, eros, pistis* . . . and *elpis.*" It is crucial to Heidegger's process of emptying the self that he withhold faith and hope in making his clearing for the advent of being; one is reminded here of Enoch Emery's preparation of his washstand for the appearance of a god as yet not even known as unknown.

Collins, speaking of that *awe* in the expectation of the advent of Being-itself, reminds us once more of what we have suggested earlier: in his discussion of Being-itself, Heidegger seems on the very threshold of talking about the advent of grace in the individual world, through which the opened world of the individual sees Being in its timelessness as permeating all-that-is, sustaining it from nothingness. We speak once more of the Lord and Giver of Life, in terror of which Rayber attempts to defend himself against all existence lest he fall down in an action of idiot worship. It is of the Lord and Giver of Life that we now speak, noticing in Heidegger an appropriation of the operations of that Person of the Trinity to his conception of Being-itself. For if he is hesitant to concede Christianity more than a popular version of Plato's nihilistic strain, he nevertheless shares with Christian apologetics those metaphors necessary to speak of his own Being-itself and of man's relation to it. The signs are there, with faint echoes of old meanings. Indeed, it is as if a subdivision-developer should bulldoze all the trees in a living landscape and then presume to name his streets in memory of them. Thus man is "the shepherd of being," and the thinker is related to being as to a "hidden presence," a "reserved treasure." The phrases are Collins's rendering, borrowed from Heidegger's figurative language, to which Collins sometimes adds in the manner of Heidegger. The following are directly from Collins, intending to show that one, in attempting to approach Heidegger's idea of Being-itself, is forced into the region of a language long since occupied by Christian mysticism.

> The danger and challenge of being are greatest precisely for those who become aware of the vocation of man to being and of his power to refuse or accept this grace.
> Homecoming for the thinker means dwelling in the proximity of the mystery of being.

And paraphrasing and borrowing figures from Heidegger's *What Is Metaphysics, Letter on Humanism, Existence and Being,* Collins summarizes Heidegger's disagreement with Sartre:

> Dasein does not signify the absurd and irrevocable fact that man *is there,* hurled up on the beach of that-which-is. . . . In its primary sense, it means that man is the *there* for being, the point of insertion for being as such amidst the things that are. Man is a focus of the relationship of being to the totality of that-which-is, the temple where being can make a clearing shelter for itself.

In that state, having emptied the self through *ennui,* man waits for the word, which is a gift, that will name the holy. The concern is "to domicile being in a human way by bringing the unspoken word of being to language in fitting words." In the clearing the word is born.

One thinking on Heidegger's thoughts, and on the explicator's attempt to find words for them is tempted again and again to break in to recall to Heidegger such old words sprung in old clearings of despair: "Be still, and know that I am God," and there is that voice to Moses at the burning bush: "I AM THAT I AM." And one recalls Christ's words to the Jews: "Before Abraham was I am." What becomes increasingly suggested is that Heidegger's mind is that of the Old Testament. Longing for proof of the transcendent, fearful of it, hesitant to go beyond the world, he waits anxiously for the miracle of the Word. Heidegger's is a climate of thought which one sees rising in the Romantic poets who, cut off from an old confidence in the transcendent, and increasingly separated from being, attempt to discover a way through the world back to the home the heart whispers of. Thus, in Heidegger's attempt to find a "completely immanent interpretation of human existence" he reminds one very much of the Wordsworth of "Tintern Abbey" who attempts to prove "Something deeply interfused in nature," a *something* rather like Heidegger's Being-itself.[1] Wordsworth's failures to establish justification of that belief, to come to terms with the curse of thought, are acknowledged in his "Intimations Ode," in which the reason tries to compensate for that feeling that he is forever cut off from communion with Being-itself. We have already remarked Coleridge's necessity of anchoring his Primary Imagination in the Great I AM to open the closed monad of the mind.

The problem for Wordsworth and Coleridge as poets is the problem of the philosopher always: the meaning of being. Collins remarks the "indetermination in the meaning *to be*, such that an analogical predication is required in order to apply it both to that-which-is and to being [Being-itself]." The analogical predication which is necessary, through new words, makes the philosopher into the poet; here one remembers how "poetic" Plato must be, even when condemning the poet in *The Republic*, or when describing him as a medium through whom the word is spoken in the *Ion*. The rationale of analogical predication from the philosopher's point of view is put succinctly by St. Thomas in the *Summa*, where he examines the necessity and limitations of metaphor in man's approach to Being. (Miss O'Connor derives her aesthetic position principally from key passages of this section, which she underlines in her copy of Pegis's *Introduction to St. Thomas Aquinas*.) It is through the "sensible imagery" of revelation that the mind "rises . . . to the knowledge of intelligible truths. . . . The very hiding of truth in figures is useful for the exercise of thoughtful minds. . . ." And sense images are the path through the senses, through the created world toward God, for "Natural things are midway between the knowledge of God and our knowledge; for we receive knowledge

---

1. I have discussed this aspect of Wordsworth's mind at some length in *The Reflective Journey Toward Order*, especially in the chapters "In a Dark Wood" and "Wordsworth and the Ghost of the Mind".

from natural things." Thus sense imagery is justified against Plato, on the grounds that the sensual world as a creature of God has existence and bespeaks its Creator, and is therefore a legitimate and necessary medium toward God for the finite mind. Sense imagery, in Miss O'Connor's term, is incarnational; spirit is recognized by finite mind through embodiment.

We are brought back to the central problem with language as Heidegger encounters it, a problem complicated by his denial of being to that world he calls that-which-is. Where Miss O'Connor shows us dramatically a "person" becoming a "Temple of the Holy Ghost" as it were, seeing St. Thomas's "nature" as brimming being, Heidegger requires as an act of faith a complete emptying of the self of that world of nature, an approach to nothingness whereby the temple of the self is prepared for the advent of Being. Where St. Thomas recognizes that the I AM THAT I AM lives always at the heart of the desert (that-which-is), that the failure to discover that presence reveals a withdrawal in man's will rather than any withdrawal of the Word, Heidegger argues that Being has withdrawn itself from that world and that it is man's task to recall Being-itself to a union through man's conjuring out of emptiness a word that names Being-itself. It is a procedure in Heidegger based on a faith contrary to our experience of being, as science and philosophy can indicate. In pursuit of that proof, let us begin with an observation by Medawar from his *Hope of Progress*. We do so because in Medawar we have a sworn enemy of such thought as either Heidegger's or Miss O'Connor's, Medawar feeling very much as Sartre and Poe do about "mysticism." ("Mysticism," says Sartre, "suits displaced persons and superfluous children.") In discussing the "mystery" of scientific discovery, Medawar says that

> The part played by luck . . . is greatly overrated. . . . The paradigm of all lucky accidents in science is the discovery of penicillin—the spore floating in through the window, the exposed culture plate, the halo of bacterial inhibition around the spot on which it fell. . . . [But] Fleming had been looking for penicillin, or something like it since the middle of the First World War. . . . A good scientist is discovery-prone.

One notices a mischievous playfulness in Medawar's diction, the "luck" that leads to the "halo" about the culture which is a revelation of being to Fleming. But perhaps neither Fleming nor "luck" is sufficient to explain the discovery in full, neither the "good scientist" as the cause, nor accident.

It is at this point that Michael Polanyi may be of service. For one finds in him a suggestion as to why Medawar's account of discovery is inadequate and why Heidegger's approach to being is misdirected. In such books as *The Study of Man*; *Science, Faith and Society*, and *Personal Knowledge*, Polanyi shows the intricate hierarchy within our knowledge, the process of a mind thinking in its relation to nature, through which process it comes to a knowledge beyond thinking. The point I wish to bring from him to our discussion has to do with the relation of the thinking process to being, as being is perceived through the senses. In *The Study of Man* Polanyi considers the attitude toward being which is necessary if we are to discover and know something of that world which Heidegger calls that-which-is. Take, he suggests, our experimental address to the animal world:

> . . . we have to dwell within the unspecified manifestations of the rat's intelligence which we are trying to detect and to understand. This indwelling is in fact but a particular instance of a more general principle. Indwelling alone can make us aware of an animal's sentience. We owe therefore our entire knowledge of the appetitive and perceptive life of animals to our powers of indwelling. . . . Ultimately we always rely on the belief that animals have feelings similar to our own in so far as their bodies resemble our own.

One necessarily proceeds from a belief, a faith in the presence of being, whether of penicillin (or "something like it," that very Socratic phrase) or of a rat's "intelligence." One sets a culture to develop; one does not set a stone to thread a maze. What is required of even the scientist at the foundation of his thought is an act of faith in being, which he exercises through a capacity which, if he were the poet, he would call "negative capability." That action of faith is necessarily one toward being as it is present in that-which-is, rather than the assumption that being is absent. "Presence" always is. The problem lies in the difficulty of bringing oneself into that presence. Seen in this light, scientific life is a vital address to being; it proceeds from presumptions of being. That is an underlying mystery in science which needs very much to be recovered to the general community; it requires prophets like

Polanyi to recall us to such known but forgotten truths, lest science be left at the mercy of superstition in the general mind.[2] For the general mind itself is largely oblivious to its dependence upon being; its thought is the gnostic shell of which Maritain speaks in "Science and God":

> . . . the impact of the habits of thinking prevalent in an industrial civiliza-
> tion, in which manipulation of the world through science and technique
> plays the chief part, results in a loss of the sense of being in the minds of a
> large number of people, who are not scientists but grant rational value to
> facts and figures.

The belief in "facts and figures" in themselves is the mark of the secular gnostic mind, that mind needing the call of prophet or poet. Polanyi will perhaps be listened to before the poet, for interesting historical reasons. He is closer to the scientist than to the poet in so far as he may be seen by that popular mind. The "popular spirit of the times" (in Miss O'Connor's phrase) is born of an old conspiracy against the poet. As Russell Fraser makes amply evident in his *War Against Poetry*, the Puritan and the Empiricist began to stand shoulder to shoulder against the poet from the time of Elizabeth's England, their principal charge not simply that poetry corrupts the spirit by leading it away from "reality," but that poetry is self-evidently frivolous and of no

---

2. In his Gifford Lectures, published as *The Road of Science and the Ways to God*, Stanley L. Jaki redresses a general failure in Western scholarship to value the "theistic contribution to science and to history," and especially the crucial contribution made by "the Christian con- creteness of that theism." Jaki brings to bear upon the point the intellectual integrity and scholarly inclusiveness necessary to show the dependence of Western science upon "the ways of God," a dependence that has allowed that science to develop its roads into the mystery of being more effectively than any other civilization has ever been able to do. His ranging com- mand of our intellectual history, focused upon an emerging science, is a considerable con- tribution toward bringing C. P. Snow's "Two Cultures" closer together. Jaki speaks for a high calling of reason beyond mere rationalism and argues that the most creative members of the Western scientific community—from Copernicus, Kepler, Galileo, Newton, down to our own day—respond to necessities beyond what is possible to a secular rationalism. Jaki's work is concerned with leaps of the mind toward the transcendent, such leaps as Voegelin finds sparked by the Hebrew sojourn in the desert, such leaps as St. Thomas finds kindled in the intellect by the fire of Love that the New Testament celebrates. Focused upon science, Jaki's lectures make a happy complement to Voegelin's study of *History and Order* and sets a larger context for Polanyi's *Tacit Dimension* and *Personal Knowledge*. Compare, for instance, one of Jaki's principal themes: "Science failed to become an open-ended avenue in the great an- cient cultures [of India, China, and in particular Greece] just as their quest for the ultimate in intelligibility, which is the quest for God, failed to go convincingly beyond man's own self and its cosmic extrapolation, an animated and self-contained nature."

practical or pragmatic use. Poetry is held suspect not only by such thinkers as a Jonathan Edwards, but by men like Francis Bacon, Newton, Locke. Bacon's attack on Aristotle shifts the Western concern for knowledge away from any virtues which knowledge has as an end in itself.[3] In the *Metaphysics*, Aristotle says that philosophy begins in wonder and is valuable for itself rather than for its utility, and St. Thomas relates the poet's concerns to the philosopher's. "The reason why the philosopher may be likened to the poet is this: both are concerned with the marvellous." But the fear is that wonder (with its accompanying awe), because one looks into the mystery of being, may lead to an arrested state like Narcissus hovering his pool. Empires of thought and power cannot be founded upon such wonder. Thus Locke, in *Some Thoughts Concerning Education*, advises parents to root out such inclinations: "If the child have a poetic vein, 'tis to me the strangest thing in the World that the Father should desire or suffer it to be cherished or improved. Methinks parents should labour to have it stifled and suppressed as much as may be." One cannot imagine what apocalyptic event would be necessary to return us to the importance of humanistic studies.[4]

3. On Bacon's radical shift of the ends of knowledge, C. S. Lewis says a very telling thing in this *Abolition of Man*: "If we compare the chief trumpeter of the new era [Bacon] with Marlowe's Faustus, the similarity is striking. You will read in some critics that Faustus had a thirst for knowledge. In reality, he hardly mentions it. It is not truth he wants from his devils, but gold and guns and girls. 'All things that move between the quiet poles shall be at his command' and 'a sound magician is a mighty god'. In the same spirit Bacon condemns those who value knowledge as an end in itself: this, for him, is to use as a mistress for pleasure what ought to be a spouse for fruit." On that magician-scientist as god, Lewis points out that "There was little magic in the Middle Ages; the sixteenth and seventeenth centuries are the high noon of magic." Magic, then, becomes widest in its followings as man shifts his attention to himself and dreams of his dominance over nature through knowledge. But, as Lewis remarks in another connection," . . . what we call Man's power over Nature turns out to be a power exercised by some men over other men with Nature as its instrument." Political, social, economic magicians replace the priest and his offices as worship shifts to the intramundane world. We remind ourselves once more of Eliade's argument in *The Forge and the Crucible* that the Enlightenment appropriates the alchemist's concern over mastering nature and time and turns it to that new dream of Progress which desacralizes both time and nature, leaving Western man isolated between the Nothingness of birth and the Nothingness of death.

4. Perhaps we should record here against our future prospects as a civilization that the 32-member Rockefeller Foundation Commission on the Humanities has just published its report, *The Humanities and American Life* (Berkeley: University of California Press, 1980). The report finds the current state of liberal education such that, unless immediate action is taken to recover humanistic studies to the academy, our country will "go down the tube as a civilized nation," as one reporter puts it in the popular press. (The reporter speaks of the

One detects in Locke's statement that double assault upon the poet, from Puritan and Pragmatist alike, which leaves the man of wonderment increasingly isolated. Faraday's consoling answer to Gladstone's question about the good of the dynamo—that some day the Gladstones of the world might be able to tax it—is a response such as the poet may be tempted to appropriate to justify his existence, if rational argument might be made to convert poem to dynamo. That it is so one may sense from the volume of apologetics for poetry that has grown geometrically since Sir Philip Sidney; that the argument has availed the poet little may be suggested also by the evil days upon which humanistic studies have progressively fallen, most particularly in higher education, with the irony increased by an activist support of the arts by the Federal government through National Humanities Agencies. At the moment there is an additional irony Faraday would no doubt appreciate. His prediction having been amply proved in the past hundred years, "pure research" is nevertheless hard pressed in the 1980's to justify itself. The history of our emphasis on the exploration of space is a most conspicuous instance, with formidable energy of mind and public treasure spent convincing the popular spirit (sometimes called John Q. Public or the taxpayer) of future benefits. The difficulty is so extreme no doubt that the pure researcher might well welcome a second Sputnik—some arresting Soviet breakthrough, of which the most likely is laser satelites.

The popular spirit notwithstanding, a particular person discovers in himself, if he will, a tacit knowledge of what Polanyi calls "indwelling," to which we find analogy not only in Keats's negative capability but in Hopkins's attempt to reveal through the poet's words the "inscape" of things. And one even notices stirrings

members of the commission as "heavy thinkers" and "pundits," in such a way as to underline the urgency of the concern.) The report itself calls for an immediate return to liberal studies in our primary, secondary, and college institutions but warns (in its words): "Blunt data show that students in the field of education are typically among the least academically proficient undergraduates." It may well be that we can't get there from here. It is nevertheless encouraging to be joined by Jeremiahs from Yale (Preseident A. Bartlett Giamatti) and Stanford (ex-President Richard Lyman), and particularly by the Chairman of the Board of Bell Laboratories (William O. Baker). We may yet rehabilitate those prophetic mavericks of Harvard at the turn of the century, Irving Babbitt, George Santayana, and others, who opposed the technological pragmatism injected into higher education at the expense of liberal education.

of that knowledge betimes in the popular spirit, so that the poet may not be eternally the outcast. For there are consequences to our forgetting that "no knowledge of nature lacks some measure of indwelling of the observer in his subject-matter." If we separate subject and object and move toward extreme isolation of consciousness from the world, it may be at least in part a failure to respond to the call of consciousness to indwelling.

There are many ways of answering that call, some of them disturbingly wrong-headed. The most immediate one rising in the scientific community is in sociobiology, which has led to a furious debate between environmental and genetic determinists, a debate erupting at the annual meeting of the American Anthropological Association in 1976, appropriately enough in Washington, D. C. A condemnatory resolution, hotly debated and at last defeated on specious grounds, would have declared the new discipline "an attempt to justify genetically the sexist, racist and elitist status quo in human society." The specious grounds may be represented by Margaret Mead's objection that to pass the resolution would be to join the "book-burning" efforts of the far right. "We are supporting the people who attack everything we believe in! We are getting ourselves into an *insane* position." Indeed so, since reason is being turned in the condemnation to the support of presumed dogma and not to the pursuit of the truth of the matter. The controversy itself may well be the most cogent criticism of both environmental determinism and genetic determinism, in that aberrant will is so conspicuously present in this staging. Neither position provides an accounting for the aberrant will displayed by the partisans.

We may observe the sociobiological position as it is represented by two proponents. Ethnologist Richard Dawkins argues, with some of the poet's license, that genes "swarm in huge colonies safe inside gigantic lumbering robots, sealed off from the outside world, manipulating it by remote control. They are in you and me; created us body and mind; and their preservation is the ultimate rationale for our existence. . . . we are their survival machines." Edward O. Wilson, the father of sociobiology, is not so absolute, holding that at most ten to fifteen percent of human behavior is genetically controlled; but his caution would seem in part against the threat of a suppression of his infant science at the hands of the popular scientific spirit of the moment. "For the moment, perhaps," he says in *Sociobiology*, "it is enough to establish that a single strong thread does indeed run from the conduct of termite colonies and turkey brotherhoods to the social behavior of man." The enthusiasts in his own camp endanger the prospects of the new science. Robert L. Trivers, for instance, believes "that every field that deals with humans is going to have to change sooner or later, whether it is economics, law or international relations. The reason is that social theory must rest in some conception of what the organism is attempting to do."

From a distance, from a perspective that sees a ground of being in the larger perspective of that relation of *ens* to *esse*, such a gathering as the one reported to the public spirit by *Time* magazine out of our capital must appear a comic farce. It might be enjoyed as such, except that in each contending force there resides the dangers of aberrant will capable of a collective force upon the world. That is, innocently implicit in each position is the assumption of a control of determinism by human will. For if there is such a "thing" as social theory, it is both anti-gene and anti-environmental, because the theory assumes the power of manipulation of both the environment and genetic makeup. The words we have quoted from the principals in the debate indicate as much. What country of our being is occupied by the eighty-five or ninety percent of our behavior that is not genetically controlled? Who are the *you* and *me* Professor Dawkins speaks of, in whom resides the kingdom of the tyrant genes? Where is that country within whose safety we may, with Professor Mead, turn blindly from a concern for the truth about reality lest we find ourselves associated with the impure people of the right "who attack everything we believe in?" What are the laws of that country in which "we" believe? It is a strange and disturbing spectacle, such a debate as this one among the very powerful and highly respected scientific community of anthropologists and biologists, almost preventing our appreciation of the theatrical farce.

Almost preventing. For at such moments of anxiety, we may turn to the popular spirit of the moment and find even in it a resistance to these absurd reductions of being. We find, for instance, an extreme satiric recognition in a recent fad—that for "pet stones," sold at high price. Rock Bottom Productions, Inc., of Santa Clara, California, sold a million rocks at Christmas 1975, each of the pets couched in grass and accompanied by a pamphlet on its proper care and feeding. An Oregon geologist provides genealogies upon request and for a fee, so that one may enjoy owning a creature whose particular history predates that of the ladies of the DAR and the histories of the oldest families of Europe. A college in the Mid-West plans a show, complete with judging and ribbons. The satirist Art Buchwald forms a Society for the Prevention of Cruelty to Rocks. Rock shelters are set up to take care of abandoned pets, which are kept awhile before being disposed of if left unclaimed or unadopted.

There is in such counter-spectacle more than a little self-mockery, a humorous recognition of that common possession among mankind, aberrant will. No doubt there are many gullible among the rocks faddists, but the significant aspect is the movement's implicit attack upon a sentimentality that enters our general deportment toward creation when we become divorced from being and the Cause of being and through pride become absolutists of a dogma centered in the self. The irony in the pet rock fad lies in bringing together, through a Dada for the masses, the inordinate concern for abstraction, for facts and figures—in this instance the ridiculous prices paid in swank stores for the pets—and the implicit low estimate of being which is reflected in the shift of sentiment to the inanimate. The absurdities of our general attitude toward our usual pets, whereby we treat a dog or cat as if it were a god, is a butt of this new national joke. (In an older, more sane world, such creatures were treated as manifestations of a god, which is quite different.) The fad calls our attention to the tremendous economic empires erected upon our sentimentality. In it our highest reach of the intellect's abstraction of the body of the world, namely money, is juxtaposed to our lowest conception of being, namely the rock. The combination speaks raucously of our spiritual poverty. If this satiric response to our current intellectual estate does not speak directly to a necessity, it nevertheless has residing in its spectacle a recognition that we are called to an ordinate reverence for the world's body. It suggests a longing at least to recover that piety of address to existence which recognizes a separateness of particular creatures who share a common ground of being—that is, which recognizes the limitations in the creature, man, who is called to what Polanyi names "indwelling." Hopkins as poet would rescue to us through "inscape" to a community of being in which particularity is not dissolved, a community in which stones and trees and cats and persons are one, but in which wholeness particularity is not dissolved.

The rock spectacle is an Absurdist commentary upon the distortion of being to which Miss O'Connor notes a prelude in a letter to Robert Fitzgerald. She writes him at Christmas, remarking that she is engaged in research "into the ways of the vulgar. I would like to go to California for about two minutes to further these researches, though at times I feel that a feeling for the vulgar is my natural talent and don't need any particular encouragement. Did you see the picture of Roy Rogers' horse attending a church service in Pasadena?" If one distorts his perceptions of being through a devotion to facts and figures, sentiment loses its anchor in being so that all being is reduced from particularity. The hierarchy of being becomes lost as well and one no longer properly distinguishes between a horse's going to church and a man's. In such a climate of mind a Jonathan Swift would despair of art's support of argument. With our perversion of the sentiment for home—that hunger for an ordinate relation to being other than the self, in a community of understanding in which multitudinous being is seen in its orderliness—we make assault upon all being, reducing it to the indefinite and general. But sentiment unbound becomes sentimentality. We destroy particularity by our "ecumenical" euthanasia of being. (Miss O'Connor speaks of pornography as one of the forms of this sentimentality in *Mystery and Manners*.) One's concern for cruelty to animals is the same as his concern for cruelty to children, animals no longer distinguishable from children in the hierarchy of being, with cruelty itself becoming a substitute enemy. A symbolically dramatic parallel to the running narrative of the rock craze is the attempt of Squeaky Fromme to assassinate the

President of the United States on behalf of trees. That diabolic manifestation of sentimentality requires only a slight adaptation of Joyce Kilmer's "Trees" to make it a theme song for the Manson "family."

It is this divorce from being with which Miss O'Connor is concerned when she remarks that the audience which confronts her looks for the redemptive act; our hunger "demands that what falls at least be offered the chance to be restored." But because our sense of evil is diluted or lacking altogether, we forget the price of restoration, expecting to be "transported, instantly, either to a mock damnation or a mock innocence." The first cost of redemption is our coming to terms with being, as it is discovered in the world through the firm reality of that-which-is. With the will, and through thought and the body's aid to thought, one may be led to a wisdom, to a stillness in which we at last have revealed to us the deepest mystery of being.

To say as Medawar does that the scientist is "discovery-prone," then, is but another way of saying that man is "grace-prone" and is not himself the first cause of either discovery or of grace. But one does not, from Miss O'Connor's position, empty himself of all to entice finite Being-itself into the temple he thus becomes; one fills himself with that-which-is, in that play between one's becoming and his gesture of love toward creation which Polanyi calls indwelling. One prepares an altar instinctively, out of a wisdom in the blood. Even if he is an Enoch Emery he may do so, in an old washstand, waiting perhaps an ablution of water and fire. The Word that comes is not a growth on the world, like penicillin on a culture; nor does it appear as tennis balls vacuum-packed in the shell of the world. It is in the world, already containing the desert, rather than yet-to-be through man's weak summoning to a presence. If we call, it is because we are first called. With Augustine and Thomas and Pascal, Miss O'Connor argues the irruption of a closed world of the self as an act of grace, through which destructive rupturing a healing occurs. *Awe* is the lingering effect of that rupture, a species of terror which Eliot remembers as "The awful daring of a moment's surrender/ Which an age of prudence can never retract." It is "By this, and this only, we have existed," not in a renunciation of that-which-is as Heidegger contends, but in the discovery of an annunciation in being. There one finds at last the true-self.

That awe-filled terror is a spiritual effect of seeing existence for what it is: the creature of God. But the spiritual burden of that recognition involves a renunciation of the self quite unlike Heidegger's conception of renunciation or Sartre's conception of the assumption of guilt. For the terrible burden is to *be*, and it is a burden because we are at once the creatures of God and free to reject our calling. That is the "enduring chill" that settles upon Asbury: the responsibility for one's life, once the Cause of life is recognized. The appropriation of guilt by Sartre's Orestes, whereby guilt comes into being (Sartre must create his own "original sin" that he may exist), has its roots in Heidegger's concept of "renunciation," that action within the consciousness whereby it is emptied in the conjuring of "Being-itself" into "presence." By this thought, the assumption is that man himself is the agent of grace; through the exercise of such "grace" man not only becomes his "true-self" but restores Being-itself to the whole of the external world. It is the final extension of that species of thought developed since the Renaissance which puts man at the center of creation.

One recalls also rather ancient inclinations to empty man of being and place him at the center. In those old inclinations, Heidegger's thought is discovered as more pervasive of modern Western thought than we might suppose when we consider that he is not so explicitly known. That is, he turns out to be one of those minds who reflect an age though the age may not be looking into the particular reflector to see itself. Helvetius in the eighteenth century, as Voegelin points out, builds his philosophy of existence on the tension between *ennui* and *passion* in man, *ennui* being "the continuous undertone of existence." But existence is seen as what-is-in-its-totality minus the Being-itself conceived by Heidegger. For Helvetius, *amour de soi* is the source of passions to stir one to an action which moves one out of the currents of "mere" existence. It is a movement which, as it invades Western thought at the level of political, social, and scientific concern, leaves a residue of boredom

in the individual breast, very like that "spleen" Baudelaire
addresses in his poetry. For the consciousness isolated becomes "a
graveyard by the moon abhorred." Each day is dully consumed and

> Ennui, the fruit of dismal apathy,
> assumes the size of immortality,
> —Therefore, living matter, you lie here
> like a granite block surrounded by vague fear,   ⁓·
> drowsy in the Sahara's hazy waste.

For when existence is seen as flat—that is, as uncaused cause,
unenlivened by that yeasty presence which G. M. Hopkins
celebrates as "deep down things"—the experience flattens the
perceiver as well, till the nearly dead spirit drifts in a world
seemingly dead, though Baudeliare is able to exclaim in protest, "*O
matière vivante!*" It is a world, in Heidegger's terms, from which
Being-itself has absented itself. To see the world as "a granite
block" is a strategy in Helvetius whereby the earth is made pet rock
of the "directors," the manipulators of collective force. Upon that
strategy social process as salvation is founded; in Comte it is the
strategy whereby God is maneuvered out of existence. And in the
wake of that restructuring of Western thought, Nietzsche looks at
man and his world and declares God is dead. The conclusion that
man is separated from being fuels the pathos of modern poetry,
particularly following Baudelaire; it is in Yeats and Eliot in
particular. Against the poet's drift to pathos one may set the rather
violent eighteenth-century reactionary, Ezra Pound, who affirms
the passions as the mover of the world through the instrument of
man's words.

In view of Miss O'Connor's celebration of Teilhard de
Chardin, we might introduce him briefly once more to see in some
respects that he parallels Heidegger. Claude Tresmontant, in his
Pierre Teilhard de Chardin: His Thought, says (in a passage Miss
O'Connor marks in her review copy):

> If there is a failure [as Teilhard sees the spiritual crises in the West] the
> fault must be imputed neither to the universe nor creation, but to man.
> In the philosophies of the absurd, Teilhard saw the disquieting signs of
> an 'ennui' which, for him is the greatest and the only danger which can
> menace evolution.

But, as Tresmontant also says a bit later,

> The tragic thing about Teilhard's destiny is that he did not know how to
> situate and define, in a historical framework, . . . this Christianity of the
> very beginning, of Scripture, of the fathers, and of the most constant
> tradition of the Church.

That remark Miss O'Connor echoes when she says, in the manuscript of her review, "His way, that of spiritualizing matter, is actually a very old way, one which throughout history is always being obscured by one form of heresy or another." She strikes that sentence out, leaving only the observation that "Actually Teilhard's work is a scientific rediscovery of St. Paul's thought." One notices the hovering cloud of heresy about Teilhard in the Church's treatment of him, and even so sympathetic a reader as Tresmontant does not "vigorously defend his orthodoxy," as Miss O'Connor says. In another passage, also marked by her, Tresmontant scores the central weakness in Teilhard's metaphysics:

> In order to avoid the Charybdis of a universe created in a purely con-
> tingent and arbitrary way, Teilhard falls into the Scylla of a well-known
> mythology. According to it God fulfills Himself in creating the world.
> God engages in a struggle with the Many (the ancient chaos) in order to
> find Himself again, richer and pacified, at the terminus of this work.[5]
> This is an old gnostic idea. . . . His criticism of what he rejects is valid,
> but the solution which he proposes does not seem to be better than the
> thesis he rejects.

We have examined Teilhard at great length in our first volume, and here we reflect that analysis. As Tresmontant's remark suggests to us, Teilhard's conception of God's relation to His creation has characteristics that are very similar to Heidegger's conception of the relation of Being-itself to what-is, a summoning of God back to His creation. Such ideas are clearly uneasy ones to Miss O'Connor, with the possibility of heresy lying in them. What she is most appreciative of in Teilhard, as we have argued, is that he calls attention once more to the existing world that it may be celebrated. His mind, "which dealt in immensities," creates a work which makes demands "on the scientist, the theologian and the poet." She considers herself the poet, and the key to her interest in

5. Teilhard says, "We become aware that in order to create (since, once again, to create is to
unite), God is inevitably induced to immerse himself in the Multitude, in order to incorporate it."

Teilhard is her remark that "the poet, whose sight is essentially prophetic, will at once recognize in Teilhard a kindred intelligence. Teilhard's view of evolution as the spiritualization of matter is close to the poet's." But it is to thinkers like Voegelin that she turns to learn "how to situate and define, in a historical framework" such thought as Teilhard's, as her reviews of the first three volumes of *Order and History* show. For she understands well enough the confusions of thought in the best minds of our age, even those thinkers within the Church of whom she speaks in reviewing Maritain's *The Range of Reason*: "The Age of Enlightenment substituted reason for revelation, with the result that confidence in reason has gradually decayed until in the present age . . . reason finds few supporters outside of Neo-Thomist philosophy."

In that same vein she remarks in another review, of Msgr. Guardini's *Freedom, Grace and Destiny*, that such concepts have been "distorted, discarded, or diluted" by modern thought "in a fashion that suggests Satanic influence." It is the result of a decay since medieval Christianity whereby "philosophy became separated from theology, empirical science from philosophy, and practical instruction from knowledge of reality." The result for the believer, in Msgr. Guardini's words which she quotes approvingly, is that he "no longer stands with his faith amid the concrete, actual world, and he no longer rediscovers that world by his faith. He has made a grim necessity of this dismemberment by constructing . . . a chemically pure faith. . . ." Such is the modern spiritual state against which both Teilhard and Heidegger react, and given the long process of separation from the world, one may not wonder that their attempts to regain the "presence" of Being in creation are not always completely satisfying to faith or reason.

CHAPTER XVI

TOWARD BRAVE NEW WORLDS: THE *RATIO* AND *INTELLECTUS* SECULARIZED

If we find Teilhard's or Heidegger's attempts to recover a presence of being to creation less than satisfactory, it may be that a significant cause of the difficulty lies in an initial influence upon them, though one we have not sufficiently traced in its invasions of the Western intellectual community. We turn to an immediate antecedent of Teilhard, acknowledged by him as an early catalyst to his thinking, a man whose ideas moved so swiftly through the Western intellectual community in the first quarter of this century as to threaten deterministic science, and then seemed just as swiftly to fade; a thinker who set himself against that Darwinian empiricism which was carrying all before it; that thinker's persuasiveness was attractive to the confused Western intellectual as the rise of fundamentalism or the Scopes Trial could not be, though he and the fundamentalist were attacking the same enemy. Henri Bergson chooses a position not only against nineteenth century determinism, but against Western metaphysics as well, a point of considerable importance to our argument. Bergson promised to be, at the turn of the century, the intelligentsia's Luther set against the Orthodox Rationalist Church of Voltaire or Bacon or Hegel or Hume. He proved most attractive to many of the intelligentsia in his reformation of determinism.

The problem in determinism, as Bergson sees it, is that Western thought has become arrested by static concepts, whether one look at Democritus' atoms or Plato's eternal forms or Kant's fixed categories. Intellectual concepts, serviceable up to a point, have for him the same limitations one finds in the latest mechanistic sciences, while classical metaphysics from Plato through the scholastics, in assuming all-embracing systems, are but self-justified by the "possible" beyond the reality of the actual. Each and all are determined, thus effectively excluding novelty. Bergson's considerable influence on art and literature includes a rising passion for "originality," we note in passing, which quickly becomes translated to novelty in a sense much reduced from Bergson's, encouraging faddishness. ("I don't know much about art, but I know what I like," feeds a considerable industry.) The word *novelty* as used to describe a small manufactured article for adornment has its parallel in literature and art, the manufactured thing indeed being one of the byproducts of sophisticated pursuits of "originality" as an end in itself. [1]

Whether one look to the classical philosophers or the modern, to classical metaphysics or to the more limited but presumptuously all-embracing systems of the new deterministic sciences, what is denied in them (says Bergson) is precisely any opening for novelty in the present moment of history. In his attempt to rescue thought from these several deterministic limitations upon thought, Bergson proposes a distinction between the *conceptual* and *intuitional* modes of thought. The conceptual is a limited, closed mode found in Western metaphysics and modern science. It is a closed thought because conceptualism is ultimately entrapped by a spatial limitation. By that entrapment the mind is able to approach existence only from a partial, restricted position which distorts the reality of existence, while seemingly providing an objective view. Image is arrested in space in a sterile objectivity. On the other hand, there are those subjective experiences which the conceptual mode deliberately sets aside in the interest of objectivity: deliberation, choice, memory are temporal and spontaneous acts in a "real"—as op-

1. Eric Gill and David Jones have cogent things to say on the point. See in particular Gill's *It All Goes Together* and *Beauty Looks after Herself* and Jones's *Epoch and Artist*, Sections I and II. T. S. Eliot, anticipating objections to his call for orthodoxy in literature, says in *After Strange Gods*, "What is objectionable, from the point of view which I have adopted, is not novelty or originality in themselves, but their glorification for their own sake. The artist's concern with originality, certainly, may be considered as largely negative: he wishes only to avoid saying what has already been said as well as it can be."

posed to a spatially determined—time. Time measured by clocks
and time endured by the mind are quite unlike each other, and the
recovery of the reality of *becoming* requires a recovery of the mind's
sense of real time, so that mind may participate in that becoming
creatively. We must realize that for the individual mind the present
is an "invisible progress of the past gnawing into the future,"
Bergson says in *Matter and Memory* (published in 1896 and in
English in 1911, its general availability thereafter of some importance to modern writers in English we shall turn to.) For the intrusion of the new science of Einstein soon after the turn of the century, its relativity of both time and space, threatened to dislodge the
individual mind from a participation in creation except in an
anarchic as opposed to creatively ordered manner. Man as creator
seemed threatened unless he could establish his power of affecting
the present, become a force counter to Bergson's "gnawing past."
(Einstein's view of creation still colors our view of the particular
conditions or situations in which we find ourselves, as for instance
the recently-established "situational ethics." We have lost a distinction through the modern tendency to describe an individual's
situation as "relative," the more accurate description being "unique," since we are particular creatures in a particular relation to
creation. The physicist's or the secular metaphysicist's attempt at a
monistic description of the personal situation is neither appropriate
nor adequate.)

Without the understanding which Bergson proposes between
the conceptual and intuitional modes of the mind, evolution can
only be seen and understood as a new arrangement made of already
existing parts. Thus Bergson's attack upon Darwinian thought as it
threatens to possess the intellectual arena in the last half of the
nineteenth century. For the Darwinian position is determined by its
spatial origins, says Bergson, the theory itself an *ex post facto*
manipulation of spatial data. The reality of creation's becoming is
inevitably distorted by the theory, which denies the introduction of
anything new into existence. The theory cannot accommodate
anything not already present in the past, but present only in the
special way of space. The conceptual approach to reality, then,
never escapes its own self-determined limits, and its value conse-

quently is a limited one, namely pragmatic survival—the maintenance of a condition in space.

Against the conceptual mode of thought, then, Bergson posits the intuitional. Intuition is an "instinct that has become disinterested, self-conscious, capable of reflecting upon its object and of enlarging it indefinitely." It is thus separated from the demands of survival action, unlike conceptual thought, and may thus affect existence. Particularly, it affects individual existences—individual minds—in which one finds of all creation the capacity for disinterestedness. Bergson seems to have found a position from which the headlong rush of mechanistic determinism may be at least slowed, with the added advantage that the conceptual mode is not rejected but commanded to the interest and rescue of the individual from the mechanistic trap. If nothing else is saved, the pride of superiority over the rest of creation will be. For, as Robert Frost is to put this point,

> Once we began to see our images
> Reflected in the mud and even dust, . . .
> We were lost piecemeal to the animals,
> Like people thrown out to delay the wolves.

We anticipate through Frost's "White-Tailed Hornet" the incipient temptation in the Bergsonian vision to a gnostic manipulation of becoming. What is important here is that the distinction Bergson makes between conceptual and intuitive thought is of considerable influence upon a wide range of intellectual concerns at the turn of the century and down to the 1980's, though he is currently little remembered. He is an important influence upon a variety of thinkers, ranging from poets like Frost to sociologists and philosophers. It is Bergson who gives us, late in his career, the terms "open" and "closed" societies, defined in such a way as to color an attitude toward tradition as reprehensible and progress as desirable, a coloring very conspicuous in the liberal mind. The closed society is dominated, he says, by the routine and mechanical. It is static and absolutist. In its religion it is ritualistic and dogmatic. Spontaneity is suppressed to conformity. The open society, on the contrary, is universalist, progressive, with its goal a maximum of diversity among individuals. Moral and religious beliefs are flexible, given as it is to the intuitional. The divine *élan vital* thus finds its fullest expression in the most open society.

Bergson's influence on our developing modern literature has received more attention, perhaps, than his influence on social institutions, and both more than his influence on emerging philosophies from phenomenology to existentialism, his thought touching Teilhard and Heidegger and Sartre. We shall indicate something of that literary influence briefly, but after first suggesting some limits to the originality of Bergson's two modes of thought so that we may consider (1) whether his vision is not rather a special adaptation of modes already established by Western metaphysics and (2) whether the very difference he makes—in the way he makes it—does not prove corrosive of a sounder approach to being. In this second question, we may discover some cause as well for the entrapment of modern literature considered earlier, in Volume I, where we contrast the sense of closure that a Joyce both reflects and recognizes in his *Finnegans Wake*. (Joyce wonders, we recall, whether that work is not rather a product of the "fancy" than of the "imagination.")

Josef Pieper, in *Leisure: the Basis of Culture*, reminds us that anciently there exists a distinction of two modes of thought, a distinction clearly enunciated in scholasticism, particularly by St. Thomas. "The Greeks—Aristotle no less than Plato—as well as the great medieval thinkers, held that not only physical, sensuous perceptions, but equally man's spiritual and intellectual knowledge, included an element of pure, receptive contemplation, or as Heraclitus says, of 'listening to the essence of things'." The distinction made by the scholastic is between understanding as *ratio*, discursive, logical thought, and the understanding as *intellectus*, "that simple vision to which truth offers itself like a landscape to the eye." It is a happy coincidence, given some of our earlier remarks about Wordsworth, that Pieper chose this particular figure to illustrate the *intellectus*. For one of the more elevated passages in Wordsworth's poetry occurs in "Tintern Abbey" as the speaker literally beholds a landscape and recalls moments of vision gained through the *intellectus*, in which

the breath of this corporeal frame
And even the motion of our human blood
Almost suspended, we are laid asleep
In body, and become a living soul:
While with an eye made quiet by the power
Of harmony, and the deep power of joy,
We see into the life of things.

Wordsworth's concern, we notice, is to reconcile thought itself to such experiences, thought having become a necessity forced upon him. In consequence, he gives a somewhat rationalist cast to the term *thought*, opposing it to that state of mind recalled as "thoughtless youth." There is then a difference between two modes of the mind's address to its object, not yet understood by Wordsworth. One might suggest that he is attempting to rescue that mode of thought described by the scholastic term *intellectus* from its suppression by the dominant mode of thought in the world around him at the close of the eighteenth century, the *ratio*. The rational mode seems to consume the intellectual community, to seduce it to a pursuit of a knowledge whose uses appear dangerous to Wordsworth. He fears a destruction in that pursuit, we suggest, such as Pegis describes in looking back from a vantage point in our century. In his preface to *Introduction to St. Thomas Aquinas*, Pegis says (in a passage we have used in another context), "European man became a thinker after he ruined himself as a knower," for thinking in this sense is "de-existentialized knowing," achieved by the deconstruction of being, separating thought unto itself and ignoring the truth that the knower "needs a body." (It is in the interest of a recovery from this dissociation from reality that Husserl will raise his cry of "back to the thing itself," through the body.)

Wordsworth complains in a poem contemporary to "Tintern Abbey" that "Our meddling intellect / Misshaped the beauteous forms of things: / We murder to dissect." Precisely because we have, we have lost as well a "wise passiveness" in the presence of creation, the immediate medium of which is the "body" of that Being murdered by thought, primarily our own body. Wordsworth is no scholastic, but clearly he recognizes the destructiveness in the excessive rationalism that had been let loose with the Renaissance to manipulate the created world and which was beginning to leave its undeniable mark upon the popular spirit, as well as upon nature, the rise of a ravenous industrialism the most conspicuous symptom. He recognizes what we may call a dissociation of our spiritual sensibilities, and he would no doubt have experienced a shock of recognition had he encountered St. Thomas's words, which Josef Pieper cites from *Quaestiones disputate de veritate:*

> Although the knowledge which is most characteristic of the human soul occurs in the mode of the *ratio*, nevertheless there is in it a sort of participation in the simple knowledge which is proper to higher beings, of whom it is therefore said that they possess the faculty of spiritual vision.

There is no question in St. Thomas's mind as to which is the higher or more profound mode of encounter with truth, though the fallen estate of man prevents an easy or continuous access to that vision and requires of us characteristically that we approach that vision through the senses in cooperation with the rational faculty, lest our very desire lead us astray. Our desire is the favorite point of entry for the demonic, a point reflected by Flannery O'Connor in distinguishing the "Protestant" from the "Catholic" address to vision: "When the Protestant hears what he supposes to be the voice of the Lord, he follows it regardless of whether it runs counter to his church's teaching. The Catholic believes any voice he may hear comes from the devil unless it is in accordance with the teachings of the church." (The considerable presence of this "Protestant" mind in the Church of Rome at this moment of history is indicated by the internal disquiet over John-Paul II, ranging from the stirrings of Hans Küng and Edward Schillebeeckx to the popular outcry on behalf of social ideologies which the new Pope opposes.)[2]

2. As I write, Hans Küng is reported as "maverick theologian" opposing John Paul's "view on sex, celibacy" on a tour of U. S. colleges, in this instance a Methodist university (Emory) in Atlanta. He is on a thirteen-city tour to warn that the Catholic church is, in his words, "losing the younger generation, especially women," who are "repressed." At the moment Küng enjoys a notoriety and attracts crowds in a way comparable to the campus phenomena of the 1960s when dissidents made the lecture circuit a lucrative aside to their activism. (The newspaper story is accompanied by a photograph of Küng autographing one of his books "for an Emory student.") To that largely Protestant gathering he says: "The Pope is against girls serving the Mass. That's crazy. The little girls think, 'Who are we?' because they have been treated differently than the little boys . . . . [The Pope] has humor and a strong personality. I only fear that the mood of the public is changing very rapidly and he is losing a lot of sympathy because of his stands on sexuality, birth control, marriage, divorce . . . ." Whatever one's position on these difficult questions, it is not to be denied that Küng's

Given the next turn of our argument, we pause upon the point made by St. Thomas to indicate that a mode of thinking not unlike Wordsworth's own sense of the intuitional which he experienced in his "thoughtless youth" is established in Western metaphysics as early as Heraclitus' beginnings. With that point in mind and without undertaking an extensive introduction and comparison of Eastern and Western Church Orthodoxy, we may with profit bring some ideas from that Eastern sister faith. To do so will help us see more clearly, I believe, in what sense it may be said that such writers as Husserl and Bergson and Heidegger and Sartre and even Teilhard are unsettling presences to traditional Western thought, adapting as they do the intuitional toward a secular use. (The intuitional mode has been neglected in Western Catholicism and Protestantism alike, except in the more "primitive" reaches of Protestantism, as Flannery O'Connor recognized.) For the adaptation is such as to disguise the shift from a spiritual vision central to the Eastern church's intuitional emphasis to a new intellectual vision of worldly limits and worldly use. The dislocations of the

---

approach is that of a demagogue rousing popular unrest, rather than that of a theologian facing complex questions. One does not put the trying questions in relation to "little girls" and "little boys" or in relation to whether the truth of the matter is popular and fits the popular mood of the moment. The question of whether the virginal conception is a legend, of whether the Resurrection is no more than a local "cult legend" (the position of Schillebeeckx) are crucial to the meaning of Christianity so fundamentally as to make Küng's approach reprehensible. If the question of the Divinity of Christ is merely one to be resolved in terms derived "from psychology and a popularized existentialism," as one critic objects, the crucial questions of our human existence and hope have been returned to the phenomenological world, a world occupied more seriously by Husserl, Heidegger, Sartre, than by Küng. The critic I mention says that "This sort of free substitution of concepts and terms in the interpreting of Christ's Divinity has been going on since the mid-nineteenth century in liberal Protestant circles. But only since the mid-1960s have some progressist Catholics been bold enough to move publicly in this direction" (Charles Atinsen, "Rome and Revisionism," *National Review*, November 14, 1980). Small wonder, then, the warm reception of Küng among Protestant colleges. A point seldom entertained by these sympathizers with him, however, is whether it was appropriate for Küng to hold the official Catholic Chair of Theology at Tübingen, in which office he was charged with presenting the established theological position of the Church. (Whether such a chair should exist in a state institution is quite another question.) Much of the Western media has treated his resignation from that post as if he had been sorely wronged, hounded out of office in blatant violation of "academic freedom" (that old 1960s cry). His occupation of the new "Ecumenical" Chair at Tübingen is the present solution, forced by theological issues of profound consequence to the Church itself. It is a solution he should himself have sought in honesty, rather than violating and subverting the responsibilities of the Chair he held. He hardly seems to have the integrity of Luther, with whom he is frequently compared.

conceptual and intuitional began at the close of the Middle Ages in the West and lead up to the tangled visions of being in modernist thought. Our guide here is Vladimir Lossky's lucid apologetics, principally his *Mystical Theology of the Eastern Church* (1944).

Lossky shows us that, "despite all its richness, the religious thought of the East has never had a scholasticism," a circumstance he finds a distinct advantage to its continuing vitality. Though one may find in it "elements of Christian gnosis,"

> the speculative is always dominated by the central idea of union with God and never acquires the character of a system. Having no philosophical preferences, the Church always freely makes use of philosophy and the sciences for apologetic purposes, but she never has any cause to defend those relative and changing truths as she defends the unchanging truth of her doctrines. This is why ancient and modern cosmological theories cannot affect in any way the more fundamental truth which is revealed in the Church: "the truth of Holy Scripture is far deeper than the limits of our understanding" [these last the words of Philaret of Moscow].

Thus Galileo, Bergson, Freud, Teilhard, or Konrad Lorenz may be the more comfortably at home in the Eastern Church in so far as their philosophy or science suits apologetic purposes. Systems of philosophy or science or pseudo- (soft) science provide what is in effect a poetic matter in support of the Church's doctrines; that is, they serve a metaphorical purpose in apologetics. Thus Lossky remarks the Russian theologian and mathematician, Fr. Paul Florensky, who suggests "that it would be possible [for the Church] to return to a geocentric cosmology on the basis of the scientific theories of our own time," since the truth of Christian theology is "sufficiently fundamental that it may accommodate itself very easily to any scientific theory of the universe" so long as it does not impertinently "deny things which are outside its own field of vision." One might raise the question here, of course, whether such a tolerance does not exact a very high price when the Eastern Church becomes threatened by a supposedly scientific theory of social reconstruction called Communism; there occurs a necessity of a violent response to that confrontation, reflected in Solzhenitsyn's war against Soviet "political science." And we set aside here an additional interesting question: whether indeed a science or philosophy may emerge directly from an Eastern spiritual climate informed by its theology in such a way as to speak with authority to Western expectations.[3] What interests us is an aspect of the Eastern Church's unchanging doctrine, or more specifically, the philosophical approach of that Church to its doctrine.

Our guide Lossky tells us that, of the two theological ways distinguished by Dionysius, positive theology (or the *cataphatic*) has been dominant in the West. The negative (or *apophatic*) is central to Eastern Orthodoxy. The negative leads "to total ignorance" and thereby to a total openness to both God and His creation. Now it is in the negative (*apophatic*) approach to being that one finds certain affinities to Western secular movements, ranging from Husserl's phenomenological approach to being, through Bergson's creative evolution to Heidegger's and Sartre's nihilism, the latter an emptying of the self in *ennui*, a self-induced emptiness given a spiritual connotation. In Husserl, I have in mind particularly the radical response to recover experience from the misdirection given experience by Descartes on the one hand and Hume and the empiricists on the other. The recapturing of an "original intuition" of the object's absolute and self-evident existence as a "bodily presence" is to be found when we return with openness to "the things themselves."

It is the Eastern "skeptical philosophy," furthered in the West by such works as Nicholas of Cusa's *Of Learned Ignorance*, following the opening made for the skeptical philosophy by Ockham's

---

3. Stanley L. Jaki's Gifford Lectures, *The Road of Science and the Ways to God*, makes interesting counterpoint to Lossky's presentation of Eastern mystical theology. Jaki, for instance, finds Eastern theology affected to the core by Platonism, where Lossky says that the Eastern Fathers resemble the Platonists only outwardly, "only in the vocabulary which was common to the age." In "The Theology of the Image," Lossky argues that the influence of Platonism reduces God as "a God of holy nature," through Plotinus and the Hermetic writers. "This is scandal to the Jews: can one admit a world without history, subject to necessity, a beautiful and ordered world, no doubt, but where nothing new can happen?" (The objection appears analogous to Bergson's rejection of Darwinian determinism. Yet there is an arresting difference: whereas the objection posed by Lossky is in the interest of freeing God of nature's entrapment, Bergson's is in the interest of freeing the individual mind of nature's entrapment.) Professor Jaki also points out that in William of Ockham one has entry into Western thought of "a claim for the exclusive validity of intuitive knowledge, which Ockham also called *notitia scientifica* and *experimentalis*." (Jaki's examination of Ockham in "Steps to God as Stepping-Stones to Science" complements Richard Weaver's approach in *Ideas Have Consequences*.) Jaki is very cautious about the mystic's negative (*apophatic*) approach to being, his sympathy ranged decisively with the positive (*cataphatic*). The negative way of Eastern thought, he says, made Byzantium vulnerable to Muhammad's Crescent, even as it prevented a development in science comparable to that in Western thought.

nominalism, that becomes a confusing presence which Western science must be wary of, says Professor Jaki in his Gifford Lectures. Ockham's separation of the two ways denies a relevance of natural theology to science, and such empirical deconstructionists of natural theology as Bacon and Hobbes will take advantage of the opportunity to isolate theology entirely, limiting existence to the mechanistic plane. On the other hand (we suggest) Descartes' rationalism, for all its emphasis upon the rational faculty, partakes of the "intuitive," but of an intuitive unanchored in complex reality, bypassing the In-between through a "Platonic" acceptance of innate ideas. Descartes' faith in the *a priori* separates material existence from idea and concludes at last that all is illusion save the consciousness within which abides innate idea. It is a position one might describe as immanent Platonism. And it is not long, says Jaki, before "science, world, God and soul . . . appear to be illusory after logic has proceeded for some time along the road charted by Descartes." What I wish to suggest is that Descartes' rationalism has as its ground the intuitive mode disoriented. The logic brought to support the position is, as Jaki shows, finally insufficient. If the old Gnostic disengaged creation from the cause of creation in an attempt to gain immediate access to the Ineffable, Descartes disengages mind from creation in order to touch, not the Ineffable, but the mind, after which disengagement even cosmology—that largest playground of the mind—must conform itself to the self-produced, rationalist formulae.

Ockham, in separating faith and reason—himself supporting a mystical faith—provides a way for the secularizing rationalism of Descartes. Meanwhile, Bacon, purporting to limit natural theology, leaving it "bound by itself" (in Bacon's words), rather incarcerates it, setting metaphysics entirely aside from physics, after which, as Jaki shows, Hobbes decapitates cosmology, rejects history, and reduces all knowledge to questions of fact and consequence within a mechanistic system. (The Fugitive poet Donald Davidson addresses the Hobbesean consequences to our sense of history in *The Attack on Leviathan: Regionalism and Nationalism in the United States*, a book sufficiently subversive of modernism that its publishers shredded it out of print.) The danger that must be repeatedly signalled is that, as Richard Weaver emphasizes, Ockham's separation of the theological ways effectively prepares a route for a rationalism set "lineally" toward a worldly city, on a road whose name becomes Progress. Man, says Descartes at a way-station along that route, is to become "master and possessor of nature" through *a priori* precepts imposed on nature. The Baconian empiricist has the same end in view along a different route. "Render to faith those things that are of faith," says Bacon, but "Out of the contemplation of nature, or [on the] ground of human knowledges, to induce any verity or persuasion concerning points of faith, is in my judgment not safe . . . ." Stewardship is thus effectively removed from man's concerns in time and place. The lineal way opened out of the Middle Ages as the road of science, although accompanied early on by a residual piety, is not always above suspicion in its motives. Thus the stance Ockham takes, a pious defense of nominalism in the name of Heaven, may be seen as providing a temporary cover under which secular reason has time to develop its independence from natural theology, whether in the line of Bacon or Descartes. From Ockham well into the seventeenth century, alarms are sounded against a growing rationalism and empiricism, each of which is increasingly bent on divorcing itself from Christian piety toward creation.[4]

We emphasize that it is affinities we discover between an Eastern theology and a Western immanentology that will rise to the authority of secular religion in the West in our century. Our point is that the Eastern "ignorance" which is achieved through negative theology is quite other than the emptiness we come to in a Heidegger or Sartre in their approach through a studied *ennui*. The crucial difference between Eastern theological thought and Western

---

4. Professor Jaki points out the Royal Society's attempt to restore natural theology to the concerns of science, against the current rising out of Bacon's slide toward atheism. One may question whether the Renaissance rationalist's or empiricist's initial piety toward the Cause of nature—toward the ways of God in the world—may not have had a considerable Machiavellian motive. Certainly as we look at recent history, it seems undeniable that modern science's escape of that classical circularity of thought which Jaki finds in Plato and Aristotle gives rise to a millenarianism in the social, political, and scientific worlds—worlds rapidly separating in their lineal developments from the old centering of a Classical-Christian vision that culminates in St. Thomas. The point is that the lineal has its own dead-ends, no less than has the circular. Life as a dance gives way to life as a race, as Chesterton said, with teleological distortions which lead the poet—the intuitive prophet—to cry out that

secular thought may be isolated precisely here in those immanentist presumptions of Western thought that triumph with the coming
of the Renaissance to the West, only partly affected by the influence
of classical metaphysics. (Voegelin has been arguing that the
West's post-Renaissance Plato is Plato misread.) The center of a
new Western religion comes to rest in the inner man, whether that
new man be advocated by Emerson or by Nietzsche. And the conclusion of this shifted center in popular religious thought must inevitably translate man into his own god, whether that center is as
patiently justified as by Husserl or Bergson or as wildly and intox-
icatingly preached as by Nietzsche.[5] When Husserl, at the close of
his *Cartesian Meditations*, quotes Saint Augustine's *De vera religione*, it
is a secularizing appropriation: "Do not wish to go out; go back
into yourself. Truth dwells in the inner man." As Richard M.
Zaner says in summarizing Husserl's position in *The Way of
Phenomenology*, the solitude necessary to the Husserlean beginning
"alone permits the systematic regressive or reflexive withdrawal
into one's self and mental life . . . . [thereby we learn] that human
life is nothing if it is not first and foremost selfhood—that strange
and uncanny reflexive solitude that relates itself to its own self . . . ."
But in St. Augustine, such reflexiveness leads directly to an encounter *beyond* the self, with that Cause of all selves, God's existence
being for Augustine an inevitable discovery which does not lead
simply to Zaner's end, the self "inwardly [relating] to the other
selves about him."

the center no longer holds. Also, Professor Jaki's cautionary approach to the intuitive way of
theology appears to leave little prospect to the prophetic poet who would share in the discovery and celebration of being—little prospect of the poet's complementary service to the
ratio through the *intellectus*. Given these two hesitations about Professor Jaki's persuasive
work, one wonders whether, despite his emphasis on revelation and a faith out of revelation,
Jaki does not leave revelation somewhat isolated to the historical aspect of the Incarnation. It
is no doubt a matter of emphasis, affected by his elected subject, the *history* of science. But
along the way of the argument one may feel that the celebration of the release of Western
thought from its classical cyclical entrapment into lineal freedom tends to overlook the
dangers within the lineal freedom. The prophetic poet, even so Byzantine a poet as Yeats,
may still be helpful to the consummate scholar.

5. On this separation of the positive and negative theologies and their secularization into a
gnosticism robbed of any transcendent object, compare Eric Voegelin's remarking in *The
New Science of Politics* the development from a

 . . . medieval immanentism through humanism, enlightenment, progressivism,
 liberalism, positivism, into Marxism. . . . The intellectual symbols developed by

If we wish to put beside this approach to being by Husserl a more excited, less cautious parallel, we could turn to Nietzsche's *Beyond Good and Evil.* That Oscar Wilde among the philosophers is more daringly shocking, impatient of the methodical approach of Husserl, Husserl's approach being too imitative no doubt of the empiricist's; that is, Husserl's is a philosophy of the self in the mode of science. Nietzsche, in his rejection of Christianity, charges that Christianity inverts "all love of the earthly and of dominion over the earth into hatred of the earth and the earthly—*that* is the task the church [in Europe] posed for itself . . . ." Thus the Church has created the modern European, "a smaller, almost ridiculous type, a herd animal, something eager to please, sickly, and mediocre . . . ." The charge is that the Roman Church is Gnostic, is Puritan, in its approach to being. But against this enemy of being, the Church, Nietzsche advances the modern secular gnostic: "The sage as astronomer.—as long as you still experience the stars as something 'above you' you lack the eye of knowledge." A transcendence of nature through the power of knowledge puts the stars *below* one. The ends toward which Nietzsche would move his New European, however, do not call for an abolition of *homines religiosi,* for the religious instinct is a very serviceable opiate of the people, the "*Volk,*" when used skillfully by the gnostic lords of power. That is, the religious impulse is just that, an impulse which is psychological and thus rooted in the biological. It is an instinct for survival in the social world so that, "For the strong and independent who are prepared and predestined to command . . . religion is one more means for overcoming resistances . . . ." Indeed, "Asceticism and

---

the various types of immanentists will frequently be in conflict with one another and the various types of Gnostics will oppose one another. One can easily imagine how indignant a humanistic liberal will be when he is told that his particular type of immanentism is one step on the road to Marxism. It will not be superfluous, therefore, to recall the principle that the substance of history is to be found on the level of experience, not on the level of ideas. Secularism could be defined as a radicalization of the earlier forms of paracletic immanentism, because the experiential divinization of man is more radical in the secularist case.

On the revolutionary import of paracletic immanentism, see Norman Cohn's *The Pursuit of the Millennium,* a study of "modernist" horrors in the Middle Ages centering around paracletic immanentism; Cohn's book is history's mirror held up to the twentieth century with disturbing self-recognitions.

puritanism are almost indispensable means for educating and en-
nobling a race that wishes to become master over its origins among
the rabble and that works its way up toward future rule." But the
evolution of a race has at its end the elevation of a very few, the
directors of that gnostic power latent in an "ennobled" race. "A
people [the *Volk*] is a detour of nature to get to six or seven great
men." (Nietzsche's general impatience would seem almost to call
for *Umschweif* to be translated as *shortcut* rather than *detour* perhaps.)
Thus Nietzsche speaks of a pragmatic application by the "six or
seven great men" of what Bergson is to call the *élan vital*, so that
through that application high points occur out of the *Volk*, a few
men above all men, the Supermen.

It is perhaps Nietzsche above all other late nineteenth-century
spokesmen for secularized gnosticism in whom we find most clearly
revealed the dangers of this new address to being. Yet there has
been an unfortunate lapse in our critical examination of that whole
spectrum of thinkers, including Husserl, Bergson, Heidegger, with
the result that we do not always see the "Nietzschean" thrust in
their thought. Hence that irony we encounter in many of Heidegger's apologists, most of whom range on the "liberal" side, when
they try to account for Heidegger's pro-Nazi inclinations, finding
the inclination an aberration rather than a symptom of a deeper
problem in his philosophy.

For Nietzsche, then, the man of power must learn to
manipulate what he calls the "religious neurosis" in man, recognizing wherever he finds it that it is "tied to three dangerous dietary
demands: solitude, fasting, and sexual abstinence." Dangerous,
that is, to the gnostic manipulator who does not see the matter
clearly. But when clearly seen by him, when he recognizes the relation of the neurosis to "dietary demands," he gains a special advantage in its manipulation. And indeed in the closing years of the
nineteenth century (*Beyond Good and Evil* is published in 1886) that
neurosis is already being shifted in a hopeful way: "It seems to me
that the religious instinct is indeed in the process of growing
powerfully—but the theistic satisfaction it refuses with deep
suspicion." That shift from theistic satisfaction means that a new
satisfaction is required; a secular teleology becomes necessary, the

diffusion of which into the popular spirit will accomplish a shifting away from the old (and for Nietzsche, debilitating) effects of transcendence. "Since Descartes . . . all philosophers seek to assassinate the old soul concept, under the guise of a critique of the subject-and-predicate concept—which means an attempt on the life of the basic presupposition of the Christian doctrine. Modern philosophy, being an epistemological skepticism, is, covertly or overtly, *anti-Christian*—although, to say this for the benefit of more refined ears, by no means anti-religious."

One does not go wrong to suggest that among these refined ears that may profit are those of Henri Bergson. As the trap of subject-object dooms the "old soul concept," it also provides access to a substitute "God," to be approached through intuition and by taking advantage of the religious neurosis now freed of its end in God. As Neitzsche puts the shift: we have moved from religion's "sacrifice of human beings to one's god," through the "moral epoch of mankind" in which "one sacrificed . . . one's own strongest instincts, one's 'nature'," (for which one may read "dietary demands: solitude, fasting, and sexual abstinence"); we have next sacrificed "God himself" so that we may turn to worship "the stone, stupidity, gravity, fate, the nothing." And so we arrive at the threshold of the new man. "To sacrifice God for nothing—this paradoxical mystery of the final cruelty was reserved for the generation that is now coming up: all of us already knew something of this." It would, however, be a mistake to suppose that Nietzsche rejects cruelty in such destructions; he is speaking in its defense. What he opposes is the failure to embrace and make use of such cruelty, without which attitude the new man cannot get beyond good and evil. It is with contempt for the shy criminal that he says, "A criminal is frequently not equal to his deed: he makes it smaller and slanders it." That is an idea whose inadequacies Doestoevski dramatizes in *Crime and Punishment*, showing in Raskolnikov the Nietzschean perversion of the religious impulse into a neurosis. On the other hand Nietzsche's is a position championed by Jean-Paul Sartre in the interest of his version of the Superman.

Nietzsche, as if he would assume the position of "Platonist" to a new secular gnosticism, sees in the *homines religiosi* an affinity to the artist; both distort the reality Nietzsche pursues. Indeed, religious man "might be included among artists, as their highest rank," as the supreme practitioner of "the intention of falsifying [the world's] image." (The poets, he says in "Epigrams and Interludes," "treat their experiences shamelessly: they exploit them." In the interest of illusion, that is.) The religious is an impulse out of an "incurable pessimism," which the Superman must recognize as such so that he may turn it to his pragmatic ends. For a people "cling to a religious interpretation of existence," through a "piety" (and sarcasm drips from the word on Nietzsche's lips) which becomes the "subtlest and final offspring of the *fear* of truth." That fear goes wrong when theistic, but since it gives an "inestimable contentment" to the lowliest it has its uses; through piety they raise themselves to "an illusory higher order" and restiveness is stilled. Nietzsche's American apologist, H. L. Mencken, makes the same point about the advantage of the religious instinct when he says (*Smart Set*, October 1923): ". . . try to imagine what the average lowbrowed Methodist would be if he were not a Methodist but an atheist!" A horror to behold.

Having drawn this message from Nietzsche, we may see what an advantage it proves to the secular gnostic if he learns to manipulate the "religious neurosis." (Freud will, of course, provide a pseudo-scientific justification of the Nietzschean argument.) It allows a direction of the energy thus reserved from "dietary demands" when transferred from a theism to a social religion. Meanwhile, with the help of a transformed Darwinian determinism (as by Bergson) a substitute object for the teleological hunger in this religious neurosis may be projected for the *Volk*. Humanity itself is the most likely naming, as the past two hundred years of our social and political "progress" shows. In that shift from theism, a secular millennialism is given a religious cast which disguises the real Nietzschean core: the whole process is in the interest of "six or seven" superior creatures who require the support of energy from the *Volk* so that they may be evolved from the *Volk*. That disguise of the real end is necessary, since the *Volk* require an object toward which to direct the agony of its religious neurosis. With no Heavenly City in prospect, with no Jerusalem to liberate from the power of the Antichrist, the Future—in the name of Humanity—becomes the New Jerusalem to be seized by force out of nature, to be liberated from the snares of history past.

One of the continuing problems confronting this Nietzschean attempt to harness the *Volk's* "dietary demands" as one might a stream rushing down a mountain is that, unlike a stream down a mountain, there is no "physics" of spirit determining its channel. Thus, having turned upon nature as material existence to be exploited (and materialism is an inevitable corollary to the Nietzschean dream), unable to hold Humanity on the high horizon of the Future, the force shatters and separates as the individual's appetites are aroused. "Freedom" of the human force to execute a millennial construction works as a slogan for awhile, but from there it becomes "freedom now," and from thence is translated into "appetite now." The evidence is present in the rise and fall of the "youth movement" that came to its climax in the 1960s and 1970s out of nineteenth-century beginnings, the fragile "idealism" of those decades now replaced by a concern among the youth for material benefits—as its academic foster-parents in the academy are increasingly lamenting. The student generation of the 1980s promises to be largely devoted to preparing itself for "getting and spending," laying waste youth's powers which were so deliberately manipulated in the past two decades toward a restructuring of political and social institutions along liberal lines. (Louis Filler has given us a survey of the youth movement with a gathering of useful historical information in his *Vanguards & Followers: Youth in the American Tradition.*)

The Western "socialist" mind which invested its faith in a revolution in the name of a generalized humanity has inevitably been disappointed by that failed god, particularly as it has been forced more and more to admit the emergence of an "aristocracy" in Russian Communism, those superior creatures elevated by the Great Experiment. Nietzsche works out the program necessary to that secular election in *Beyond Good and Evil*, and the lords of the Kremlin have executed it. He provides a textual expansion to satisfy the necessity anticipated in France by a decree of the Committee of Public Safety (1794): "The transition of an oppressed nation to democracy is like the effort by which nature rose from nothingness to existence. You must entirely refashion a people whom you wish to make free, destroy its prejudices, alter its habits, limit its necessities, root up its vices, purify its desires." The committee must of course determine the nature of those negative aspects of a *Volk*'s character as well as dictate the positive substitute, with the results we see in the Russian experiment in "democracy." The ends toward which this new freedom will be directed awaited Neitzsche's explorations and Marxist executions, but the line of this evolution toward democracy is clearly present in the workings of the Committee of Public Safety of 1794, as that Committee's own antecedents are to be located along that line of thought through which the positive and negative theological ways became separated and secularized.

What is to be the "metaphysical" justification whereby, in order to allay their troublesomeness, a people may have its theistic fixation shifted to an end that yet allows those people a sense of participating in raising themselves to "an illusory higher order"? Well, the deterministic, mechanistic implications of Darwinian evolution are hardly encouraging, unless there may be introduced into that system provision for the "new." The Superman is a *new* creation, not just a transformation of the old man; for Nietzsche there is a leap in being beyond good and evil. But how to go about such a leap? It is at this point that the mystery of the apophatic becomes translated to a serviceable use: "To sacrifice God for nothing," that final cruelty. And here we return to our statement that the "ignorance" of theology in the Eastern Church is quite unlike the emptiness that is to be built into Western man, out of which emptiness there is to be conjured a new energy. Lossky is quite aware of the distinction between the Eastern Orthodox and Western secular uses of the negative way, though he does not put it in our context: "The apophatic way does not lead to an absence, to an utter emptiness; for the unknowable God of the Christian is not the impersonal God of the philosophers." It ought to be remarked, then, that the deliberate shift of the Western philosophers to an "impersonal" God (whereby He may be the more comfortably killed with the weaponry of the new Western sciences) is a strategy necessary primarily for the reformation of the intelligentsia; the shift is not aimed at the "lowliest," in whom a belief in the "unknowable God" is fundamental and not easily dislodged. The revolutionary fervor of the intelligentsia in Russia and the West has invariably encountered difficulty in associating itself with Nietzsche's "lowliest," with the peasant or worker whom it is forced to use. (A symptom of the problem no doubt is the general shift of political lines in the 1980 American election.) It takes a long time for the intellectual transformation to reach these lowly creatures, and even when it does, it is not likely to take. Dostoevski makes fictional capital of the problem in several of his works, but we may cite closer to home the popular outcry after World War II against the supposedly new "God Is Dead" theology which appeared at the heart of the Protestant churches in their academic centers. Also there is the troubling emergence of the New Fundamentalism in the 1980s, a direct development out of that shocking declaration by the new theologians that God is dead. Fundamentalism generally lacks a persuasive articulateness, in consequence of which it is widely and wildly fragmented. With no clear center from which its position can be laid out, it presents a disturbing spectacle, particularly to the eyes of the remnants of the liberal establishment. But we should not overlook an important aspect of this supposedly new movement: it comes bearing witness to a reality which has been lost by gnostic distortions. It attempts to recall us to known but forgotten truths which it is not able to enunciate succinctly in any self-clarifying and unifying way. In this respect, it is akin to the radical movement of the 1960s, in which the young (as we argued in earlier pages) also bore a confused witness to realities distorted by forces it could neither name nor exactly describe.[6]

6. The word *fundamentalist* first appeared on the American scene after World War I. It was a term attached, as the *Daily Mail* (May 8, 1924) says, to anyone holding to a "literal inerrancy of scripture—opposed to *liberalism* and *modernism.*" This distinction of the *fundamentalist* from the *liberal* or *modernist* is of telling importance, as is the characterization of K. Lake (*Religion: Yesterday and Tomorrow*, 1925) of the fundamentalists as the least well-educated. The London *Times* (August 25, 1955) says the word "appears to have been used first in connexion with the [American] Northern Baptist Convention of 1920 to describe the more conservative delegates who desire to restate, reaffirm, and re-emphasise the fundamentals of our New Testament faith." But now, says the *Times*, " 'fundamentalism' . . . appears to describe the bigoted rejection of all Biblical criticism, a mechanical view of inspiration and an excessively literalist interpretation of scripture. . . ." What the *Times* does not say is that the term has

To enforce the point without a general survey in support of it, let me ask that we test it in the In-between, in the *metaxy* of our experience of this moment. What is the typical attitude of the Biblical critic in the post-World-War-I period? What position would he take to 1) the fundamentalist himself and 2) the theory of evolution. (The scientific approach to the Shroud of Turin, which has been much in the news this past five years, may well change that attitude, but the question still signifies.) Toward which position, the fundamentalist's or the evolutionist's, would the Biblical scholar be the more reluctant to stand in opposition? My appeal is to the reader's experience of the post-World-War-I intellectual community, in which Darwinian evolution is largely accepted as scientific, whereas fundamentalism is considered the dying throes of superstition. In defense of the fundamentalists, or rather by using the current outcry against the fundamentalists as a point of departure in showing Darwinian evolutionism untenable, Tom Bethel in a recent *American Spectator* ("Evolution Now," November 1980) suggests that the sudden surfacing of fundamentalism as a potent force in the civil arena is "a straightforward grass roots assault on materialism." These mavericks, says Bethel, have "simply taken it upon themselves to declare materialism bosh." (Bethel's use of *bosh* reminds one of Mencken, and his argument's appearing in *The American Spectator* is occasion for a wry smile, since that periodical's patron saint is H. L. Mencken, whose ridicule of the fundamentalist in the 1920s and his championing of Nietzsche is notorious.) What is overlooked by the fundamentalist's antagonists, says Bethel, is that "Scientific theories . . . must dwell permanently in the shadow of defeat." That is to say, a theory is a formulation in which, as Owen Barfield shows us, an attempt is made to "save the

---

become what Richard Weaver would call a "devil" term, as opposed to a "god" term like the new "Biblical criticism." (See Weaver's *Ethics of Rhetoric* and John Bliese's helpful guide, "Richard M. Weaver: Conservative Rhetorician," *Modern Age*, Vol. 21 No. 4 (Fall 1977), 377-86.) Fundamentalism, one might suggest, is an extreme reaction to the construction built upon Scripture by revisionists who are as often as not dominantly influenced by the liberal, modernist secular spirit. What might be said also is that fundamentalism has caught the attention of that spirit in a way that a Chesterton or C. S. Lewis or Weaver seem not to have managed to do. A more respectable designation, emphasizing the action and less the reactionary aspect of fundamentalism has been of late "Evangelical," a term struggling to escape the "devil" word *fundamentalist*.

appearances.'"[7] As Bethel says, "[W]hen one thinks of the theories of Newton, Einstein, Kepler, et al., one can think of numerous outcomes in nature which, if observed, would destroy their theories immediately."[8] But Darwinism is logically immune, simply because it is precisely *not* a scientific theory. Its evidence is suggested as self-evident proof of its statement, and contrary evidence is impossible to produce. Whatever survives, *because* it survives, is fittest. But what is *fitness* but survival? Thus a logical tautology. The currently volatile argument of evolution versus creationism misses the point on both sides. Creationism, says Bethel, belongs in the department of theology, not science. And by the same arguments, Darwinism belongs also in the department of theology—as theology has been reconstituted since Bergson. As an aberration in the body politic,

7. Owen Barfield, attacking the modernist presumptions, points out in *Saving the Appearances: A Study in Idolatry* that certain sciences—geology, biology, and physics, for instance—look at prehistory of the cosmos with foreign eyes. Man, being a later addition to the cosmos, is transplanted by that looking into a pre-human world. The reality of prehistory is therefore compromised. In the same way, and in varying degrees, the attempt to see any past moment—our own childhood for instance—is compromised and limited. The idea of time past, when we see it, is already changed, so that the "self" we were can never be clearly seen by the "self" we are. Of prehistory, the pre-human world, Barfield says, ". . . at the time the unrepresented was behaving in such a way that, *if* human beings with the collective representations [i.e., symbols] characteristic of the last few centuries of western civilization had been there, the things described would also have been there." But much of that imported vision of the prehuman is analogous to settlers bringing smallpox to the Indians, changing its reality. We have "notional 'models' " of prehistory whose nature is that of "artificial imagery," which when taken as natural become *idols*. Given the modern climate of idolatry, then, says Barfield, we understand how the Darwinian theory becomes established—"by borrowing from the experimental by the non-experimental sciences." For, looking at earthly creatures, the appearances on earth so much lack the regularity of the appearances in the sky that no systematic hypothesis will fit them. But astronomy and physics had taught men that the business of science is to find hypotheses to save the appearances. . . . saved they were by the hypothesis of—chance variation. Now the concept of chance is precisely what a hypothesis is devised to save us from. . . . Yet so hypnotic, at this moment of history, was the influence of the idols and of the special mode of thought that had begotten them, that only a few . . . were troubled by the fact that the impressive vocabulary of technological investigation was actually being used to denote its breakdown; as though, because it is something we can do with ourselves in the water, drowning should be included as one of the different ways of swimming." (p. 64)

8. An interesting example of the "falsification of a theory" is in the news. Professor James S. Clegg of the University of Miami has presented his evidence that certain life forms may cease "life" and resume it. That is, if the criterion of life is metabolism, creatures ranging from nematodes to brine shrimp die and return to life. The older position that these creatures are only in hibernation is called into question by Professor Clegg's experiments, so that either a revised theory of what constitutes life in such organisms must be advanced or they must be considered to die and return to life. A drop of water is sufficient to restore them into

then, fundamentalism in the 1980s is a telling indictment of intellectual failure on the part of the academic community.[9]

Fundamentalism might better name and describe its antagonist, and thereby more effectively purify the new Biblical criticism (an alternative to burning that criticism, which seems the inclination of many within the movement): its enemy is the secularized negative way of theology. For in this Western distortion a subtle trick has been played upon such *Volk* as the fundamentalists. Haze Motes, we recall from *Wise Blood*, speaks for that trickery when he asserts that "Jesus is a trick on niggers." The secular gnostic denies the faith posited in an unknown God by translating it out of existence through *unknowable*, through eighteenth- and nineteenth-century science. But a stream of modern gnostic thought companionable to that stream, rising out of the conceptual (the rational), substitutes the "Unknown Negative," about which a considerable secular "theology" of the self has grown since Nietzsche. That new body of scripture has made the task of secularizing the spirit of the age much easier, particularly since the poetry of the negative way is delectatious to the intelligentsia.

We see this temptation to a secular gnostic religion as implicit

life. The "fundamental aspect of life," says Professor Clegg, "is the structural integrity of the organism," as the "fundamental aspect of a clock is its mechanism." The engagement of analogy here toward mystery and the interest in that mystery are encouraging. But says Professor Clegg: "Contemporary biologists are not very historically or philosophically oriented. . . . This generation of commercial intensity is almost a nonintellectual atmosphere where everything has to have some commercial use. It's a very myopic view." (Athens *Banner-Herald*, November 9, 1980). In the same news is the report of *Voyager I* and its spectacular visit to Saturn. Saturn's rings are baffling close up, not to be accounted for in the laws of astrophysics as presently understood, with the result that those "laws" must undergo adjustment. "We may," says Bradford Smith, head of *Voyager's* camera team, "have to develop a whole new breed of celestial machinations" to suit "the dynamics of the ring system." It is more probable that it will be necessary to deduce the celestial machinations already in operation.

9. Bethel introduces an aside to this point which needs currency. Why has there not been a firmer critique of the Darwinian pretense? Because there is a "vigilant yet subtle . . . censorship imposed by peer review. Authors of academic articles aren't really 'censored' . . . . They merely want to be published. They therefore tailor their views, if necessary, to avoid displeasing the high and mighty on the editorial review boards. Precisely because these journals aren't really read by anyone at all, a purely authoritarian system of publication prevails, based on credentials and expertise." When the notorious "publish or perish" rule is imposed, while not all published work succumbs to the pressures toward mediocrity, most of it does, as any academic's honest appraisal will tell him. The criterion of publication in a referred journal removes from the local academic community the pressure of reading and judging,

in Bergson's words on "The Meaning of Evolution" (*Creative Evolution*):

> The animal takes its stand on the plant, man bestrides animality, and the whole of humanity, in space and time is one immense army galloping beside and before and behind each of us in an overwhelming charge able to beat down every resistance and clear the most formidable obstacles, perhaps even death.

That vision, dynamically expressed, sounds strangely like the scholastic concept of the Great Chain of Being, except of course it is divorced of any anchor or end in the transcendent and denies any limit to becoming. The vitality is presumed intrinsic in nature, and that aspect will prove a considerable obstacle to Teilhard when he comes to build his own evolutionary vision on the Bergsonian model. For what we have in Bergson's words is a presumption of man's self-elevation through his willed becoming. "There are no things," he says, "there are only actions." Again, "If I consider the world in which we live, I find that the automatic and strictly determined evolution of this well-knit whole is action which is unmaking itself, and that unforseen movements represent the action that is making itself." Thus he must speak "of a center from which worlds shoot out like rockets in a fire-works display—provided, however, that I do not present this center as a *thing*, but as a continuity of shooting out. God thus defined, has nothing of the already made. He is unceasing life, action, freedom. Creation . . . is not a mystery; we experience it in ourselves when we act freely." Anticipated here is the assertion made in *Morality and Religion*: "The universe . . . is a

---

taking recourse instead to elevation of the work by the evidence of an editorial board over the judgment of a responsible editor who lacks these services. On the title pages of publications within the humanities one can discover the increasing presence of "names," either as members of a board, or as "contributing" editors. This is not, of course, to suggest that such are invariably a sign of a transfer of authority from the editor or the judgment of the local academic "peer group": I would estimate the percentage to run only up to about ninety. But the intellectual status quo is thus preserved, leaving to maverick journals the loosening of intellectual mediocrity. There is, incidentally, an interesting commentary in *Beyond Good and Evil* on the indifference of the academic world to the crucial intellectual struggle that Nietzsche engages, the "industrious scholars and the other accessories of the universities" who are effectively removed from the intellectual ferment of the age: "boundlessly clumsy naïveté lies in the scholar's faith in his superiority, in the good conscience of his tolerance, in the unsuspecting certainty with which his instinct treats the religious man as an inferior type that he has outgrown, leaving it behind, *beneath* him—him, that presumptuous little dwarf and rabble man, the assiduous and speedy head- and handiworker of 'ideas', of 'modern ideas'."

machine for the making of God."

Such, no doubt, is the immediate source of that disquieting element in Teilhard's thought of which Claude Tresmontant speaks: Teilhard falls into "the Scylla of a well-known mythology. According to it God fulfills Himself in creating the world . . . . This is an old gnostic idea." We hear Bergsonian echoes when Teilhard speaks in a letter to Zanta of the " 'panchristizing' of the Universe" or when he expands later upon his "Christogenesis." The gnostic dimension of this idea appears more clearly in its secular guise in Bergson: ". . . consciousness is essentially free; it is freedom itself; but it cannot pass through matter without settling on it." Because it settles on matter, "It will . . . always perceive freedom in the form of necessity; it will always neglect the part of novelty or of creation inherent in the free act . . . ." Or at least it will so neglect novelty until the negative way of Heidegger and Sartre can dispel matter from consciousness. Teilhard's attempt to rescue creation in his Point Omega, through his radial and tangential energies, owes something fundamental to Bergson's evolutionary vision of the "whole," particularly in that aspect of his argument in which matter appears as a falling away from a radial energy's ascent.

Teilhard might have found a helpful corrective to Bergson's immanentist limitations in Eastern theology. Consider, for instance, Lossky's comparison of the Eastern Church's distinction between God's "energies" and His grace: "God condescends towards us in the 'energies' in which He is manifested; we mount towards Him in the 'unions' in which He remains incomprehensible by nature." That is, the Eastern conception of the "energies" is precisely a distinction preventing that *identity* of the created and uncreated that threatens Teilhard's argument crucially at Point Omega. (One might be reminded by Lossky's comparison of *energies* and *unions* of G. M. Hopkins's *instress* and *inscape* respectively; there is an Eastern aspect to Hopkins's approach to poetry.) The Eastern concern does not embrace the elevation of all creation through its concentration in the Noösphere, with a further concentration at Point Omega, a hypostatic union of God with creation as in Teilhard. Its concern is rather with the rescue of the particular soul. Eastern Trinitarian theology "presupposes a continuous and progressive series of changes in created nature, a more and more intimate communion of the person with the Holy Trinity." That language seems echoed by Teilhard's perhaps, but the Eastern sense of a rising and converging cautions that "the divine nature must be said to be at the same time exclusive of, and in some sense, open to participation," the words of caution spoken by St. Gregory of Thessalonia. (The Eastern concern is an exploration of St. Peter's words that we are destined to be "partakers of the divine nature.") The "union to which we are called," says Lossky, "is neither hypostatic—as in the case of the human nature of Christ— nor substantial, as in that of the three divine Persons: it is union with God in His energies, or union by grace making us participate in the divine nature, without our essence becoming thereby the essence of God. In deification we are by grace (that is to say, in the divine energies), all that God is by nature, save only identity of nature . . . according to the teaching of St. Maximus."

These are troublesome distinctions to the modern mind, but ultimately crucial beyond what they may seem to promise. They are consequential ideas in the history of our age, so that the brave may not falter, though their guide stumble and lean on firmer guides like Lossky. "The divine and deifying illumination and grace is not the essence but the energy of God," says St. Gregory of Palamas. The energies thus distinguish themselves from the Western sense of grace on the one hand and from Teilhard's immanentist sense of energies on the other. For in comparison, Teilhard's radial and tangential energies seem much closer in conception to Bergson than to St. Gregory. "Creation is the task of energy; it is for energy to beget," says St. Cyril of Alexandria, and Lossky remarks that those energies are understood by the Eastern Fathers as not "created, formed *ex nihilo*" as in Western theology. Rather, they "flow eternally from the one essence of the Trinity." It is as if Eastern theology sees in the Western conception of grace a sort of passive allowance of becoming that occurs through an energy inherent in the created world, whereas for the Eastern view the energies are a more pervasively active presence *in* creation, though not *of* creation. The emphasis is upon a more dynamic sustaining presence than the language of the Western Church seems to suggest.

In addition, says Lossky, the Western conception of grace

"implies the idea of causality, grace being represented as an effect of the divine Cause exactly as in the act of creation." For Lossky the energies are a "shining forth eternally from divine essence"—before and after creation if one may put it metaphorically.[10] The objection to the Western sense of grace as Lossky sees it is very like Bergson's objection to Western metaphysics in general: it appears to be a concept which, if it does not rob being of its free participation and limit God as well, at least casts the relation of God to becoming in a less remarkable immediacy for a mind trying to touch that mystery. The crucial difference always between the Eastern Orthodox and the Western secularized vision, however, is that the one centers upon the individual soul's participation with God through God's energies, while the other centers (in Bergson conspicuously) upon the participation of the individual consciousness with the existing world. In distinction from Teilhard's concern for the "panchristizing" of creation, then, the Eastern vision holds that "All things were created by the Logos who is as it were a divine nexus, the threshold from which flow the creative outpourings, the particular *logoi* of creatures, and the center towards which in their turn all created beings tend, as to their final end." Teilhard's

10. In Eastern theology, the position defined by the "energies" is such that the term serves as a restraint upon the inclination to dissolve the created into the Uncreated, or the Uncreated into the created—the latter the direction largely taken in the West since the Renaissance. That is, the loss of distinction means the loss of the Uncreated, a development culminating in the death of God for Hegel and Nietzsche. Through the conception of God's energies, the deification of matter and of person is carefully distinguished from the deifying force itself (which force, as the Uncreated is removed from the account, comes to be posited in man by Western secularism). For the Eastern Church, the energies of the Godhead are distinguished from the essence of the Godhead. Thus the position may, says Lossky, presuppose "a continuous and progressive series of changes in created nature," through the energies, and "a more and more intimate communion of the human person with the Holy Trinity." But there does not occur that amalgamation of the human person and the whole of creation that seems under way in Teilhard, with everything rising to a convergence at Point Omega in a new version of the hypostatic union. (The difference one might say is suggested as between becoming God-like and becoming God.) There is (again Lossky) "a continuous and progressive series of changes in nature," and it is "in creatures . . . that the infinite and eternal energies abide, making the greatness of God shine forth in all things, and appearing beyond all things as the divine light which the created world cannot contain." Here Wordsworth might find encouraging support for that sense of a disturbing "presence" he addresses in "Tintern Abbey" 's nature, his "Sense sublime of something . . . deeply interfused" in nature. For Wordsworth, that something's "dwelling" is "the light of setting suns, / And the round ocean and the living air, / And the blue sky, and in the mind of man." Here lies the danger the Eastern Church (and the Western no less) would avoid: a shift of residence for that "something" to creation itself, to an immanence. This is not, in

emphasis, to the neglect of this first aspect of the Logos (the "creative outpouring") is upon the tendency toward an end but a tendency whose prime mover seems an immanent energy.[11]

Wordsworth, Teilhard's 'panchristizing', his systematic development of a "Christogenesis": it is rather a 'pantheizing.' But the position in both Wordsworth and Teilhard is resisted in the Eastern Church's distinction between essence and energy. Hence St. Gregory of Palamas says emphatically "The divine and deifying illumination and grace is not the essence but the energy of God." (The Western Church provides clarification as well in its distinction of "natural grace," though the Eastern position quarrels with the distinction.) Of course, such concerns as these seem foreign and refined beyond endurance to most sensibilities in our world, to the popular spirit of our age. At the same time one notes (with what equanimity and charity possible to muster) how generally we warm ourselves at the Winter Solstice with that seasonal scripture (in America), "Yes, Virginia, there is a Santa Claus," though we're prepared in other seasons to ridicule scholastic pursuit of Love in the human condition. In general, we seem to be prepared to accept an immaterial existence, an immanent force in humanity which may be given a psychological "reality." We project that force by sentimentality through an image of Father the God in a Red Suit. Questions of essence or energy, of whether there is any order of being other than the Uncreated and created no longer even seem esoteric, but only antiquated. Such concerns, says Mrs. Lucynell Crater, show a mind not "as advanced as we are."

11. It must be said that, while there are troublesome aspects in Teilhard's formulations, the formulations in Eastern thought face similar problems. The difficulties Lossky finds with Western scholasticism are not completely removed in the Eastern, which must be said finally to have a scholasticism, though it may be generally true that "The question of the relation between theology and philosophy has never arisen in the East." That question rises more troublesomely in the West after St. Thomas than before—that is, in the decline of scholasticism, for to Thomas theology clearly holds primacy. A quotation from Lossky perhaps makes our reservation clearer: "The goal of Orthodox spirituality, the blessedness of the Kingdom of Heaven, is not the vision of the essence, but, above all, a participation in the divine life of the Holy Trinity." In thus distinguishing Eastern Orthodoxy from Western, I suspect Lossky undervalues the Western view of spirituality. For to speak at all of blessedness (as Lossky himself must) involves a disengagement, a separation. Thus, while "the vision of the essence" implies a distance of the visionary from essence, so too is there a distance when one speaks of an Eastern "goal" of "spirituality." My point does not hinge upon a distinction between essence and energy and grace, but upon the problem of bearing witness, of *saying*. The Western orthodoxy recognizes a necessity to overcome the separation, and the impossibility finally of expressing the separation when it is overcome. One expression of that recognition centers on the metaphor of movement, a movement in excess: the Kingdom of Heaven is to be seized by violence. It is as if Lossky, in some of his otherwise helpful distinctions between the East and West, would take St. Thomas as a Socrates, who talks (through Plato) as if his aim in transcendence is to observe Idea, that action involving a separation of Socrates from the Idea even at the ultimate level.

CHAPTER XVII

BERGSONIAN VISIONARIES AND GUSTS OF BEING

Bergson, we might put it, has given us a version of the coming to be of the Noösphere, self-elevated by the action of its own creative becoming. He sees that action as like the dancing upward of a constantly rising fountain, whose force shatters at its upper reach in a display of spectacle—the present moment—the exhausted matter falling away. Just what that hidden force is and just how man relates to it must be approached, says Bergson, not by the conceptual mode of thinking, but by the intuitive, through which man's consciousness discovers itself into the force. Thus the conceptual approach to being may be reduced to a subordinate role and controlled by the liberated mind. This is the necessary way to the subversion of the dominant metaphysical, conceptual limitation of being established as primary in the Western mind. Having said this, let us place beside Bergson's position a comment by Lossky: St. Thomas, he suggests, transfers Dionysius' distinction between positive and negative theology, the *cataphatic* and *apophatic* ways, to the plane of dialectic and thus "reduces the two ways . . . to one, making negative theology a corrective to affirmative theology."

With what we have said of Bergson, and with Lossky's comment on St. Thomas in mind, we return to our earlier remark that in the Middle Ages there occurs a dissociation of spiritual sensibility. When St. Thomas, after Ockham, is largely repudiated by Western thought (and particularly through nominalism) there develops a breach in the Thomistic dialectic. In one direction, through the cataphatic theology purged of the apophatic, there increasingly develops a secular conceptual mode of thought leading (among its other effects) to empiricism and thence to the establishment of the authority of the "hard" sciences. It is this strain of the divided spiritual sensibility which Bergson discovers as his antagonist, without understanding, however, how deep are its roots in medieval theology. His own way, the intuitive, is not lost to the West in that separation that occurs in the Middle Ages. We note, for instance, that a negative theology is still very much alive in St. John of the Cross, whose dark night of the senses and of the soul requires an emptying of the self in the interest of a convergence with being, under the auspices of grace. That negative mode of the spiritual sensibility will become increasingly dissociated from the conceptual and will itself become secularized, running alongside, but independent of, the positive. We see Pascal in his gamble attempting to hold the two together—himself a very active participant in the emerging sciences. (It is one of many ironies in our spiritually-troubled world that Pascal is one of the fathers of our computer.) In this line of development along the negative way, we have Descartes' doubt as a spring of the self, and his attempted proof of his own particularity as a sign of the increasing secularization the negative way is undergoing. That way will lead to a variety of manifestations in the nineteenth and twentieth centuries, in the negativism Bergson wrestles to deny, for instance. In his chapter "The Idea of 'Nothing' " he presents his version of the apophatic way, a still point at the center of the turning consciousness as it rotates between the outer and the inner. He concludes that the seeming emptiness at the turning point is an appearance only and not a reality.[1]

---

1. Briefly, action, says Bergson "fills a void, and goes from the empty to the full, from an absence, to a presence, from the unreal to the real." (This sense of filling a void we will encounter again in Heidegger, in whom action in a void creates the *Dasein*.) But "I see myself annihilated," says Bergson, "only if I have already resuscitated myself by an act which is positive." Bergson, no more than Heidegger or Sartre, seems to distinguish between the possibilities of (1) a willed negation in which the self persists, a backward motion against matter in Bergson, against all being other than consciousness in Heidegger, and (2) a willed participation in being, in which action the self forgets itself in an openness to all being. "The void," says Bergson, "is, at bottom only the absence of some definite object, which was here at first, and is now elsewhere, and in so far as it is no longer in its former place, leaves behind it, so to speak, the void itself. . . . what is perceived, is the *presence* of one thing or of another,

If Plotinus, Dionysius, and the Fathers of the Eastern Church are various in their descriptions of openness to God, they nevertheless share in the negative way as the only approach to that openness. And if Husserl, Bergson, Heidegger, Sartre are various in the details of their approach to discovering the springs of their own being, they too share a negative way. But there is an incommensurate distance, we must be reminded, between the Eastern Orthodox and modern Western versions of the negative way. The secular Western way is directed toward the end of one's own becoming, and ultimately provides not an openness to being but a closure of individual being upon itself. We shall, in our next chapter, pursue this Western way in more detail in Heidegger, placing him beside Edgar Allan Poe. Let us here rather follow further Bergson's introduction of that negative way, because through it he exercises a direct influence on American literature comparable to Poe's influence on European. That good New Englander Robert Frost proves a useful bridge on this byway.

When Robert Frost read *Creative Evolution*, having been already prepared for that encounter by his interest in William James, the effect was immediate and long-lasting. Taking the book with him on a long winter train ride just after Christmas in 1911, he became intoxicated by the arguments to such an extent that Bergson's ideas pervade his poetry from that point on. Perhaps the most signal display of Bergson's presence in Frost's poetry is his "West-Running Brook," though we might use "Mending Wall," "Birches," "The White-Tailed Hornet," or "One Step Backward Taken" equally well. In "West-Running Brook," the young protagonist takes a stand counter to that of his young wife's as they speculate on their relation to nature. Most specifically, his argument is "against" matter, against matter's pull downward toward the abyss. For, he says, existence "seriously, sadly runs away / To fill the abyss' void with emptiness." It is a "universal cataract of death / That spends

never the *absence* of anything. There is absence only for a being capable of remembering and expecting." That is, the void is an after-image of some thing. "I can by turns imagine a nought of external perception [an after-image] or a nought of internal perception [a memory removed], but not both at once. . . . In this coming and going of our mind between the without and the within [the Other as an object and the Self as an object of consciousness] there is a point, at equal distance from both, in which . . . we no longer perceive the one, and that we do not yet perceive the other: it is there that the image of 'Nothing' is formed."

to nothingness." But there is a counter force, a resistance in the very pull itself, "Rising a little." And it is in "this backward motion toward the source . . . that most we see ourselves in." Frost's poetry will argue from this point on to the end of his career (see "In Winter in the Woods Alone," the final poem in his last volume), that through this force we transcend nature, though he never dwells upon the initiating "source," never quite brings himself to confront the question of the two antithetic forces in matter, the "energy" that pulls to the abyss and the "energy" that reacts against that pull. It will lead him to say with a seriousness disguised by playfulness, that "nothing not built by hands of course is sacred." (That ambiguous playfulness is finally more than Yvor Winters can abide, as his "The Spiritual Drifter as Poet"—a reading of "The White-Tailed Hornet"—shows.) This backward motion, through which order is brought to bear upon nature's disorder, is centered in man as the holy of holies for Frost. Against Emerson's monistic attempt, he will affirm that "A melancholy dualism is the only soundness." ("On Emerson," *Selected Prose*) But enough of Frost, the poet most lastingly converted to Bergsonian creative evolution.[2]

Bergson's distinction between real and clock time has had a great deal of critical application in the study of the fiction of writers like Dorothy Richardson, Virginia Woolf, James Joyce, Faulkner, and many others, so that we need not be detained with the concern. It is worth mentioning, however, a literary influence of the Bergson-

---

2. At sixty, Frost writes a letter to *The Amherst Student* (March 25, 1935) revealing how steady the influence of Bergson has been since his 1911 discovery of *Creative Evolution*:

> We people are thrust forward out of the suggestions of form in the rolling clouds of nature. In us nature reaches its height of form and through us exceeds itself. . . . The background is hugeness and confusion shading away from where we stand into black and utter chaos; and against the background any small man-made figure of order and concentration. . . . To me any little form I assert upon [nature's chaos] is velvet, as the saying is, and to be considered for how much more it is than nothing.

This assertion of order, creation of form, is the constant theme of Frost's poetry, usually dramatized in a tension between the pull of the heart against the head. "On the Heart's Beginning to Cloud the Mind" is a clear instance, if not one of Frost's better poems. The same opposition is in "Stopping by a Woods on a Snowy Evening," Frost's playfulness allowing the "little horse" the role of horse sense—the necessity of a return to order. The animals in his poetry vary from those which nature controls to those man controls and his farmers are engaged steadily to maintain domestication. The *head* is presented as a masculine attribute, the *heart* a feminine, sometimes battling within a single consciousness, sometimes dramatized

ian real time not often touched upon, his influence on the Imagist Movement. The primary point of entry of that influence is T. E. Hulme, often cited as Imagism's founder. Hulme's published writings are minimal and, for the most part, late, the movement having lost most of its impetus by the time his *Speculations* is published in 1924, edited posthumously by Herbert Reed. But he was a lively presence in London just before World War I, an intimate of Pound and Eliot and many of the young literati in whom stirred an awakening. Hulme lectured on Bergson, and he published a translation of *Introduction to Metaphysics* in 1913. In his posthumous *Speculations* appears not only his "Bergson's Theory of Art," but for our immediate use "Romanticism and Classicism." In this essay he argues that the "fancy" is crucial to a recovery of poetic activity, indeed a necessity to that "classical" mode which Hulme champions. The necessity of fancy in the creative evolution of a poem is, he says, "all worked out in Bergson, the central feature of his whole philosophy." That central feature is precisely the distinction between the conceptual and the intuitive modes of the mind, Hulme advancing the intuitive as the decisive mode to poetry. For, he says, the intellect can "only represent complexities of the mechanical kind." The act of creation in art is "intensive" rather than "extensive," the terms Bergson's. "To deal with the intensive you must use intuition."

We have here to turn back to Bergson for some clarification, to that concern of his with the intensive action of the intuition as opposed to the extensive action of conception. There is in the individual an inner, directing principle, says Bergson, not to be accounted for in physico-chemical formulations such as would reduce the account of being ultimately to the spatial. But through our in-

---

in separate consciousnesses, as in that battle between Mary and Warren in "The Death of the Hired Man." (Consider, for instance, the two definitions of home posed in that poem.) It is the backward resistance by this "masculine" energy in nature that brings order to the degree that the "feminine" pull to chaos can be accommodated. Thus a slight rising above matter's pull upon consciousness, through which, a Bergson would say, "consciousness . . . will always perceive freedom in the form of necessity." There is no promise in Frost of an ultimate triumph in this battle. At best it is a draw, as argued in the last poem of his last volume, its title also significantly *In The Clearing*; resistance makes an arena in nature for one's becoming. The poem casts its protagonist as going *against* the woods like a lone soldier, *marking* a maple as victim, *laying* it low. But there is no *defeat* for the woods in one tree's *overthrow*, as there is no lasting victory for the speaker in his "retreat for yet another blow."

tuitive consent we come upon *un élan original de la vie*—an original impetus of life that is in the individual. And let us not overlook the locus of that impetus: it is not to be ascribed to any cause beyond the self.[3] It is through this *élan original* that one enjoys a special relation with all existence other than the mind itself, if one exercises the intuitional mode as opposed to the conceptual. For the intuitional mode, he says in his *Introduction to Metaphysics*, involves an immediate, nonconceptual, direct participation in the intuited object. It is an act "by which one is transported into the interior of an object in order to coincide with what is unique and consequently inexpressible about it." (One hears in these words a near description of what John Keats calls "negative capability," Keats illustrating his term by saying that in reading the *Iliad* he is with Achilles shouting in the trenches, or in watching a sparrow peck about the gravel he enters the creature in such a way as to experience that action.) But this intuitional act has standing in its way always the pervasive distortions of the conceptual, so that some radical action of the mind seems called for if the intuitive mode is to be recovered. And this Bergsonian necessity brings us back to Hulme on "fancy," back to the influence of Bergson on Imagism.

The radical action necessary is to restore "fancy" to a supremacy over the "imagination" as understood by the early Romantics. For in his separation of fancy from imagination, Coleridge seems to denigrate the fancy, reducing it to a wayward inclination, useful but to be carefully commanded. When he says of the fancy that it is the "aggregative and associative power" which "has no other counters to play with, but fixities and definites," a suggestion of the fancy's manipulative powers over reality seems implied in the description. "The fancy is indeed no other than a mode of memory emancipated from the order of time and space; while it is blended with, and modified by that empirical phenomenon of the will which we express by the word Choice." For

3. Much later, his influence considerably waned, Bergson comes to make some room for a first Cause in his view of evolution, though hardly in a formulation that would gain the consent of either Eastern or Western orthodoxy. It is relatively late that he says, in *The Two Sources of Morality and Religion*, that evolution is God's "undertaking to create creators, that He may have, besides Himself, beings worthy of His love." Man, "or some other being of like significance . . . is the purpose of the entire process of evolution." Early, "The universe . . . is a machine for the making of God"; now it is a machine for the making of a playmate for God.

Hulme, Coleridge must here seem to side with the conceptual mode over the intuitive. What Coleridge is saying is that the fancy has the capacity to distort the spatial occurrence of objects so that the cause-effect relations of objects become distorted in the mind, become unreal, even surreal in appearance. One's anchor in place is slipped by fancy. Bergson might rejoin (and he does, though not directly to Coleridge) that only through such slipping of the chains of space upon the object is it possible to experience it in the fullness of being, in the time stream of consciousness. For it is precisely an emancipation of consciousness "from the order of time and space" that Begson is seeking as the way to reality. It is this Bergsonian direction that Hulme would have the poet take in his approach to image. For, from Bergson's or Hulme's position, Coleridge's concern for the organic nature of the poem is hampered by his dominant imagination, itself dictated by the conceptual. "A mechanical complexity," says Hulme, "is the sum of its parts. Put them side by side and you get the whole." But the "vital or organic is . . . a convenient metaphor for a complexity of a different kind," a complexity approached through intuitional action. It is only by new metaphors, that is by "fancy," relieved of spatial arrest, that a poem can be made "precise" in such a way as to pay tribute to the true organicism that a poem must reflect. For that reason, "fancy will be the necessary weapon of the classical school" that Hulme would call into existence. In leading his argument toward a conclusion in the authority of Bergson, Hulme says, "The leg of a chair by itself is still a leg. My leg by itself wouldn't be." That is, from his point of view his leg is an organic presence of a whole held and made organic by the mind. By his intuitive knowledge it is an ever-present presence in a manner beyond concept, beyond spatial limitations. (And in this idea one recognizes as well Bergson's influence on that new painting which rises in Cubism and ranges as widely as Picasso's developments and Salvador Dali's. Indeed Dali's work is a deliberate comment on the conceptual, spatial mode of thought.)

In Imagism, then, one is brought into the image (so runs the argument) in the immediacy of real time. Or one might say that the image is informed, participated in, by one's being transported into it. If the Imagist Movement becomes static and finally sterile, it is in part because most of its participators do not realize the necessity of a dynamic, "creative" address to the object by the "fancy." We see Pound and Wyndham Lewis attacking this stagnation of Imagism when they launch a new movement, Vorticism, publishing *Blast* (which survives two numbers) to advance that cause. Vorticism centers upon the image and a multiplicity out of that image, an address to image which Pound describes in *Gaudier-Brzeska* (1916): "The image is not an idea. It is a radiant node or cluster; it is what I can, and must perforce, call a VORTEX, from which and through which, ideas are constantly rushing." There is a suggestion here of a life within the image, a creative force, uninhibited by the anchor of the image in space, as if time is liberated to its Bergsonian "real" dimension by releasing the image in an imaginative act. Whether or not the images of a poem may be so liberated is in doubt, a concern we shall turn to in our next chapter when we consider in particular Eliot's "Preludes," a poem first published in the Vorticist's *Blast*. But for Pound the image takes on the powers Lossky describes as Christ's in the continuous creation of beings; Christ as a "divine nexus, the threshold from which flow the creative outpourings, the particular *logoi* of creatures" has given way to the poet's image as the creative center of the world's becoming.

Donald Davie in his *Ezra Pound* (Penguin Modern Masters) gives a brief but revealing exposition of the role of Vorticism in Pound's evolving *Cantos*, beginning with crucial passages from Allen Upward's *The New Word* (1908). Some of Upward's words we may appropriate, to see another aspect of Bergson's influence through Upward. But we give those words a different implication from Davie's, since the "new word" Upward champions is not St. John's *logos*, except in so far as that idea is secularized. In discussing *idea*, Upward locates a sense of "thrownness" in it that Heidegger might appreciate; he anchors that sense in folk thought on the one hand and attempts to baptize it by citing a parallel in St. Thomas on the other. It is a reduced St. Thomas, however, since any relation of idea to first cause is excised: idea is "the builder's plan of a not-yet-built house." The illustration is Thomas's, but this sense of idea or *form* is restricted to the human mind as origin. Upward concludes that "The idea is not the appearance of a thing already there, but rather the imagination of a thing not yet there," hence the sense of house thrown into nature by idea. "Now my Dutch word-book renders 'idea' . . . by *ontwerp*, which is to say, out-throw. And in Holland a builder's plan is called an *ontwerp* . . . . the mind of a great Roman theologian jumps with the common mind of a Dutch folk . . . ." The Bergsonian requirement that room be prepared in nature for novelty underlies the argument, the mind itself throwing forward "a thing not yet there."

Upward makes a significantly distorting appropriation of a traditional Christian symbol to support his position, and in following his lead, Pound takes a direction which he will come to question in the last of the *Cantos*, a direction quite other than Eliot's. (That Pound is increasingly aware of the parting of ways between him and Eliot is testified to repeatedly in the *Cantos* in his remarks on and allusions to Eliot, a development that reaches a climax in the *Pisan Cantos*.) What Upward says is that "The Cross is the Sign of Matter, and as such it reminds us of the nature of Matter. Not only is it the rude picture of a knot . . . but it shows us how the knot is made. . . . Thus it reminds us that two Ways of Strength must meet cross-wise to become entangled. And their entanglement is their arrest." But the two ways are lines of inter-mundane forces, and thus the perversion of that traditional symbolism in which one of the lines points Heavenward. That is, Upward's cross lies horizontal. (Contrast Dante's cross at the top of Purgatory Mountain or Eliot's in the *Four Quartets*.)

Upward's uses of the word, then, perform an exorcism of spirit, except in so much as spirit may be spoken of as a power of mind over matter, a power resident in man. And thus he prepares for that somewhat mystical approach Pound is to make to existence through the Vorticist's image, a development fundamental to the *Cantos* and one Pound argues with the conviction of an eighteenth-century rationalist, expecting complex reality to conform to idea. In image the idea meets the object; the result is a creative transformation whereby the entangled and arrested energies of nature are released by the imaginative mind. At a first level the release allows the mind itself to grow in its power; at a second level, the release allows a pragmatic force to be exercised by mind upon nature. Thus the human mind becomes the rescue of that being which is frozen in matter, or what is the more common in Pound, the energies frozen in history by art, which thus must be "made new," his famous battlecry. Fundamentally, this is a Bergsonian idea, advanced by Pound with rationalist conviction.

I think one may understand in this context why Pound believes that there is a literal power in the image which may be harnessed to work, why he is so much convinced that when the right word is said an inevitable consequence of general good results. That image-word is a "radiant node . . . from which and into which, ideas are constantly rushing," so that when it is in the control of the activist poet it functions like a .nuclear reactor, providing the light and energy necessary to the building of his city, the City of Dioce. One sees as well the reason for Pound's antipathy to metaphor as commonly understood, for instance to metaphor as used by a poet like Wallace Stevens, whose metaphorical fictions can but appear frivolous to Pound. In Pound, idea is the imagination of a thing *not yet* there, implying a necessary action of bringing something to be more positively than as a fiction. Wallace Stevens's playful interest in image is to bring into being for a moment's entertainment of mind a "supreme fiction" independent (in so far as the power of the imagination can manage it) of any ordinary reality. For Pound, imagination must meet matter in image and disentangle matter's energies so that a "progress" of becoming is effected, particularly in the intellectual and social structure of community. That is, Pound desires to establish the poet as king, rather than Plato's philosopher as king, precisely because he believes the key to nature's and man's becoming lies in the exercise of the imagination. (His belief is closer to Shelley's than he would be comfortable with.) In the tamer use of image for the making of metaphor as entertainment, Pound sees a perversion of mind; one is removed from the images themselves, and image is the medium through which reality is established and controlled. The secondary nature of metaphor is its emphasis upon "likeness" in "unlike" things, so that metaphor builds a shadow world. (Note that Pound finds Plato most amenable of all Western

classical philosophers.) In traditional metaphor, says Pound, there
is a certain beauty of form, the "result of 'planes of relation.' " But
the "Poet, whatever his 'figure of speech,' will not arrive by doubling or confusing image." (*Gaudier-Brzeska*) That is but to entangle
energy in images at cross planes.[4]

Such violently anti-romantic men as Pound and Hulme and
Lewis, as we gain a perspective upon them, seem to be more and
more caught in a close continuum of Romanticism. Eliot as well,
and no doubt that is what he has in mind in looking back in 1961
("To Criticize the Critic") and saying, "as for Classicism and
Romanticism, I find that the terms have no longer the importance
to me that they once had." Hulme's Neo-Classicism certainly
seems to be rather a Neo-Romanticism, though intentionally a
reaction to the nineteenth-century poetry that he is so scathingly
contemptuous of, as was Pound and, less bombastically, Eliot.
Indeed, in separating fancy from the imagination (as the Romantic
after Coleridge tends to do), fancy is denigrated as if it were
poetry's Original Sin, a tendency which finds an extreme reaction
in surrealism and eventually in Dada, in comparison to which we
discover a "classic" restraint in Coleridge and Wordsworth.
Wordsworth goes to some trouble to redress the Romantic reduction of fancy in his "Preface to the Edition of 1815" of his poems.
The fancy, he admits, "is as capricious as the accidents of things,
and the effects are surprising, playful, ludicrous, amusing, tender,
or pathetic, as the objects happen to be appositely produced or fortunately combined." The imagination on the other hand "is conscious of an indestructible dominion;—the Soul may fall away from
it, not being able to sustain its grandeur. . . . Fancy is given to
quicken and to beguile the temporal part of our nature, Imagination to incite and support the eternal." Fancy is characterized as
that power in the poet "insinuating herself into the heart of objects

---

4. For Wallace Stevens, that is exactly how one does arrive at the uses of poetry, Stevens
especially valuing the confusion of image in the making of metaphor. See Stevens's "essay"
on the subject in *The Necessary Angel*, "Someone Puts a Pineapple Together." Such an inclination suits only a private pleasure, from Pound's position. Pound's is an activist role that
makes him appealing in the 1960s and 1970s. If one examines the flood of anthologies that
collect the work of beginning poets in those decades, the rise of Pound's influence is evident,
as is the decline of Eliot's. Especially one finds Pound's name coming up in those brief "ars
Poetica" entries in the "Contributors" appendices to such anthologies.

with creative activity," less controlled by "fixed laws" than is the Imagination. But while praising the fancy when employed within its proper limits, Wordsworth is nevertheless careful to suggest the dangers in it when it is not complemented by the imaginative power. He gives an honorable place to his "Poems of Fancy" in the collection, but they are a small portion of his work. Fancy's freeing of images from nature's reality may "beguile" the temporal part of our nature if unchecked, even beyond the province of poetry, as suggested by those operations of the mind that attempted to restructure a whole nation in eighteenth- and nineteenth-century France, a spectacle that might well give Coleridge or Wordsworth pause in the formulation of their poetics.

Henry James will address the Romantic's problem of the fancy's relation to imagination, but under the rubric of "romance" and "realism." In a passage of his preface to *The American* (1907) he says that romance is "experience disengaged, disembroiled, disencumbered, exempt from the conditions that we usually know to attach to [experience]. . . . The balloon of experience is in fact of course tied to the earth, and under that necessity we swing . . . in the more or less commodious car of the imagination. . . . The art of the romancer is, 'for the fun of it,' insidiously to cut the cable, to cut it without our detecting him." Both Wordsworth and Coleridge are concerned to anchor the experience-imagination balloon, not only in nature as is James's object, but in the Cause of both nature and the imagination, the I AM THAT I AM. Thus the dignity of the imagination might itself restore a respectability to poetry, which had fallen into disrepute among those intellectuals whose devotion had become focused on the conceptual approach to reality, whether in science or government or business. (Henry James's own anxiety to validate fiction as "real" is surely in part to satisfy his searchingly skeptical, science-minded brother William.)

Technology increasingly becomes the poetry of the triumphant rationalism, as intellectual process tends to become the nineteenth-century's substitute for religious rites. But in so becoming, the particular intellect is increasingly removed from that community of consent that is necessary to viable rites. A strong and active intellect can effect a movement, within which rites become established. That happens out of Marx into Marxism, out of Freud into Freudianism. But the consent here required is to a secular gnostic religion which presents itself as being scientific. Wordsworth, on the other hand had insisted, in 1802, on the close relation of poetry to science, but it was a complementary relationship not often tolerated in the nineteenth century, despite the considerable labors of Matthew Arnold and John Ruskin. Between Coleridge and T. E. Hulme, then, the "poetry" of existence, the dynamics of becoming associated with the spiritual, had been largely excluded from any version of existence that seemed reasonable. Hulme's fancy is an attempt to recover the zest for things, the delights that Wordsworth speaks of, but in the name of a profound approach to reality, calling to its support the new science as rescued by Bergson. Fancy is the new realism, spoken to by a shifting relativity in nature which Einstein was advancing in physics, but, more important to Hulme, by the shifting reality of consciousness which Bergson advances as metaphysics. Hence Hulme summons Bergson in support because Bergson seems to be, in a persuasive way, rescuing being as dynamic from its threatened arrest by rational, conceptual limitations upon being. Hulme is attempting to recover joy, and this new joy he thinks requires as agent the fancy whose power (in Wordsworth's words) is that of "insinuating herself into the heart of objects with creative activity." (Husserl's own return to the things themselves is also an attempt to recover consciousness from the disorienting effect of its removal from reality, its removal from the object, a removal inaugurated by Descartes.)

Such, then, is the use the poet and aesthetician may make of Bergson's *élan original de la vie*. We turn now to another aspect of it which will lead us back to our concern with certain philosophical positions developed out of it. Bergson remarks of this vital impetus—a force which determinism has not discovered because of its conceptual approach to the object—that it does not generate energy of its own. It rather serves to "engraft on to the necessity of physical forces the largest possible amount of indetermination." Thus *being*, he holds, becomes progressively opened and determinism corrected. Matter drags against the impetus of this creative force and is spent (in Robert Frost's words) "in sending up a little" special life. What one discovers here is a speculative vision by Bergson of an immanent gnosticism: for matter, though a necessary antagonist, is an antagonist to be transcended. Bergson's speculative vision, though he will not pursue cause, requires him nevertheless to speak of the earliest life, physico-chemical, into which the vital impetus "insinuated itself." Thus if he will not begin at a beginning, he cannot begin simply yesterday. Questions of origin and cause in Bergson are in suspense, then, until Teilhard advances upon the Bergsonian argument his own version of leaps of being in matter.

Bergson was a catalyst for Teilhard's thought at about the same time his work also served Hulme and Frost. Teilhard says in 1917 (*L'Union créatrice*): "By the mere fact one sees in universal becoming a pattern of convergence, one eliminates the Bergsonian idea of a vital thrust without finality, a *vis a terge*. A dynamism such as his allows indeed for a centre of divergence at its starting point, but I do not see how it would produce a fusion of the elements which it drives before it." What seems missing to Teilhard, then is that Point Omega he will himself eventually posit, but it is important that we notice in the range of his thought that he does not diverge at last so far from his Bergsonian beginnings as his words suggest. He is concerned with a "creative union" as a step beyond Bergson's "creative evolution." Christopher F. Mooney, in dissociating Teilhard from Bergson, remarks that Teilhard "always speaks of Christ as an object of faith; Bergson always as an object of philosophy." The intended dissociation of Teilhard from Bergson, however, I believe too strongly put. As Teilhard says in his *Appearance of Man*: "We have good reason to smile at Bergson's 'élan vital.' But have we not at the same time thrown it overboard too lightly? Extended to the initial phases and the present totality of the biosphere, the expression has certainly a disagreeably anthropomorphic flavor. But restricted to the reflective zones of the Noösphere, it does no more than express the dynamic rigour of a situation."

Again, the primary weakness Teilhard finds is the failure of the Bergsonian system to posit a teleological resolution of the *élan vital.* Bergson's complaint against Darwinian determinism is that it does not allow the new, the novel. Teilhard would enlarge that allowance toward a convergence of the Noösphere with the transcendent at Point Omega. And he suggests an intrusion of the novel short of that end, as he has suggested several intrusions along the road to the present—life into matter, awareness into life, self-awareness into awareness—in the long development to modern man.

In *The Appearance of Man*, Teilhard speaks of a "*New Evolution*" which has become capable of "utilising for its ends an equally *new* form of *heredity*, much more flexible and richer, without being any the less 'biological' on that account." It is a hereditary force of "*educative* transmission of a complex continuously modified and augmented by conduct and thought." We are not far removed here from that Bergsonian strategy of a separation of intuitional and conceptual thinking whereby one steps outside space in the interest of real time, though it is a more actively conscious activity in Teilhard's formulation. (The intuitively exercised mind is not in Bergson a subconscious action either.) In this "educative transmission" of a new heredity, "individual human beings are so subtly developed through the centuries that it is strictly impermissible to compare any two men who are not contemporaries. . . ." Teilhard footnotes the remark by a comparison of Bergson and Plato. "As a 'brain' and a 'heart,' Bergson was not perhaps the equal of Plato. But, living two thousand years after Plato, he perceived and felt things that Plato could neither know nor see. Something like the principle of relativity applied to history." What is incipient here, one fears, is a *gnostic* transmission in a new heredity, subtly developed through the centuries, an *ex post facto* view, but one easily transferred from observation of the past to manipulation of the future.

We have examined in our first volume the weaknesses in Teilhard's vision of evolution toward Point Omega and need not revisit too long that old ground. But we may conclude our observations on his thought by reminding ourselves once more, as Tresmontant does in his study of Teilhard, that he "falls into the Scylla of a well-known mythology" in attempting to provide the

Bergsonian vision with a teleological completion. He construes being as immanent and attempts to reconcile his faith in Christ to the immanent. "According to this myth," says Tresmontant, "God fulfills Himself in creating the world. . . . This is an old gnostic idea." But what we notice is that it is an old gnostic idea arrived at by way of the new gnosticism which Teilhard would oppose in Bergson. There is a poignant note struck in Teilhard's letter from Song-chou-tchoolz (May 24, 1927): ". . . this contact with the real does me good. And then, amid this complexity and immobility of the rocks there rise suddenly toward me 'gusts of being,' laborious unification of things, and it is no longer myself thinking, but the Earth acting." What is missing, one fears, is that awareness found in a similar experience of Gerard Manly Hopkins; for Hopkins the "Earth acting" is a sign of the "grandeur of God," not of an *élan vital* immanently perceived.

CHAPTER XVIII

OLD BOSSY DISGUISED AS THE WHITE STAG

It is a curious aspect of Heidegger's life that, in so far as it can be separated from his philosophy, he reminds one of an Agrarian like Donald Davidson. His quiet attachment to his native Swabian land, his private life close to the local, going dressed in peasant garb, with his brother farming nearby. But the more telling parallel is to Poe, in whose "Domain of Arnheim" one sees the difference between Mr. Davidson's anchor in Christian tradition and Poe's and Heidegger's rootlessness. As Strauss observes, Heidegger's pursuit of a "being at home beyond the most extreme homelessness" is built in "fantastic hopes, more to be expected from visionaries than from philosophers." The pathos of the position is that there is neither the comfort nor the confidence of having rested the attempt—the quest for the quest—upon an acceptable base from which the "worlds" of individuals can be reconciled. Nor does any pattern of reassuring meaning in existence emerge from history conceived as a succession of ravenous moments in which each consumes the moment before like hungry Chinese boxes. What one has is a "resolve" (Heidegger's term) out of the *given*, directed toward that given—that is, directed inward upon the self—but with questions of faith in any *giver* set aside. Ostensibly, such questions are set aside in favor of a respect for the formal limitations of philosophy in its pursuit of ontological proofs. Yet there is also that accompanying refusal to admit fundamental questions such as Strauss, Voegelin, Collins, and Roberts bring to bear. In Heidegger's "resolve" lies (as Roberts puts it) "the extreme potentiality of existence," which is "renunciation." It is a renunciation of the self and of all being, as we observed, fundamentally different from that renunciation we are admonished to practice by St. Paul and the Gospels. For Heidegger's renunciation has as its reward the prospect of an encounter with Nothingness rather than that new being St. Paul posits. The promise is that we arrive at our "true-self." But it seems rather that we arrive at a spiritual state like that Miss O'Connor dramatizes in Rayber as he stands waiting a terrible pain that does not come. That is certainly a prospect, in so far as one is a "realist of distances" in the meaning of that phrase as understood by Miss O'Connor. We recall that Poe's Monos explicitly rejects "the explanations of the priesthood," as Heidegger rejects the Christian position because it is a Platonism for the masses. Heidegger's call to us is an enticing one, as siren songs always are, luring us to assumptions of power through consciousness which promise to make one the arbiter of his own being.

What evidence have we of the consummation Heidegger promises? The evidence, he says, is anchored in our sense of the totality of Being. It is not a cumulative sense of the whole of existence as might be measured by that mind "infected with system, and with abstraction" or "enwrapped . . . in generalities," as Monos puts it, the result of which infection is the "rectangular obscenities" of the harsh "mathematical reason." Now "Being-itself" is for Heidegger separate from the particularity of things, and is to be approached (to borrow from Monos) by the "sentiment of the natural" which is served by the poetic imagination. In moments when "what-is-in-its-totality" (the phrase-noun from Heidegger) is accessible, it is with a sense in Heidegger that the "finite is contained in this unknowable whole." But one's reaction to that awareness is less likely to be joy, as in Miss O'Connor, than boredom. (Boredom as a state becomes a technique, characteristic of the *poète maudit*, we might add.) "Not boredom," Roberts says in explanation of Heidegger's sense of boredom, "with a particular book or play or form of work, but finding oneself drifting in the abyss of existence as a mute fog which draws everything into a queer indifference. The sense of wholeness here comes out in the

fact that *everything* is meaningless, pointless, tasteless, colorless."
But whether one deals with *fact* or *illusion* is a question to be raised
to Heidegger, a question we have earlier raised to Poe. What we
should remark is a gentleness in this address by Heidegger to
Being-itself through boredom, in contrast to the wildly excessive
and satanic uses of boredom by some Absurdists.[1]

Roberts says in his redaction of Heidegger's argument:
" 'What-is-in-totality' is like a bottomless sea into which all
distinctions vanish. . . . there is 'nothing' to hold onto. While
everything positive slips away, the only thing that remains and
overwhelms us is 'Nothing.' We also slip away from ourselves so
that what remains is not a definite 'I,' but a pure 'being-there'
(*Dasein*)." That pure "being there" is an instance of consummation
of the "true-self" such as death must finally seal in us, a moment in
which the "true-self" is found. "Our thought systems and our
practical activities are attempts to run away from this encounter.
The proper way to express what happens when anxiety reveals
Nothingness is to say not that 'what-is-in-its-totality' has been
annihilated, . . . but that it has become untenable. This 'making of
what-is repulsive' is not annihilation, but nihilation (not
Vernichtung but *Nichtung*)." It is a distinction which Heidegger
makes so that he may set himself apart from the activist nihilists,
and we call attention thereby to the ascetic gentleness that leads
Heidegger to his mountain top retreat.

These words in paraphrase and exposition by Roberts, while
reflecting a more refined argument in Heidegger than Poe makes,
show nevertheless how closely Poe anticipates Heidegger. The
peroration and conclusion of "The Colloquy of Monos and Una" is
an attempt to give some sense of the senselessness of that
consummation in Nothingness. Monos gives an account of a
transcendence of the senses into a sixth sense, admitting the
difficulty of reporting it since "Words are vague things." It is not a
thing that is being expressed anyway, but an encounter with

---

1. Recall, for instance, Aldous Huxley's satire on the cult of boredom in *Antic Hay*, particularly its malignancy in his diabolic character Coleman; the novel is a comic treatment of
spiritual bankruptcy.

nothingness. We may cite some of Monos' concluding statements, whose parallels to Heidegger seem obvious:

> The consciousness of *being* had grown hourly more indistinct [after the body's death] . . . mere *locality* had . . . usurped its position. The idea of entity was becoming merged in that of place. The narrow space immediately surrounding what had been the body, was now growing to be the body itself. . . . all was void. . . . The sense of being had at length utterly departed, and there reigned in its stead—instead of all things—dominant and perpetual—the autocrats *Place* and *Time*. For *that* which was not—for that which had no form—for that which had no thought—for that which had no sentience—for that which was soulless, yet of which matter formed no portion—for all this nothingness, yet for all this immortality, the grave was still a home, and the corrosive hours, comates.

"Apathy" as Baudelaire puts it, "assumes the size of immortality," in which emptiness the journey is made. Poe's colloquy journeys into nothingness, by argument at least, in an assumed elevation beyond the created world; yet one is not separated from that world. The "rest" for nothingness is in the grave, in corrosive hours. The autocrats Place and Time are the grounds for the transcendence of what Heidegger calls "Being-itself," described by Poe as "temporal Eternity." One notices particularly the divesting of personality in Poe, an attempt to deny the permanent self that we try to capture with the pronoun "I," though the very act of dramatizing the argument commits Poe to some symbolic positing of speaker. The best he can manage is *Monos*, a substitute perhaps for that old naming of Monos before his entry into Nothingness through death, an old name which may have been something like Jonathan Woodbury, but was more probably simply Edgar Allan Poe.[2]

Poe pursues an idea in his "Colloquy of Monos and Una," but from a fictioneer's stance. We allow him, at least initially, a suspension of our disbelief, even though we may conclude at last with James Russell Lowell that he is "two-fifths genius, three-fifths

---

2. The Greek *monos* is rendered *single, one, alone*; it is balanced by the Latin feminine *una*, which bears the same meaning. One has in Poe's "Colloquy of Monos and Una," then, Poe's ironic adaptation of the traditional literary dialogue of the self divided, as ancient as the Egyptian "Dispute of a Man, Who Contemplates Suicide, with His Soul," c. 2000 B.C.

sheer fudge." But Heidegger's position is that of the philosopher; his ideas and arguments aren't advanced as occasions of fiction. One hesitates to suggest that he deliberately manipulates language for effect, as Poe does. His manner speaks a high seriousness which suggests that he misleads himself as well as the reader as he pursues that quarry he would entrap by words, that elusive creature he calls *Being-itself*. It is well to recognize in advance the "three-fifths sheer fudge" in him, so that we may better come to terms with whatever genius remains. He engages in a game of words whose issue is of profound consequence to the struggling consciousness attempting to deal with his words. Now when we examine the game Heidegger plays out with high seriousness, what we discover is that the words he uses disguise simple country truths so that they appear as original discoveries. The trick through which *Being-itself* is to be surprised at its watering hole is to construct an elaborate net of jargon, in the building of which trap our attention is shifted from the distortions of individual words by our excited anticipation of closing the net upon the phantom quarry. Thus we are led to stated propositions whose harvest turns out to be either the self-evident or the unsubstantiated, or some combination of the two: the self-evident distorted by the proposition's language. The family cow, we may conclude, has been decorated to resemble the White Stag. Consider, for example, what Heidegger makes of one commonplace of our social experience.

We know that Person A may be delegated by Person B as his representative to some gathering or in some action. One's boss may send one to "stand in" for him at a meeting. Person A may thus act for B within the limits of a delegated representation. He may be accepted in that capacity by Person (or Persons) C. We have described abstractly an experience as simple to the individual as his fetching the evening paper for his father or a piece of chalk from the supply room for his first-grade teacher. Or the "representation" may be as complex as a technician's service, on behalf of his computer company, to an international conglomerate. Now Heidegger, in *Being and Time*, puts this commonplace as follows:

> Indisputably, the fact that one Dasein can be *represented* by another belongs to its possibilities of Being in Being-with-one-another in the

world . . . . Representability is not only possible but is even constitutively for our being with one another. *Here* one Dasein can and must, within certain limits, *"be"* another Dasein.

The murky language leading up to the emphatic conclusion, the qualifier within the conclusion itself ("within certain limits"), and the doubling of punctuation of the crucial verb *be* (using both italics and quotation marks) all conspire to obscure the hocus-pocus of language. For there has occured a radical distortion in the verb *be*; one speaking for or acting in the name of another does not *come to be* that other in any *essential* way, except within the pseudo-statement. (Poe's and Heidegger's inclination to italics, it appears, becomes infectious.)

The first-grade student sent for chalk is *not* his teacher, though he may mistake himself as such as he dawdles down the hall. He may even be taken as a "sign" of the teacher or of the whole class by the keeper of the chalk treasure: "What do you all do with chalk? Eat it?" The dragon of the chalk-horde, however, makes no mistake: the child is not the teacher, else the words would be otherwise framed and most likely only muttered. That is, the child's being is not "constitutively" affected in such representation, except as he may allow himself to be metamorphosed by self-esteem or metamorphosed by an irritated keeper of the chalk. (I have resisted using the librarian as instance, since librarians are anciently abused in such dramas.) A fiction writer, let us suppose, might well build a slight epiphany upon the child's encounter with the chalk dragon, but the epiphany would involve precisely the child's recognition that he has not been "constitutively" affected by the authority delegated by his teacher. The deflation of his self-importance is the most likely denouement, though the sentimental approach might focus rather on the terrible dragon and imply an innocent child. There is a considerable body of our literature which turns on just such representational errors. There is the Man in the Gray Flannel Suit, the Company Man, the Soldier, Citizen X. But the burden of the literary theme is colored by pathos or irony, implying a distortion in the agent of the fiction which has been thrust upon him or courted by him. Such fiction's resolution turns on the degree of our recognition that a Heideggerian "representability" has distorted the agent's being. One could collect a considerable anthology to the point, perhaps beginning with Melville's "Bartleby, the Scrivener," and featuring Kafka's *Metamorphosis.*"

The point is that Heidegger suggests that a literal, i.e., essential, transformation occurs through the action of representation, while the transformation is only a fiction of the philosophical statements made about the social situation. And what we begin to notice about his philosophical position is that it depends for its persuasiveness upon words individually dramatized to the point that the word seems to be the name of particular creatures. A human being becomes *Dasein* (being-there), a social encounter becomes *Being-with-one-another. Being-itself* becomes the antagonist of *what-is-in-its-totality.* We find ourselves, depending upon the degree of skepticism we maintain—the degree to which we fail to suspend our disbelief—journeying into Swift's Laputa as Gulliver does or accompanying Bunyanesque (but secularized) personae toward an Omega encounter with *Being-itself,* though we come to that point only as a fiction. That is, we stage encounters between *Dasein* and *Being-itself,* as Poe stages an encounter between *Monos* and *Una.* But we find ourselves nevertheless removed from the experience of a dramatic encounter by the very word-projection. We witness a drama that does not return us at last to the reality of the In-between in which such drama finds its ultimate test independent of words. (In contrast, we may note the effectiveness of Plato in such dialogues as *The Phaedo* or *The Banquet,* in which the country of the Idea is anchored in a realistic setting, which in turn points to our existence in the In-between.)

It is not, of course, that philosophical questions are not at issue, but rather that through words so dramatized as to become characters themselves we are increasingly removed from that which philosophical words presumably aim toward. Words as creatures increasingly constitute a shifting veil between consciousness and the "Being" which consciousness pursues. This confusion is conspicuous in Heidegger's dealing with that most sacred of "objects" to Poe, death. Death, Heidegger tells us in *Being and Time, "is* always one's own." And an enthusiastic explicator of the line remarks in glossing it, "in relation to his death no individual human being can be represented by another." Indeed, a whole academic industry is founded upon marketing such a commonplace filtered through Heidegger's word-characters, as Professor Paul Edwards shows us in his *Heidegger and Death: A Critical Evaluation.* Professor Edwards demonstrates the intolerable structures built on this proposition about death, its only validity the true but platitudinous assertion that each creature of nature dies in nature. A country spiritual puts the point much more succinctly:

> You gotta walk that lonesome valley,
> You gotta go there by yourself,
> Ain't nobody here can go there for you,
> You gotta go there by yourself.

Even the adverbs *here* and *there* are as profound philosophically and spiritually as Heidegger's formulations and scarcely need glossing at all.

What is of interest to any reader who has a predilection for dramatic irony is that Heidegger, in pursuit of being, confounds the trail left by Being within the In-between—the Platonic *metaxy*—through distortions that center largely upon his misuse of the copulative verb. It is an ancient problem, perhaps more ancient even than its tricky presence in Plato's *Parmenides*, that early attempt at an accommodation of the one and the many so that consciousness is not entrapped in its own *one alone*.[3] But the very ancientness of the problem ought to disallow our modern innocence in the matter. Still, after obfuscation of terms, the Heideggerian proposition announces as conclusion that A *is* B, and with the electric presence of italics in the distorted verb. It is refreshing, then, to hear Professor Edwards state an inevitable conclusion. After examining Heidegger's arguments concerning "being-

---

3. Of that brave attempt a poet (a wearied student no doubt) has written "A Possible Solution":

> Wise Plato's brother in his youth
> Worked hard to learn Parmenides'
> And Zeno's arguments toward truth—
> Of Sameness, of Pluralities.

> And having learned their speeches through,
> He marvelled learning's benison;
> But he bred mares in learning's lieu,
> Did wise old stable Antiphon.

toward-death" as leading to an ultimate fulfillment of the
"Dasein," Edwards says: "all that is meant by the Heideggerian
statement that life is being-toward-death is, first, that human beings die, and, second, that unlike plants and animals they know
and are, fugitively or nonfugitively, concerned about their death.
The objection to this statement is not that it is false, but that it is a
platitude."

Let us suggest here that the fugitive concern for the meaning of
death has as its origin, in Heidegger, a modernized concept of
freedom, one which has had removed from it any suggestion of
limits such as were anciently associated with freedom. I do not
mean *freedom* as it has become entangled in the social or political or
economic arena, though those divisions within community existence have been decisively affected, one fears, by the liberated
concept. I mean the immediate sense, interior to the individual
soul, of its own absoluteness. That sense of absoluteness, dominantly modern, though an ancient temptation in the soul as the story of
Lucifer suggests, affects the soul with an apprehension of the void.
For it seems an imperative of such freedom from which the limits of
being have been dissolved that it somehow fill the void, touch some
absolute limit in an action whose import to the soul is that it alone
creates—must create and self-fill the void. That, as we have seen, is
the import of Poe's *Eureka*. We can see that impulse championed
with evangelical zeal by one of Heidegger's disciples. Professor
Werner Marx of Freiburg, pointing to Heidegger's action out of
this ambiguous freedom, declares that Heidegger leaps "onto the
shores of Being," thus becoming "imbued with a strong conviction
[that] he is the voice and instrument of Being." He is trying to "attain a 'second becoming' for mankind." Professor Marx seems
oblivious to the ironic distortions through which Heidegger is thus
made into the Third Adam, a millennarian Christ. Or rather, the
declaration is of an immanent position from which all traces of the
transcendent have been removed, with Heidegger becoming Point
Omega by a violence of language. This act of a "second becoming"
has its analogue, not in Christ, but in Prometheus (and one has
repeatedly in reading Heidegger a sense that the philosopher is pre-
Platonic in his pursuit of Being). This second Prometheus would

seize Being so that *Being-itself* will have appeared to be transcended, an action we shall presently pursue in Heidegger. But just what this ultimate Being beyond *Being-itself*, seized on mankind's behalf, turns out to be in simple country terms, must give us pause. With death, Heidegger says of this capture, "Dasein stands before itself in its ownmost potentiality-for-being." This standing is "at the same time the uttermost one," i.e., *eigenst*—"most my own." But this finality of death as the absolute of being seems less than a paradox when we realize that what is being celebrated as the *fullfilment* of the human being is an absolute *emptiness*, a consummation very like the one Socrates considers and rejects in *The Apology:* "a state of nothingness and utter unconsciousness . . . like the sleep of him who is undisturbed even by dreams . . . ."

This Heideggerian vision of individual perfection deviates widely from both the Platonic and the Christian conception of a becoming pursued through freedom. The distance can hardly be delineated, as even Heidegger's struggle with Nothingness as a closure of particularities shows. What we recall to our profit here is our antithetic concept of freedom as it relates to man's being, freedom as a condition, a limit itself within the limits of the particular gift of our being, the individual person. For freedom is not a *thing* one uses as an instrument, a shovel to dig the soul's grave or build its monument, though our frustrated namings of freedom these past three hundred years sometimes suggests that it is palpable: it is, to repeat, a condition of our potential being within the contingent *metaxy*. One's completion of being is the action of fulfilling a limited gift, actions inescapably within the conditions of freedom. This is the proposition Miss O'Connor has in mind when she speaks of one's life as "a good under construction," with the implied possibility of deconstruction as well. Put another way, freedom is a condition of openness in the soul which calls for a complementing action of the will, the effect of which is a *fulfilling* in so far as good may be constructed in the soul. For without the *filling*, freedom is but an uneasy condition of the soul, within which a terror rises out of a contingent prospect of meaninglessness.

The exception we are taking to Heidegger's sense of freedom, in which freedom his *anxiety* or *dread* arises to compel *Dasein* to its encounter with *Being-itself*, is not easy to make plain. Let us contrast an anxiety that T. S. Eliot dramatizes in his poetry. (We shall use Eliot as Heidegger uses Hölderlin: the poet most effectively reveals the fundamental nature of being's relation to consciousness.) Eliot's early poetry reflects a state of mind in which he takes mind itself to be trapped in time and place; time and place as present in the mind appear static and mind consequently arrested. We see that condition put simply in his "Preludes," with the "evening" coming to consciousness of arrested images. It is now "six o'clock." Put another way, it is now the "burnt-out ends of smoky days." Yesterday, tomorrow are each now, but in a deadly arrest of the present moment that will only be dissolved at last in those famous (or infamous) opening lines of *Burnt Norton* concerning a new way of seeing how time past and future are contained in time present. At this early point in the poetry, however, there arises an anxiety, a dread out of a sense of the arrest of one's becoming. From the "Preludes" forward in his poetry, Eliot begins to engage the problem of memory as a clue to disentangling time and place as the arrest of being; it is a concern that has collateral expression in Eliot's quest in his prose for tradition, a concern modified and clarified at last in the distinction he comes to make between tradition and orthodoxy in *After Strange Gods*.

The initially troubling problem with memory, for Eliot, is its relation to desire, for there is unmistakeably a desire in the consciousness to break free whatever "paralysed force" (the phrase is from "The Hollow Men") yet resides in the consciousness. Eliot, too, is beleagured by the intellectual spirit of the age, so that any attempt to reconcile desire and memory as St. Augustine or St. Thomas might do seems *déclassé*. That intellectual climate of modernist thought is entrapment enough, courage lacking. But more decisive is the enigma of desire's relation to memory within the limits of the mechanistic view of mind in nature which was so generally accepted by the intellectual community at the time of this early poetry. One can well imagine how exciting was the prospect Henri Bergson presented to such struggling minds as Eliot's and Robert Frost's and Teilhard's and Voegelin's, all of them troubled by mind's entrapment in matter, each of them affected by

Bergson's signal of an imminent force breaking out of mechanistic existence. For Eliot, who heard Bergson during the period when the "Preludes" and "Prufrock" were under construction, but does not find him answering the problem adequately, the initial fear is that desire in the consciousness is but an afterglow of past experience.[4] If so, desire may be nothing more than nostalgia weighting the present moment of consciousness like a Boston or a London fog; its only identifiable object appears to be a past experience, which one may pursue with desperation, but only through repetition, into a boundless future. Every six o'clock is like every other, and *now* is always and only the burnt-out ends of smoky days.

Such is the theme of spiritual arrest in Eliot's "Preludes," in "Rhapsody on a Windy Night," a theme so arrested in its development as to threaten Eliot's poetry with monotony to the aesthetic sensibility. But that very doggedness in pursuing the theme is an indication of how serious a problem Eliot the man (as opposed to the poet) is wrestling. The theme comes rather sharply into focus, with new complexities, when dramatized in "Gerontion," the poem Eliot at first thought to use as prologue to his *Waste Land*. In "Gerontion" we have a persona placed very near the point of convergence of consciousness with death. If Heidegger were describing the imminent encounter, he would speak no doubt of the *Dasein's* nearness to *Being-itself*. But we are not in a Heideggerean world in "Gerontion," as we shall see.

Pulled by the prospect of annihilation in "fractured atoms," Gerontion is yet held by those "Vacant shuttles" that "Weave the wind"—by ghostly images of past experiences which, though they reveal no pattern, linger still as prophetic signs. Eliot's speaker, the consciousness of "a little old man," may be at the edge of extinction, but he does not surrender desire to that threatening oblivion. He revisits the signs—the residue of memory—since memory's images somehow hint of a way of seeing the self in a time past, a way involving more than the present attempt to protract a "chilled

4. In the *Criterion* many years later (April 1934), Eliot remembers his days in Paris in 1910 and 1911: ". . . there was a most exciting variety of ideas." He sets the names of those active in literature and art and philosophy and science—Gide, Claudel, Anatole France, Remy de Gourmont, Barres, Peguy. All were "more or less Bergsonian *and* Catholic *and* Socialist . . . . and over all swung the spider-like figure of Bergson."

delirium" of the senses. More seems at issue than this present clinging to images through desperation as the body fades. A disturbing
concern to Gerontion now is that he seems to have misread signs at
a first encounter. That old contingent address long ago, which
lingers only as memory, might be somehow recovered in spite of the
final, historical resolution of the contingent moment by what appears in retrospect to have been a wrong action. Fräulein von Kulp,
in memory, is arrested as she once turned in the hall, "one hand on
the door," and the door is once more unopened.

If one regains such a past contingent moment, while knowing
as well the subsequent false resolution of the moment, that
knowledge is condemnatory. "After such knowledge, what
forgiveness?" Gerontion asks. And the villainess seems to be Cleo,
history, in the light of a present knowledge. For she gives "when
our attention is distracted . . . with such supple confusions / That
the giving famishes the craving." Gerontion's old attempt to fill
that craving appears now as an attempt to devour existence; it has
led only to the world's and the self's empty existence, vacant images
in "memory only." Memory still seems only "reconsidered passion," as the dying man's being seems only "Thoughts of a dry
brain in a dry season." But in spite of that terrible knowledge, the
desire for some secret opening of the self persists. It is a desire for
some consequential action of becoming, focused in memory but accompanied by the hard-gained knowledge that neither "fear nor
courage saves us" in the contingent moment.

In *The Waste Land*, the same question of desire's entanglement
in memory opens the poem explicitly, but by "Ash-Wednesday" we
find the question changed, as if some answer to the problem has
been given. In "Ash-Wednesday" we come to the prospect of hope
as threatened by the abyss of despair. Desire, it now appears, has
discovered its true object beyond history, a discovery made through
reconsidered passion—by revisiting points of contingency in the
past through memory and learning to "sympathize," "give," and
"control" spiritually. By the end of *The Waste Land* the struggling
spirit has moved beyond Gerontion's condition. His decayed house
may at least be set in order, its fragments of memory "shored
against [his] ruin." For, although one cannot alter the past actions

within the dimension of history, one may yet through memory recover a state of being which we may call right-mindedness toward those old actions. "Great is the power of memory," says St. Augustine in his *Confessions*, a work which figures significantly in Eliot's own spiritual journey as it does in the poetry he writes, particularly *The Waste Land* and "Ash-Wednesday." (I have developed this relationship in my *Eliot's Reflective Journey to the Garden*, and a most illuminating support of our point here is to be found in Gerhart Niemeyer's "History and Civilization," *Anglican Theological Review*, November 1976.) In his paean to memory, St. Augustine adds, "its deep and boundless multiplicity is something fearful . . . . And this is the mind, and I am this myself." For, just as through our senses we engage the created world and through the created world are moved toward the Creator of that world, as St. Thomas says, through memory we engage the fragments of our past encounters with creation and are led thereby toward the cause not only of existence separate from consciousness but to a Cause of the very consciousness in which the fragmentary experience of creation stored by memory is shored by image against our ruin. As St. Augustine argues, memory is itself an inevitable route we follow toward the Cause of all effects when the will is righted. A *present* encounter of *past* encounters is the key to the opening of the self, to the necessary sympathizing and giving to existence whereby one becomes.

When Eliot has come to this understanding of these chapters on memory in the *Confessions*, he will be prepared to say that "What might have been" is "always present" to the seeking self. For by an act of the will, consciousness may participate once more in an event of its own past, as freely as before, though it is a participation no longer within the dominion of time and place—no longer a matter of history. History itself may and must declare that moment past, and that is an aspect of history's subtle confusion that troubles Gerontion; fascinated by history, he has supposed that forgiveness is an action in time. But from a different prospect upon history, Eliot has come to see that "History is a pattern of timeless moments." Perhaps here one has, if but faintly, an analogue between the self's attempt to rescue its history and that mystery deeper than memory through which all time is said to have been rescued, the Incarnation, the Ineffable Intrusion into time whereby the world is restored. For though an event *in* one's personal history may not be altered, edited out of one's history, the individual soul may nevertheless participate in that past moment in such a way as to celebrate, through consent, that time's redemption. That is, a right-willed consent—still and still moving within the limits of the soul's freedom—addresses the spent moment in a new contingency, but a contingency now out of time. That is the moment of vision Eliot celebrates when

> The new years walk, restoring
> Through a bright cloud of tears, the years . . . .

What is redeemed as well is the old but "unread vision" restored to the "higher dream." For there lies an opening upon a transcendent vision that haunts Gerontion's fragmented images, to which he is drawn against the pull to oblivion.

It is here, then, that the past moment becomes redeemed. Or put more particularly, more personally, more crucially to any "Dasein," it is here that one's being is restored. Such revisiting of past moments is the necessary condition (we are instructed) within the spiritual realm for the exercise of confession, contrition, amendment, through which we are strengthened so that we may "live with" our past. And as the self is restored, the world is also returned to us restored. As Eliot puts it, in that moment of recovery

> . . . the lost heart stiffens and rejoices
> In the lost lilac and the lost sea voices
> And the weak spirit . . .
> Quickens to recover
> The cry of quail and the whirling plover . . . .

The blind eye sees at last; the wasted sense of smell, lamented by Gerontion, has restored to it "the salt savour of the sandy earth." Christ's question is resolved; the "salt of the earth" (Matthew 5:13) has its savour of being restored, for it is the individual man that Christ speaks of as the "salt" in that crucial text following the Sermon on the Mount. Not of course a restored youth to the always changing body in any literal way.

These passages from Eliot's "Ash-Wednesday" and the

reading we here give them suggest why Flannery O'Connor could be so cheerful about her own changing body. For where Gerontion is able to understand only decay, she understands a change, a transformation in the mystery of becoming. She was not arrested in her spiritual development as, say, Dylan Thomas seems to have been, if we may take "Fern Hill" for a moment into our present concern. Thomas, like Gerontion, is haunted by a memory of having once been "Golden in the heydays" of time's eyes, the goldenness now as sear and yellow as autumn. The attempt to recapture that lost Eden in his memory, through images revisited with a presumption of the will's power to restore the self as "prince of the apple towns," proves doomed. For, though creation is remembered as having been daily restored to its primal state in the innocent boy, who could awake to the world come back "all Shining" and "Adam and maiden," Thomas can no longer escape the chains of time's sea. He cannot finally move beyond history to reconcile memory and desire, any more than Gerontion has managed to do.

Thomas's poem is moving in its pathos, and we see how near he is to Gerontion's condition when he recognizes that he has followed time "out of grace" and cannot recover the moment. The failure, the source of pathos in the poem, is perhaps the attempt to erase interceding events in time past, to seize a youthful innocence by the violence of metaphor that denies the interval between. But the will may not, as we have said, erase times past from time, even through the instrument of poetry—any more than it can command grace.[5] The desire is profound, but one questions whether a sufficient restoration of right-mindedness allows Thomas's speaker (and one fears Thomas himself) to relive a past moment in a new becoming of the self. For the moments to be relived are not simply those moments of primal consciousness, themselves already in decay since even the child

> "*lordly* had the trees and leaves
> Trail with daises and barley
> Down the rivers of the windfall light."

5. I trust that my reader understands that my concern here is not with the relative aesthetic values of Thomas's "Fern Hill" and Eliot's poems, though one might consider whether the inclination which I find rather general among my brighter students to value "Fern Hill" over "Ash-Wednesday" may not be in part explained by Miss O'Connor's

Eliot celebrates a recovery out of an anxiety he has experienced very like Thomas's. In *Little Gidding* he proclaims the delivery through memory from history seen as either "servitude," Thomas's enslavement by the chains of time, or a "freedom" such as Heidegger supposes in the projection of *Dasein*. The use of memory, Eliot says, is

> For liberation—not less of love but expanding
> Of love beyond desire, and so liberation
> From the future as well as the past.

We have now to contrast Eliot's sense of anxiety, dramatically played out to a resolution in his late poetry, to the sense of anxiety met in Heidegger, the temptations to which are incipient in both "Gerontion" and "Fern Hill." Heidegger's disturbed anticipation in the consciousness, in the *Dasein* whose resolving object he declares to be death, is crucial to his whole vision. (The "trail" leads "down" all through Thomas's poem also, be it noted.) What we deny is that the object of anxiety is so simply identified as the obliteration of consciousness itself: *Dasein* perfected by its being dissolved in *nihilation*. For that approach to self-transcendence can be understood only as an erasing of the self from history, a condition of *l'âme close* as opposed to Eliot's *l'âme ouverte*, to borrow Voegelin's companion poles from the complex In-between. The anxiety that rises from our experience of contingency within the *metaxy*, the In-between, may be rather resolved than terminated when one understands the possibilities in memory as presented by St. Augustine.

If we put beside St. Augustine's understanding of memory's disturbing presence Heidegger's description of the source and end of anxiety (or "dread") we may see, even through the murkiness of the language, that what Heidegger aims toward is indeed a closure of the self, an absolute alienation, whose resolution must be oblivion. We understand then how he comes to the conclusion that death is the perfection of *Dasein*. In *Being and Time* he argues:

> What dread dreads for is being-in-the-world itself. In dread, the nearest
> handy things, and within-worldish beings as such, sink away. The

---

remark that "a prophet gone wrong is almost always more interesting than your grandmother," who has gone right, as it were. Joy seems bland compared to agony, especially to the young waking spirit. Childhood is attractive after it is lost. (And Dante's *Hell* seems far more "dramatic" than his *Heaven* to the Huck Finns, as we suggested in our first volume.)

"world" can offer nothing, any more than the existence of others [can offer anything]. Dread thus deprives man of the possibility of understanding himself from the "world" and from the explanations [of within-
worldish beings].

Such is the procedure of alienation through dread, until one
reaches that state of emptiness described as *ennui*. Thus "Dread in-
dividuates man into his ownmost being-in-the-world, which, as understanding, essentially throws itself forward into possibilities."
What is most curious about this conception of dread is that, in supposing it the first cause toward one's being, Heidegger implies that
one's early existence is really a pre-history, a "B.C." (Before self-
Creation) a state which, though it haunts one, must be exorcised.
That is, in relation to our interest in "Fern Hill" and "Gerontion"
(and in relation to many of the poems by Hölderlin which Heidegger uses to support his position), the moment of coming to be is not
that moment of Thomas's "windfall light" but the moment when
its loss is discovered in turning away. One *isn't* until he has reached
sallow youth. History is not to be revisited, even as in Thomas, but
expunged so that there is no "B.C." That is the necessary condition
described by *ennui*. Thus Heidegger creates, but only verbally, his
own *metaxy* for his *Dasein* to inhabit, the poles of which are the *Dasein* on the one hand and "his ownmost being-in-the-world" on the
other. But the latter is projected—"essentially throw[n] forward
into possibilities" by the *Dasein's* "understanding." The past is
obliterated, leaving only a future in the suspended, alienated world.
And the informing spirit of that self-made closed world, its "Holy
Spirit," continues to be dread.

What seems evident from our common country experience of
existence is that the withdrawal Heidegger counsels is only possible
through an action of the individual's will in purging consciousness
of all images of past experience, thereby presumably purging the
self of all "feelings" about existence separate from the impending
"ownmost being-in-the-world." What is first necessary is the death
of the memory, after which one consequence may be that *Being-itself*
can be declared withdrawn, not present. Such is Heidegger's refinement of Nietzsche's proposition of God's withdrawal from existence: Heidegger "purifies" consciousness of all traces of

memory, as if there might otherwise continue a threat of an intrusion of some force through the memory such as Augustine would call grace. (We have remarked Sartre's own struggle with this problem, his long battle with the lurking "Holy Ghost" that remains even after he has thrown "God" out of the cellar of his mind.) What we must insist is that the very action of withdrawal is already an operation upon what Heidegger chooses to call "being-in-the-world," an attempt to be "born grown" as a country phrase might put it. It is an initial denial of existence and of being itself, presumably in the interest of the *Dasein*. But the denial seems inescapably tinged by the diabolical.

Except as a desperate act of the will (and *deconstruction* is also a part of the contingency of our being), the experience of contingency in reality—in the *metaxy*—allows no such simple resolution of the tensional stress in consciousness as this withdrawal and emptying of the *Dasein* so that it may declare its own universe into existence, create its own *metaxy* suspended between the simplified poles of the *Dasein* and its "ownmost being-in-the-world." Within that world, whose spirit is dread, dread is denied its object. There is no such simple a resolution, even of the pseudo-tensional world, as the consummation of *Dasein* in *nihilation*, the self obliterated. Certainly such consummations rarely seem tolerable to the *Dasein* who is more than a creature of this web of words. Empedocles on Etna of course makes *an* ending, but that does not mean he makes *the* ending. ("We have not reached conclusion, when I/Stiffen in a rented house," Gerontion fears.) Heidegger's freedom appears at last quite limited, partial, though it may be mistaken as an absolute by a given human being. And one hears, faintly echoing within the *Dasein* our philosopher has projected, those discomforting words so emblematic of our world:

> The mind is its own place, and in itself
> Can make a heaven of hell, a hell of heaven.

Emblematic of our world, we say. The self-limiting state which Heidegger advances (and it is not so much that he influences our world as that he reflects it) is in the last analysis a description of that spiritual state which Voegelin sees as conspicuously modern. It is a state in which man finds himself "condemned to be free and urgently [wanting] to be arrested for editing a Maoist journal."

But we may conclude nevertheless that even in that desperate state, there is yet some hope, short of *Dasein's* leaping into Etna or plunging into the whirlpool of nothingness. (Neither Heidegger on his mountain nor Poe in his maëlstrom researches chooses the plunge of suicide.) As we may see from Gerontion's struggle with the problem, the very hunger for an arrest—a rest of the soul beyond history—suggests a capacity for a becoming which is at a tangent quite away from oblivion. We have seen Miss O'Connor dramatize this hunger, which is also a dread, in many of her characters: they violently pursue being even as they attempt to deny it by clearing an arena in being, creating a vacuum in existence which they would declare their own. Haze Motes in emptying himself also seeks his come-uppance by conjuring "Being" through blasphemy, for instance. And Young Tarwater seeks an end through his attempt to "do No," not simply say no. In those dramas, what each discovers is that a stronger, more violent calling of an answerable Yes pervades creation, though its terror of mercy is more devastating than Heidegger's angst or dread or anxiety. That mercy requires a death also, but a death more complexly taken than Heidegger's death. And when we test Heidegger's fiction and O'Connor's against our experience of our own existence, it is O'Connor's which corresponds more nearly to what we know of ourselves now and of our past.

It is possible that Poe's and Heidegger's dramas are less colloquys or monologues in the isolated self, the mirroring of the self in words, than the creators of those fictions seem to suppose. For the words are from one *Dasein* or *Monos* to others, not simply to an "ownmost being-in-the-world" or an *Una*. Each undermines the position he proposes by this very fact. But even if it were otherwise, even if there were such isolated halls of mirrors of the self as our fiction writers project, the shifting images within those isolated worlds are susceptable of disquieting turns, just as they are to Gerontion, just as the roses in the garden Eliot comes to at last prove disquieting to the beholding eye. For the self's image of itself may suddenly put on the look of an object that is looked at, become a focal point where an "unseen eyebeam" intrudes other than the staring self. Certainly possible, whatever the degree of the probable. If such should occur, it seems most probable that it would occur at a point "which is always present." And at that point the fugitive self may well hear, as Gerontion does without fully understanding what is happening to him,

> Footfalls echo in the memory
> Down the passage which we did not take
> Towards the door we never opened
> Into the rose-garden.

That rose-garden is surely only a turn of the will away, a turn into a new fullness of the In-between.

CHAPTER XIX

THE SHROUDED "I"
AND DECAPITATION OF BEING

Such a colloquy between mirror images of the poet named *one alone* is quite foreign to anything we find in Flannery O'Connor. For her, concerned as she is with "the entrance of love into the world through the medium of human character despite its natural distortions," it is necessary to maintain "the mystery of the person as against any kind of determinism," but particularly such self-determinism. And she cites Fr. D'Arcy's *The Meeting of Love and Knowledge*, a Thomist argument distinguishing Christianity's commitment to fulfilling "individuality and desire." She quotes from D'Arcy a passage which casts light on her use of "person" and "personality" in her essays: "Without persons and personality there is no Christian religion, and its philosophy centers around this thought. . . ." The difference between her and Poe on this point leads to the paradox of their technique: Poe is able to write best from a first-person point of view, whatever he names his agent; Miss O'Connor does not use that device at all. And even in her first-person essays she usually talks of herself by speaking of the "poet," or the "Southern writer" or the "Catholic writer in the South."

Monos' or Poe's argument makes of him what Eric Voegelin calls a "parousiastic gnostic." The interpretation of *parousia* (presence) as *being* by Heidegger leads Voegelin to describe "parousiasm as the mentality that expects deliverance from the evils of time through the advent, the coming in all its fullness, of being construed as immanent." If we relate that address to being to

Why Poe Drank Liquor

the gnostic positions out of the Middle Ages and Renaissance, says Voegelin, we discover "The long history of post-classical Western gnosticism . . . in its continuity as the history of Western sectarianism." Voegelin's point is one complemented by Brice Parain's comparison (in *A Metaphysics of Language*) of the Age of Immanence to the Age of Transcendence which preceded it. Both arguments reflect upon our earlier discussion in Volume I of the effect of the separation of faith and reason in that intellectual war at the University of Paris in the late thirteenth century, after which nominalism gains ascendency. Such are the grounds that prepare the rise of "ersatz religions," says Voegelin, which prepare for the so-called "death of God," the idea central to Heidegger's thought, but to Poe's as well. It is an idea very important in its antagonist role in the fiction of Flannery O'Connor.[1] Just how a way was made, says Voegelin, is as follows:

> The aim of parousiastic gnosticism is to destroy the order of being, which is experienced as defective and unjust, and through man's creative power to replace it with a perfect and just order. . . . In order . . . that the attempt to create a new world may seem to make sense, the givenness of the order of being must be obliterated; the order of being must be interpreted, rather, as essentially under man's control. And taking control of being further requires that the transcendent origin of being be obliterated: it requires the decapitation of being—the murder of God.

If this is the case, then it matters little whether the assumption of man's control of being is exhibited in Utopian attempts upon society as in Condorcet or Comte, or through the utopian attempt

---

1. Miss O'Connor's extensive interest in this background is apparent from those reviews of theological and philosophical books she did for *The Bulletin*, the Georgia diocesan weekly. Thus, in remarking Gilson's attack on nominalism in *The Unity of Philosophical Experience*, she calls the book "indispensable to an understanding of the modern age." She is reviewing *Reason c d Revelation in the Middle Ages*, which properly prepares one to read the other Gilson book. Voegelin's treatment of the Sophists in *Plato and Aristotle* reveals Socrates' arguments as still classic ones against "that sophistic philosophy of existence which characterizes positivism and the age of enlightenment." Bouyer's *The Spirit and Forms of Protestantism* shows the negative principles of Protestantism (as opposed to the positive ones of Luther, Calvin, and John Wesley, of which both she and Fr. Bouyer approve) as spawned by "the decadent scholasticism of the 15th century." In reviewing the *Writings of Edith Stein*, she suggests that the reader will be interested in the philosophical essays included if he has "a background in the phenomenological approach to existence of Edmund Husserl," and Denis de Rougemont (who understands the Protestant mind better than the Catholic, she says) is very helpful on Nietzsche and the "God is dead" argument. Indeed, her reading in the intellectual and literary heritage of the West is impressive in its range, and she incorporates it quietly and inconspicuously in her art.

of the imagination to make its own private world as with Poe. Poe and Heidegger are cousins to Condorcet and Bentham and Comte, though they react sharply against the empirical or utilitarian gnostic. In Sartre the family is brought closer together again. For the gnostic political or economic activist and the gnostic poet have the same initial goal—the "decapitation of being." That murder accomplished, imagination is then freed to supply order and trumpet its own sense of being through that order. Such, we must observe, is the role envisaged by Poe for the imagination. And as John Casey remarks of Sartre as well, the "imagination is not a contingent and super-added power of consciousness; it is the whole of consciousness as it realises its freedom." But in the illusion of absolute freedom of the consciousness lies the sense also of an absolute alienation, the end to which sectarianism tends (at its logical extremity, the myriad sects of *one alone*).

"Science," says Heidegger in *Existence and Being*, "has to assert its soberness and seriousness afresh and declare that it is concerned solely with what-is. . . . science wishes to know nothing of Nothing." Voegelin also attacks science's conception of "what-is" but on different grounds: as developed out of Bacon and turned to positivist uses, the result of which is that "The transcendental pneuma of Christ is replaced by the intramundane spirit of man, and the change of heart by the change of opinion." That change of opinion affects being by its temptation to a ravagement of the world's body in pragmatic exploitations. On the other hand, "a change of heart" may lead to the intellect's operation upon being so that the whole of existence comes into focus as an estranged, closed monad desperately emptying itself, the direction in Heidegger. Either position is the same in its killing effect upon the spirit—the soul—of the manipulator of being. From Voegelin's point of view, Heidegger's attack upon "science" is an instance of the pot calling the kettle black.

" 'What-is in totality,' " says Roberts in explaining that term from Heidegger, "is like a bottomless sea into which all distinctions vanish. . . . there is 'nothing' to hold onto." The metaphor he elects to describe the process of emptying the world and the self to conjure "Being-itself" is suggestive of Poe's own metaphor employed dramatically to project nonexistence at the conclusion of his *Narrative of A. Gordon Pym.* We recall that Pym, having reached a point where all passion for survival in an empirical world has been spent at the extremity of reason, encounters a revelation of Nothingness.[4] He has moved to the very edge of "What-is." Pym's own account, as managed by Poe, ends at a time and place: March 22, the furthest reaches of the South Pole. It is the beginning of a new "year" beyond those marked by local cosmologies of solstice or the precision of longitude and latitude. Darkness at that point is "materially increased." The air is full of "gigantic and pallidly white birds" which fly out of the veil ahead of the drifting boat as if one were approaching the central void out of which there is a continuous creation. The boat breaks through that veil, and "now we rushed into the embraces of the cataract, where a chasm threw itself open to receive us. But there arose in our pathway a shrouded human figure, very far larger in its proportions than any dweller among men. And the hue of the skin of the figure was of the perfect whiteness of snow." Thus far Pym's account, which suddenly breaks off with these last words. The "editor" adds a note saying that Mr. Poe, the intermediary mentioned in the narrative's preface, has declined "to fill the vacuum" left by the interrupted narrative. Pym is mysteriously dead, but a second man on the expedition, Peters, is still alive, "a resident of Illinois." Perhaps "the governmental expedition" about to set out for the pole will be able to confirm or deny details of the report with its collection of empirical evidence.

Meanwhile, the "editor" presumes to decipher those fragmented characters reported by Pym from the island of Tsalal, seeing in them an "Ethiopian verbal root." As deciphered, they are from "to be shady" and "to be white," which combined are taken to express "The region of the south." What they really try to say is

---

2. Pym, unlike Haze Motes, is by design forced to engage the world through handicapped senses, his hope made to rest in reason. His food is rotten, a challenge to overcome; the surface of a piece of paper must be felt as he searches for words without a light; sounds are submitted to the reason for explanation. But it may be a question whether Pym is more closely enchained by circumstances in the dark bosom of the whaling ship than Haze in Taulkinham through his own angry will. The difference is that Pym is put in a situation, while Haze appears at least to have put himself in a similar situation. The concern of each writer differs, because each reads man in the world differently.

that same message we read in Poe's prose poems "Shadow" and "Silence"—the ultimate reality of Nothingness. Poe's mystical vision reached by a journey, one might say with a shifting of cosmology, is at a pole opposite Dante's after his long journey called the *Divine Comedy*, a journey which ends with a vision of the Rose of Paradise rather than of cataracts, chasms, and the shrouded human figure so white that its lines against the white world hardly allow the eye to discern them except in the estimate that the figure is "very far larger in its proportions than any dweller among men." The vision of Nothingness it would seem proves more challenging to the poet's art than the vision of Perfect Being.

Poe does not, as suggested earlier, make Heidegger's distinction between *annihilation* and *nihilation* in *Eureka*. One suspects him incapable of doing so, for that distinction is one possible only to a more passive "resolve" toward an empty state of being, from which the "I" is removed, than Poe can manage. Though we have seen him working toward such a removal in his "Colloquy," we remember from the general body of his work a tenacious clinging to the "I." It is as if he cannot submit to such a dark night of the soul as Heidegger requires. Still, one cannot escape in Poe any more than in Heidegger a homesickness for Nothingness. In Death, says Una, "we have . . . learned the propensity of man to define the indefinable." It is a homesickness of which one has a vague idea through "the mystic parable that tells of the tree of knowledge, and of its forbidden fruit," a warning against the dangers of such knowledge as is relentlessly pursued by "the mathematical reason of the schools." Knowledge may yet be possible under the autocracy of Place and Time, but only through that "sentiment of the natural" such as Poe quotes Pascal as supporting, in which "all our reasoning reduces itself to a yielding to sentiment." What one has in such sentiment as Poe understands it is a movement of consciousness in that direction which Husserl will attempt to define more rigorously. In "the sentiment of nature" lies the possibility of regaining, in the present world, as Poe's "Colloquy" puts it, that state of man of "ancient days when our wants were not more simple than our enjoyments were keen—days when *mirth* was a word unknown, so solemnly deep-toned was happiness—holy, august and blissful days when blue rivers ran undammed between hills unhewn, into far forest solitudes, primaeval, odorous, and unexplored." Monos' version of the "mystical parable" is that it expresses a homesickness for a state of being in nature, un-self-conscious, such as Wordsworth is pursuing in "Tintern Abbey." But it is also that state which, not long after Poe's words, Edmund Husserl is to pursue in his phenomenological arguments. Husserl's ground is in the "Original Intuition," his cry is "back to the things themselves," by which he means a return to the immediate data of consciousness whose formula, in order to prove itself the ground of departure, might be put: "I experience therefore there is the 'bodily presence' of what I experience." But Heidegger, Husserl's student, pushes away from that attempt to recapture an Edenesque state of un-self-consciousness in nature, toward an encounter with Nothingness, and we discover in Poe that Monos also must give over that lesser longing for a return to the first birth in order that he may be "born again" into the mystery of Nothingness. The recovery for Heidegger and Poe is not of something lost and found again as Husserl assumes; it is a discovery of a destiny which the action of seeking calls into a present. Only when the indefinite quest has emptied the self and the world does the object appear, dispelling the anxiety of that modern malady Pascal calls the "quest for the quest."

One supposes Pascal's yielding of reasoning to sentiment to be a first step necessary in that journey toward the "true-self's" coincidence in Nothingness, but that is a direction Pascal would reject forthwith, though as a reader of the *Pensées* knows, he was familiar with such terrors. We have spoken already of a similar homesickness for Nothingness in Miss O'Connor's Rayber, an inclination which she, like Pascal, recognizes as a diabolic temptation. As she knows something of the mind of Pascal, Kierkegaard, Husserl, and Poe, so too she knows Heidegger's. She underlines that passage at the end of *Existence and Being* which we cited, in which Heidegger rebukes the hesitancy of the rationalistic mind to confront Nothingness:

> Science . . . has to assert its soberness and seriousness afresh and declare that it is concerned solely with what-is. Nothing—how can it be for

science anything other than a horror and a phantasm? If science is right then one thing stands firm: science wishes to know nothing of Nothing. Such is after all the strictly scientific approach to Nothing. We know it by wishing to know nothing of Nothing.

This rebuke is not far removed from Tarwater's rebuke of Rayber, who hovers tempted out of his empiricist, determinist comfort in the world, but unable to act out the logical extension of its implication. "I can do NO," says Tarwater. Rayber can only say No. It is Tarwater who drowns Bishop, forthwith, good Baconian that he is in this matter.

Miss O'Connor stands opposed to the rationalist mind as does Voegelin, on the ground that it reduces the fullness of being; she sees a reality in Nothingness, but it is to her the reality of Evil, as it is to Voegelin. Heidegger says his is an approach to mystery, but as Miss O'Connor says explicitly, Evil too is one of the mysteries we contend with, being "not simply a problem to be solved, but a mystery to be endured." One is not required to seek out and embrace that particular mystery. She and Pascal stand firmly on the point, though one may not deny the existence of evil as an escape of evil. The dragon is by the side of the road, she reminds us in an epigraph from St. Cyril which she adds to the paperback edition of *A Good Man Is Hard to Find*. "We go to the Father of Souls, but it is necessary to pass by the Dragon."

For our purpose of distinction between Flannery O'Connor and Poe on this point, we may make a final comment through Heidegger's more carefully constructed metaphysics which contains the position incipient in Poe. In building his ontology, Heidegger is in reaction to both classical and Christian metaphysics—the classical position holding that nothing comes of nothing (*ex nihilo nihil fit*), while the Christian position is that God creates out of nothing. Heidegger, asserting "Being-itself" as the ultimate, asserts as well that it is conjoined with Nothingness. But, in Roberts's emphatic words, Heidegger concludes that "*Being-itself is finite in essence.*" "And because man (Dasein [being-there]) can transcend itself as projected into Nothing, he can see the essential finitude of Being." In Poe's terms, man becomes the "earth-angel," he who appears to be a madman in the world's eyes—such an earth-angel as he dramatizes in Monos. "Against the Christian doctrine of *creatio ex nihilo*," says Roberts, "Heidegger declares that every being, in so far as it is a being, is made out of nothing (*ex nihilo omne ens qua ens fit*)." Even though Heidegger holds that "Being-itself" and "nothingness" are conjoined, the "true-self" has risen beyond "Being-itself," which makes possible its realization that "Being-itself" is finite. In other words, it is from the Nothingness side of the conjunction that Heidegger's own "earth-angel," the "true-self," looks upon "Being-itself." That is the position from which Poe has Monos and Una speak directly. It is the same position Poe plays with satirically in "Mellonta Tauta," his dramatization of "things that belong to the future," in which the narrator makes commentary on mid-nineteenth century intellectual life from his advantage of speaking a hundred years later. Though he admits to being "almost devoured by *ennui*," he finds some amusement in the quaintness of the 1840s. But he realizes that even in those benighted days "many of the long established axioms had been rejected. For example—'Ex nihilo nihil fit.' " From the same position Monos comments more seriously on those concerns which are now unimportant from the perspective of himself as the new man. They become unimportant when we realize that (as Roberts says in concluding his survey of Heidegger's thought) "The things and concerns which seem so . . . and which seem to give significance to our lives, come from nothing and return to nothing." Or, as Poe expresses it in his fundamental principle of *Eureka: "In the Original Unity of the First Thing, lies the Secondary Cause of All Things, with the Germ of their Inevitable Annihilation."*

Flannery O'Connor recognizes those principles as dominant in atheistic existentialism, but she realizes as well that they are far more pervasive of the popular spirit of the age than that spirit itself realizes. She dramatizes the consequences of those ideas upon the community of man, the ideas being part of the "unreasonable" that she means when she says that as fiction writer she is committed to "the reasonable use of the unreasonable." Julian, in "Everything that Rises Must Converge," is sentimentally attached to the safety of a bubble of intellectual abstraction, which proves insufficient protection from the world. Julian, Asbury, Rayber, Hulga among others find that their simplified pre-answers are inadequate to existential circumstances when they are forced out of themselves to confront ultimate questions at the personal, immediate, local level—when they are forced to the experience of the In-between. But what may be most humiliating and irritating of all about Miss O'Connor's fictional revelations is that she weaves these sophisticated intellectual currents intricately into the sordid and banal commonplaces of a supposedly backwoods region, the South. That petty con man who makes off with Hulga's wooden leg is sardonically devastating when Hulga expresses outrage at the contents of his hollow Bible and his spiritual hollowness. He says the most stunning thing of all at this point, shaking forever her image of "good country people": "you ain't so smart. I been believing in nothing ever since I was born." He hasn't had to attend the Sorbonne to learn that possibility, and that is an almost unforgivable argument in our author.

CHAPTER XX

POE'S EMPTY BOTTLE

In his work Poe's details are not so precise in their empirical register as those of Alexander von Humboldt, nor so imagistically concrete as Flannery O'Connor's, a matter of deliberate technical strategy in Poe. How seldom we see the object he presents us. Where factual description seems at issue in his text, one has an impression that there is no concern for the particular but only for species. Except for the tone that sustains the presentation, with some modulation of volume, it is sometimes as if one were encountering descriptions of farm implements in an old Sears, Roebuck catalogue—precise words under shaded woodcuts, leaving the farmer's experience of the In-between to make the object substantial to his practical eye, those harrows "made with seasoned oak frames, riveted at each tooth and strongly braced." Such are the characteristics of much of the imagistic detail provided by A. Gordon Pym in his account of his experiences aboard the whaling ship, from the beginning of his strange voyage nearly to the end. Poe's preferred handling of detail, however, we find in one of his better, tighter tales —"William Wilson"—where detail exists sparely and its empirical referent is asserted rather than presented to our senses through images. There is here little of the line-drawing upon which we may lean our subjective feelings about the things of the senses.

Nevertheless, as the story gets under way, the narrator promises his reader a "minute recollection" through explicit details of his own past experiences in the world. What we are actually given are such phrases as "extensive grounds," "Neighboring fields," a "high and solid brick wall," a wig "minutely powdered," robes that are "glossy" and "clerically flowing." Now this early promise of a minute recollection acknowledges a technical necessity to the drama which our narrator apparently recognizes but which our writer studiously avoids providing. What is missing in consequence is an initial sense of the particularity of the narrator himself—and this in a story whose climax depends upon a surprise whereby the external world as it touches upon consciousness is to prove illusional and consciousness itself thereby called in question. Poe, in other words, is dealing with that madness which repeatedly draws his imaginative interest, a madness whose effect depends upon spectacle, since the effect of disorientation depends upon orientation. And spectacle, alas, depends upon some common ground with the reader's senses. Before the grotesque mask can signify, one must be familiar with faces. Aside from the philosophical dilemma in Poe, the aesthetic one is formidable in its own right. Or rather say, because of the philosophical dilemma, the aesthetic is well-nigh insurmountable. For the message in Poe's bottle is that the bottle is empty. If that be so, what then of the bottle itself?

In order to surprise one with a fiction about emptiness, the vessel must be enticing, must promise at least its own substantiality. It seems then that for the dramatic effect, Poe's tale must show initially a world of objects and events as they impinge upon a consciousness in whom we rest some confidence. But the narrator names himself William Wilson in order to deny us the substantiality of his real person, a person notorious under another name the world over, he assures us. The narrator's coyness about his own credibility, about his particularity, multiplies the burden upon our belief in the minutia of the story's texture, since that texture is out of the narrator. We are nevertheless expected by Poe to give consent to the existence of a substantial, even historical world, inhabited by Wilson. From the beginning our narrator is to develop a narrative sequence whose key is the image, ultimately the image of the narrator himself as he becomes emptied of all substantiality.

He becomes a suffering malignity—a negation of being. The movement one expects as the tale unfolds, particularly since it is the promise the narrator makes, is one from a "minute" and precise recollection anchored in a world which in some wise is common to reader and narrator, to its culmination in a mirror image of a mirror image. The mirror image of our narrator—his double—is the image upon which the story comes to focus in an acceleration toward what the narrator at one point calls his total collapse as a "victim to the horror and the mystery of the wildest of all sublunary visions."

We ought to notice a vocabulary in this phrase which is very deliberately supplied by Poe, particularly so since we are to look at his imagistic strategy in comparison to Flannery O'Connor's. For, as we might demonstrate amply from the body of Poe's work, his use of a word like *mystery* or *vision* rather certainly has to do with a puzzle proposed, but a puzzle which refuses to yield to the rational intellect. But *sublunary* suggests a limiting of the region of our concern from any transcendent implications, Poe being particularly wary of any suggestion of outer mystery. He is suspicious in large part because of the intellectual vogue of New England Transcendentalism, a movement commanding an audience and the means of publication Poe felt denied to him. Poe is interested in detail—in fact—but in facts as details; that is, as counters at the disposal of reason. His is not *fact* as in Emerson's mystical use of the term: "an Epiphany of God." His opposition to Emersonian flirtations with outer mystery leads him on one occasion to ridicule the Transcendentalist's distortion of detail in the interest of the transcendent. One should proceed, Poe mockingly advises, by indirection.

> Above all, study innuendo. Hint everything—assert nothing. If you feel inclined to say "bread and butter," do not by any means say it outright. You may say any and every thing *approaching* to "bread and butter." You may hint at buckwheat cake, or you may even go so far as to insinuate oatmeal porridge, but if bread and butter be your real meaning, be cautious, my *dear* Miss Psyche, not on any account to say "bread and butter."

It is as if Poe cannot see that *buckwheat cake* or *cornbread* is a more direct and particular image than *bread* and anchors the idea of bread in its tendency to abstraction. The tendency he attacks is the very one to which he is himself extremely vulnerable.

The narrator of "William Wilson," we note with our own irony directed at Poe's abstractionism, comes to give us a minutely particular description of the English boarding school at which he spent five years of his life and of which he has—he tells us— something like total recall in matters of particularity. But he describes the remembered school building for us in such terms as a "house . . . old and irregular." The "psyche" of which we are to be convinced by Poe's story proceeds by such an indirection that the story becomes vaporous before it is well under way. Let us observe nevertheless that the story struggles throughout with the necessity of particularity. Though he does not give a precisely concrete image of himself from which we may proceed, the narrator attempts to convince us of an antagonist who is a precise duplication of himself in every naturalistic detail. His double bears his own name, a circumstance "doubly" disgusting. He has the same features and mannerisms and even the same birthday, which is incidentally Poe's own. This uncanny duplication, strange to tell, completely escapes the notice of the rout of boys at the school, though the only distinction our acutely perceptive narrator can make between himself and his "arch-enemy and evil genius" is that the double can speak only above a "very low whisper," a characteristic which returns to the narrative repeatedly in an italicized form. It is not of course that we would deny our narrator an illusion which he mistakes as a reality objectively present in the outer world. The point is that we require some firm anchoring of the strange events, otherwise the strangeness itself escapes. The narrator, we reflect, is rational, even if madly rational. He has a sufficient intelligence to have found it worth discussing with his lively companions that they have not in five years noticed similarities between their two classmates, William Wilson and William Wilson. Or is the existence of all the narrator's companions in the story to be taken as an illusion?

The "evil genius" of the story, the narrator's rival, is inescapably associated with a traditional conception of man's conscience. His "insinuated counsel" is always a "moral" one; his repeated role in the action is very much that of Socrates' own familiar spirit. For Wilson's double is intent on preventing some "bitter mischief" Wilson himself is bent upon. His intrusion insultingly denies our narrator his "natural rights of self-agency." Poe's clever device in the story is to turn traditional though fading concepts of good and evil upside down and thus elicit an initial sympathy for his evil narrator. Indeed, Wilson is a creature one is tempted to compare at length to Miss O'Connor's own Misfit, though a brief suggestion of the parallel must suffice. William Wilson was from childhood, he assures us, "distinguished" by an "evil propensity." As the Misfit's father might remark of him, he was "a different breed of dog" from those around him. As the story opens, we learn from Wilson that, following the climactic conclusion of the tale he is about to tell us, he has become notorious, an outcast who is "to the earth . . . forever dead." He is the victim of a possession so total that he lives perpetually in "unspeakable misery, and unpardonable crime." The only extenuation he begs is that the reader grant some degree of "*fatality*" "amid a wilderness of [his own] error." The dark Greek sense of fate is thus summoned to stand as explanation of the evil that possesses him. But the fate is vaporously vague, while good is malignantly active so far as the narrator reads it for us.

Given our present concern for his use of detail, we must resist the temptation to pursue Poe's ideas here, though we may not avoid them entirely. The epigraph itself entices us to idea, the words very likely Poe's own invention though he attributes them to "*Chamberlayne's 'Pharronida.'*" The epigraph asks:

> What say of it? what say [of] CONSCIENCE grim,
> That spectre in my path?

The story suggests that the hated rival is the conscience, externalized by a divided mind; that second haunting presence is grimly opposed to the protagonist's exercise of his "natural rights of self-agency." This phrase, too, is a complication of that hint of Greek fatalism as a justification of evil, the most interesting complication of idea in the story. If we were to pursue the matter, we should have to consider why our narrator speaks of his infamous history as having left him in a state of "unpardonable crime" rather than of unpardonable sin.

But with the hint of a parallel in Miss O'Connor which is suggested by Poe's epigraph, let us rather turn to one of her protagonists who also encounters "conscience" standing in the path of his own pursuit of self-agency, a pursuit Miss O'Connor unhesitatingly associates with sin. Her figure of conscience stands in a highly visible form before the reader no less than before her protagonist. Haze Motes on a crucial dark evening is confronted by a mirror image named Silas Layfield. Silas seems identical to Haze, being dressed in the same clothes and hat, standing on the hood of a car preaching, as Haze is doing—indeed mouthing Haze's very words. Silas, like Asa Hawks, "ain't true," but he is terrifying to Haze. In the scene that contains their encounter, Haze says with grim determination as he looks at Silas, "You've got to hunt it down and kill it." If we look for the antecedent of Haze's *it*, we discover it to be *conscience*, though the rabble gathered on the dark street of Taulkinham do not catch the reference. Haze has just been insisting with angry desperation that the conscience does not exist, that "your conscience is a trick." His listeners, unlike William Wilson's acquaintances, do, however, understand the external comedy of the scene. A "fat woman" asks Haze with a grin, "Him and you twins?" She concludes that Haze is "nuts," since she "never seen no twins that hunted each other down." Haze does follow the hapless Silas and murders him on a country road, in a scene itself rich in imagistic detail. Out of this scene there emerges a comedy of confessional dialogue so widely dissociated from the literal action—especially dissociated in Haze's mind—that the murder is highly comic, a matter of confusion to some of Miss O'Connor's readers, since thus she seems to take murder lightly.

When we turn to a similar scene in Poe's story, the contrast is very marked. For five years William Wilson has been plagued by William Wilson, the circumstance that has passed unnoticed by his associates. Then one night the narrator goes with a lamp into his rival's room where his "evil genius" lies sleeping. There ensues an encounter of wild proportion, but during which the rival continues sleeping undisturbed. The narrator makes a discovery so horrifying that he leaves the school in the dead of that very night, "never to return." He recalls his moment of vision for us to make the horror vivid:

> I looked; and a numbness, an iciness of feeling instantly pervaded my frame. My breast heaved, my knees tottered, my whole spirit became possessed with an objectless yet intolerable horror. Gasping for breath, I lowered the lamp in still nearer proximity to the face. Were these—*these* the lineaments of William Wilson? . . . Was it, in truth, within the bounds of human possibility, that *what I now saw* was the result, merely, of the habitual practice of this sarcastic imitation? Awestricken, and with a creeping shudder, I extinguished the lamp. . . .

The excited language here attempts to convince a reader of a profound revelation. The clause *what I now saw* is given in italics, but we are allowed to see nothing specific for ourselves. The effect is loud in the context of the story, but not dramatically persuasive. Certainly it is not so persuasive as a similar scene in *Wise Blood*. There Haze creeps into a rival's bedroom, strikes a match, and leans over that false prophet Asa Hawks. Haze too is awe-stricken, but by discovering what he has suspected all along: Asa Hawks stares back at him out of eyes that have only pretended to be blind. And at this close proximity, Haze must see as well a reflection of his own face in Asa's eyes. Miss O'Connor's scene is very quiet. It is also imagistically available to us, both in its immediate images and because she has so carefully prepared for this scene through that enlarging metaphysical conceit of *eyes* and *seeing* which holds her novel together. Her metaphor is scrupulously anchored in the natural world as well. Similarly, in the scene with Haze and Silas on the streets of Taulkinham, she has made the suits, hats, automobiles convincingly real before Haze encounters the mirror image of himself. Even Silas's repetition of Haze's words has been abundantly prepared for, Haze's arguments having been turned inside out by the argument and action that comes before. The futile emptiness of those words now strikes Haze what promises to be an immortal blow, though it seems to his immediate senses, particularly to his eye, that it is a duplication of himself in nature that accuses him.

Poe might object that Miss O'Connor has allowed herself a more considerable canvas upon which to paint the illusion of a substantial world, neglecting thereby the single emotional effect that Poe sets as the highest end of his fiction. But the problem I find in Poe's imagistic technique, by contrast to Miss O'Connor's, is not simply that in the one we are given a very tightly constructed short story and in the other what appears to be a loose novel. As we have been saying, Poe's narrator attempts to convince one of his antagonist as an objective duplication of himself; at the same time there is the dramatic necessity of only gradually revealing the duplication. The baffling horror descends upon the narrator as his double is revealed over a considerable span of years. The story ranges widely in its pretense of place as well—from the boarding school to Eton to Oxford to the continent, and even so far afield as Moscow. But Poe's economy here proves false. The traditional unities of time, place, and action—followed much more closely in *Wise Blood* than in Poe's tale—have substituted for them a unity of voice. That voice allows only a steady dropping of bare nouns or excited adjectives and adverbs whose force too often depends upon their being italicized. The words carry no sensual referents that might convince one of a modulated *duration* (in Aristotle's sense of the term). As much as he might wish to proceed without commitment to a substantial world, Poe must start with images that echo such a world if he acknowledge any reader at all. For the world of time and place alone give the necessary anchor a reader must have for an imaginative sense of an action rising to a climax. Even the experience of music does not escape the necessary bounding by time and place. Concerning Aristotle's argument on dramatic unity, we might observe that they must apply in some degree not only to drama but to the individual scenes or episodes which form the sequence of small dramas in a narrative—if there is to result that necessary sense of duration that encourages one's "willing suspension of disbelief."

If Poe assumes a listener, then, he must speak of some world common to his listener, though he himself believe the world of nature—our common source of image—an illusional one. One might better say *particularly* if he believe that world an illusion, assuming he is concerned with producing an emotional effect upon an innocent listener. In this light we observe that the dramatic movement which Poe's story assumes is a reversal: a movement from a presumption about the reality of that world separate from consciousness to the reality of Poe's own vision. That is, the movement is from an apparent concrete objective world available to the senses and through them touching upon consciousness, to an emptied subjective world in which any objective naming is futile because ambiguous at best—whether the naming be the apparent blood stains on a murdered idea at the tale's conclusion or the repetition of the empty name of William Wilson. A reader, one might suppose, must be better prepared by his narrator for the weird surprise of objects, initially accepted as certified by the narrator's senses, rapidly dissolving all those distinctions which images ordinarily provide for our rational or emotional responses. The apparent strategy Poe chooses is that the images progressively prove empty and illusional by the very duplication of image and the repetition of phrases and words. At the climax of the story, which is also its resolution, the world of objects and consciousness itself dissipates, losing even the faint effect of the line-drawing. The intent is to leave the listener touched with horror by an alien madness— by a voice out of an empty bottle. But to make the emptying of image the dramatic action of the story requires that the image first be acceptable at the imagistic level. It must, again, speak more closely to one's senses at the outset. We must be convinced of the existence of the bottle before our thirst may be disappointed by its emptiness.

CHAPTER XXI

OF HATS AND CLOAKS
AND POCKETBOOKS

In Poe's "William Wilson" the narrator, at a point where he has yet another unsettling encounter with his mysterious "double," has his whole attention suddenly

> arrested by a fact of the most startling character. The cloak which I had worn [to a gathering] was of a rare description of fur; how rare, how extravagantly costly, I shall not venture to say. . . . When, therefore, Mr. Preston reached me that which he had picked up upon the floor, and near the folding doors of the apartment, it was with an astonishment nearly bordering upon terror, that I perceived my own already hanging on my arm, . . . and that the one presented to me was but its exact counterpart in every, in even the minutest possible particular.

We are at a point in the narrative at which the reader no less than the narrator is to be shocked almost to terror by an inexplicable encounter, and the persuasiveness of that encounter would seem to depend heavily upon this duplication of coats "in even the minutest possible particular." To the degree that one is moved, however, it is by the tone of the speaking voice and not by the immediacy of any imagistic detail. Poe as artist depends but slightly upon any detail concretely summoned by words to an immediate presence in the narrator's memory. Still, there is a constant insistence upon the vividness of those details as revisited, upon a revival of the original emotional burden of an old event or situation through remembered particularity. The narrator of "William Wilson" has promised us from the beginning a "minute recollection."

It is tone, we discover, which must bear and transmit an

emotional effect to the reader. But under the authority of tone, whose medium is a vague imagistic report of "costly" cloaks of "rare description," a reader is at last persuaded only of an amorphous, disturbed consciousness. Put more baldly, characters in Poe do not develop or change in relation to situation or event; they but continue the hollow mediums for Poe's ideas of emptiness, ideas whose horror must be certified to the reader by the excited voice of the purported witness to emptiness. It begins to appear that Poe's first-person point of view is a necessity out of the artist's dependence upon tone to arouse emotional response in the reader. Emotional effect is determined by the level and pitch of sound and not by any symbolic burden of sound, in which respect Poe's tales are closely akin to his poems. Hence, also, the importance of typographical devices, most particularly his use of italics at key points in the tales; even his "humorous" pieces find the locus of humor in typography, as in his famous "X-ing a Paragrab."

In Flannery O'Connor's fiction, on the other hand, imagistic details are of crucial importance as they reveal the presence of a world external to the character, a world which Poe is at pains always to deny in his ambitious tales. The concrete world inhabited by Miss O'Connor's characters reveals itself to the reader no less than to her character, so that the character is dramatized by his response to that world. For she intends her character to signify beyond the more simple end of stirring a reader to a fleeting emotional horror. It is through images bearing an immediacy to the reader because they are anchored in the real world of the senses that she dissolves the spiritual tensions built in her character. That double presence of the world—to the character and to the reader—is present through a skillfully manipulated point of view, so that a range of emotional responses is played, from ironic comedy to poignant terror. There is a most careful attention paid to minor objects and to peripheral characters, the effect of which is to give her fictional world a substantial weight in our imaginations.

She remembers that very early she read "a volume of 'The Humorous Stories of Edgar Allan Poe,'" and adds, "I think that started me thinking of a writing career." But she adds at once, "I'm sure Gogol influenced me." It is evident that the comic eye of

Gogol, with its hunger for imagistic detail, teaches her more than the distortions of consciousness in Poe. In *Dead Souls*, for instance, one recognizes immediate affinities between her fiction and Gogol's. Chichikov, Gogol's comic Mr. Shiftlet who speculates in dead peasant souls, encounters his own Mrs. Lucynell Crater in the widow Nastasia Petrivna. The widow's attitude toward her possessions, including even her property rights in dead peasants, reminds one of Miss O'Connor's small property holders. Later Chichikov encounters a once-grand landholder named Plushkin, whom he mistakes for a peasant woman because of dirty, torn clothing. Plushkin, a miser whose own soul is near extinction, is revealed in his spiritual poverty through the squalor of his person and his surroundings. The dramatic point of the episode is reached when his dying spirit flickers for a moment at the faint recollection of a last friend in the world: "He's an old friend of mine. Of course! We used to eat out of the same trough." The folk cliché, so constant a device in Miss O'Connor, is spoken amid Plushkin's refuse of life. There is a heap of rubbish scavanged from the countryside and thrown in one corner of his dark room, out of which protrudes a broken shovel and an old bootsole. On a dusty bureau lie scraps of paper, a lemon dried to the size of a walnut, a wine-glass with three dead flies, quills with ink dried in blobs "consumptively" on them. Plushkin's words are poignant, depressing, and they are so because the world in which they are spoken reveals so concretely his spiritual waste. The effect achieved is largely through the telling images that make the fiction's world uncomfortably palpable as it reveals the character's spiritual state. There is more of the terror of Dante's Hell here than of the psychological horror in Poe's tales.[1]

---

1. Miss O'Connor shares with Gogol a playfulness with character names and with metaphor that goes deeper than mere playfulness. For instance, Chichikov's troika, which bears him through all his shady adventures, becomes at the very end a symbol through which to address Mother Russia. "Who conceived thee? Methinks 'tis only among a spirited folk that thou couldst have come into being," whereupon there is an elaborate and at the same time concrete enlargement upon the vehicle as it rises from the earth. "Whither art thou soaring away to . . . Russia?" Haze Motes's Essex and Chichikov's troika bear interesting parallels, though Miss O'Connor is more indirect, less explicit—as she is more careful to avoid author intrusion. The author's intrusion becomes a deliberate and delightful device in Gogol's *Dead Souls*, and several of the brief essays compare interestingly to what Miss O'Connor says in essays such as "The Fiction Writer and His Country," "Some Aspects of the Grotesque in Southern Fiction," and other pieces in *Mystery and Manners*. In Chapter 7 for in-

To see this difference is to understand the reservation about Poe implicit in Miss O'Connor's remark that most Southern writers (and she means herself most particularly) "are considered, I believe, to be unhappy combinations of Poe and Erskine Caldwell." It is our purpose here to explore that difference through her uses of details, and we may begin by looking at her excitable child in "A Temple of the Holy Ghost" in contrast to Poe's excitable scoundrel, the narrator of "William Wilson." In her story we see through an irascible child's eyes, though the child does not narrate, a rich gauche farmer who courts a boarding teacher. Mr. Cheatam always brings Miss Kirby

> . . . a little gift—a bag of boiled peanuts or a watermelon or a stalk of sugar cane and once a wholesale box of Baby Ruth candy bars. He was bald-headed except for a little fringe of rust-colored hair and his face was nearly the same color as the unpaved roads and washed like them with ruts and gulleys. He wore a pale green shirt with a thin black stripe in it and blue galluses and his trousers cut across a protruding stomach that he pressed tenderly from time to time with his big flat thumb. All his teeth were backed with gold and he would roll his eyes at Miss Kirby in an impish way and say, 'haw haw,' sitting in their porch swing with his legs spread apart and his high-topped shoes pointing in opposite directions on the floor.

These are the bold strokes of a cartoonist, but made with meticulous imagistic care. The effect of presenting Mr. Cheatam in this way is not only to make substantial the milieu within which the story's action occurs, but to convince one as well of the child's acute

---

stance, Gogol intrudes a defense of the writer against the popular spirit of the age: "that [popular] judgment will consign him to an ignoble place in the ranks of those writers who have insulted humanity . . . . For the judgment of the writer's own times does not recognize that equally marvelous are the lenses that are used for contemplating suns and those for revealing to us the motions of insects imperceptible to the naked eye; for the judgment of his times does not recognize that a great deal of spiritual depth is required to throw light upon a picture taken from a despised stratum of life . . . ." In the final chapter, just before the ironic and agonized address to Russia through the figure of the troika, the intruding author attacks the general reader's complaint that the writer peers too deeply into his character's soul, rather than being content merely to show the character "as he appeared to the whole town" in the fiction. For "had the author restrained himself the readers' souls would not be troubled by anything after reading the book through . . . . Yes, my good readers, you would rather not see mankind's poverty exposed." (*Dead Souls*, tr. by Bernard Guilbert Guerney. New York: The George Macy Companies, Inc., 1948.) One is reminded of Miss O'Connor's response to the lady from California who complained of her depressing portraits "that when the tired reader comes home at night, he wishes to read something that will lift up his heart . . . . I think that if her heart had been in the right place, it would have been lifted up."

awareness. We see Mr. Cheatam with her limited eyes, though from a position reserved to us by the third person point of view. We thus see that she, more convincingly than William Wilson, is (to borrow Wilson's words) of an "imaginative and easily excitable temperament." Our seeing the world she inhabits so minutely through her eyes helps persuade us that her observations of the sun are valid, the sun being a more important presence in the story than Mr. Cheatam.

A selection from this sun imagery will show the point. While her country friends, invited as dates for the teenage convent girls, are singing "He's the lily of the valley," the child is aware that "The sun was going down and the sky was turning a bruised violet color that seemed to be connected with the sweet mournful sound of the music." There is no apparent rational connection, only an association in the breast of a puzzled and restless child. Alone after the young couples have gone to the country fair, she looks out over "the dark slopes, past where the pond glinted silver, past the wall of woods to the speckled sky where a long finger of light was revolving up and around and away, searching the air as if it were hunting for the lost sun. It was the beacon light from the fair." The action reflects the child's own quest, one which she does not yet know she is set upon and the impressionistic vagueness of detail suits the reflection.

The intricate pattern of the child's observations of the people around her and of natural phenomena, colored by her restless curiosity about life, comes to a climax and resolution in the last few sentences of the story. The mystery of the hermaphrodite at the sideshow, reported to her by the silly convent teenagers, the experience of the mass at the convent—a whole fabric out of the child's associations is brought together when on her way home she looks at the back of the driver's neck and then out the car window. Alonzo, the driver, as well as her mother, inhabits an adult world the child resents. He appears grotesque and repulsive in his physical presence, and the detail becomes fittingly precise and repulsive. The child observes "three folds of fat in the back of his neck and noted that his ears were pointed almost like a pig's." When Alonzo and her mother drop their talk of the sideshow freak,

remembering her presence, the child looks out "over a stretch of
pasture land that rose and fell with a gathering greenness until it
touched the dark woods. The sun was a huge red ball like an
elevated Host drenched in blood and when it sank out of sight, it
left a line in the sky like a red clay road hanging over the trees."
How terrifying in its grotesqueness is the Incarnation to the
opening eye. It rises beyond the comprehension of mere
incarnation—of man the spiritual creature—which is already a
sufficiently frightening mystery to the child in Alonzo and in her
mother.

Disturbed by the mystery of outer existence, the child begins
to waken to the mystery of her own existence. She is leaving
childhood, discovering that change in her body which marks her
passage into the adult world. But she is also aware of much more
than a physical change. She cannot articulate this mystery of
herself as "a temple of the holy ghost," yet her awareness reaches
its climax in an epiphany in which the inner world is for a moment
brought into an enlarging relation to the natural outer world, and
both to something higher. The effect is a celebration of being, not of
emptiness as we find in Poe—a celebration of that being which
includes the child along with the created outer world and its
strange nuns and priests and farmers and hermaphrodites, as well
as its pines and ponds and stained and threatening sunsets. For the
created world is for Flannery O'Connor, as it was for Pascal (as he
says) "an image of grace." Particular segments of that world and
images received out of that world have a way of coming suddenly
alive with a life beyond the accounting of reason or the senses. One
of the effects of such an experience in the created world, as Miss
O'Connor dramatizes it often in her fiction, is a panic in her
protagonists—a terror in the presence of that mercy which reduces
presumptuous man, woman, or child.[2]

Poe also leads us to an epiphany, but one in which there is the
recognition only of an inevitable annihilation. At the conclusion of
"William Wilson," the speaker faces his own image in a mirror

2. We might recall the origins of our word *panic*: the sudden, unreasonable and overpower-
ing fear which the ancients supposed was caused by the god Pan. American poets have felt
the absence of such explanations, partly because they have tended to enspirit nature with
their own consciousnesses and partly because Puritan thought purged nature of old imagin-

after delivering that image a death blow. The mirror stands "where none had been perceptible" during the struggle. In it his own features appear "all pale and dabbled in blood." He cries out to us that they are "in the most absolute identity" his own features. The pale image speaks in whispered italics the concluding words of the story, so that the narrator "could have fancied that I myself was speaking while he said:

> "You have conquered and I yield. Yet, henceforward art thou also dead—*dead to the World, to Heaven, and to Hope. In me didst thou exist—and, in my death, see by this image, which is thine own, how utterly thou hast murdered thyself.*"

Such is Poe's shocking encounter with what Heidegger would call perhaps the "true-self, the *Dasein's* encounter with its "ownmost being-in-the-world."

What Poe requires of his reader, in order that he may work his emotional effect, is that we hang on every word for the word's sake, but be impressed by its literal articulation and not by its meaning. Hence the importance of the italics in this passage, and of the capitalization of *World, Heaven, Hope*. He is dependent upon a melodrama, effected by diction and by a typography used like musical notes to sustain a tone. One is expected to ratify an impression on the authority of the act of speaking itself, as opposed to sheer and empty silence, not on the authority of what any words convey. And that incidentally is a principal reason that Poe must commit himself not only to first-person point of view but to the short lyric and tale, since impressions are fleeting. One has the uncomfortable reflection, after the experience, that he has been held—in the words of the German poet Hölderlin—by "lyre music,

ings. An occasional writer has celebrated our deliverance. Sylvester Judd, for instance, in his novel *Margaret* (1845), says:

> There are no fairies in our meadows, and no elves to spirit away our children. Our wells are drugged by no saint, and of St. Winifred we have never heard . . . . The Valley of the Housatonic is beautiful as the Valley of Tempe, or of Cashmere, and as oracular. We have no resorts for pilgrims, no shrines for the devout, no summits looking into Paradise. We have no traditions, legends, fables, and scarcely a history . . . no chapels or abbeys, no broken arches or castled crags. You find these woods as inspiring as those of Etruria or Mamre. Robin-Good-Fellow is unknown, and the Devil haunts our theology, not our houses, and I see in the last edition of the Primer his tail is entirely abridged. (Quoted by F. O. Matthiessen, *American Renaissance*, 13-14.)

Hawthorne, as we shall see at some length in Volume III, was not so content with nature's exorcism as is Judd or the more influential Emerson. For not only faeries, but the devil and saints were also cast out, and in the process the very ground of being itself. In the absence of such a ground of being, Poe comes to long for "earth-angels" to rescue an empty world, and comes to believe himself such a one.

a song without words." For it is a necessity of Poe's limitations as artist that his tone be initiated at a high pitch and maintained at that pitch, largely through repetitions in which there is little variation.[3]

We have in Poe, then, no such subtleties of language as in Miss O'Connor, who foreshadows her revelations in such device as the structure of her sentences as well as in metaphors that often seem at first merely casual or comic. When young Tarwater visits the city the first time and leans too far out of the lawyer's window, high above the busy street, "he saw his new hat drop gently, lost and casual, dallied slightly by the breeze on its way to be smashed in the tin river below." That hat, his badge of authority and pride, has to be removed, but not by such accident as this, nor by his Uncle Rayber's concern for social appearances. It must be removed by an act in which Tarwater willfully participates, an act which issues in a submission and humility. If he will not be made humble, because of his angry independence, that very independence will make such an act a dramatic necessity. That is, by calling our attention to the refusal, Miss O'Connor commits the story to the refusal that must be tested. In one important respect, Tarwater is like Poe's William Wilson, or rather like Wilson's report of himself. As a child Tarwater too is distinguished by "evil propensities." In his frantic attempt to say NO—to serve as minion of evil—evil undoes him in the person of the stranger in the lavender car, who after raping the drugged boy, takes his hat "as a souvenir." Later when Tarwater goes to warn the children of God in the burning city, he journeys bareheaded.

3. If one compare his prose poems "Shadow" or "Silence" to Wallace Stevens's "Seascape Full of Clouds," the weakness of Poe's devices becomes more apparent. One sees how much he depends upon agitation at one speed in his speaking voice, as in a washing machine, to perform what his words will not accomplish through any signifying presence. Stevens's subtle shifts in perception, through very minor variations in his repetitions—but variations that measure shades as in an impressionistic painting—are far more effective in establishing a sense of the changing seascape of the mind than Poe's elaborate idea of *identity* (in Stevens's sense of the term) between such words as "DESOLATION" and "SILENCE." In addition, the identity Poe develops is largely through the use of the vestigial imagery of a literary vocabulary. Poe's speaking voice must therefore begin in a trance-like state that allows few possibilities of that modulation necessary either to make a particular work dramatically effective or to create in the reader a convincing sense of verisimilitude which would justify any willing suspension of disbelief. For dramatic effect depends upon a development and revelation such as enlarges perceptions rather than accumulates facts—facts in Poe's work being paradoxically the assembled evidence of emptiness.

Miss O'Connor thus builds with her play on Tarwater's hat an intricate pattern of imagery which functions at both the level of naturalistic detail and at the symbolic level of her spiritual theme, Love. The hat is not simply a literary gimmick imported for the surprise of imagistic doubling as Poe's cloak in "William Wilson" seems to be. In the structure of that sentence in which we see Tarwater's first lost hat, we see vividly echoed in the diction the casual drift of the hat downward in the literal air. In the rhythm of that diction the words settle to a flat dead ending in the sentence. Once more: "he saw his hat drop gently, lost and casual, dallied slightly by the breeze on its way to be smashed in the tin river below." The sentence gives a comic parabola of Tarwater's prideful course through the novel, up to his encounter with the stranger in the lavender car.

Tarwater's hat is but one image in the dramatic weaving of Miss O'Connor's novel. Water, fire, bread, hearing aids, bottle-openers, the sun, the moon, silence, noise—if one take any of these (or others) and explore them carefully, he will discover an intricacy of emerging symbolic meaning, controlled by a very careful eye to the naturalistic detail; it is through the naturalistic surface that one penetrates to the spiritual depth. When Old Tarwater lies in his wooden coffin and instructs Young Tarwater in the proper burial ritual, the boy (looking at the box) sees "nothing showing but [Old Tarwater's] stomach which rose over the top like overleavened bread." Christ as the Bread of Life, that constant thread in the novel, is echoed in comic cliché; it is an empty phrase to Tarwater as he remembers the scene and the discussion with the old man. For at this point, Tarwater can comprehend only literal food. He sees his hunger as literal, though mysteriously insatiable by literal bread. Hence his own diagnosis of "worms" as his difficulty. In his final vision, he is looking out across the young, freshly plowed field of corn. With that promise of cornbread and liquor out of nature's and Buford's constancy as a foreground of time and place, Tarwater comes to see the loaves and fishes transformed, though they carry still a very physical weight in his understanding. The boy is approaching a point where he can sense the sacramental complexity of bread. For bread is neither simply symbolic nor

naturalistically material, this fiction suggests. It is <u>real in both its</u>
<u>spiritual and sensual dimension</u>s. The natural world can never be
what it has been to Tarwater, since in that vision which Miss
O'Connor celebrates the whole world becomes transformed. The
world about him becomes a different country in the same way that
Rome becomes a different city in that vision which sees it borne in
the City of God as St. Augustine does, and in that new world he
comes to see the possibility of becoming <u>a new man</u>. That is, he sees
it inadequate to conclude himself as simply mirrored by the external world or the external world a mirror of his own thought, which
in either perspective means isolation from the outer world, the turning of image in upon itself as in "William Wilson."

For O'Connor, image is window not mirror. In her fiction she is
constantly attempting to reveal a double presence in the brief image
that she is concerned to capture. It is of this attempt she speaks
when she says, "The longer you look at one object, the more of the
world you see in it; and it's well to remember that the serious
fiction writer always writes about the whole world, no matter how
limited his particular scene." <u>Catching in an image the large world</u>
<u>as it is implied by an object was her principal devotion as artist,</u> for
which reason she requires as close a reading as we are accustomed
to give the metaphysical poets. But the double presence her
principal characters encounter is the small world of <u>their wayward</u>
<u>selves.</u> When Haze sees Silas Layfield standing on the hood of a car,
mouthing Haze's own attempts at blasphemy, he becomes
obssessed with destroying his own conscience, which Silas seems to
manifest. "Your conscience is a trick," he insists, seeing Silas. But
he adds almost at once, "If you don't hunt it down and kill it, it'll
hunt you down and kill you." Whereupon he pursues the hapless
Silas and murders him. Tarwater's stranger echoes Tarwater's
inclinations as well as his language and haunts him as a stern
rebuke to his willfulness, turning him with Rayber's help toward
the possibility of rescue. "The prophet-freaks of Southern literature
are not images of the man in the street," Miss O'Connor says,
"They are images of <u>the man forced out to meet the extremes of his</u>
<u>own nature.</u>" It is <u>man in his spiritually fallen nature that her</u>
<u>characters discover as images of themselves.</u>

The device of <u>doubling personae</u> has been fascinating to writers in the modern world, at least since the German Romantics, in whom perhaps Poe encountered it through Sir Walter Scott's interest in <u>E.T.A. Hoffmann</u>. It comes to be of increasing thematic interest as the spiritual and physical worlds become dissociated in Western thought and as the problem of identity of the self grows in the popular mind toward the agony of alienation, <u>a consequence of an increasing insistence on</u> (in Poe's phrase) the "<u>natural rights of self-agency</u>." We see a coincidence of these concerns in Poe's "William Wilson," a story which probably owes something to tales like Hoffmann's "Sand Man." Miss O'Connor also makes complicated use of the double in *Wise Blood*. Haze encounters his fallen self through images that come to him from the external world; there is the figure of the mummy, for instance, and Asa Hawks's eyes seen by match light and Silas Layfield in a full imitation of Haze including his blue suit. But it is important that we distinguish between Miss O'Connor's doublings and Poe's.

She makes the distinction repeatedly, often through her use of her characters' eyeglasses. Haze has his mother's lensless glasses; the Misfit wears glasses; Rayber does. What she suggests is that <u>our vision of the world is divided</u>, requiring to be brought into focus. It is one way of dramatizing <u>the Manicheanism</u> we moderns are given to, a charge Miss O'Connor makes against us repeatedly in *Mystery and Manners*. The Misfit is in one world but disturbed by rumors of another, the world as rescued in Christ. His cleaning his glasses, a natural enough act, means more through the conversation with the grandmother which accompanies the action. *Seeing* <u>in its literal and prophetic senses is a constant in</u> Miss O'Connor's fiction; what she attempts is a proper focussing upon the world whereby one becomes a "realist of distances." When we reach the conclusion of Poe's "William Wilson," the recognition, the focussing, is upon empty being, the narrator having become no more substantial than his own illusion in the mirror. But Miss O'Connor's protagonists come to enter a silent yet resonant country, an action which Haze or Tarwater resists until they must capitulate; they are <u>forced to abandon the illusion that existence is simply explained by 19th-century naturalism</u>. Thus they enter upon the complex ground of being where the new temptation is to deny the naturalistic world, a temptation as ancient as Plato or the Gnostics and as modern as Poe or Jean-Paul Sartre. It is through her own detachment as story teller that she dramatizes the necessity of this focussing. Indeed, it is in the disparity between her characters' initial vision of reality and Miss O'Connor's own that the ground for both her comedy and tragedy is established, though readers persist in mistaking her characters' views for her own. As her characters move toward seeing the world as she sees it, the comic element diminishes. Poe on the other hand, when comedy is afoot in his work, moves in a different direction, toward farce as a rescue from intellectual dilemma as in "King Pest," of which tale Constance M. Rourke remarks that Poe transmutes "terror into gross comedy" in the manner of the frontier tall tale. One is hardly inclined to laughter after Haze loses his Essex, or at the resolution of "A Good Man Is Hard to Find," or in the third section of *The Violent Bear It Away*. Nor is laughter stirred at the end of "Everything that Rises Must Converge."

We may conclude our point by examining her use of the double in the title story of the posthumous collection, seeing here that her comedy also turns grim as illusion fades in the protagonist. In the story the protagonist Julian thinks he discovers a comic double of his mother in a Negro woman who boards the bus. The comedy, however, is more nearly that of the bad joke: it is at his mother's expense. What Julian does not perceive is the degree to which he himself is reflected in that woman, the imagistic details disguising the kinship from him, but not from the reader. The initiating device Miss O'Connor uses to this end is very like Poe's cloak in "William Wilson," though much more intricately employed. That pseudo-intellectual realist, Julian, is much embarrassed and irritated by his mother, who he supposes hides her emptiness in antique manners and false recollections of family history, the pride of generation. He must ride a common city bus with her, a bus awash with hoi polloi of mankind who are more repugnant to him than to his mother. As they set out for the bus stop, he bears the indignity of her new hat in a martyrdom ill-concealed:

It was a hideous hat. A purple velvet flap came down on one side of it and stood up on the other; the rest of it was green and looked like a cushion with the stuffing out. He decided it was less comical than jaunty and pathetic. Everything that gave her pleasure was small and depressed him.

The mother and son encounter a variety of people, Julian progressively irritated by his mother's friendly stupidities. He plots some public outrage to embarrass her, and so intent is he on his petty revenge that when the large Negro woman gets on the bus with her child and pays her fare, though he observes them minutely his sullenly reflective mind is on his mother. He does not at first realize what his senses have taken in:

> . . . a large, gaily dressed, sullen-looking colored woman got on with a little boy. . . . Julian hoped that he would sit down beside him and that the woman would push in beside his mother. He could think of no better arrangement. . . . There was something familiar-looking about her but Julian could not place what it was. . . . Her face was set not only to meet opposition but to seek it out. . . . Her bulging figure was encased in a green crepe dress and her feet overflowed in red shoes. She had on a hideous hat. A purple velvet flap came down on one side of it and stood up on the other; the rest of it was green and looked like a cushion with the stuffing out. She carried a mammoth red pocket book that bulged throughout as if it were stuffed with rocks.

A Poe could not have resisted italicizing the repeated sentences, but Miss O'Connor is careful to submerge them in Julian's rambling eye and his arrogant sullenness which allow him only surface observation; the final sentence about the pocketbook, an object which figures dramatically at the story's climax, allows the reader a moment longer to enjoy the irony at Julian's expense. One's attention as reader, then, is on Julian. With the advantage of his delayed recognition, we see him suddenly realize that the woman's hat is identical to his mother's. He is delighted beyond containing himself. But what Miss O'Connor has revealed to the reader in her management of Julian's recognition is the childish superficiality of his awareness, which contrasts sharply with his own estimate of his worldly and intellectual sophistication. What is more crucial, we see his petty arrogance unmistakably as he projects it upon the world, and we begin to realize that there is another world yet for Julian to recognize.

The hat after this point in the story is mentioned only once more, almost passing unnoticed when it is. When the Negro woman knocks Julian's mother down, out of anger at her gesture of love to the little boy, Julian picks up his mother's pocketbook and hat and helps her up, interpreting the Negro woman's action as just and righteous and lecturing his mother on the lesson she should have learned. The story has now come to focus upon the impending change in Julian, while very skillfully subduing the devices that have made us see both him and that possibility. We are left with Julian struggling toward light out of his spiritual darkness. It is also, as one learns to expect of Miss O'Connor's fiction, a literal struggle on a darkening city street in those concluding lines. "The tide of darkness seemed to sweep him back to [his mother lying dead in the street], postponing from moment to moment his entry into the world of guilt and sorrow." A lesser writer would have been sorely tempted to make a final use of the hat, that apparent catalyst to the violent action in the story. But Miss O'Connor's delight is not primarily in her mastery of concrete images for the purpose of irony, though one is delighted by those qualities. The end those images serve is deeper: it is the revelation of that mysterious love at the center of all being which makes such terrifying demands upon us. Julian, childish throughout the story, at the last calls "Mama! Mama!" like a child being forced alone into a real world he has so far managed to avoid, that world of guilt and sorrow in which he must discover and come to terms with a common humanity, but a humanity which is insufficient to its own rescue through "self-agency." Julian, that is, is being forced to put off the old, egocentric self. But the suggestion is quite other than that he will be left with only a mirror image of himself—with what Wallace Stevens might call an "identity," the empty and meaningless duplication such as that with which "William Wilson" ends. Julian has been emptied too, but only so that he may be filled in ways different from Poe's conception of the possibilities of man's being; and it is in a manner quite unlike that which Heidegger envisages as developing out of boredom—ennui, although those "modern" symptoms are nevertheless apparant in Julian as the preliminary signs of his spiritual and intellectual poverty. Earlier in the story he thought himself safe. He could withdraw behind his newspaper

. . . into the inner compartment of his mind where he spent most of his time. This was a kind of mental bubble in which he established himself when he could not bear to be a part of what was going on around him. From it he could see out and judge but in it he was safe from any kind of penetration from without.

But the vacuum in which he has attempted to maintain himself, his "bubble," is ruptured by a devastating intrusion from an outer world, an intrusion through the world he has sat in judgment upon, in an action of that Agent of all being and action. That intrusion, as we know, Miss O'Connor speaks of as the action of the mystery of grace.

We have come a world away from Poe in Miss O'Connor's fiction, for as we discover in reading Poe carefully, his concern is to establish just such a "bubble" as Julian builds. Poe, like Julian, would deny any world separate from the self by building an intellectual bomb shelter, a mental bubble in which to hide. And so Miss O'Connor's words concerning the rootless modern man, particularly the writer who denies the created world as Poe does, are apt. "The borders of his country are the sides of his skull." It takes something stronger sometimes than an atom bomb to open the old self-centered Adam in us which would retreat inward from the world. From her realization of the dramatic possibilities in the tensions of that necessity, Miss O'Connor writes her Dantean comedy, a comedy rich also with Chaucerean playfullness about man's struggles with the created world. And a part of the comic in her fiction springs from the protagonist's discovering likenesses of himself in the outer world—likenesses which he cannot explain as a projection of his own making. It is one thing to take bored delight in one's singularity as Julian does. But it is devastating to be forced to acknowledge a world one cannot claim to have made and then encounter the haunting presence of that world's Creator. Poe gives us the baffled horror of the inexplicable; the mind plays tricks upon the senses with a momentary emotional shock. Miss O'Connor raises up terror out of a deeper mystery: the mystery of self-agents who are not self-caused at the deepest level of their being. We are more deeply arrested by her fictions than we are sometimes comfortable in admitting.

CHAPTER XXII

REALITY AS
THE SHADOW OF UN-BEING

Poe's fascination with annihilation is very specifically analyzed at the climax of "The Imp of the Perverse." The surface of the story is simple enough. A man who has murdered another—who by that act becomes the murderer's "worldly" benefactor—is brought to confess his deed, his guilt, but with no sorrow associated with the deed. He awaits execution, reflecting upon the cause of his confession, since his reason proves to him beyond doubt that, except for his own confession, he would never have been discovered. We are to understand that the murderer did not kill out of greed or envy or hate or passionate anger or for revenge. The deed has as its sole reason a perfect X, a problem devised so that it is beyond solution by ordinary reason; it thereby celebrates the narrator's superior reason, making him an "earth-angel" of that faculty.[1] The doomed man tells us that he abhors the "rabble," those of inferior intelligence whom he supposes to constitute the rest of mankind. That he inherits the dead man's estate is simply the added triumph of a private irony, since the venture has had nothing to do with "the mere worldly advantages accruing from my sin." And as an added fillip to the affair, the coroner has ruled that death was "by the visitation of God."

But whence the confession that dissolves this perfect X? We have overlooked, our narrator tells us, through "the pure arrogance

---

1. "Unmotivated treachery, for the mere intent of injury," says Allen Tate, "and self-violence are Poe's obsessive subjects. He has neither Purgatory nor Heaven, and only two stations in Hell." *The Man of Letters in the Modern World,* 141.

of the reason" the impulse to the perverse, an inexplicable quirk among "the faculties and impulses—. . . the *prima mobilia* of the human soul." The nature of the soul is an invention of the reason, and reality follows the invention. Thus we determine "naturally enough" (a phrase not explained) that "man should eat." We therefore "assign to man an organ of alimentiveness," through which the detailed alimentary system comes into being. Thus it is "with every organ, whether representing a propensity, a moral sentiment, or a faculty of the pure intellect." Man's reason is the creator of all that is called *man*. The argument thus obliterates the physical body by a series of actions of the reason through which the natural, moral, and spiritual are reduced to a common level, namely the level of intellection. This is an existentialism more extreme than Sartre's, for Sartre does allow an existence at the physical level as independent of the reason or imagination. Poe's speaker invents the world by reason, but his invented world exists only as an *illusion* of a thing, which means that the imagination is the ultimate power: out of nothing, the imagination creates an illusion of a something. And here we come to the fateful point in man's creation of illusion. The narrator, misled by reason, comes to invent the non-reasonable, the perverse, which by that "invention" has an existence that feeds his madness. It is an inevitable invention, as black proceeds from white, night from day, left from right. The "tensional" grounds in Poe's story are unlike those tensional grounds described by Voegelin as desirable. For there is no In-between here within which one experiences the pull "between *amor Dei* and *amor sui*, *l'ame ouverte* and *l'ame close;* between the virtues of openness toward the ground of being such as faith, hope, and love and the vices of infolding closure such as hybris and revolt," and so on. We have, rather, a split in Voegelin's "pairs of symbols"; in his terms the poles have become "hypostatized" as independent en-tities with an effect he describes for us. For with such hypostatiza-tion, "we destroy the reality of existence as it has been experienced . . .; we lose consciousness and intellect; we deform our humanity and reduce ourselves to a state of quiet despair[2] or activist confor-mity to the 'age,' . . . of suffering from the absurdity of existence or

2. Voegelin's phrase "quiet despair" is made pregnant by Poe's constant concern for "quiet" as "silence," for "despair" as hope of annihilation, evidence of which we have been adducing from the poems, tales, and essays.

indulgence in any divertissement (in Pascal's sense) that promises to substitute as a 'value' for reality lost. In the language of Heraclitus and Plato: Dream life usurps the place of wake life.'' In Poe's story the narrator finds himself trapped by his separation of the tensional poles by his reason. As if he is become a perverse image of St. Thomas's God, who cannot unwill a willed thing, the narrator by his "invention" of the non-reasonable, the perverse, dooms himself, though *doom* is hardly a word with any meaning within the argument's context. (God, in our analogy, may be spoken of as "doomed" to perfect being, perfect good, but only metaphorically; figurative language is our inadequate attempt to speak of a mystery beyond the comprehension of our finitude.)

Poe's narrator thus confesses the murder, not because it was a premeditated evil requiring confession, contrition, and amendment for the soul's health, but because an irrational perversity has been given a kind of existence by the rational. Evil, in the argument of St. Thomas, has existence as an absence of good, as negation. It is allowed residence in the soul through the will's freedom to say or do NO (as Tarwater perceives). But St. Thomas's evil has no such aspect in Poe's story. It is a created antithesis, leading to a Manichean dilemma within the creating consciousness, which is itself the whole world. Evil, the perverse, becomes haltingly operative, a Frankenstein's monster in the "soul" that made it. Its existence has no cause which might relate it to events external to the consciousness; consciousness is the only god against which it can rebel. Still such ideas of consciousness may not be imagined as absolutely self-contained by Poe, in spite of the clever argument. Even the chase at the story's conclusion is an action in an external world necessary to the resolution of the story, a concession Poe must make consequent upon the necessary assumption of an audience. In those assumptions the argument founders. What happens in the course of such thought is that the irrational must devour the rational, leading toward madness. For even the assumption of an audience is irrational if the narrator's arguments are to be consistent, a point that might have given a more clever turn to the tale than it bears had it been developed by calling in question the reader's existence as more than illusion.

Now to move toward madness, as Poe's stories so often do, requires a measure of madness against some assumption of sanity; that measure is neglected. Poe is surely as interested in the idea of the perverse as he is in writing the tale, but he finds himself in the dilemma of every solipsist who feels compelled to speak. Even so, he might have made the madness in this tale more terrifying. Does the crowd in his story, by its act of chasing the murderer, without any reason for the chase, make the murder itself *exist* and thereby make the murderer exist? By such dramatic extensions of the dilemma, the reader might be drawn for a moment into the vortex of the story's movement by a passive if not willing belief (in contrast to a suspension of disbelief) and the reader himself thereby be threatened by the perverse. But such interesting complications of the drama are not implied, though Poe might have gladly turned his fiction into a revenge upon his reader, as Baudelaire turns his *Flowers of Evil* into a spiritual Venus' flytrap in his introductory sonnet. (That Poe longs for such a sweet revenge is suggested by the conclusion of "Hop-Frog," in which the twisted, but abused, dwarf escapes with the dwarf Beauty and lives happily ever after.) By consenting to the argument for the existence of the perverse impulse, the narrator might argue, one brings that impulse into being in the mind that follows such reasoning, even as it is said to have sprung from reason in the narrator's mind; therefore it might be said that by the reader's passive consideration of the argument, the perverse impulse comes into being in *his* mind. The closest we come to this idea, however, is in the narrator's appeal to the reader's reason when he begs that we give an assent to the argument. The appeal is made, however, not to the reason, but to "one's own heart."

The murderer's confession has nothing to do with the health of the soul then, with entering that world of guilt and sorrow as Miss O'Connor's Julian must. The idea that one's conscience exists, let alone that it may be purged of guilt, is foreign to Poe. (Haze, we remember, in a similar dilemma, tries through violence to destroy his conscience.) Satan can say, in Milton's portrait of the great Imp of the Perverse, "Evil, be thou my Good." In Poe's story and in his thought in general something very like this perversion is in operation, though I do not believe Poe fully understood it to be so.

"We might . . . deem this perverseness a direct instigation of the arch-fiend," the learned narrator tells us, not having read his Milton carefully, "were it not occasionally known to operate in furtherance of good." Evil is presented as random, as sometimes a cause of good, and its consequences are discomforting only to the reason. This "overwhelming tendency to do wrong for the wrong's sake," however, will not "admit of analysis, or resolution into ulterior elements." Perverseness by definition is "a *mobile* without motive, a motive not *motivert*." The description might well fit such an enigma as Iago, except that one has a considerable measure of Shakespeare's particular characterization of evil: Iago is cast against a human world, peopled with characters who stand in measure of evil and good. But Poe's tale is not one which sounds human character in concrete action; it is an expansion of an idea. Yet it is nevertheless an idea which purports to be an attempt upon a truth about evil, through the highest reason—a reason not separated very far from Poe's own faculty though this purports to be only a "tale."

The admitted existence that makes the idea of the perverse possible in words is the consciousness, consciousness being assumed common among us through what Poe declares in *Marginalia* to be "the identity of construction in the human brain."[3] It is under the guidance of this self-created perverseness, says Poe's

---

3. It is a curious conjunction to place Poe's contemporary, Kierkegaard, beside Poe on this point. For Kierkegaard, who knew some of Poe's work, philosophy is also inadequate to the problem, but precisely because it assumes an identity of construction in the human brain; but additionally there is an assumption of an affinity between the human mind and ultimate truth such as reduces man. Socrates, Kierkegaard's representative philosopher, would hold knowledge a rediscovery of intrinsic knowledge in the mind, a discovery of the affinity of mind to truth. But that tie, says Kierkegaard, is broken by sin and cannot be restored by reason. Recreation of being is necessary, not a recovery of thought. Kierkegaard is resisting a modern trend, to which Poe gives aid and comfort. Once more I urge consideration of St. Thomas' solution to the problem with which Poe is contending: how to reconcile what Gilson calls "the twofold fact that there is intellectual knowledge and that the world of nature is intelligible to the mind." It is the paradox of the unintelligibility of intelligibility itself which Einstein sees as the great mystery, a problem not dissolved by a reduction of nature and the substitution of idea in consciousness, the idea declared by Poe to be created ex nihilo by the imagination. The intellibibility of even intelligible ideas of this stamp is still unresolved. The reader is particularly referred to Gilson's "A Metaphysics of the Name of God," *The Spirit of Thomism* as clear exposition of the problem. If one chooses to consider Thomas' argument only as rational wit, it still puts Poe's argument in its shade and is more challenging to one's reason than Poe is capable of being.

narrator, that we "peer into the abyss," lured by the "delight of horror" to "this rushing annihilation." And "because our reason violently deters us from the brink, *therefore*, do we the most impetuously approach it. There is no passion in nature so demonically impatient."

Pascal has already looked at Poe's version of evil as presented in "The Imp of the Perverse," but his reading of it finds the culprit to be quite other than reason or a spiritual gene in which is programmed the soul's obliteration. In *Pensées* (82) he speaks of an "arrogant power, the enemy of reason, who likes to rule and dominate it." The power "has established in man a second nature to show how all-powerful she is. . . . If the greatest philosopher in the world find himself upon a plank wider than actually necessary, but hanging over a precipice, his imagination will prevail, though his reason convince him of his safety." He will jump, and thus reason appears at the mercy of imagination. The imagination gains its awesome power out of that inclination in man through which he falls by pride. If no Satan from the outer world tempts him to hurl himself from the pinnacle of the temple to test his divinity, his own imagination will serve the purpose nicely.

"He would make himself his own centre, and independent of my help," says God's Wisdom, in *Pensées* (430). "He withdrew himself from my rule; and, on his making himself equal to me by the desire of finding his happiness in himself, I abandoned him to himself. . . . It is vain, O man, that you seek within yourselves the remedy for your ills." Pascal is characterizing the same inclination that Kierkegaard will later describe as the arrogance of "being oneself," which attempt leaves one vulnerable to the seductions of impulses; and this development in our thought in part helps explain that growing emphasis upon the imagination in Romantic letters. For one sees an increasing attempt since the eighteenth century to raise imagination to omnipotence over the world. It is an impulse conjured and fed by some romantic minds, Shelley's for instance, leading to the dangers of a dominance by impulse. In this process of thought, Satan becomes transmogrified into Prometheus, a process one observes as pervasive of our literature from Milton's day to our own. The new public image of the Old Rebel appropriates, through the arrogance of his disciples, a holy cause to justify his powers to man and thus over man. Usually that cause is a social one, sufficiently vague to be catalyst to an emotionalism in the popular spirit to turn impulse into a force that may be focussed upon the vague cause by some "director" of the cause. But one is not always convinced of the same degree of self-sacrifice for mankind in our new Prometheus as in the Greek hero-god. The modern version of Prometheus seems too easily possessed by a hunger for revenge, a characteristic which reminds one rather of Milton's antagonist. There is some reason, then, to approach with caution sudden causes—whether Common Cause, environmentalism, Nader's Raiders. Especially we should pause with caution before aberrations such as Squeaky Fromme. The attempt to assassinate a President of the United States in the name of clean earth, air, and water is a spectacle of spiritual significance to a whole people. If Satan cast out Satan (we are told) he is divided against himself and his kingdom cannot stand. But within his kingdom of chaos such a strategy exacerbates chaos; the kingdom is increased by dissolution, as it were. Evil fades into a confusing anti-Deism in universal chaos. Such, one fears, may be a strategy of the diabolical which led Baudelaire to say that Satan's cleverest wile in the modern world is to convince that world he does not exist. For, though "it is more difficult to love God than to believe in Him," says Baudelaire in his first preface to *Flowers of Evil*, "it is more difficult for people nowadays to believe in the Devil than to love him. Everyone smells him and no one believes in him. Sublime subtlety of the Devil." Against that devilish strategy Miss O'Connor insists that "we need a sense of mystery which sees the devil as a real spirit who must be made to name himself, and not simply to name himself as vague evil, but to name himself with his specific personality for every occasion."

The danger that imagination may seduce one to the control of impulse is a reason that Coleridge and Wordsworth, the elder ambassadors of the imagination, were so concerned with refining the concept of the imagination by separating fancy from it, however much they disagree on the distinctions to be made. One notices that the rejection of Coleridge and Wordsworth by their younger successors touches partly upon this concern. Coleridge seeks to anchor man's imagination in the great I AM, an attempt which a Shelley will hardly accede to. Coleridge's is also an anchoring point which one finds in those cryptic notes Pascal wrote after his mystical experience, notes discovered after his death in the lining of his jacket. For it seems evident that the experience Pascal responds to in those fragments clarifies for him that struggle between faith and reason he has been undergoing.

These passages in Pascal's secret history suggest that Miss O'Connor was not only familiar with the fragments but has them in mind explicitly in the experiences of her two prophets, Old and Young Tarwater. Pascal's emphatic word FIRE, followed by "God of Abraham, God of Isaac, God of Jacob, not of the philosophers and scholars" are figured in Tarwater's burned eyes after his vision, as they are in the Old Tarwater's being touched by a finger of fire in the revelation he remembers.[4] In "Novelist and Believer" she quotes Pascal's words, "God of Abraham, Isaac, and Jacob and not of philosophers and scholars," as attaching to "an unlimited God and one who has revealed himself specifically. It is one who became man and rose from the dead. It is one who confounds the senses and sensibilities, one known early on as a stumbling block. . . . the object of ultimate concern and he has a name." These insistent words are spoken as her judgment of the limitations in the art of the latest of the romantics who also wrote fiction: Hemingway, Kafka, Gide, Camus. They are caught up, she says, in "a kind of sub-religion which expresses its ultimate concern in images that have not yet broken through. . . ." It is Pascal, she recalls, who said "If I had not known you, I would not have found you," words she applies to that struggle in Camus which suggests a knowledge locked in him which cannot break out of his closed self through images so that they may name the "object of ultimate concern." Though she did not live to see Sartre's use of Pascal's statement in *Words*, in the passage in which Sartre speaks of his own struggle to exorcise the Holy Ghost from the cellar of his mind, she knows it a

---

4. Compare also Pascal's "Eternally in joy for a day's trial on earth," echoed in its dark aspects by Tarwater's stranger: "Every day is judgment day." One notes Haze's "penitential practices" are like Pascal's, who wore an iron girdle with sharp points turned in.

necessity of the radical existentialist to root out that whispering temptation of the Holy Ghost. It is a necessity Haze is aware of, cursed by that presence in the "blood." Sartre puts it: "the Holy Ghost whispers its staggering words in my ear: 'You would not seek me if you had not found me.' " Dedicated "unbelieving searchers" like Camus, Miss O'Connor says, force the believer to purify his notions in "the heat of our unbelieving neighbor's anguish." Their anguish leads her to focus our attention on the instruments of that anguish, the words that express it, the images that fall short of the ultimate and do not "show any recognition of a God who has revealed himself."

The point is that Miss O'Connor, like Pascal, comes to terms with reason, as Poe and his successors cannot. Reason is not an enemy to be made the captive of imagination. One does not cast out the "God . . . of the philosophers and the scholars." One rather recognizes the limits of reason, as one discovers that it is faith which takes one at last into that silent country to the borders of which reason can only direct one. Grace is necessary to the reconciliation of faith and reason, to the bridging of that otherwise impassable gap between natural reason and the true end toward which natural reason moves. For through grace the reason comes to see that, as St. Thomas says, "grace does not destroy nature, but perfects it." Because this is so, "natural reason," that reason employed by Pascal's "philosophers and scholars" must minister to faith "as the natural inclination of the will ministers to charity." Faith, which is in the heart through revelation, does not stand opposed to reason, which is of the mind as it is fed by "natural knowledge" to its incomplete end. For "faith presupposes natural knowledge, even as grace presupposes nature and perfection the perfectible."[5] As Roberts says, in presenting Pascal's position in *Existentialism and Religious Belief*, "Faith and reason belong to different orders, but

---

5. *Summa Theologiae*, I, q 1, Art. 8, Reply Obj. 2; Q 2, Art. 2, Reply Obj. 1. That Miss O'Connor read these sections of the *Summa* closely is shown by her own arguments. She has also marked key passages in Thomas' argument in her copy of Pegis' *Introduction to St. Thomas Aquinas*. One is encouraged to read Gilson's lucid explication of the passages quoted above as they are related in the *Spirit of Thomism*. Especially helpful are Chapter II, "The Master Plan of Creation," and Chapter III, "A Metaphysics of the Name of God." The latter is a particularly helpful exposition of Thomism as it aids Miss O'Connor's critique of modernist errors in Existentialism.

they need not come into conflict. Rational demonstration is capable of employing principles which are basically similar in all men. But only faith can reach what is unique in each man; its appeal is concrete instead of general, and it is addressed to the whole person instead of just to the intellect." Pascal the mathematician does not abandon mathematics after his conversion, that "harsh mathematical reason of the schools" which Poe rejects in words that immediately follow his quotation from Pascal.

Poe would have it that reason is an effect of "the identity of construction in the human brain"; through reason there is a possibility of explicit communication, especially through the "tyranny of fact" as he says somewhere, though as we have seen he takes an excessive pride in the superiority of his own analytic reason over most men's. His faith, transferred to the imagination, carries with it reason's appeal to the abstract and general instead of to the concrete, so that he is given to dramatizing idea. He attempts an emotional effect of idea upon a reader by "using words for the obscure harmonics which resound about them and which are made up of vague meanings which are in contradiction with the clear meanings," to borrow Sartre's excoriating words once more. With no clear distinction between an imagination freed of a reality larger than the consciousness itself (through which the imagination operates) and an imagination anchored in such a reality, Poe cannot finally distinguish between the demonic and angelic inclinations in himself, giving himself to either impulse as the occasion most easily allows. The "Imp of the Perverse" and "The Domain of Arnheim" are out of the same mind; their significant denominator is a conception of the imagination which makes a god of the artist. It is a conception of the imagination as described by Pascal in its spiritual dangers. The imagination is "that deceitful part in man, that mistress of error and falsity, the more deceptive that she is not always so. . . . she compels reason to believe, doubt and deny. . . . she fills her devotees with a satisfaction far more full and entire than does reason. . . . How insufficient are all the riches of the world without her consent!" For Flannery O'Connor, the imagination is one of the avenues to man's heart, not simply to his emotions. And it is the novelist's heart that is spoken to no less than the reader's. "The Lord doesn't speak to the novelist as he did to his servant Moses, mouth to mouth. He speaks to him as he did to those two complainers, Aaron and Aaron's sister, Mary [Miriam]: through dreams and visions, in fits and starts, and by all the lesser and limited ways of the imagination."

Poe clearly believes otherwise. "And because our reason violently deters us from the brink," says Poe's narrator in "The Imp of the Perverse," speaking of the abyss of the Absurd, "*therefore*, do we the most impetuously approach it. There is no passion in nature so demonically impatient." But such terms as *nature* and *demonically* are either empty words in Poe's use of them or so distorted from their usual meanings as to confuse us. By such usage, one supposes evil in us as an instinct, perhaps, through which man is determined to self-destruction. Ordinarily when we say of someone, through irritation or anguish, that he is "determined to destroy himself," we mean that he wills his destruction. But Poe suggests that we are evil-prone, as we say of someone that he is accident-prone, the escape of the deterministic implications of which we have taught ourselves to call subconscious will. But Poe does not seem to mean to suggest any participation of the will in evil at all. If we take Poe's premise in *Eureka* seriously, as he commands us to do—namely that all things are out of nothingness and have in them the germ of nothingness, an inclination to return to the source of all things—what we are left with is the conclusion that his conception of the object of the perverse is likewise his conception of the ultimate goal of all things.

Its germ is in us, a premise somehow revealed to Poe. The full growth of that germ is the return to nothingness from which "all" has sprung. We have no alternative given us in his thought, so that his cry in the margin of *Eureka* that it is a work which "cannot die" rings with the pathetic irony of contradiction. Life is a walking shadow, a tale told by a madman rather than the idiots of the schools; it is a dream within a dream. And Poe is left in a desperate situation. For we can have at least a vague understanding of Socrates' argument that the world of our senses, which we mistake for the reality, is but an insubstantial shadow of perfect being— Idea. But what meaning is possible to a conception of that supposed reality as a shadow of an absolute unbeing, nothingness? Even if one should say, yes, but what if Poe *does* see the truth, the answer is still that there is no certitude in that truth. For if Poe sees emptiness, unbeing, as ultimate reality and attempts to acclaim annihilation as our only hope, perhaps even using Pascal's words for his perverted vision—"certitude, feeling, joy, peace"—his very acceptance of nothingness is larger than the emptiness he accepts. Therefore nothingness cannot be "all" or the source of all, for it is otherwise contained.

CHAPTER XXIII

FAITH LEAPING—
TO BEING OR ABYSS

Here begins a necessary diversion. We must address ourselves, albeit fearfully and in faint degree, to the question of questions, "*the* problem of problems," as Gilson calls it, namely: What is Being? It is a question "which men have been asking for twenty-four centuries without finding the answer." Gilson adds, "Very wisely, our students—and sometimes their professor—forget about it and get rid of the problem by that simple method." But that old problem is one St. Thomas thought to have solved, though his solution is subsequently denied by philosophers of the immanent, including Heidegger, and culminating in that most immanent of immanentists, Jean-Paul Sartre. By virtue of our theme we are committed to the question, indeed the question is our theme, and we must make the attempt, most grateful to Gilson and Maritain in so far as they accompany us into those grounds St. Thomas established on the question. It is a necessity to our argument also because Miss O'Connor declares herself so resolutely a Thomist explicitly in this question and insists that the particular virtues of her art are dependent upon St. Thomas's position. The following pages will, I hope, reveal something to us of her conception of art as a "vocation" through which she realizes herself as a "realist of distances," a "prophetic poet" intent on rescuing the lost ground of Being to the popular spirit of our age. At the very least we must be convinced that her interest in St. Thomas is not a casual one, that her acquaintance with his mind is much deeper than the surface of her statements in *Mystery and Manners* at first reveals. And we shall certainly see how radically removed from the traditional grounds of being developed from the Greeks through St. Thomas our world has become.

We may begin by seeing St. Thomas's answer to the question *What is Being?*, relating certain immanentist thought which is counter, and come at the end of this chapter to a consideration of Heidegger's late thought on the question, expressed in *Identity and Difference* (1957). Initially, in Gilson's exposition of the problem in *The Spirit of Thomism*, we are dealing with this "problem of problems" from the position of man's "natural reason." Through that reason, as we grapple with the distinction between St. Thomas's *esse* and *ens*—*beingness* and *that which is*—we are brought at last to the point where the grace of revelation must be turned to the aid of natural reason. We should be false to our natural reason not to attempt the distinction, though to express it through reason alone leaves the distinction intellectually dissatisfying, for the difference between *thatness* (*esse*) and *whatness* (*ens*) is reconciled by grace and grace alone. The "*whatness* of things," says Gilson, "differs according to their respective natures," whether one see things of different species and orders, or things within the same species differing in particularities. Now "concerning their *thatness*, only one of two things can be done [by our intellect]—it can be affirmed or denied." Thus Poe's conception of being as "a dream within a dream" constitutes a denial. For what we are speaking of here is *being itself, the esse*, which differs from perceptible being, the *ens*. And what is of crucial significance in the distinction is that *esse* differs from *ens* not in degree, but in kind. It differs, but not as "one more perfection in the same line as . . . other perfections" of *ens*, for it is "entirely different." And here we quote Gilson without interruption:

> In Thomas' technical language, actual existence, which he calls *esse*, is that by virute of which a thing, which he calls *res*, is a being, an *ens*. It is the being-hood or being-ness of being. It is *be* in being. It is *to be* that makes a certain thing to be a being. *Esse* is defined by its essence, namely that which the thing is.

What may initially confuse one in this distinction, if he can get beyond those suspicions of scholastic thought that are a currency in the popular spirit, is a haunting "feeling" that in the definition *esse* is only a name of an idea deduced by natural reason from its encounter with the natural world, and so a creation of the reason itself; and that is Heidegger's position on the question as we shall presently see. For certain things in experience seem to be what we should prefer to call "actual existence." But here is the point where St. Thomas goes beyond his mentor Aristotle, who reaches a dead end (as Thomas sees) in his attempt to see the true ground of being. Thomas nevertheless supposes Aristotle to have gone as far as the natural reason can go in the attempt. It is an attempt Thomas values very highly, and he is in agreement with St. Justin on the point, a point which the first three volumes of Voegelin's *Order and History* may be said to examine. "Saint Justin," Gilson reminds us, "held the astonishing view that God had given philosophy to the Greeks even as He had given his Law to the Jewish people. . . . According to Justin, it was God's intention that philosophy should play for the Gentiles a role similar to that which his own revealed Law had played for the Jews. In other words, both the Greek philosophy and the Jewish Law were included in the general economy of the divine providence." It is in the development of this idea that Thomas comes to bring faith, and the revelation of the New Testament, into a relation with both the Law and philosophy; it is by this means that Thomas advances beyond Aristotle's impasse on the question of being.

For Thomas, it is the *esse* which is "actual existence." It is the existence within all existences, or more accurately once more, it is that by virtue of whose act all things are caused to be. "To posit the existence (*esse*) of a being (*ens*) is to posit at once as real all the qualities included in its definition; to take away existence (*esse*) is not merely to deprive that being of one of its attributes, it is to suppress them all at one fell stroke." That latter course, the removal of existence, yields Poe's denial, which we may state in a parallel opposition: all (*res*) is a dream (Poe's *ens*) within a dream (Poe's *esse*), in which Poe's *esse* is *nothingness*, a *not-being-ness*.

Now *esse*, says Thomas, is not *a being* (an *ens*); it is that which makes such-and-such an *ens* to be an *ens*. *Esse* is a universal force, so to speak, by virtue of which *all* is. It is "a sort of static energy in virtue of which the being actually is, or exists." What Sartre does is to steal St. Thomas's *esse* and rename it the *imaginative will*, in which respect he is Poe's intellectual heir. For Thomas, "*esse* is fixed and at rest in being." (These are Thomas's own words.) But for Sartre, the imaginative will fixes being and only thereby may it rest in the being it makes, its own temple so to speak. The imaginative will is the action whereby being exists. For Thomas, the *to be* of a being is "at its very core," Gilson says. But for Sartre, it is the action of the imaginative will which is at the core of being. (We recall John Casey's statement that for Sartre the "imagination is not a contingent and super-added power of consciousness; it is the whole of consciousness as it realises its freedom.")

In addition, Thomas argues that "God is innermost in each and every thing, just as its *esse* is innermost in the thing." But for Sartre, the "I" is the innermost of everything, just as the *imaginative will* is innermost in everything. For Thomas, it is the *esse* in man that is the "temple of the Holy Ghost": but for Sartre it is the imaginative will that is the temple of the "I."

Thomas's *esse* and Sartre's *imaginative will* may be taken as poles of tension defining the ground on which Miss O'Connor's fiction unfolds, a fact implicit in that fiction and in some of her remarks on that fiction. We may observe as well that these poles are echoed by the names Voegelin uses to establish the tensional grounds of being: for instance, his "*atmor Dei* and *amor sui*, *l'âme ouverte* and *l'âme close.*" And we recall once more Sartre's argument in *Words* that he was at last successful in his attempt to expel, not simply God the Father, but the Holy Ghost. Having descended into the cellar of his mind and collared that Recreant, he threw Him out, after which he became free to assert "I" as the ground of being. On Sartre's confident assurance of his success we have already expressed ourselves as unconvinced. For Sartre in the final analysis compromises as Heidegger does in the intellectual dilemma: he pursues nihilism and not the purer annihilation of Poe.

One might compare Miss O'Connor's description of this necessary descent into the self and the issue as she sees it in contrast to Sartre's or Poe's descent. The problem for the novelist such as she supposes herself to be lies in the use of being without abusing being.

> The problem . . . will be to know how far ne can distort without destroy-
> ing, and in order not to destroy, he will have to descend far enough into
> himself to reach those underground springs that give life to his work.
> (*Mystery and Manners*, 50)

And again, "The writer operates at a peculiar crossroads where time and place and eternity somehow meet. His problem is to find that location" (*Mystery and Manners*, 59). And in "The Fiction Writer and His Country" she says,

> When we talk about the writer's country we are liable to forget that no
> matter what particular country it is, it is inside as well as outside him.
> Art requires a delicate adjustment of the outer and inner worlds in such a
> way that, without changing their nature, they can be seen through each
> other. To know oneself is to know one's region. It is also to know the
> world, and it is also, paradoxically, a form of exile from that world.

In her careful use of such words as *nature, world, self,* seen in the light of Thomism, one comes to understand more fully what she means when she says that the longer one looks at an object, the more of the world one sees in it. Her looking, her vision, is a penetration to *esse* through her natural reason, as it is supported by faith. Thus she sees that nature and grace are not separated.

Now in Thomas's argument, it is through the fundamental ground of being, the *esse*, that God is present in things. He is pre-sent (as Thomas has it) as the cause is in its effect. Being (*esse*) derives its "actual existence" from its cause, God, and the mul-titude of beings, God's *creatura*, exist as effects of *esse*. The relationship between *esse* and *ens* touches deeply upon "nature" as a revelation of the Cause of nature, for nature through this relationship bears deep in itself an image of its cause. It is that image which man's "natural reason" approaches through the first knowledge of the senses. (We have several times cited Thomas's remark that "A perfect judgment of the mind obtains through turn-ing to sense-objects which are the first principles of our knowledge.") With the aid of revelation, faith discovers the in-timate relation between the Cause of all being and all being; faith comes to "see" that being is continuously sustained by its Cause and that the effects of that Cause appear fully to the "natural reason." The fiction writer who lacks faith, Miss O'Connor says, is trapped by "images that have not yet broken through to show any recognition of a God who has revealed himself," and she is speaking explicitly of Camus, who seems to have been able neither to collar the Holy Ghost and throw Him out nor accept Him; thus Camus remains suspended by arrested images. There is something of a recognition of this circumstance in his remark cited earlier from the *Diaries of Julian Green*: he finds himself, he said, in the condition of St. Augustine "before his conversion." (Czeslaw Milosz reminds us, in *Emperor of the Earth*, that Camus' first work was his university dissertation on St. Augustine.)

In Thomas's argument lies the possible ground on which the analogy of the artist's relation to his art is seen paralleled by God's relation to His creation, and seen with a vision neither blasphemous nor presumptuous. If the cause were not in some manner in its effect, if the cause were withdrawn from its effect, then the effect (the *ens*) would cease because the "being-hood" of that effect would have ceased. But "to take away *esse* is not merely to deprive [a] being of one of its attributes," Gilson reminds us, "it is to suppress them all at one fell stroke." It is in this understanding of the relation of *esse* to *ens* that the Thomist rejects the central arguments of Husserl, Heidegger, Nietzche, Sartre, in so far as both nature and art are understood by them. Gilson uses an analogy to clarify the point at issue, an analogy out of art: "Man or bird, when the singer ceases to sing, the song ceases to be; the being of the cause really is *in* the effect." And in that remark lies a clue to the desperate anxiety in the poets of the intramundane, of the immanent. Anxiety (that important concept in Heidegger's thought as we have seen) prompts to the necessity of a continuous song, for if the song should cease, the cause of the song thereby ceases. Silence, quiet, has a terror for a Poe or Nietzsche or Heidegger or Sartre that it doesn't hold for Thomas or O'Connor, because silence as the one side and the other understand it is radically different. In the fear of silence lies a recognition of the finiteness of man's being. That is the spring of Keats's melancholy, for he believes he recognizes the inevitable cessation of the cause of his poem, namely the poet, and the cessation he suspects is annihilation. Thus neither the urn nor the poem confers immortality upon the artist. The art object at best becomes the foster child of Poe's silence and the philosopher's slow time.

But one may see the circumstances of man's being in an entirely different perspective, as Thomas does and as Flannery O'Connor does. From her perspective, Miss O'Connor as artist does not discard that imperfect analogy of the artist as creator to God as Creator. That is why she can see a validity in Maritain's argument that art does not imitate nature as a mirror imitates the object, but rather imitates the *operations* of nature, that action which may be said constituted by the relation of *esse* and the *ens*. The poet "imitates" God in relation to his art, and the faith that he is made in God's image is the necessary clue. Thus the poet is not an "imitation" god, as modern poets have tended to make him; he imitates the actions of God as the finite may imitate the infinite perfection; he does so through that salient parallel of his being to God's being, the intellect. He calls an artifact into being, not *ex nihilo* but *ex esse*. The artifact is an imitation of "nature's" *thatness*, not of nature's *whatness*, and hence art is not a mirror of objects. And that is the truest reason that Miss O'Connor is, as artist, concerned with the *possible* and why she sets the *probable* aside in so far as it is a consideration of the action of art. For the *probable* may lead one into the temptation of imitating *whatness* as its highest aim, in which imitation the artist is limited. The "naturalists" of whom she speaks as possibly producing great "naturalistic" art do so, she says, in so far as they are true to nature. Notwithstanding the limitation, the *ens* of their art, in so far as it truly reflects the *ens* of nature, may very well in consequence speak something of *esse* beyond what they understand. But it is better, since man is a rational creature, to understand. That is, the artist is well advised to make reasonable use of the unreasonable, art being (in Thomas's definition as she quotes it) "reason in making."

To avoid the unnecessary limitations of art by the artist, extreme instances of which are deadly error to the artist, the poet must resist the divisive separations of the tensional poles of being; they must be held dramatically dynamic by reason and faith in concert. The artist must not ignore *esse* in favor of *ens*, nor the reverse; nor may he abandon faith for reason, or reason for faith. As Miss O'Connor says,

> St. Thomas called art "reason in making." This is a very cold and very beautiful definition, and if it is unpopular today, this is because reason has lost ground among us. As grace and nature have been separated, so imagination and reason have been separated, and this always means an end to art. The artist uses his [natural] reason to discover an answering reason in everything he sees. For him, to be reasonable is to find, in the object, in the situation, in the sequence, the spirit [*esse*] which makes it itself [*ens*]. This is not an easy or simple thing to do. It is to intrude upon the timeless, and that is only done by the violence of a single-minded respect for the truth.

Thus she speaks, showing in what sense she goes beyond Eliot's concern for the "objective correlative," a concern which at the time of Eliot's definition still found him very much thinking as Poe had thought.

Miss O'Connor as artist is willing to risk a violence that may bear Heaven away. It is the risk St. Thomas himself was willing to take. Gilson warns his reader not to misunderstand Thomas's argument—that *esse* is (as we may put it) the Temple of the Holy Ghost—as a form of pantheism in Thomas. He quickly adds:

> Thomas Aquinas was not a particularly safe Thomist; rather than safe, he preferred to be right, which is not the same thing. The safe Thomist prefers not to state the whole truth if asserting it without qualification would risk misleading his readers.... Thomas means that God is present in all beings because he is their cause; so he is in them as the cause is in its effect.

The poet is in his poem in something of the same manner, which is why Miss O'Connor reminds her reader that "You have to get the writer's view by looking at the novel as a whole." For both Thomas and O'Connor there is a constant faith such as allows the free and full exercise of natural reason. Thus Thomas out of his faith can be bold in the pursuit of the truth, his natural reason being measured by the truth and not the other way round. He can be fearless in appropriating from the philosophers, even the "pagan" philosophers, for "The study of philosophy [he says] does not mean to learn what others have thought but to learn what is the truth of things." In learning the truth of things, the learner moves toward perfection, is made more perfect in his love of the cause of all truth.

In Miss O'Connor, one finds the same faith assuring her that truth, while it tests faith severely, does not destroy it. Intellectual error encouraged by aberrant will alone can do that. Thus naturalism by its truth (its being true to nature) may produce true art. That truth to nature through the natural reason is the first responsibility of the artist to his vocation. She says, "because I am a Catholic, I cannot afford to be less than an artist." But in being an artist we must remember that "the explanation for any good writer is first that he knows how to write and that writing is his vocation." It will follow inevitably that "The Catholic novelist doesn't have to be a saint; he doesn't even have to be a Catholic; he does, unfortunately, have to be a novelist." If he is the novelist she intends, he may well endanger his reader by that refusal to be a "safe Thomist." He knows all too well the danger "of corrupting those who are not able to understand what he is doing. It is very possible that what is vision for the writer is temptation and sin to the reader." But he cannot be true in his vocation and be deterred from the truth by such fears. His safety, his certitude, lies in his refusal to separate judgment from vision, or to see nature as separated from grace by separating his reason from either faith or the imagination.

We come now to consider Heidegger's attempt to overthrow the Thomist position, in reflections that add to what we have already seen of Heidegger's thought as a development out of immanent suppositions. In a late attempt at a solution to the problem of Being, Heidegger returns once more to Parmenides, his argument in his lecture on "The Principle of Identity" (1957) based on a fragment of that ancient thinker: "For the same perceiving (thinking) as well as being." That is, he says, "Thinking and Being belong together in the Same and by virtue of this Same." Western thought required more than two thousand years to overcome the interference with Parmenides' insight, the culprit an intrusion of metaphysical thought which holds that identity belongs to Being rather than the reverse. Only with speculative Idealism, beginning with Leibniz, does Western thought begin to overcome the handicap and establish "an abode for the essence . . . of identity." Identity is "the unity with itself" of "every being," and by being is meant here thinking-Being, an appropriation and shifting of the Thomist's *esse*. The question for Heidegger is how one arrives at that necessary synthesis of *thinking* and *Being* which constitutes *identity*. He recognizes, though I do not believe he solves, the dilemma Brice Parain expresses in *A Metaphysics of Language*: thinking is antithetic to being, since to think is not to be but to wish to be. (Parain also, we might recall, takes as his own point of departure the problem as it is bequeathed Western man by Parmenides.)

Heidegger's solution to the dilemma is that one must move "away from the attitude of representational thinking," that attitude which has been the curse of Western thought and permeates language itself, a curse requiring not a purification of the language of the tribe but the creation of a new language by the poet. Thus one may leap into a beyond. This "spring leaps away . . . from the habitual idea of man as the rational animal who in modern times has become a subject for his objects." This "spring" is also a leap "away from Being," in order to escape the entrapment by Western metaphysics that intrudes between our age and Parmenides' thought, a metaphysics which takes Being "as the ground in which every being as such is grounded." Thus for Heidegger identity is prevented in Western metaphysics by the supposition that man thinks out of the ground of Being rather than that *thinking-Being* is a synthesis of identity, whereby the ground is identity and not the reverse. That is, Heidegger takes a position antithetic to Thomas. The leap—the "spring"—is into "the abyss," into thoughts "belonging to Being." For "only with us can Being be present as Being, that is, become present."

What we have in this argument is the necessity of a leap of faith or, as Pascal might call it, a "gamble" on identity. It is a gamble on a conclusion already anticipated by Heidegger. Having "felt" or "sprung" toward the desired conclusion through all his thinking life, he turns his rational faculty to support the anticipated conclusion. This is to say that Heidegger devotes reason to the support of a conclusion already reached in his leap of faith. But when we digest the conclusion, we still find ourselves occupying a

closed world. For Heidegger's concern is that thinking and Being
be opened to each other by the leap of faith so that each assumes
the other through (in his phrase) an "event of appropriation."
They become the Same, as suggested by Parmenides in his
fragment from which the argument sets out. In this realm of the
"event of appropriation" we find a "vibrating within itself, through
which man and Being reach each other in nature, achieve their
active nature by losing those qualities with which metaphysics has
[falsely] endowed them."

This "self-vibrating realm" as he calls it is the same one which
Eliot found himself occupying when he wrote his "Preludes" out of
phenomenologist reflections. It is the one Poe earlier rationalizes in
the "pulsing" of the "Heart Divine" in *Eureka*. But Heidegger's
spring into the abyss, he insists, is neither into an "empty
nothingness nor murky confusion." (The phrase seems a rebuke
intended for Sartre on the one hand and the "metaphysical" such
as St. Thomas or Gilson on the other.) The abyss is "the event of
appropriation" in which "vibrates the active nature of what speaks
as language." The " 'principle of identity' means now," he says, "a
spring demanded by the essence of identity because it needs that
spring if the *belonging* together of man and Being is to attain the
essential light of the appropriation": if, in other words, consciousness is to achieve a condition we may describe critically as
self-sufficient.

The discouraging aspect of Heidegger's thought, of his
solution to the problem of identity as he considers it formulated by
Parmenides and (in Heidegger's view) subsequently distorted by
Western metaphysics, is that it can only assert a self-sufficiency by
its leap. It is a solution which remains within a private world, the
individual consciousness, and which therefore has failed to break its
enclosure, its alienation. For to have reached a conclusion in
reconciling the "*belonging* together of man and Being" as Heidegger
does is only at best to have resolved identity of the consciousness
that makes the leap to resolution; it does not solve the problem of
multiplicity of consciousnesses, though it gestures toward language
as the mysterious house of beings (*res*). (Language, he says, was "at
one time called the house of Being.") There is a pathos in the
concluding lines of this essay on "The Principle of Identity":

> Whatever and however we may try to think, we think within the sphere of tradition. Tradition prevails when it frees us from thinking back to a thinking forward, which is no longer a planning.

The pathos in this solution to the problem of time past, present, and future is in the *we* and *us*, and one recalls the dramatic occasion of the words, the 500th anniversary of the University of Freiburg, Breisgau (1957). One of many in the audience, though stirred, might well object to the plural inclusion. For the argument is not out of 500 years of tradition but out of the tradition of Heidegger's three score and ten, out of the "sphere of tradition" of an "I," which remains essentially isolated by the argument. It is the argument perhaps of *a* unified world, but not of the world—not *the* world of multiplicity contained by a reality higher than the particular thinking consciousness that is the "I" we call Heidegger. To conclude that "only with *us* can Being be present as Being . . . become present" is to leap into a closed world and plead to be accompanied.

We conclude with two observations growing out of these objections to Heidegger's attempt upon a solution to the problem of the one and the many. Heidegger's translator and interviewer, Joan Stambaugh, observes in her introduction to *Identity and Difference* that Heidegger sees a recovery in Western thought through an "epochal clearing of Being reached with Hegel." Being becomes "the absolute concept grasping itself, the 'absolute' has become the absolute Idea." We thus enter (we might suggest) a realm analogous to the one Teilhard projects in *The Phenomenon of Man.* (Maritain remarks an extreme realtionship between Hegel and Teilhard in *The Peasant of the Garonne,* cited in our first volume.) In Heidegger's version, *Idea* becomes *I.* In Stambaugh's summary: "This absolute Idea moves forward through history toward an absolute total result of history in which all individual distinctions are at once negated as being merely individual, preserved in the essential being, and elevated into the higher reality of the whole." Such is the concept of Heidegger's Point Omega, in which thought and Being—opened to each other by the leap beyond thought—become "the Same." They fold together in identity. But the negation of individual distinctions is a "murky confusion" in spite of Heidegger's denial because it is not a resolution of distinctions in any reality separate from the leaping thought of the particular consciousness: it is rather an interior dissolving to an illusion of wholeness, in which consciousness turns in upon itself in a species of action which appears more Eastern than Western. We recall here Heidegger's continuing quarrel with Western modes of thought, the villains being Plato and Aristotle primarily. That is, the enemy to Heidegger is those thinkers whose leap of faith is made out of an assumption also, but toward existences separate from consciousness. The leap of such thinkers is to the conclusion that identity belongs to Being rather than the obverse which Heidegger insists upon.

Our second conclusion concerning Heidegger's thought is to recall the poet Ezra Pound solving the problem in his own leap of faith whereby he certifies himself as poet. Pound's is a leap which establishes the authority of the "I." It is a clearer move then Heidegger's in that it reveals its consequences in the existential world, the world of the many, more immediately. For Pound sees the necessity of an appropriation of power out of the "sphere of tradition" to the immediate uses of the poet—the "I." In a very early poem "Histrion" (1909), more interesting for its argument than its poetry, Pound asserts the principle which will lead him eventually to champion the poet-king over the philosopher-king. For the poet, through the power of words, commands the Being he dreams into a presence. At least, that is the conclusion Pound acts upon with faith. It is no accident of his thought that he comes to see Mussolini a "poet" in whom to rest confidence. (One remembers as well the shaded question of Heidegger's relation to Nazi thought.) Pound's words:

> Thus am I Dante for a space and am
> One François Villon. . . .
> 'Tis as in midmost us there glows a sphere
> Translucent, molten gold, that is the 'I'
> And into this some form projects itself:
> Christus, or John, or eke the Florentine;
> And as the clear space is not of form's
> Imposed thereon,
> So cease we from all being for the time,
> And these, the Masters of the Soul, live on.

It is, alas, a formula for possession by a spirit other than the self whereby the self wins a power to be exercised upon the world. This is a use of the "self" which might give the exorcist a frightening turn when so boldly expressed. That the same attempt may be made in innocence, out of the desire for unity of the self, does not lessen by its innocence the incipient dangers. Kierkegaard might see in Pound's formulation a conjuring of the Devil such as leads the Scandinavian to suggest that the poet accomplishes his work through compact with Satan, as we earlier quoted him as saying. One supposes St. Thomas would likewise see in Heidegger a trespass upon dangerous ground in which the self would establish itself as a "self-vibrating realm." To adapt another poet on the question: The self becomes its own place thereby, thought becoming the temple of Being and the two infolded together. But that is a sort of limbo of the self, neither Heaven nor Hell. It suggests the disturbing circumstance of Blake's Urizen, we might conclude. For the "self-vibrating realm" is suspiciously like that

> Dark resolving in silent activity,
> Unseen in tormenting passions,
> An activity unknown and horrible,
> A self-contemplating shadow,
> In enormous labours occupied.

We might add that Heidegger's late solution is neither novel nor solution. It is a pass reached in Western thought from Hegel into the nineteenth century well enough, as Heidegger suggests. Or rather an impasse, which leads Baudelaire to attempt an escape into a larger world through correspondences. He says (in Allen Tate's translation):

> All nature is a temple where the alive
> Pillars breathe often a tremor of mixed words;
> Man wanders in a forest of accords
> That peer familiarly from each ogive.
>
> Odors blown sweet as infants' naked flesh,
> Soft as oboes, green as a studded plain,
> —Others, corrupt, rich and triumphant, thresh
>
> Expansions to the infinite of pain:
> Amber and myrrh, benzoin and musk condense
> To transports of the spirit and the sense!

The transport is back into the mysterious complexity of a world larger than the centering "I," the "self-vibrating realm," and we find it a world of guilt and sorrow in which thinking man attempts to recover the ground of Being, *esse*, lost in his willfulness. The flowering out of such evil manipulation of Being is not through the agency of evil—not for St. Thomas nor for Flannery O'Connor. It is through grace, which restores identity, particular being in the ground of Being, *ens* in *esse*, till one becomes still and knows the cause of *ens* through the cause of *esse*, the Presence which is not called but which calls. The call to the "leaping" or "springing" *I* says to that *I* from of old: "Be still and know that I am God."

CHAPTER XXIV

BEING IN TRAVAIL

Our excursion, though brief, will have helped reveal how serious Miss O'Connor's comedy is. As she says, "when a writer's moral sense coincides with his dramatic sense, when his judgment coincides with his vision, he is in a position guaranteeing his respect for mystery." And that maximum amount of seriousness allows a maximum use of comedy. Her comedy underlines a serious movement in her principal characters, most conspicuously those pseudo-intellectuals of an Existentialist persuasion such as Julian and Hulga. They are forced to the edge of the abyss by existential reality because of the contradiction between that reality and their ideas. It is the pressure of *being* itself, not Heidegger's term but St. Thomas's—that deepest something in *ens*, without whose abiding presence nothing would exist. It is St. Thomas's "actual being" that gives the lie to the pretense of being in her characters. And they are at last brought to confront the implications of their intellectual position by the necessity of an action of assent. In Julian's case, for instance, he must assent to enter the "world of guilt and sorrow." Miss O'Connor sees the depths of terror in that predicament. From her point of view, the character is brought to a most stark point of removal from being, and therefore from the Cause of being. The terrors of that alienation she recognizes as out of a perversity, seeing the accomplishment as the Devil's handiwork, though it is a work which prepares the ground on which grace intrudes. When her character is forced out of himself "to meet the extremes of his

nature," as she says, what he discovers is a double danger—and the
necessity of choosing the one over the other. For the abyss is not the
only threat to man's inordinate regard for his freedom. If through
his dream of an absolute independence he comes to the brink of
annihilation, there is another way yet. But it is a way seemingly no
less difficult. Here is the terror of that *positive* of which she speaks
when she says:

> There is something in us, as story-tellers and as listeners to stories, that
> demands the redemptive act, that demands that what falls at least be of-
> fered the chance to be restored. The reader of today looks for that mo-
> tion, and rightly so, but what he has forgotten is the cost of it. His sense
> of evil is diluted or lacking altogether and so he has forgotten the price of
> restoration. . . . He wants to be transported, instantly, either to a mock
> damnation or a mock innocence.

That early recognition raises a terror in Tarwater which seems
more devastating than he wishes to endure. In this respect he is like
"Today's reader" of whom Miss O'Connor speaks who,

> if he believes in grace at all, sees it as something which can be separated
> from nature and served to him raw as Instant Uplift. This reader's
> favorite word is compassion. . . . There is a better sense in which [the
> word] can be used but seldom is—the sense of being in travail with and
> for creation in its subjection to vanity [as in Christ's compassion, his
> sacrifice for creation]. This is a sense which implies a recognition of sin;
> this is a suffering-with, but one which blunts no edges and makes no ex-
> cuses. When infused into novels, it is often forbidding. Our age doesn't
> go for it.

It is evident that she is speaking of the compassion she herself
infuses in *The Violent Bear It Away*, in which she means to dramatize
the agony of Tarwater's travail with and for creation. Tarwater is
not, of course, Kierkegaard's reflective tragic character, the man of
faith who—having renounced the finite and temporal—has them
restored to him as Job has his losses restored. No doubt she believes
in a restoration; for that is the mystery of the Resurrection. But the
attempt to infuse the restoration in fiction is what leads to a
tractarian piety which distorts the limits of art. It leads to such
novels as Charles B. Flood's *Tell Me, Stranger*, "fictionalized
apologetics," which introduces that "depressing new category:
light Catholic summer reading." One is nearer reality in such a
book as Julian Green's *The Transgressor*.

It presents the kind of situation which emphasizes the mystery of evil in its starkest aspects and it offers no solutions by the author in the name of God; nor does it offer the solutions of faith for those who do not believe. It is completely lacking in false piety. . . .

In other words, it emphasizes the terrors attendant upon the temptation to surrender the self and the price of that surrender.

We have observed that Miss O'Connor's most complete portrait of that perverse spirit which Poe explores is in her figure of Rayber. Because Rayber is conceived by her as an intellectual, it is possible to present more directly through him the ideas she is holding up for examination than is possible through Tarwater. If old man Tarwater is a true prophet, "a crypto-Catholic" as she calls him, young Tarwater seems by inclination a natural servant of Satan. He is dangerously near that point in his development which Rufus describes to Norton in "The Lame Shall Enter First." "Right now," he says to Norton, he would go to where his mother is if he should die, to Heaven, "but if you live long enough, you'll go to hell." Tarwater has lived almost long enough. But not quite. He is one of those mediums Miss O'Connor speaks of who, in spite of "natural distortions" is capable of providing an entry into the world of love; he becomes the immediate ground for the dramatization of the deadly battle between being and nonbeing. The dark spirit takes easy residence in his mind as the "stranger," though Tarwater is such a maverick at this turning of his being that he tries to occupy a world separate from the one in which rages the conflict of good and evil. Rayber on the other hand can rationalize his position, an ability which fascinates Tarwater, even as it irritates him. Rayber's attack upon being, by a deliberate action of his will, aligns him with the satanic, though in explicitly denying God, the cause of being, he thinks he denies Satan as well. For Rayber as for Sheppard, faith and the Bible is "for cowards, people who are afraid to stand on their own two feet and figure things out for themselves." Rayber is more set in the way Rufus warns of than Tarwater can force himself to be. For Tarwater has not yet lost the good of the intellect as has Rayber, who "figures" being in abstractions.

Though there is this similarity between Tarwater and Rayber, a similarity Rayber attempts to exploit, Tarwater is acutely aware of a resemblance between his friendly stranger and Rayber. Miss O'Connor's text subtly supports that alignment by gradually changing the stranger's diction, for if initially he speaks with the old man's and Tarwater's language, he comes at last to use Rayber's. Given the freedom of intellect and his faith in it, Rayber considers that he has a certain claim on Tarwater, he is a sort of secularized godfather to the boy. The subtlety of that perversion of responsibility, whereby it becomes a self-defined obligation, will eventually haunt Rayber as he hears himself echoed in Tarwater at the lake just before the drowning of Bishop; but before that time we see Rayber working out the meaning of the world and his own role in the world through a pride of intellect. It was in the interest of Rayber's sister (Tarwater's mother) that he brought to her that strange ministerial student. In the country boy Rayber had discovered the same intense hunger burning as the one we see in old Tarwater. Rayber encourages a "natural union" between the two in the interest of his sister's "self-confidence," the issue of which union is Tarwater. Rayber cannot see the old man's curse upon the Tarwater clan as larger than an inheritance of the particular blood line, in spite of his fascination with the same curse in the ministerial student, in whose destruction Rayber participates.

What we discover in the spiritual actions Miss O'Connor gives us in *The Violent Bear It Away* is that, while man may be a medium of love to the world, he may also be a medium of its opposite, evil, whose existence Miss O'Connor insists upon. "The Christian drama is meaningless without Satan," she says in her review of Christiani's *Evidence of Satan in the Modern World.* "Although the modern reader will find his credulity strained by some of the macabre instances of possession described, he will be required by a strictly scientific attitude not to dismiss this evidence out of hand." Even a Rayber, should he turn his attention upon such evidence, might be hard pressed to explain the existence of such evil in terms of psychology. This is a point of difficulty Miss O'Connor rather more heavily emphasizes in the companion story to *The Violent Bear It Away*, "The Lame Shall Enter First." In the story Miss O'Connor's modern gnostic, Sheppard, experiments with the enigmatic Rufus to Sheppard's own destruction. Explicitly, Sheppard is more concerned with redefining malignant evil than is Rayber. As for Miss O'Connor, she is confident that "the reader leaves [Christiani's] book with his belief in Satan considerably fortified."[1] Her own belief long since settled on the matter, she is not given to the spectacular as Christiani finds it in the existential world, but approaches the Satanic through a psychological realism to see to what extent it may reveal the operation of evil in ways more suitable to her fiction. Thus Rayber, a manipulator of people, tries to get inside people's heads as Old Tarwater protests, and to freeze the mystery of personality in scientific study. He makes of his subject what he would have it be, excluding the inconvenient. He becomes intent on moulding Tarwater in his own image when the boy comes to him out of the night, thus revealing himself as one of those Dr. Frankensteins of the psyche spawned by Freud. That is, he is a radical enemy of *esse*, of *being-ness*.

We are surely meant to notice that, so long as Rayber is Tarwater's principal antagonist, the "stranger" has a more restricted and refined call upon Tarwater's consciousness. Rayber is helpful surrogate to evil, since Tarwater has a grudging admiration for this man whose "guts are in his head." Rayber's devotions are to the abolition of man, though not till the moment of his collapse does he come close to realizing it. Falling so heavily on the modern side of the distinction C. S. Lewis makes on this point, he would think Lewis's distinction nonsense:

> For the wise men of old the cardinal problem had been how to conform the soul to reality, and the solution had been knowledge, self-discipline, and virtue. For magic and applied science alike the problem is how to subdue reality to the wishes of men: the solution is a technique.

Rayber's own self-discipline is practiced through his scholarly technique; for him it is a virtue springing from his knowledge of a mechanistic universe; he is an alchemist of personality. In the service of that universe he is as fanatically enrolled as the modern reader imagines the medieval monk to have been to the service of

---

1. Leon Christiani under the pseudonym of Nicolas Corte also writes *Pierre Teilhard de Chardin*, a book in Miss O'Connor's library. We are again reminded of the difficulties Teilhard has with the problem of evil, difficulties considered in our first volume.

God. Rayber is even ascetic in his devotion. But it becomes clear,
even to Rayber, that his practice of self-denial is but an increasingly
frantic attempt to keep insanity at bay; at last his attempts to
transform being to fit his dream of reality fail.

To Rayber all existence, including persons, is by his chosen
mechanistic principles suitable to the manipulations of intellect,
and he devotes himself to remaking existence in his own image,
violating the human heart in that unpardonable way that
Hawthorne abhors. Because he does not consciously delight in evil,
he is not a Roger Chillingworth, but he is even more frightening, as
blind malignance always is. It is an empty world he builds, one
which at last falls about him, leaving the exterior world and
Tarwater more or less intact. For Rayber's actions are all, in spite
of his denials, turned at last to God's service. Even his lack of
courage, his inability to murder Bishop, is ironically instrumental
in bringing Tarwater to his vision through that paradoxical action
of Tarwater's rescue through murdering Bishop.[2]

Rayber, to Tarwater's disgust, participates vicariously in
those journeys to the edge of the abyss which are so inviting to both.
For he is touched by a madness, though he does not truly see in
what his madness lies. That is, he is touched by the love he
struggles to refuse. For if to Poe the appeal of annihilation must be
dramatized as madness, to Rayber the pull of Love must be
rationalized as madness if he is to preserve his position as
rationalist. If the pull to perverseness violates reason in Poe's
argument, the pull to Love violates reason in Rayber's. He must for
consistency reduce that pull to the clinical level and treat it as a
psychological disturbance. It runs in the family; it is in the blood or
in the genes. Miss O'Connor speaks directly to such an aberration
as Rayber in "Novelist and Believer." She rejects several strains of

---

2. Miss O'Connor remarks in her review of *Further Paradoxes* of H. de Lubac (for the *Bulletin*)
that "paradox is the search for synthesis. It faces toward fullness." We may add: and so it
faces partly away from us; thus through paradox we may proceed toward the ineffable. One
comes closest to a penetration of mystery by entering paradox with faith. I have suggested
elsewhere that Eliot makes this discovery. It allows him to abandon the detachment irony
reveals in him well into *The Waste Land* and to risk the country of paradox in which, as Haze
Motes feared, one might "be walking on the water and not know it and then suddenly know
it and drown." "Death by Water" in *The Waste Land* and *Ash-Wednesday* becomes quite
revealing read in this context of thought.

deterministic devotions which operate in the modern world as a "sociological" or "naturalistic" bias. The problem is not that they are wrong, but that such biases tend to be exclusive, pressing their limited insight as absolute. However, "there is an even worse bias than these two, and that is the clinical bias, the prejudice that sees everything strange as a case study in the abnormal . . . . the novelist will be interested in psychological or cultural or economic determinations only as he is able to go through them to give us a sense of something beyond them." As is usual when she speaks so strongly of the novelist's interest, she is speaking primarily of her own. In the case of Rayber (if we may borrow terminology) she is interested in revealing that those seeds of love in him are there in a way quite different from what his "science" is capable of explaining.[3] Rayber's madness touches him as an inheritance larger than determinations through the blood of the literal family of the Tarwaters, being an inheritance from the Crucifixion. Tarwater insists to Rayber that "It's you the seed fell in . . . . It ain't a thing you can do about it. It fell on bad ground but it fell in deep."

Rayber, then, is pulled in two directions, only one of which appears to him to threaten sanity. But as Kierkegaard in his *Concluding Unscientific Postscript* argues, an imbalance in the direction of denying the realities of either the inner or outer worlds which man inhabits may lead one to madness. There are then, as David E. Roberts says in his *Existentialism and Religious Belief*, in summarizing Kierkegaard's argument, "two kinds of madness." Roberts's summary is so incisively applicable to Rayber's situation that we are justified in presenting it at some length. One kind of madness

> . . . takes the familiar form of retreat into a private world of hallucinations where there is no contact through thinking and feeling with other persons and the external world. [Cf. Poe's world of "a dream within a dream."] The second is not so easily recognized as insanity in our day because it is intimately connected with attitudes we thought were leading toward enlightenment and the triumph of critical intelligence. It is found in the sort of man who knows a great deal about natural science or psychology, and who can therefore manipulate physical processes or human beings with extraordinary expertness, but who himself has somehow

---

3. Note Miss O'Connor's clever use of World War II shrapnel in Haze Motes's body as his handy substitute for Original Sin in *Wise Blood*, analogous to Rayber's genetic madness as substitute for love.

become dehumanized. His habit of viewing the world as raw material for
experiment, observation, and the dispassionate discovery of laws has
made him insensitive to those dimensions of nature and man that can
only be apprehended as the unique and mysterious *thisness (esse)* of each
individual which awakens in us an answering response of feeling. This
man has, like a chameleon, taken on the color of his view of the world. It
is as though he had a card file, a calculating machine, a laboratory inside
of him instead of a heart. And he is crazy.

This summarizes exactly what Old Mason Tarwater has
recognized in Rayber, but in the absence of a common ground
between himself and Rayber, and no common language, he cannot
articulate his recognition of Rayber's madness. The whole world
outside old Tarwater seems similarly mad, and it exerts its force on
Rayber's behalf. Hence it is that the old man is confined to the
asylum, until he realizes that the way to be considered sane is "to
stop prophesying on the ward." He recognizes, as does Tarwater,
Rayber's obsession with manipulating human beings. Both
Tarwaters see Rayber as a man who has "a card file, a calculating
machine, a laboratory inside of him instead of a heart," as young
Tarwater's biting questions about Rayber's hearing-aid show:
"Does your head light up? Do you think in the box . . . or do you
think in your head?"

But Old Tarwater recognizes also the spark still smoldering in
Rayber. Rayber is not absolutely immune "to those dimensions of
nature and man that can only be apprehended as the unique and
mysterious *thisness* . . . which awakens in us an answering response
of feeling." "Once, and only once" does the old man tell Tarwater
the dark secret in Rayber: "He loved me like a daddy and he was
ashamed of it!" Rayber, like old Tarwater, has a fixation, but one
which love denies. "The old man had not known when he went
there to live that every living thing that passed through the
nephew's eyes into his head was turned by his brain into a book or
a paper or a chart." But no matter how strongly Rayber may
protest that his "guts" are in his head, his head will not dislodge
the gnawing love, though this is not to say that Rayber is "saved"
in spite of his will. As if countering this supposition, Miss O'Connor remarks, in "Catholic Novelists and Their Readers,"

> . . . the novelist does not write about general beliefs but about men with
> free will, and there is nothing in our faith that implies a foregone op-

timism for man so free that with his last breath he can say *No*. All Catholic literature will be positive in the sense that we hold this freedom to exist.

We are not encouraged to believe, in spite of the powerful pull of Love upon Rayber, that he will necessarily relinquish his timid *No*. Indeed, our final witness of him suggests the opposite— suggests that he has resisted being pulled into that country to which Tarwater is drawn and so is left to dissolve in his emptiness. (He wills away his *esse*, one might say.) We see him revisiting Powderhead and being visited there by intimations of Love through nature. Walking through the woods to overlook the old homesite on his last visit to Powderhead, he stares "as if he were in some vast overwhelming edifice. . . . out of the silence a bird sounded four crystal notes." As he stares up at the trees, he dislodges his hat, which Bishop recovers for him. Tarwater's own struggle for an absolute freedom is dramatized in part by his obsession with hats, a motif we have touched upon; the final segment of his journey back to Powderhead he makes bareheaded. Remembering this dramatic motif of hats, we see here in Rayber a moment of openness in which a new vision of reality is possible to him. But when he puts his hat firmly back on his head, the spell is broken and he thinks that his near vision is but the old madness stirring in his blood and that he has once more escaped it. Now he is the owner of this place: "Quickly he reduced the whole wood in probable board feet into a college education for [Tarwater]." It is an act by the mind to recover his freedom from the threat of love, a love which nevertheless continues always at hand, even (St. Teresa would say) in a forest reduced to board feet. That evening, as Tarwater is about to drown Bishop, Rayber sees the two walking to the boat.

> The sky was a bright pink, casting such a weird light that every color was intensified. Each weed that grew out of the gravel looked like a green nerve. The world might have been shedding its skin.

But if the world is doing so, Rayber will have none of its revelation. He will not see the world transformed from what he wishes it to be. At this point in the narrative, one has still ringing in his ears Rayber's talk with Tarwater about "rooting out" the compulsion to baptize Bishop, the necessity of cutting down the "weed" every time it appears. Rayber remains still suspended, unable to act, though Tarwater has understood Rayber as encouraging him to drown the child. Rayber knows, too, that he has been so understood, so that when he hears Bishop bellow out of a silence in which he thought himself made secure by turning off his hearing aid, it is as if he concludes with a perversion of Christ's last words on the cross, it is finished. He has succeeded in emptying the external world by denial, being at this point "indifferent even to his own dissolution. It seemed to him that this indifference was the most that human dignity could achieve. . . . To feel nothing was peace."

It is at this point that he discovers what torment lies in the peace of the abyss. Our final account of Rayber has him at the window, looking out over the dark world:

> He stood waiting for the raging pain, the intolerable hurt that was his due, to begin, so that he could ignore it, but he continued to feel nothing. He stood lightheaded at the window and it was not until he realized there would be no pain that he collapsed.

Thus he comes to that spiritual condition he has always struggled toward with his intellect, his natural reason, as the only way to avoid the madness of love. He collapses in his emptiness.

If we are to understand what Miss O'Connor is saying through Rayber, we must I think go to those ideas we have already presented out of St. Thomas and Pascal, with some addition perhaps from Kierkegaard. Both faith and doubt, says Kierkegaard, are manifestations of freedom. One supposes, however, that in respect to action out of freedom, doubt is the act of withdrawal, faith an act of approach to mystery. Some action is necessitated in a situation where the reason cannot demonstrate either eternal life or annihilation. Rayber wants, finally, a certitude without risk, he lacking the courage of a faith that would justify an act. He can neither embrace annihilation nor allow himself to be embraced by love. He shares the common lot of man, caught in the tangles of being, between the tensional poles of the ground of being, where as Pascal says, "Nature confutes sceptics, and reason confutes the dogmatists." "Humble yourself, weak reason," Pascal goes on, "be silent, foolish nature. . . . Hear God." Rayber too is, in Pascal's words, "sustained between those two abysses of the Infinite and Nothing," unable to accept human weakness without despair or human greatness without pride. The argument of Pascal's *Provincial Letters* hinges on the point that "faith involves inescapable decision in the face of inescapable uncertainty." But if either element of the dilemma is removed, faith is destroyed; faith is the one freedom in man which gives any other freedom significance. "I believe" is the mark of grandeur in man because it is the point where the consent of will to believe makes possible that risk without which man is mere automaton. If one act at all, out of the center of himself, he falls—either into the abyss or into Abraham's bosom. Rayber is capable of flirting with action, but not of moving ahead into that territory Kierkegaard holds to be occupied by the man of faith. For if one is to remain sane, he must move beyond the aesthetic state, in which he is "suspended by intellectual skepticism and metaphysical speculation," a stage in which the meaning of life is left hostage to fate and fortune; the victim of external event. He must also move beyond the ethical stage, with its temptations to a religiousness that takes refuge in abstractions such as social problems, "universal" demands that threaten the person of the seeker. In Kierkegaard's version of the Abraham-Isaac story, the differences between the ethical man and faithful man are brought into conflict, demonstrating to Kierkegaard's satisfaction at least the mystery whereby the man of faith has returned to him all that he has renounced through faith.

Rayber never approaches that conflict decisively. Intending well, he is a victim of the paralysis of will; he is a more complex figuring of that spiritual state Eliot dramatizes in "The Love Song of J. Alfred Prufrock." He longs for annihilation romantically, but hasn't a faith to support his longing. Thus he becomes a victim of his own sentimentality. To elect No and do No, as Tarwater does, is an act of faith which reaches to embrace annihilation. It is an activation of the will with consequences Tarwater does not and cannot anticipate. We are not to conclude that Tarwater's searing rescue was inevitable, that he is absolutely predestined as God's prophet. As Miss O'Connor says, the ways of grace are mysterious even as are the ways of evil; "if he appears to have a compulsion to be a prophet, I can only insist that in this compulsion there is the mystery of God's will for him, and that it is not a compulsion in the clinical sense." The distinction she makes here, which she declares herself incapable of explicating, is one that may be somewhat resolved in those distinctions Pascal makes about "efficacious grace." The final remark to make here, in returning to our interest in Poe, is that Poe is less a victim of frozen will than Rayber, though he too rather flirts with making the leap of faith to embrace annihilation than actually making the leap, as one of his French disciples, Rimbaud, seems to have done. Poe too is detained by metaphysical speculations and intellectual skepticism within what Kierkegaard calls the aesthetic level of being. In Kierkegaard's terms, Rayber too is an inhabitant of that level, in spite of the appearance of intellectual action in his assault upon the world. Tarwater recognizes at once, however, that Rayber's action is all talk; Rayber lends support by inaction to the popular spirit of the time, being a distorted figure of St. Thomas's man, the crown of nature and medium of love in the world. That is, Rayber is a grotesque; he is man with his "guts in his head."

CHAPTER XXV

ORIGINALITY:
THE BURDEN OF THE FALLEN

Reason in Poe's thought has no more cause than perversity; it too is an accidental effect of consciousness—that fundamental given which Poe also has difficulty accounting for. Even so, reason as accident of consciousness may be a cause of madness. For in particular it is the principal conjuror of annihilation. Such conditions as these affect the very terms of Poe's arguments as they appear more widely than in his tale of "The Imp of the Perverse," and because they appear widely in him, they call our attention to yet another given with which Poe is forced to contend: the given language of consciousness, impressions, images, but most of all the very words with which consciousness attempts to come to grips with itself. *Good, evil, soul, moral, archfiend, demonic*—such terms are an inheritance to consciousness from a stream of thought preceding the particular awareness named Poe who presumes to use them. He does not wish them to bear the significations of their old association of idea and reality, the burden upon any language older than its user. Poe's boldness in manipulating a given language to his own uses is no doubt the main point William Carlos Williams has in mind when he praises Poe. Poe's "greatness is in that he turned his back and faced inland to originality, with the identical gesture of a Boone." Again, "What he says, being thoroughly local in origin, has some chance of being universal in application . . . . Made to fit a *place* it will have that actual quality of *things* anti-metaphysical—." What one might find confusing in Williams's praise is his failure to realize the limits of man's originality, history itself (as reflected in our language) being a constant warning of limits. Boone, seeing a virgin West, invades it with axe and rifle, a "language" out of Europe and not indigenous to Eden. These are the instruments of fallen man, and unless one recognize them as such, they may escape ordinate control in the frenzy of Eden pursued. One carries the past with him wherever one goes, an inescapable burden in the pursuit of "originality." The failure to recognize that burden finds a parallel in those intellectual axes and rifles wielded by the Puritan mind in its effort to build New Eden, a subject we shall address in our final volume. Williams, in seeing Poe's originality as counter to that New England mind, does not recognize the underlying similarities between Poe's mind and that of a Jonathan Edwards, being distracted by antagonistic surfaces, by spectacle in the language of each.

We suggest here (for future development at length) that the epistemological inheritance of the two minds—Poe's and Edwards's—is fundamentally the same. Not realizing their mutual intellectual origins, the critic of Poe may well credit him with originality and thus mistakenly see in him "the astounding, inconceivable growth of his locality." Thus Williams reaches the conclusion that "in him American literature is anchored, in him alone, on solid ground." But to the contrary, Poe's "originality" is anchored in that thought flourishing out of the Enlightenment. Consider Williams's instance, Poe's exegetical proposal: the "fiery serpent that bit the children of Israel . . . possibly the guinea worm . . . . The mysterous is so simple when revealed by science!" Poe's words, and spoken like a true son of the eighteenth century, even when we allow some residue of an older sense of *knowledge* to lie in his use of *science*. We have seen that for Poe the *mysterious* in a tale is that which is made to yield to analysis. Poe can see Hawthorne's "mystery" only at one level, that of empirical science and strict rationalist logic. The axe and rifle of reason made a clearing in nature no less for Poe than for his New England counterparts, thereby denaturing nature. That, at its base, is the effect Williams calls originality.

More than American literature is anchored in this ground,

adhering most particularly in our words, those sometimes anguished ransom of the past to the future. That ransom we tend to waste with the abandon of spendthrifts upon the present moment, leading the alarmed poet to declare again and again the necessity of purifying the language of the tribe. A brief disquisition upon the effects of wasting language, as we see it evidenced in the abuse of a term like *originality*, may show something of the popular spirit of our moment of history with which Miss O'Connor found herself contending. What we share in this distortion with our contemporary wastrels is that old failed will in Adam, who would be equal to the gods. And a sign is the attempt to divorce a present moment from its origins—a provincialism of mind. It is exhibited in our blindness to the depths in such a word as *originality*. Because we would be self-generated, we share the aberrant presumption, not only with compatriots of the moment, but with the generations of man reaching back to that first who revolted against the Giver, in concert with Lucifer, whom we romanticize as Prometheus in recent centuries.

Now it is in our abuses of the language that old origins of aberration find echo in the present moment. We need not go so far into our past as the mists of the first Eden to discover that mortal decay. Poe's own abuses of words may serve as exemplum, and we keep in mind particularly the shift of emphasis, Poe's primary concern for the immediate emotional effect upon a presumably passive consciousness—the reader. In Poe, the prime mover of emotional effect is presumed to be the poet: the manipulator, the maker, the originator of effect, the cause of language. But what is conveniently ignored is that the poet is not the cause of a language *ex nihilo*. *Originality* as the poet's seduction flourishes out of the Renaissance, in science no less than in art. It is inevitably elevated to the respect of a cardinal virtue as we come to devote ourselves to a progress, the evolving God of immanence which must secretly feed upon the created world. That concern affects literary reputations, even as it fuels the machinery of criticism. There has been, for instance, a considerable industry built not only upon Poe's "originality" but (an instance only) upon Chaucer's *lack* of originality. The Father of English Literature is revealed as a plunderer of European literature. The demonstration of Chaucer's borrowings (not in itself an unworthy contribution) may inordinately give an "effect" of originality in the critic while settling the matter of Chaucer as "creative." In the ordinate address of the critical mind to such a problem, Chaucer must surely be elevated, if for no other reason because it recalls that charm in him that is an effect of an open telling of old tales to an innocent audience. It is, in Pound's phrase, a *making it new*, with the *it* a constant and the poet the servant of continuity in community. For Chaucer's poetry is superlative in that, without shunting aside the poet's responsibility for the good of the thing made, it is devoted to a community gathered in aesthetic pleasures. It binds the tyranny of time in the ground of our common humanity.

It is an arresting reflection then that, in the name of Progress, we elevate originality beyond its limited virtue. Such is the consequence of our general usurpation of the Divine prerogative of creativity. If such a shifting of the First Cause to that secondary cause in creation—man—affects the artist in our society so radically—as it clearly has—it affects even more the scholar in those institutions which of old were devoted to knowledge, to a pursuit of the truth for its own sake—the universities. I have at hand a set of "guidelines for promotion" of faculty, setting the criteria for judgment. As for "research," it is not the truth which is central, but "new knowledge." Research then must be "original" research. How that attitude toward truth affects the scholar's responsibility to the mind, his responsibility to a continuity of mind in time, is clear enough in philosophy or the history of literature. A new theory is presumed more valuable than truth itself; "innovation" becomes the operative concept, just as a new food additive or the development of a new serum becomes worth more than yesterday's solution to physical or physiological concerns. Not long since, a conference of poultry experts was proclaimed at my institution, their theme advertised as "The Chicken of Tomorrow." A Platonic wag threatened a rival conference, with application for Federal funds, under the title "The Egg of Today." But wit has little effect against the drift of institutionalized thought. The "chicken of tomorrow" is the high goal which colors the intellectual community of universities, a direct effect out of Enlightenment thought. Such an emphasis must inevitably make it seem less important in the popular spirit of the age to know what Plato or St. Thomas have to say about chickens, or what the consequences of Bacon's or Voltaire's thought have been upon that popular spirit. The possibilities in Socrates' definition of *man* which prompted a clever opponent to present a plucked chicken, a nine-holed biped without feathers, and declare that Socrates thought it a man are that easily turned aside. What matter St. Augustine's or St. Thomas's considerations, let alone Aristotle's, on Socrates' questions. That is old knowledge, and the successful academic very quickly learns the advantage Chaucer's monk enjoys: "This ilke Monke leet olde thinges pace."

Now if we look about us carefully, with the eye of Plato or Aristotle or Thomas, we discover interesting consequences of that climate of thought in which the popular spirit is virtually the only spirit extant, a creation of reason gone amuck. And in the products of progress, the things of creature comfort and entertainment such as autos, houses, breakfast foods and popular novels, we discover a punishment of our "enlightened" presumption: a deadly sameness. Particularity becomes the victim. The relation of Thomas's *esse* and *ens* having been set aside, sameness becomes the principal threat to the dream of happiness fostered by our dream of progress. It is as if there really were a unique self in each of us that we are bound to treasure, which might (Thomas argues at least) be discovered in the uniqueness of nature, in the particularity of the *ens* which speaks of cause whereby the thing is what it is and no other thing. The sameness of our art—our autos and cereals and books—mocks us as vocationists precisely because it is not a celebration of the abiding. It is a sameness bred of an aberrant appetite for newness as a virtue in itself, an originality for which man may claim exclusive credit as creator. Thus we begin to practice in a rather frenzied way a rescue, which is but an extension of error. We would stamp upon our creations some claim through "innovation," in the process of creation or in its design or contents, with (as often as not) only superficial attention to the final end. Oh, cries the monk out of the desert, looking at the strange city circus we call our civilization—oh, could we but recover to our service Aristotle's four causes that we might begin to think again. As in the children's twilight game, we find we must go back and start over, having forgotten to ask "Mother, may I?"—the question which at least acknowledges something given by "Mother Nature," that limit upon pure originality in man.

But, objects the innovator, our mass products do not cater to the masses. The object, the products exists in infinitudes, but the end of each is a particular self. One might illustrate that plea from political, social, economic, even spiritual realms of our community, but the most persuasive, obvious, and generally symptomatic presence is thickly about us in the assault of the media upon us as consumers. There one finds brought into focus all the intellectual innovations bred and nurtured in the universities in support of the chicken of tomorrow. Thus a perfume (and how many academic reputations rest upon the development and distribution of a perfume), though made for the millions, is presented as uniquely effective. A queue of lovely ladies is flashed upon us from the screen, but the confident voice—carefully modulated between that of the scientist, sociologist, and prophet—assures any captured female "you" that she shall smell like none of these lovelies, as no two of them smell alike, though each eagerly uses the same magic potion.

Thus sameness is given the magic of *uniqueness* by words abused, and deliberately abused. Originality is transferred by the wizardry of science to the possession of the lonesome self, a laying on of mystical formulae which is the open sesame of the self's closed world. What a gay, happy community is shown to issue from perfumes (or deodorants). Who dares contend ours is not a religious age? But what is recognized in such manipulation is a truth worth rescuing. The self must be a new self. On that rock of truth are built such perversions of Peter and Paul. In a perverted parallel, the self must be continuously new with the rising of each sun. NEW becomes the crying point for breakfast cereal, soap, or books in the mouths of those prophets and poets of the new mysteries who make a product "go." Thus the public relations conjurors of the holy public spirit. But this diabolic perversion of nature and man is in fact an attempt to practice alchemy upon our innate desire for the rescue of the self; it turns—or keeps turned—the self to self-rescue. And the key instrument to the successful practice of that alchemy is the perversion of the gift once thought to set man somewhat above the general run of creation, the intellect. Not intellect, but the faculty of reason in that intellect; carefully separated from the other aspects of mind. For as the Enlightenment demonstrated quickly in the political realm, reason so isolated is the quickest medium to quicken pride. And thus, accompanying that studied abuse of one's attempt at self-rescue through the quest for the "new," there is given a sop to the mind—the elevating praise of reason's "objectivity." Objectivity becomes, through our willing participation in this manipulation, a concept whereby we dissociate ourselves from both responsibility and commitment. For when we prove the objectivity of our view, we may then lay claim to a credit of an inordinate degree. Objectivity has had removed from it by our dissociation both wonder and awe, not to mention a healthy doubt. We stand flattered by our separation from all that is not the self. Now the self, already under transformation, may become vicariously the beneficiary and hence the possessor of objectivity. One may enjoy the confidence he imagines in a Newton or Einstein (or whomever he will) by watching those experiments with headache powders in glass stomachs and graphs of scientific effects prepared by "leading medical authorities." One may be induced to swallow the results of comparative taste-tests of soda pop—through the mind.

Objectivity, as we are tempted to distort it in self-justification, tends to become the dark shadow of our presumptive claim to omniscience, which the popular spirit still presumes justified to the man of science as he is popularly understood. When these two distortions are brought into conjunction—the romance of objectivity and the romance of originality—the self is amply provided a routine for exorcising itself from the large creation, all that which is not the self, and gain as its reward the illusion of its own transcendence. The self thereby becomes easy victim of the manipulations of the directors of such abstracted selves, for that is how the self becomes a powerless unit of power, suited to conglomeration. And that is the secret of power in Enlightenment thought. Consider specific evidence of assaults upon the self, the sore of our spiritual disease: one sees a lovely blond Medusa's head, shaking its long hair to show its loveliness. It is lovely because it is washed with an expensive cosmetic rinse. And it says, "It costs more, but I'm worth it." The perverse incarnation draws one to a death of spirit in matter—through abstractions manipulated by the reason and given an appearance of reasonableness. Or, next frame, the self-made Pygmalion, in swim suit at her pool side. She is what she is, and the world is what it is, as a consequence of drinking non-caloried pop—the magic potion of her transformation, not practiced by external manipulating agents of the media, but by a creative act of her own will. She tells us, with a Puritan echo of Eve's seductiveness, "Be good to yourself. There's only one you." There is a handsome Adam at her elbow, grinning like a presidential candidate, so that any "you" may be vicariously present in Eden, male or female. Thus the popular conjurings to spiritual suicide. The manipulation is reduced to its bare principle in that journal of sophisticated intellectuals, *The New Yorker*. A full page liquor ad, for a St. Valentine's Day issue, colorful with filigree and arabesques—those old first devices of the grotesque in art in the early Renaissance. In the center of the page stands the only Word, in discrete type: "Love Thyself." That becomes the first and great commandment, and the second is like unto it: "Drink brand X: Deny all else."

What we witness here in the manipulations of the lonely selves of our age is not simply the machinery for the generation of Power—in the instances cited the power of wealth through the sale of pop or liquor or hair rinse. (Lest I be misunderstood, I ought to say that pop and hair rinse and liquor are not in themselves "evil.") What is destructive in an absolute degree is the individual spirit as it wills to be wooed to annihilation. It is a species of spiritual suicide. That is the heinous effect upon individual creations, whether practiced in the political, social, or economic realms of community. The individual is encouraged, and wills to believe, that the self which he calls "I" is the ultimate reality. Such trading on the popular myth of the self-made man hides the reality beneath its surface: that there is only the self-unmade man. (It ought to be mentioned as doubtful that in the final moment one may successfully plead destruction by brainwashing.) The pride of the self is the only suicide, whether it be slowly accomplished or instantly by the reflex of a finger on a trigger or swallowing an ultimate potion—those last acknowledgments of the dependence of the self upon its location in time and place, the body. Suicide is the ultimate egotistical act. The most apocalyptic act granted man, more apocalyptic than the atom bomb when seen in the perspective of the individual, in whose name we have come to worship. The monoxide of "I," when it is not reciprocally related to the dioxide of the Other in a community of being, gradually drowns itself. That version of spiritual suicide is spoken of from Pascal through Baudelaire and into our century under the rubric of *ennui*. Of course, there are the more spectacular exits, reported in the evening news, suicide with a bang rather than a whimper. But the point remains: whether gradually accomplished or on the instant, suicide is surely the ultimate egotistical act in that it presumes to deny all being—first of all creation not the self, and finally the self itself.

Yet we see that creation survives such attempts at its denial. Gerard de Nerval could not eradicate his memory with his apron-string noose. If you read these words, even in doubt of them you prove my point: the world survives. St. Thomas, we remember, holds that ultimate attempt of annihilation as itself frustrated. One cannot destroy absolutely what he himself has not absolutely created. Dante dramatizes the argument in the sad wastes of the *Inferno*. And in the light of this argument, we return once more to Poe and his pathos, to his attempt through *originality* to deny the *other*, to an abuse of words by the poet which must be seen to have had a considerable influence upon the popular spirit of our age beyond his "literary" influence. The manipulations of the emotion through sound, under the pretense of reason, in the interest of a controlled effect: that is the *end* of Poe's art. It is an end adapted as means in the manipulation of sound for power. *Originality, objectivity, innovation*: we must beware the demonic potential in such old ideas.

CHAPTER XXVI

ON REDUCING
THE IRREDUCIBLE X

In spite of Poe's attempt to make the annihilation of the self substantial by emptying old words and filling them with emptiness, signification remains still "the shadow which prevails" against him. Poe's fascination with the "irreducible x" of annihilation (to borrow a phrase from his disciple Wallace Stevens) gives rise to his fascination with hieroglyphics, for in such signs one finds the meaning so long absent that they become the tempting compromise between the desire for originality as a creation *ex nihilo* and the burden of that preëxistence amid which the consciousness finds itself. Similarly, the manipulated conformities of landscape become a sort of new language. But in his fascination, one finds him possessed of the very mathematical mind he attacks in the "Colloquy," those literary structures themselves a borrowing of form from the debates of the schools. Poe is forced, as are we all, to accept some givens, though against the desire of his will, whether the given be the world's body or a language floating through generations of mind. In respect to language, his revenge is to drain usual meaning from words, in so far as he can. Thus actions toward being are declared actions toward annihilation, the idea to which he gives narrative plot in "The Imp of the Perverse." "The impulse increases to a wish, the wish to a desire, the desire to an uncontrollable longing, and the longing . . . is indulged."

When W. H. Auden reaches our shores a hundred years after Poe, he looks about him and concludes (though without reference to Poe) that we are heavily infected with "West's disease" (the allusion is to Nathanael West): "This is a disease of consciousness which renders it incapable of converting wishes into desires. A lie is false; what it asserts is not the case. A wish is fantastic; it knows what is the case but refuses to accept. All wishes, whatever their content, have the same unvarying meaning—'I refuse to be what I am.' " We have seen that such a characterization fits Miss O'Connor's Rayber and his condition of paralyzed will rather well. If Auden is right, we may find Poe has affected consciousness beyond his own private struggle with it in that he helped call into being that malaise in which we hesitate before the consequences of annihilation. For not many of us can be tempted over the edge into the abyss, can be tempted to indulge the longing for annihilation, though we are fascinated by the prophets of destruction. "A prophet gone wrong," says Miss O'Connor of her Misfit, "is almost always more interesting than your grandmother, and you have to let people take their pleasures where they find them." Certainly the idea of the abyss has been conjured into the general consciousness, whatever or whoever the Imp, and magnetic fear draws to malaise. What was necessary to this particular fear was discrediting the existing world; but the discrediting was not accomplished by characterizing the world's abuse as sinful "worldliness" as Hawthorne or Old Tarwater might do. One had to undermine the worldly science of empiricism as well. For the "Puritan Perplex" is not the only stream of our perplexity. If a Rayber abuses reality by his clinical bias, another form of rationalism is capable of abusing the limited virtues of the clinical.

Human uses of empirical data, says the narrator of "The Imp," go astray by "deducing and establishing everything from the preconceived destiny of man, and upon the ground of the objects of his Creator." The particular scientist named to illustrate the error, the phrenologist, has a particularly ironic suggestiveness in relation to Poe's rejection of Humboldt in *Eureka*. Humboldt it might be said devoted himself to reading the bumps and crevasses of the earth's body. Now one may not simply dissociate Poe from the narrator of "The Imp of the Perverse" on the grounds that Poe is merely being satiric of the doctrines of Utilitarianism and is arguing the

absurdity of that position from an exaggerated position in his narrator. It is not empirical data as pursued by science since Bacon,
with its secularizing propensity, that Poe's murderer would reject,
on the grounds that it abuses nature by presuming to detect in
nature God's secular ends. Though "Deity" and "God" are mentioned, piety or humility in man's uses of the created world is not at
issue; the point of attack is rather man's following his reason to the
exclusion of the god that holds Poe enthralled by wishes, desires,
longings: the Imagination. The point he insists upon is that "God"
cannot be comprehended at all "in his visible works." It follows
that rationalization of man's actions in nature under the pretense of
reading God's intentions for nature is but the height of reason's fol-
ly. Any god other than man's own operative imagination is a false
god.

Yet a perspective upon "all things" is as necessary to Poe as it
is to Humboldt, and that necessity eventually calls forth *Eureka* as
an attempt to sustain a rationalization of that god Imagination, to
which the central act of worship by Poe is the body of his work. He
says, in "The Domain of Arnheim," that "no position can be attained on the wide surface of the *natural* earth from which an ar-
tistical eye, looking steadily, will not find matter of offence in what
is termed the 'composition' of the landscape." What is required, as
we have seen, is those "earth-angels" who are "a class of beings,
human once but now invisible to humanity," who from a distance
perceive as humans do. Only from such a position may the bumps
of "all things" be artistically managed. To such a spirit, "our disorder may seem order." The garden of the hemisphere "may have
been set in array by God" for the earth-angel's especial "death-
refined appreciation of the beautfiul." Thus Poe becomes member
of a new body of the elect. Such argument has interesting echo in
Wallace Stevens's justifications of the imagination as the "necessary angel" through which one achieves a death-refined appreciation of the beautiful. Stevens's grand visions of the hemispheres in
his building of metaphor assert order as the province of the
imagination. For Stevens as for Poe it is through the imaginative act
that one gains a levitation and detachment from what Poe calls the
"ground of the objects of his Creator." Stevens calls that ground
"reality," but it is "mere" reality.

Undoubtedly Poe felt himself such a creature as his "earth-angel."[1] In *Marginalia* he says:

> I have sometimes amused myself by endeavoring to fancy what would be the fate of any individual gifted, or rather accursed, with an intellect *very* superior to that of his race. Of course, he would be conscious of his superiority; nor could he (if otherwise constituted as man is) help manifesting his consciousness. Thus he would make himself enemies at all points. And since his opinions and speculations would widely differ from those of all mankind—that he would be considered a madman is evident. How horribly painful such a condition! Hell could invent no greater torture than that of being charged with abnormal weakness on account of being abnormally strong.

Not only must Poe create a whole universe; he must create Hell as well, without which the fullness of his created experience would be incomplete; he must be the misunderstood artist. But the worst hell of all is that even so strange an angel as he proposes cannot create its world except by borrowing from the preëxistent. He is repeatedly forced back to an indignity: he must borrow words, with their implicit structuring of language and language's images, in which hover not only the ghosts of other minds but in which also lie the temptations of consciousness toward the exterior world at the present moment of consciousness. He could not "(if otherwise constituted as man is) help manifesting his consciousness," and so he must be considered by all men a madman.

The "Domain of Arnheim," as we are encouraged to see it, has "a weird symmetry, a thrilling uniformity, a wizard propriety. . . . Not a dead branch, not a withered leaf, not a stray pebble, not a patch of brown earth was anywhere visible." *Weird, thrilling, wizard* do not, however, remove his landscape so far into an imagined world but that we detect the remnants of the eighteenth-century formal English garden at its base, just as the diction of his prose in general is haunted by that century, as in such words as *symmetry, uniformity, propriety.* Our perspective upon this domain reveals it a

---

1. Similarly, Wallace Stevens celebrates the poet as "major man" in his "Notes Toward a Supreme Fiction." His position is strikingly similar to Poe's. As with Poe, God is "simply a projection of itself by a race of egoists." (*Letters,* 349) Again, "God is a postulate of the ego." ("Adagio," *Opus Posthumous,* 171) He writes of himself, "The author's work suggests the possibility of a supreme fiction, recognized as a fiction, in which men could propose to themselves a fulfilment." In that work he considered his most important one, "Notes Toward a Supreme Fiction," one might say that he is "trying to create something as valid as the idea of God has been," to use his own words. (*Letters,* 863)

dead place, called *perfect* as a circumlocution. But from it every hint of mortality that nature gives us is removed by denial, except that by calling attention to no "dead branch," "withered leaf," or "brown earth" those realities of the existential world are introduced. Because they are present by the very attempt of denial, they undercut the imaginative denial of them so that we have our attention called to Poe's world as a product of wishful thinking.

Gilson in his *Spirit of Thomism* tells a little story about a horse, to illustrate the inadequacy of natural reason alone to account for "actual existence" (*esse*): It is "a popular story, in France, about the horse of the knight Roland. He was a wonderful horse; he had all possible characteristics, all possible qualities. He was fast, he was strong, he did not eat, he did not drink. He had only one defect. He was dead." Actual existence (*esse*) is what Poe cannot give to his world, as man cannot give it to Roland's horse. From Roland's horse, through that fabulous horse in Chaucer's tale, through the fabulous machines of science fiction (out of the Enlightenment, including Poe's own) through Yeats's golden nightingale, down to Haze Motes's Essex (*esse* with an irreducible *x*, the cause of its being): the temptation to man is to make a world; the frustration in such worlds is that he cannot provide "actual existence." The flood of cartoons and jokes about the machine turn upon that impossible task. The machine, even the computer, can express confusion, but not anger. It can spew detail or nonsense, but not unifying love or disintegrating invective.

On Poe's lake, that "inverted heaven," one floats in a miraculous canoe "stained with arabesque devices in vivid scarlet, both within and without." That canoe turns itself, propels itself into the setting sun. The landscape in and out of the lake impresses the observer with "a miraculous extremeness of culture that suggests dreams of a new race of fairies, laborious, tasteful, magnificent and fastidious." It is "the phantom handiwork, conjointly, of Sylphs, of the Fairies, of the Genii, and of the Gnomes." It is the imaginative attempt of one Edgar Allan Poe, the Prometheus of the imagination, to seize the Heaven of beauty by the violence of an imaginative act which destroys existential reality. The force used is a commandeered language distorted by its enslavement. What one is struck by is that Poe appropriates an emerging nineteenth-century technocracy and translates it to the service of an eighteenth-century aesthetic, calling the hybrid agents Sylphs, Fairies, Genii, and Gnomes. The canoe, in spite of its psychedelic camouflage, is a miniature paddlewheel with automatic pilot.

Twain will make more raucous use of Poe's strategy a little later, in *A Connecticut Yankee at King Arthur's Court*, exaggerating by outrageous juxtaposition. He chooses the medieval world as seen by his disaffected nineteenth-century imagination, which he is also somewhat inclined to satirize. He adds to that imagination those techniques of nineteenth centruy mechanics he wishes to celebrate as his homage to the new god emerging in the popular spirit. But already technocracy is deadening sensibilities, as Twain is forced to acknowledge in the dark conclusion of his novel. "For magic and applied science alike," we hear C. S. Lewis saying in *The Abolition of Man*, "the problem is how to subdue reality to the wishes of men: the solution is technique."

But if Twain is pulled toward the technical magic in Yankee mechanical ingenuity on the one hand and toward the appeal of a nature unviolated by man's techniques on the other (an appeal celebrated by Huck on the raft), there is no comparable division in Poe. Poe will use the magic of words to subdue Twain's conflicting worlds and remove them by soaring above them on the wings of poesy. To see the earth from the perspective of "the angels that hover between man and God" allows one to imagine earth a single animal, like Roland's horse, suspended in the pastures of space, but under the command of the imagination; thus all nature becomes domesticated by imagination, though *dead* is another word for this particular domestication. Troublesome realities are housebroken by Poe as "earth-angel," so that they may dwell in the large house of consciousness. But one can't help recalling another imaginative perspective upon our tiny planet turning in the vastness of space. Dante sees it a shiny apple toward which we hungrily reach, but he sees also the worm of evil buried at its core. As committed as Dante is to the powers of man's imaginative use of knowledge, he does not suppose the imagination also a sufficient insecticide. Man unaided cannot slay the dragon, liberate himself,

and restore the garden as he would have it. That is the position
Miss O'Connor holds against the assaults of the popular spirit of
her age.

"The imaginative game of liberation derives its momentum
from an intensely experienced alienation and an equally intense
revolt against it," Voegelin remarks in *The Ecumenic Age*. Voegelin is
addressing himself to the larger movements of thought in history,
upon which float the drifting empires. But he has come to consider
that the paramount measure of history is not the "conventional
belief" in history as "a meaningful course of events on a straight
line of time." The peculiar structure in history "originates in the
stratification of man's consciousness through the process of differentiation." Revelation is the key to history, and it is a revelation
within the movements of the individual soul—and to that soul—of
"the Hidden or Unknown God." Man discovers "something in his
humanity that is the site and sensorium of divine presence; and he
finds such words as *psyche*, or *pneuma*, or *nous*, to symbolize the
something." We are talking with the aid of Voegelin with the terms
of philosophers like Plato and Aristotle, but they touch also upon
the mystical Word of St. John—upon the *logos*. And we are talking
also about those grounds in the soul which Miss O'Connor approaches in saying that man, even given his "natural distortions,"
is the medium for "the entrance of love into the world through . . .
human character." The truth Voegelin has come to in his
monumental study "pertains to man's consciousness of his
humanity in participatory tension toward the divine ground, and to
no reality beyond this restricted area." Thus he concludes that
"History is not a stream of human beings and their actions in time,
but the process of man's participation in a flux of divine presence
that has eschatological direction. . . . The process of history, and
such order as can be discerned in it, is not a story to be told from
the beginning to its happy, or unhappy, end; it is a mystery in
process of revelation."

These remarks from Voegelin are helpful to us in several ways.
First, they give us a further perspective upon the linear conception
of history as it emerges out of the Enlightenment in tandem with
the ideal of progress. ("Historicism," says Eliade in *Image and Sym-*

bol, "is a product of the decomposition of Christianity: it could only
have come about insofar as we had lost faith in the trans-historical
reality of the historical event.") Poe's reaction to such an entrapment by time, we have seen, is to elevate his own imagination. For
he is uncomfortable with the determinist aspect of history conceived as a blind force external to the imagination, a conception
(we may add) which includes nature as well as man in its control.
The shift in Voegelin's focus from that of his earlier volumes reveals
his own break with a nineteenth-century visionary conception of
history he seems to discover as residual in himself. It is a conception
such as affects Teilhard, as we argued earlier. Teilhard is still committed to the linear, leading Tresmontant to observe that he "did
not know how to situate and define, in a historical framework, . . .
this Christianity he had discovered." He could not see the affinity
between the revelations he experienced and the revelations inherent
in Christianity from the beginning, "of Scripture, of the fathers,
and of the most constant tradition of the church." Voegelin means
to designate such affinities in the complexities of history in his term
ecumenic, a word expressing a common perception of the divine
ground of being which is independent of historical periods or circumstances. (Voegelin's *ecumenic* is a more precise term than its
popular use since Vatican II.) In consequence of Teilhard's
historical view, there is an inordinate emphasis in his work upon
the evolution of the whole of creation toward Point Omega; in that
emphasis, individuality is subdued and the particularity of the
creatura of God distorted. The distortion affects most particularly
the conception of the personal soul in its relation to both creation
and its Creator. It is in this respect that Voegelin's latest approach
may be seen as a criticism of Teilhard. For Voegelin begins to give
an emphasis to the divine presence in its relation to the individual
soul as being separate from the constrictions of time and place. The
millennial impetus in Teilhard seems born of his attempt to accommodate revelation to nineteenth-century scientific thought; but it is
modified by Voegelin's perspective (though Voegelin does not mention Teilhard):

> the substance of the creative action is the "word." From the beginning,
> reality is the divine word speaking in succession the evolution of being

from matter through plant to animal life, until it speaks man who, in the persons of patriarchs and prophets, responds by his word to the word spoken by god in history. The reality of the cosmos, thus, becomes a story to be told by the man who participates responsively in the story told by the god. . . . The word of man when he articulates his consciousness of reality emerges from the reality that is the word of god.

Eric Voegelin's position may at first strike one, as he reads *The Ecumenic Age*, as confusingly independent of traditional thought, and there has been one review at least that harbingers an alarm which will no doubt grow. In the Fall 1975 issue of *Modern Age*, Professor Thomas Molnar raises questions about the direction Voegelin takes in his two recent books, *The Ecumenic Age* and *From Enlightenment to Revolution*, putting questions to those works: "is Voegelin a philosopher, a historian, or a political scientist? If a philosopher, is he Christian, a classical Greek, or a German idealist?" Voegelin, says Molnar, "appears to be retreating from the transcendental exploration and to be integrating mankind with history, with only ambiguous hints at transcendence." An answer to Molnar's questions and his observation lies, in part, in Voegelin's attempt to work himself out toward the transcendent by a firm control of reason as it examines the history of man's experiences in nature. Miss O'Connor would surely understand the tentative position he takes, whereby he avoids being at once inhaled into any established position, that he may establish a position. In the *Bulletin*, Miss O'Connor regrets the critical approach in which "a 'Catholic structure' [is] used like a bulldozer," and in another of her reviews, addressed in the direction of literary criticism, she regrets in the title *Catholic Review of Books and the Arts*, "the implied assumption that there is a brand of criticism special to Catholic rather than that any good criticism will reflect a Catholic view of reality." What she is expressing, as we have seen, is her faith that any sound address to nature through natural reason, whether its object be seen scientifically, philosophically, or artistically, will reflect what is or should be orthodoxy in proportion to the soundness of the address, the clarity of the eyes. That is surely also a position implicit in Voegelin's approach, in which he discovers the necessity of an integration of the various disciplines of mind upon the question of being, so that Molnar's question of whether he is philosopher, historian, or political scientist is not initially to the point.

We have considered this problem in Voegelin's new position at length in our first volume, but it is helpful to put the question in a slightly different perspective by suggesting that Voegelin's approach is, by analogy, rather like Wordsworth's approach to the problem of being as contrasted to Coleridge's. Coleridge makes certain assumptions about the transcendent, from which he moves. Wordsworth attempts to avoid assumptions, in so far as he can, in pursuit of revelation in the world. In this distinction lies the principle upon which the imaginative tasks of *Lyrical Ballads* are given division by the poets. Wordsworth's "Tintern Abbey" is the principal exemplum of this approach, in which he addresses himself as immediately as he can to that world of nature external to his consciousness, as Voegelin approaches the history of nature—human nature—as revealed by man's words in the long course of time. As to whether Voegelin is Christian, Greek or German idealist, the observation must first be that he sets aside labels as he sets about examining the evidence of a transcendent Creator of the cosmos in the testimony of mind—the history of thought in the world. In this respect he is well within "the spirit of Thomism." The Creator in the mystery of His ways, Voegelin concludes, speaks in different ways to different minds. In the differentiation of history Voegelin discovers a common evidence of transcendent presence speaking through the created world, a world he calls the "word of the god" in the passage quoted above.

One cannot disregard his suggestion of a "divine presence that has eschatological direction." Nor may one ignore the severity of Voegelin's indictment of Gnosticism in that presumption which ignores the spoken word of the Creator, the created universe. And here again we find him close to Thomas Aquinas, though as we noted he has some reservations about Thomas in other respects. He also has severe words to speak on the failure of the Church since the Renaissance to comprehend its role in restoring order and opposing the destruction of the grounds of being by that gnostic thought born of the Enlightenment. In "Immortality: Experience and Symbol," for instance, he speaks of "theologians, who ought to know better," who are nevertheless "softening under constant pressure and display a willingness to demythologize their dogma, to abandon the most charming miracles, to renounce the Virgin Birth, and glumly to admit that God is dead. The attitude is regrettable; for a truth whose symbols have become opaque and suspect cannot be saved by doctrinal concessions to the Zeitgeist." Although on another occasion he calls for a new Thomas rather than for a Neo-Thomism, here he adds that "the exegetic language will make the older symbols translucent again," and a major part of his labor has been to make lucid once more the older symbols of the philosophers, particularly Plato's. His emphatic insistence upon the obligation of man to participate in the "mystery which is in the process of revelation" through the spoken word of the transcendent god (that word being the created cosmos) certainly speaks an orthodoxy very old in the Church.

We may place Poe against this background to strengthen our suggestion that, in spite of himself, he is a child of the Enlightenment. His imaginative game of liberation, "The Domain of Arnheim," can be seen in the light of Voegelin's remark as a game which "derives its momentum from an intensely experienced alienation and an equally intense revolt against it." Voegelin adds that "gnostic thinkers, both ancient and modern, are the great psychologists of alienation, carriers of the Promethean revolt." Poe, we have been arguing, is a Prometheus of the imagination, rejecting the world from which he feels alienated, refusing participation in the revelation of which Voegelin speaks in favor of his own created revelations. By a violence to language in an assault upon Beauty's heaven, he would become sole possessor of that heaven, casting out all Sylphs, Fairies, Genii, and Gnomes. But for all the attempt, he is hampered by the necessity of *trees, stones, water, light.* And even his psychedelic paint does not make the *canoe* disappear, nor does the multitude of *miraculouses* in the text remove his world from the mundane existence of oars and muscles and broken limbs or bare stones. That is to say, it is finally impossible for him to escape what Voegelin calls the Word of the Creator, the existing cosmos, through which—as Miss O'Connor repeatedly affirms out of St.

Thomas—limited man discovers the presence of the Creator. Poe's assault upon Beauty's heaven in "The Domain of Arnheim," then, impresses one at last as the action of a Walter Mitty as artist, of a mind whose dream is of being a miraculous impressionistic painter, transforming through the mistiness of language that fearsome other, the substantial world. And so it comes to pass that Poe paints himself into a corner of a world he has tried to deny as existing, removed from the doors and windows that open toward a transcendent.

We see now that Poe's allegory rests upon an assumption that language is a primal fluid which may be dissociated from the body's world so that the consciousness may constitute its universe. But the housing body thereby becomes rather a flat envelope of consciousness, punched outward into a shape; through it burn the fires of a highly volatile, private mind. Or, put another way, Poe's phrenology reads bumps from the inside. And here we see the meaning of that point on which, as Tate says, so many of Poe's tales revolve: the spirit's battle to inhabit bodies. There is horror in such allegory, not just at the level of that sensationalism which makes Poe's tales periodic fare of cinema or television; his is a radical divergence from traditional allegory. Dante too attempts to arouse us in his narrative of the soul's journey into Hell. At one point he too shows us an instance of the body possessed by a foreign spirit. It is a body still alive as body, but inhabited by a demon, since the particular soul is so vile as to have been snatched away to Hell before its appointed time. The terror Dante would raise in his figuring of death in life is that of the soul excluded from rescue by its willfulness. Poe uses the term "life in death," but it does not touch upon transformation or transmigration. Life in death aptly describes the state of consciousness as it is in contention with what we ordinarily conclude to be a world separate from consciousness and adjacent to it. That world is the one which we understand ourselves as perceiving through the agency of the senses, whereby we discover in varying degrees (according to one's "sensibilities," we say) a life in that adjacent world, a hint of divine presence. But in both Poe's poetry and his tales, we find what Tate calls "the consuming fire of the abstract intellect, without moral significance."

Poe is fascinated by the prospect which abstraction permits. Yeats and Eliot, realizing Poe's dream as more generally pervasive of the world by the century's end, will become exceedingly distressed. For *The Waste Land* mind is an extension of Poe's "death in life." The condition seems a general one in which the souls of men have been snatched out of the world. The sense of incompleteness—the feeling of emptiness, of something lost—is an enlarging force of despair, affecting not simply individual man but the community of men.

But that sense of emptiness was for Poe the condition necessary to sustain consciousness as the center of the world; that is, his is an elected, not an inherited, alienation. That is what D. H. Lawrence criticizes so sharply in Poe. Of Poe's version of Prufrock, Roderick Usher, Lawrence says his "nerves are so strung that they vibrate to the unknown quiverings of the ether. He . . . has lost his self, his living soul. . . . When man becomes self-less . . . how much can his elemental consciousness express . . .? Roderick Usher quivers on the edge of material existence." Roderick, says Poe, is caught in "some struggle with the grim phantasm, Fear." But such a struggle can yield only the horror of despair. And "We must insist," as C. S. Lewis says in *The Problem of Pain*, "that dread and awe are in a different dimension from fear. They are in the nature of an interpretation man gives to the universe, or an impression he gets from it." That is, awe and dread are responses by consciousness to an existence it does not believe itself the agent of.

Since secondary causes, Poe's "All thing," are secondary to Nothingness in Poe's vision, it is in them that the struggle for unity with the source occurs. Hence intellects devour intellects that they may be identical, an incestuous hunger which must finally result in an obliteration in Nothingness. The surface situations in Poe, which speak of matters incestuous (as in the relation between Roderick and his sister) are the concessions necessary to Poe's inverted metaphors, the price the Gnostic mind must pay for that pride of intellect through which it cuts itself off from the whole of creation. The central point in Poe's metaphors as he describes it in *Eureka* is preponderantly such "attraction" and "repulsion" of warring intellect as lies in the conflict between Roderick and Madeline Usher. "His heart is a lute hung on the wall," the story's epigraph says, "and as soon as it is touched it sounds." But vibrations by a stronger power than itself must shatter the whole. Roderick and Madeline are left twisted grotesquely in mutual death, their bodies collapsed; then the whole "house," that ancient metaphor for the body, sinks in oblivion into a nameless swamp.

Attraction and *repulsion*. The former, we are told in *Eureka*, is the body; the latter the soul. The one is the material, the other the spiritual principle of the universe. "*No other principles exist.*" But all Poe's camouflage talk about Newton, gravity, electricity, atoms, planets, stars is gesture to avoid the haunting question of existence as it relates to any possible cause separate from the mind which projects *Eureka*. The humbug in Poe, with which James Russell Lowell charges him in a witty verse, is in considerable measure a stratagem to avoid a terror greater than that of annihilation. Poe's discussion of irradiation, "part and parcel of the *sphere*," when seen as metaphor for the burning light of consciousness such as breaks forth from the eyes of his characters at the high points of physical dissolution, reveals the desperateness of his position. How necessary it is that he maintain himself an intelligence differing in kind and not simply in degree from his fellows. He must be, and be the cause of, his own *esse*. His center, which is the light of consciousness, is the source of an infinitely exploding sphere which, without objects to satisfy its reaching outward, would mean unfulfilled reaching; yet if those objects prove *like* in some manner, the self-center must collapse.

In "The Domain of Arnheim," the hero of the piece has four elementary principles to be satisfied if *being* is to be maintained. The first three are rudimentary concessions to the body of the world, though they are worded so that they might be concessions to communities larger than the individual consciousness. Indeed, they are principles which one finds Faulkner dwelling upon in the development of his world, and which one finds also in the Fugitive Agrarians. The first is "free exercise in open air," and our hero points to "the tillers of the earth, the only people who, as a class, can be fairly considered happier than others." But as a class they are reduced to peasant, their harmony being at the animal level. The second necessity is "the love of woman." Nothing is said of the nature of that love, or whether the necessity is the love of a "good" woman. That is, _woman_ is once more an abstract, a creation by the imagination of a thematic object. (It has nothing to do, surely, with the current objections to male exploitation of woman as sexual object.) The third, and most difficult of realization, is a "contempt of ambition." An Ike McCaslin, in his contempt for ambition, hardly conforms to Poe's principle here, for Ike's is a concern for expiation through nature, a self-sacrifice to the violated presence he has mystically experienced in nature. In Poe's principle there lurks the old danger to his position: ambition requires the good estimate of some consciousness other than the ambitious one; a concession to ambition is a reduction of the omnipotence of the individual consciousness.

Still the fourth principle is such, by its very nature, as to make a control of ambition possible: "he held . . . the extent of attainable happiness was in proportion to the spirituality of this object" which he pursues. And here lies the real center out of which flows the energy of Poe's hero, as if a fountain of perpetual youthful rebellion. One might once more compare the principle involved abstractly in Poe's argument to a dramatizing of that temptation in *Go Down, Moses*. Old Ben, finally fallen, ushers Ike into the fallen world, the world of guilt and sorrow in which world he becomes a reflective to whom ambition appears quite other than it does to Poe's protagonist. His cousin-father McCaslin pulls from the library shelf that poem of John Keats which dwells upon the imagination's attempt upon immortality. "The Ode on a Grecian Urn" reflects images in a manner that echoes Ike's youthful fascination with the pursuit of Old Ben, against which there is now only an emptiness with Ben killed and gone.

> She cannot fade, though thou hast not thy bliss,
> Forever wilt thou love, and she be fair.

Faulkner's suffering reflective who cites these lines, Ike McCaslin, is still anchored in the concrete reality of an external world by the pieties of those rituals through which one acknowledges those separate existences of which one is not the cause. But Poe must restlessly seek a perspective from a position that cannot be "attained on the wide surface of the _natural_ earth."

In effect Poe refuses that piety described by Frank Sheed as our "love offered to that to which one is bound by obedience."

If the concern for audience, which is a temptation to one's ambition, is a contradiction of the position Poe would maintain, it too is a convenience somewhat like the necessity of a pursuit of an object not to be obtained. A hostile audience allows a shift of attention from the threat of the dream's collapse, as the pursuit of an inaccessible object allows the sustained ecstasy of a love "forever panting, and forever young." One notes Poe's toying with audience in his more solemn moments as well in his satirically humorous ones, those hoaxes in which the peasantry of mind is ridiculed. For the frantic necessity is at once to preserve the dream and to save the consciousness from it, since it is not so much an exploding universe as a universe collapsing outward in a dissipation, an annihilation of consciousness. Poe's fallen world is the mind at war with the body, its "haunted palace," and the metaphor he repeatedly extends does not so much display the ingenuity of a metaphysical conceit (we have the same metaphor handled with arresting ingenuity by Shakespeare and Donne) as it constitutes an attempt by Poe to preserve himself from the consequences of his gnostic spirit, whose modernity is that it denies a transcendent in which mind may come to rest. Reluctantly he consents: reason must be employed. Reason addresses itself to a mystery whose solution is the discovery of the disjointing trickery of the senses upon the mind; thus what is required is a subjection of the senses by reason so that the mind may assert its victory in a pattern whose only cause is itself.

If any object exists independent of the light of consciousness, serious questions about the limitations of consciousness arise. For one, the omnipotence of the imagination, in which Poe would rest his faith as a protection against the devouring threat of reason, is called in question. But if objects can be accepted (with reason's help) as creations of the imagination, the light of consciousness may be reflected back upon itself from such pseudo-objects without concession to a separate existence, and the consciousness thereby protected in its closed system. We will have then "a novel Universe swelling into existence, and then subsiding into nothingness, at every throb of the Heart Divine." And "this Heart Divine—what is it? *It is our own.*" (The plural *our* is a rhetorical concession to the reader.) Poe denies the heart of darkness that troubles Hawthorne and Conrad and Faulkner and Eliot, with which the fiction of Flannery O'Connor is concerned; it is only in that heart that these writers find community of consciousness, though it is a fallen community. In contrast, Poe's heart of light, whose throbbing will subside into nothingness, may fulfill for him the "Germ of . . . inevitable annihilation," a final rescue from those threats of community that, at different levels of the same territory of the human spirit, trouble Arthur Dimmesdale, Ike McCaslin, the Misfit, and those awarenesses that inhabit *The Waste Land.* Still, no more than Keats is able to do can Poe embrace directly the oblivion that makes him more than half in love with easeful death, that still-to-be-pursued object for Poe. It is an object at a pole removed from that object of our homesickness of which Pascal or Kierkegaard or C. S. Lewis speak and about which our writers concerned with the community of humanity dramatize in verse and story.

If "Matter *is* only attraction and repulsion," as Poe insists in his notes in the margin of *Eureka,* that assertion does not make him so much a forerunner of particle physics as it makes him the destroyer of his own constructed "unique Universe." A "finally consolidated globe of globes, being but one particle, would be without attraction—i.e., gravitation." The argument, disguised as a synthesis of science since Newton, concludes that "the final globe would be matter without matter—i.e., no matter at all: it must disappear. Thus Unity in Nothingness." Nor is this prescient of our own recent fascination with Black Holes in the new astronomy, for Poe's black hole is not a collapse of matter upon itself with the acceleration of gravitational force; it is, once more, an outward collapse of consciousness, an action of annihilation. But to talk about this outward collapse, we must first de-matter matter that we may then de-spirit spirit. And once more reason becomes an avenging angel visited upon the material world, through whose action that world is turned to dead statue, like Ligeia's head, since it cannot be destroyed by denial. It is a principle of denial that by its action gives the denied object a sort of existence, as evil certifies existence. Since existence (*esse*) is good, evil depends from good. That is the old agony in the satanic spirit; for it shores up the good, as it were, by its attempt to erode it. This impulse is in Poe, and it is so suicidal in him that one marvels that he did not end it all, as did Gérard de Nerval, though one may consider his peronal history a prolonged self-destruction like Rimbaud's. Mallarmé speaks of Nerval as one of those "exaggerated heroes who have gone so far in drollery as to hang themselves on lampposts."[2] Mallarmé's praise of Poe honors a slower self-decay.

Poe concludes his epic, *Eureka* (which we might subtitle *Consciousness as Victor over Existence Through Its Own Annihilation*) with a rather caustic comment about our usual perception of the material universe. At our first encounter we might take it a rebuke such as Wordsworth is capable of; it appears to be Poe's denial of our argument. "All these creatures—All—those which you term animate, as well as those to whom you deny life for no better reason than that you do not behold it in operation—*All* these creatures have, in a greater or less degree, a capacity for pleasure and for pain:—*but the general sum of their sensations is precisely the amount of Happiness which appertains by right to the Divine Being when concentrated within Himself.*" The emphatic statement might also appear a faint echo, though somewhat sentimentalized, of scholastic argument about the relation of God's *creatura* to their Creator. Or one might take it to carry pantheistic overtones, the happiness of creatures being the throbbing sensation of deity. But one must not overlook the repeated separation of creation from Creator and the insistence that one can detect through the creatures nothing of the Creator. What is really constituted here is a radical deism of the individual consciousness. Happiness for the All as spoken here is an accident of that deity's operation. When one reads "William Wilson" or "The Imp of the Perverse" or "To Helen" or "The Raven" in this light, it is borne out once more that the creatures are of Poe's own creation, through which he satisfies a hunger to be *the* Creator. Life exists by the beholding of *what is* as extended by the beholder, that action which feeds the "Heart Divine," which is the self. The darkest happiness

---

2. C. F. MacIntyre, *French Symbolist Poetry*, 115. MacIntyre remarks that Rimbaud is "like those men of violence who, as St. Matthew tells, take the kingdom of heaven by force. He . . . wrote with a violence at times brutal, often with the set purpose of shocking his readers." (136)

of all—the bliss of non-being, annihilation—is presented repeatedly as the downward movement to an incredible darkness at the vision's end: descents into maëlstroms, that incredible darkness of white at the end of *Pym*, the decay in mirror images of "William Wilson." The final message in Poe's bottle is not a torn piece of paper with fragments of words, nor broken hieroglyphics discovered on deserted islands. His beatific vision is that the bottle is empty. And with that prestidigital gesture, the bottle too disappears: "the fever called living is over at last."

CHAPTER XXVII

TONE AS SUBSTANCE:
THE ESCAPE OF BONES AND
BLOOD

We are familiar with the concern of modern poets such as Yeats and Eliot for the general cloud of lifelessness that seems to hover over our world; and we have mentioned Eliot's particular fascination with Poe, the many attempts he makes to isolate the inadequacy he feels in Poe in spite of being drawn to him. From the close of World War I almost to the end of his life, Eliot returns to Poe again and again. He remarks in a relatively late revisiting, "From Poe to Valéry," that Poe's prosody has the effect of being "immediate and undeveloping," relying on "the incantatory element in poetry," a sign merely of a youthfulness such as one finds evidence of in the early work of Eliot himself, particularly in those *Poems Written in Youth*, published in 1967. Eliot might have said, had he not reached a point where he is ready to abandon those favorite terms of his early criticism—*Romantic* and *Classical*—that Poe's prosody is "romantic." It is that prosodic inclination one finds in a high degree in a Shelley, another of the youthful Eliot's heroes.

Eliot makes his point about Poe by demonstrating the "irresponsibility towards the meaning of words" reflected in a phrase like *immemorial years*, as contrasted to Tennyson's *immemorial elms*. The *year* is anything but *immemorial* in Poe's use, but Tennyson's phrase combines the "felicitous sound value" of a word which is "exactly the word for trees so old that no one knows just how old they are." One might defend a possibility in Poe's phrase by suggesting that Poe is narrating an event in which the event that makes the experience memorable is yet to be revealed; that is, at the point of the phrase's use in the poem, the recollector is at a low point of a low year which, except for the experience about to happen, would indeed have remained immemorial. But one would not have succeeded in rescuing the poem by a rescue of the phrase. As Aldous Huxley demonstrates rather conclusively by his analysis of the whole texture of "Ulalume," it is an exercise in the "Vulgarity of Literature." Eliot's general conclusion is valid if his evidence is scant.

But if Poe's prosody is undeveloping, so too is whatever thematic burden the poetry carries. Allen Tate, in "The Poetry of Edgar Allan Poe," suggests that all Poe's poetry is a projection of his mind, that he is "the demon he tells us he saw take shape in a cloud." And Tate goes on with a just judgment, complementing Eliot's:

> A non-theological view of demonology would tell us that a demon is simply a person who cannot develop—a fierce determinism has arrested the rounded growth of his faculties, so that the evil he does other persons is not a positive malice but an insistence that they remain emotionally and intellectually deprived as he himself must remain. . . . All of his poems might have been written in any one year of his life, at age fifteen or age forty . . . .

The small demurrer I would enter on the judgment is to the phrase "must remain," since Poe does not seem so much constrained to his position as to have deliberately chosen it. A contrast to Keats's intense engagement with constraint in the memorable year of his famous Odes, issuing upon the somewhat calmer waters of "Ode to Autumn," supports my caveat to Tate's statement, the greater poet engaging risks beyond what Poe will attempt in his poetry.

One might consider that Poe's prosody is simply out of the innocence of an arrested development, that Poe is rather a Tom Sawyer as poet, recognizing dangers to be guarded against. For the limits of one's imagination reveal themselves when one is drawn into that outer world, as Huck Finn chooses to be drawn and as Keats is.[1] But most important, as we have shown, the arrest is a

1. I am in part tempted to this yoking of Huck to Keats as poets by Eliot's own fascination with both. In his analysis of *Huckleberry Finn*, Eliot's concern with the novel's structure involves the limits of Twain's artistry. Twain one might say is tempted by Tom Sawyer as poet on the one hand and Huck as poet on the other.

necessity of the angelic mode Poe is committed to by the very nature of his ideas. Eliot's incantatory aspect is demonic in Tate's sense, if not diabolic in Kierkegaard's; the deliberate distortions of the created world by the imagination constitute a predisposition to the camp of the fallen angel. Nevertheless, the meaning in the words of the poems is always undermining the arrogance of sound in spite of Poe's attempt to empty them. Sound is for Poe that necessary catalyst to the suspension of tone in the intellect, whereby he would bypass language's anchor in the outer world, the world of ordinary reality experienced by the sensations, a world in which bodies do live and a multitude of *creatura* seem to have particular existences that at least (as Wordsworth would say) half create the mighty world of eye and ear.

But Poe's deepest suspicion is of sensation. In his satiric piece on "How to Write a Blackwood Article," more is at stake for him than an attack on sensationalism used as an appeal to an audience easily attracted by spectacle. "Sensations are the great things after all. . . . Should you ever be drowned or hung, be sure and make a note of your sensations—they will be worth to you ten guineas a sheet." In rejecting that species of public titillation, which we have magnified since his day by the public press with photos added, Poe chooses an arrested sensibility. His objection isn't to the obscenity involved. I mean *obscenity* as Richard Weaver recalls us to its meaning: that which is unfit for public exhibition, which "with the rise of the institution of publicity . . . makes a virtue of desecration." Nor is Poe concerned with Weaver's "propriety," in which resides the manners of the piety with which we face the created world. For if he satirizes sensationalism in some of his spoofs, he practices his own species of it in his most serious work, in his distortions of reality which denature nature and humanity alike and constitute his grotesquery. In rejecting sensationalism of the popular variety, he eschews the senses as well, the effect of which is to make him dependent upon tonal associations in words, the cause of which tone lies as much in the misty past experiences of man in the world as in the pure sound. Poe assumes, that is, a stock response to the sound of utterance, and he posits as substance an intellectual abstraction— the death of a beautiful woman, for instance. The search for biographical sources in Poe casts but faint light, for the source is primarily intellectual, and its borrowings are not from experience itself but from echoes of those experiences which Poe would exclude. That is, Poe—far from being so original as Williams would credit to him—is a "literary" poet, his vocabulary, rhetoric, diction heavily weighted with the historical. Had he not lost mother and stepmother, he would have dreamed them dead in the interest of that universal sense of loss to which he attempts to give his own meaning: the homesickness for oblivion, as ancient in man as his first sense of loss. Nostalgia is the easiest of our "feelings" to manipulate with "tone," as pathos is easier to arouse than tragedy, since nostalgia and pathos attach to a loss in which one does not recognize himself as a cause. (Nostalgia and pathos usually precede an indictment of the gods.)

Tone is the message in Poe's poetry, the closest he can come to the angelic mode, the intuitive as opposed to the rationally discursive which man is burdened by. He will not undertake the arduous and possibly crippling descent into the dark secrets of material existence such as stain words indelibly. He attempts rather to pipe to the "spirit" those ditties of notone, which by that mischief in language which betrays him turn out to be one tone. That is why Poe must inevitably parody himself, writing one poem over and over. The bathos in him, the failures of style, are a consequence of his refusal to acknowledge that the nature of language is such as to commit its user to its full resonance, in which the poet's very being is engaged with being other than the self. ("In the last analysis," Eliade says emphatically, "*the world reveals itself as language*. It speaks to man through its own mode of being, through its structures and its rhythms." *Myth and Reality*.) That commitment moves one to the borders of mystery, not only the mystery of the individual mind, but toward that which St. John speaks of when he says, "In the beginning was the Word. . . . And the Word was made flesh." As if haunted by that old mystery, Poe parodies that message from the Gospels, the last instance being in those notes in the margin of his *Eureka*: "*What I here propound is true*: . . . if by any means it be now trodden down so that it die, it will 'rise again to the Life Everlasting.' "

We may here make an additional observation about Poe's concern for what is "true" which will enlighten our reading of his work in the context of his poetic and philosophical theories. For as we look at the question of the mind's relation to truth from a Thomistic position, we begin to discover the way in which an inordinate concern for truth may itself separate one from reality. One of the byproducts for the reader out of this inordinate concern has been modern poetry's primary concern for form. That concern in Poe gives rise to William Carlos Williams's excessive praise of Poe's originality, as we have seen. A little later than Williams's acclaim, Eliot comments on the problem the poet has with the temptation of originality. The time of Eliot's comment, in relation to his own development, is important. It comes in 1933, after "Ash-Wednesday" and before the *Four Quartets*. This is to say that Eliot is discovering a way to truth on his journey back to reality; his "natural reason" is beginning to enjoy the support of faith. His comment, in *After Strange Gods*, anticipates an objection to his call for "the standard of orthodoxy to contemporary literature." He rejects in advance the charge that he means "that novelty of form and of substance" is "to be deprecated." He adds, "What is objectionable, from the point of view which I have adopted, is not novelty or originality in themselves, but their glorification for their own sake. The artist's concern with originality, certainly, may be considered as largely negative: he wishes only to avoid saying what has already been said as well as it can. . . . To assert that a work is 'original' should be very modest praise: it should be no more than to say that the work is not patently negligible." Miss O'Connor, in answer to the question asked by an interviewer whether fiction is evolving new forms, answers: "I wouldn't know about literary questions like that. So-called experimental fiction always bores me. If it looks peculiar I don't read it." If we put her remark into the whole of her work, as she suggests is necessary in arriving at an author's meaning, its foundations will appear more solid than when the remark is taken out of context, and Eliot's remark casts a helpful light as we do so. Always for her, the artist's eye must be on nature. When that eye wanders toward form as an end, the artist begins to lose that source of being without which art becomes an abstraction which struggles to make form its substance, though one be so audacious as to call it "concrete poetry" as occurs of late.

It seems to me an observable phenomenon that the poet whose emphasis is upon originality is the poet who takes himself most seriously as the kingpin of creation. The poet who makes significant contributions to the enlarging of art's possibilities is less likely to exude that arrogance of superiority, whose authority is his novelty, novelty being a sign of the poet's self-election to the role of earth-angel. It is perhaps a difference one marks between those two brother poets, poets concerned with a quest that leads each in a similar philosophical direction—Rilke and Poe. Nevertheless for Rilke, the pursuit of being is a primary end, and his enlarging of form—his novelty—a necessity of that pursuit. In Poe one discovers a more decided temptation to form itself. There is a similar difference, I believe, to be observed within the single poet on occasion. Consider as instance James Joyce. The early Joyce, it seems to me, in his enlargements upon the instruments of fiction, also has as an end a quest for being through form. As exile for the sake of exile becomes more obsessive to him (the satiric treatment of this inclination in Stephen is not finally able to save Stephen's creator from that temptation) Joyce is drawn to form as end. *Finnegans Wake* is the product of that aberrant quest.

There is a recognition in St. Thomas of this danger to the natural reason. A marvellous gift, the natural reason is so marvellous that one may be tempted away from its proper end to contemplate the natural reason itself as the highest good. That is, intellect may become the surface of the pool of reality on which the Narcissus of the Ego finds itself frozen, unable to penetrate beyond the surface. On one occasion (Thomas is in contest with Siger of Brabant) he insists that "The purpose of the study of philosophy is not to learn what others have thought, but to learn how the truth of things stands." We have said these words repeatedly, and we summon them again to argue that truth stands out of reality. Thus on another occasion he says, "truth can be predicated not of what really exists but, in the strict and proper sense, only of what is thought." Now, the fascination with "truth" ("Beauty is truth, truth beauty') leads one inevitably in the direction of natural knowledge as an end, if one does not protect oneself from excess. Thus Thomas reminds us that "The opinion of those who say with regard to the truth of faith that it is a matter of complete indifference what one thinks about creation, providing one has a true interpretation of God . . . is notoriously false. For an error about creation is reflected in a false opinion about God." The argument holds, whether "God" be the Christian God or the god of the consciousness elevated by Poe. If truth is "of what is thought," it takes only a subtle alchemy in thought to believe that truth is thought; from thence the contemplation of "truth" becomes a turning away from reality. One becomes isolated by his own abstraction, since truth is a separation from reality by the intellect. But recognizing this limitation of "natural reason," one may well find one's faith energized by grace and return to reality. Something like this is involved in the meaning of that paradox out of Heraclitus: the way up and down are the same.

Thomas gives careful warning of the danger that natural reason will separate one from reality. The warning is directed, as Gilson says, to an audience of baptized men, but one can see it as crucially decisive in the subregions of man, among the self-baptized, the egocentric. And thus we may see the pertinence of Thomas's remark, in *Quaestio Disputatae de Veritate*, to our concern with the artist and the problem of originality. "The ultimate felicity of man cannot consist in the contemplation which depends on the understanding of the principles, for that is a most imperfect contemplation, being most universal and limited to the knowledge of things in potency. Besides, that is only the beginning of human inquiry, not its end, since we owe it to nature, not to our own effort to discover truth." We owe it to the gift in us which we call "natural reason," man's nature whereby he is created in the image of God. This is the given, with which we begin the journey out of potency towards being; self-reflection is not an end proper to contemplation. The artist whose end is "experimental fiction" bores Miss O'Connor for this reason, not because she opposes the enlargements possible in art in its homage to reality: she opposes those enlargements being made an end and not the beginning for the artist, an end of vision rather than the means of vision.[2] In this vein Gilson complains of the modern Thomist who distorts Thomism in the same way, seeing truth as removed from reality and thereby making a system of truth, its intellectual formula the end of natural reason. Such a mind is "like unto a man holding a lamp, lost in the contemplation of its light and complaining that he sees nothing." Thus Thomism has ceased to be dynamic because it has ceased to be Thomism. It is this objection that may also be brought against the poet's shifting to form as end, his audience complaining more loudly than he that nothing is seen with his light. The "nothingness" *in* the light he holds is not sufficient answer to the reader's objection. Nor is the reader necessarily a Philistine when called one because of his complaint. These considerations return us to Eliot's remark on the question of the poet's originality, to his objection to the "glorification" of "novelty and originality" by poet or critic "for their own sakes."

Fifteen years later, Eliot returns to the question, just after World War II and just as Miss O'Connor turns seriously to the writing of fiction as her "vocation." Eliot concludes about Poe, seeing him once more through the eyes of Baudelaire and Valéry, that he is "thoroughly convinced of [Poe's] importance, of the importance of his work as a whole." What he finds of importance is Poe's setting Baudelaire, and subsequently Valéry, upon that road which leads those poets to conceive the primary work of art to be the *process* of its construction. "The subject is little, the treatment is everything." But Baudelaire's distillation from Poe that the "poem should have nothing in view but itself," while it sounds firmly objective as a consideration of his own intentions as poet, does not account for Baudelaire's intense engagement with the demon that haunted Poe: the meaning of the materials of poetry as they attach to the threat of the abyss on the one hand and the mystery of existence on the other. Baudelaire's use of correspondences, his

---

2. For the same reason she is bored by the "social sciences" which "have cast a dreary light on the public approach to fiction." For under that influence "novels are considered to be entirely concerned with the social or economic or psychological forces that they will by necessity exhibit" as "means to some deeper end." The writer must "make his gaze extend beyond the surface, beyond mere problems [including problems of form], until it touches that realm which is the concern of prophets and poets."

poetry's attempt at being at least a negative of some brighter positive beyond the fragmented intellectual and spiritual world he inhabits, considerably qualify the poetic principle he enunciates. Man wanders the temple of nature, "where the alive/Pillars breathe often a tremor of mixed words." And the phrase Miss O'Connor picks up from Baudelaire to relate to her own subject matter is of importance, not only to her reading of the modern state, but to Baudelaire's own troubled reading of our world: "The devil's cleverest wile is to convince the modern world that he does not exist." The prince of evil thus obscured, we find ourselves confused on the question of evil, mistaking in nature itself an evil presence heightened to confusion by our senses. We are buffeted not only by odors "blown sweet as infants' naked flesh," but by "Others, corrupt, rich and triumphant" that "thresh expansions to the infinite pain" through which we seek "transports of the spirit and the sense." We shall want to remember Eliot's conclusion that in both Poe and Valéry one has a meeting of extremes, especially as we come to consider Hawthorne and Nathanael West, in whom it may also be said that such extremes meet: "the immature mind playing with ideas because it had not developed to the point of convictions, and the very adult mind playing with ideas because it was too skeptical to hold convictions."

The separation of faith and reason in the thirteenth century, which we explored as the wellspring out of which issues our own troubled waters, is reflected in Eliot's statement. That it has wider application than his discussion of Poe, Baudelaire, and Valéry seems not to have suggested itself to him. We may anticipate a future discussion by suggesting that the battle between Shrike and Miss Lonelyhearts in West's novel is a battle between these two extremes. And the battle in Hawthorne over the mind's invasion of the heart, the "Unpardonable Sin," is very much out of a spiritual milieu Poe found himself caught up by. For Poe is made uneasy by Hawthorne, not simply by Hawthorne's inartistic use of allegory, but by what is implicit in the allegory that Hawthorne attempts: the possibility he would suggest of a world transcending the self and its private meaning. Hence Poe finds " 'The White Old Maid' . . . objectionable, even more than 'The Minister's Black Veil,' on the score of its mysticism." Certainly Hawthorne's uses of white and black in relation to sin are considerably removed from Poe's interests. "Even with the thoughtful and analytic," Poe concludes, "there will be much trouble in penetrating its entire import."

The real difficulty is not that Hawthorne's mystery is impenetrable. It is rather that the conception of sin each poet holds lacks correspondences. Sin for Poe is that mistake whereby one becomes victim to the illusion that death is a passage into another state rather than into annihilation, for all his sensationalism of disembodied spirits attempting to inhabit bodies. For that is merely the spectacle in Poe's fictions, which incidentally engage for him a large audience who do not penetrate his meaning and think the better of him because they do not. Valéry's perception of Poe's meaning is far removed from that of the audience of television productions of the tales. In "The Sleeper," highly praised by many of Poe's critics, the beautiful girl is "a child of sin," but not in the sense that the epithet might be attached to Hester Prynne's Pearl. She is so because as a child she imagined that the noises issuing from the ancestral vault against which she threw stones were voices from beyond the grave. The poem concludes that the dead girl shall "nevermore" force an echo with her idle stone, "Thrilling to think, poor child of sin!/ It was the dead who groaned within."[3] The second version of the title of "The City in the Sea" was "The City of Sin," in which poem the same presumption of existence after death is rebuked in the city's dissolution in the closing lines. Poe's conception of sin is not that which reflects a willful violation of one's own existence in revolt against the Cause of being. It is rather the same sin as that Wallace Stevens develops in his poetry, as for instance in "Sunday Morning": a violation of one's own integrity as self-caused cause whose Word is the imagination.

Mystery necessarily yields to the analytic for Poe. And it does so through a thoughtful examination of the evidence. The child's imagined groans from the family tomb signify no more than the "wanton airs" that wave "the curtained canopy" under which a

---

3. A poet whose themes and their accompanying melancholy seem particularly close to Poe is E. A. Robinson. "Luke Havergal" is far more convincing as a poem capturing Poe's conception of death and annihilation than Poe ever manages. *Cavender's House* is a tale by Poe in verse, and Poe's "Sleeper" with her "closed and fringed lid" is echoed in Robinson's "Dead Lady."

body lies. If Wallace Stevens were putting the point, it would be a "mimic motion" that was not hers, "inhuman," the "meaningless plunging of wind." Poe's *Narrative of A. Gordon Pym* is largely built upon a reduction of such mystery. In that narrative, we begin an adventure such as would delight the heart of Tom Sawyer. Indeed Augustus, who inveigles Pym upon his journey, is very much a Tom, devising plans as elaborate as any Tom dreams up to free Nigger Jim. In Poe's "narrative" boys are pitted against men, from Augustus' careful trickery of the adult world in getting Pym out of his house and into the ship, to the elaborate accommodations for Pym below decks. The adventure is rich with juvenile attractions, which Poe from time to time makes fun of, knowing the incipient boy in the adult reader. (Pym nevertheless appears old—almost ancient—by the end of his adventure.) Poe enjoys also a Swiftean irony, in his use of shipboard jargon, for instance *orlop decks, main hatchways, double-reef sails, trysails, larboard bulwarks*—on and on beyond the necessities of verisimilitude in an age better acquainted with sailing ships. The novel is in one of its aspects a long shaggy-dog tale, bearing comparison to his famous hoax played on the *Brooklyn Eagle*. The tricks are garnered largely from Poe's reading, though a study of his sources would prove less rewarding than of Coleridge's that lie behind "Kubla Khan." The long garrulously tedious section on stowage, the case histories complete with names and dates and ships and their cargoes; instructions for cargo stowage whether cotton, corn, or oil. All this technical information pretending to underline verisimilitude not only plays upon the reader's credulity, but upon the typical American inclination to justify Tom Sawyer by a show of pragmatic interests. (Tom Sawyer becomes Horatio Alger in a later rescue.) The point is rather directly made by Poe's own intrusion as "editor" in the narrative's notes: learned paraphernalia, accompanied often by the device of italics to emphasize the banal. The reader is victim of a long leg-pull.

Yet there is something more. The reader almost has his leg viciously pulled off. We have it suggested that "ill and good" are "strictly comparative," the comparative instrument being the imaginative intellect, which might presumably save one from being taken in by the hoax of the *Narrative*. There are illustrations, clues, along the way. The "thread of destiny" depends upon an "incident" whose coincidence to the intellect must be seen by one's reason as the consequence of events. Thus, as in Poe's conception of the highest art as the act of production of art, the highest adventure is in the process of analysis of events, whose significance as event is of at least a secondary importance, even as is the question of whether or not the events literally transpired.[4] One overlooks the primal devotion of mind to itself if he allows the senses to mislead him into writing such sensational material as might please the editors of *Blackwood*. The unravelling of the mystery of the supernatural in the *Narrative* has as its principal concern the justification of Tom Sawyer as poet.

The young man Pym is buried three days and nights in his box-tomb in the ship's hold. He rises on the third day, but to darkness and to confusing mystery. Because his senses are disoriented, he reads perception with imagination too much anchored in past experience. He finds himself in a world seemingly incomprehensible, but as it develops, he is only reading a very ordinary world falsely. The disjointed events, experienced after his long sleep, slowly dissolve before analytic reason into a pattern which the reason certifies to the restored imagination. The grotesque "phantasms" he encounters have simple explanation; either the senses have been distorted by the body's incapacities or some elementary fact is missing from the puzzle of events. Thus the weird jungle of the ship's hold yeilds to the mind at last as stowed cargo; the fearsome wolf that threatens Pym, causing his desperate preparation for a bloody encounter, turns out to be his faithful dog. The awe of mystery is simply the effect upon a superstitious mind of events not understood by the proper concert of imagination and reason in the analytic mind. Poe's reasons, when he allows them to surface in the narrative, simplify his narrator's anxiety. It is this aspect that leads Tate to say that his stories give "the adolescent mind the illusion of analytic thought."

If, through distortions of the imagination's powers by disoriented sensations, Pym has come to see the simple situation—

---

4. Once more we might compare Wallace Stevens. It is perhaps to be understood that the girl "we" hear singing on the beach at Key West is a projection of the narrator's imagination, the pretense of reporting an actual experience merely a part of the poem's supreme fiction.

that mutineers have seized the ship—the experience provides the means for undoing the mutineers themselves through a supreme fiction of the imagination. Pym's resurrection from the hold of the ship as a ghost (since the mutineers have made an error in simple arithmetic, not having counted all the "souls" aboard) allows the trick. When he descends into the presence of the mutineers to confront that black leader of mutiny, who "in all respects was a perfect demon," the "demon" is literally frightened to death. We are noting once more a playfulness in language in Poe, which has a serious implication. Pym earlier reads by a light, which his ingenuity provides him, the cryptic message on the torn paper, ". . . blood—your life depends upon lying close." Pym reflects after the experience that had he known the literal desperate situation above deck, it could not "have imbued my mind with one tithe of the harrowing and yet indefinable horror with which I was inspired by the fragmentary warning thus received." For blood is "that word of all words—so rife at all times with mystery, and suffering, and terror." Being "disjointed . . . from any foregoing words to qualify or render it distinct," it falls with intolerable burden into "the innermost recesses of my soul!" The language, and Pym's three-day burial, combine to show Poe very deliberate in a parody of the Resurrection. When the mystery is resolved, when the circumstances of the note's composition become clear, it turns out to be another Tom Sawyer adventure, Augustus having written, "I have scrawled this with blood, etc."

Poe has consciously employed Christian dogma as an ironic commentary upon mystery as it affects his superstititious narrator, Pym. The failure of Pym's reason to see through such "mystery" is made the butt of his later charade as the poisoned sailor Rogers, returned to life. Superstition about ghosts, says the now older, reflective Pym, is to be attributed to "such remnants of doubt about the reality of apparitions" as the reason has not succeeded in dispelling. Such remnants "have been at the bottom of almost every such visitation, and that appalling horror which has sometimes been brought about, is to be attributed . . . where most suffering has been experienced, more to a kind of anticipated horror, lest the apparition *might possibly* be real, than to an unwavering belief in its reality." *Ecce signum*—the body of the chief mutineer. It is the same message concerning the nature of sin as carried by "The City in the Sea" and "The Sleeper."

Concerning her own uses of mystery, Miss O'Connor comments upon the difficulties with audience, for the audience she speaks to is one committed to Poe's conception of mystery, with a hundred years of accelerated science since Poe to justify the belief that all mystery yields to analysis.

> If I write a novel in which the central action is a baptism, I know that for the larger percentage of my readers, baptism is a meaningless rite; therefore I have to imbue this action with an awe and terror which will suggest its awful mystery. I have to distort the look of the thing in order to represent as I see them both the mystery and the fact.

Her procedure is quite the opposite of Poe's. He presents one with the distortions as mystery, dissolves them with the intellectual solution which reduces the mystery to puzzle, and then solves the puzzle. She enlarges upon accepted fact, which she certifies with a concreteness of detail (such as is not necessary to Poe's purposes) in order that she may leave the story and the reader open to mystery, where the reader has formerly been content with what he presumes simple observations about the nature of reality, observations accepted as sufficient to the full meaning of reality. If we compare Poe's use of a primate in his famous murder mystery to Miss O'Connor's use in *Wise Blood*, we see this difference clearly. Enoch acts out a reversion through one pull in the blood, a pull of our blood which antedates Bethlehem back toward naturalistic existence. But Haze is finally overcome by another pull of the blood, containing and transforming that aspect of his being which he shares with Enoch. He goes back to Bethlehem, leaving us with the mystery of that pinpoint of light at the end of the novel. Poe's resistance to the Enoch in mankind is not through the heart, but through the mind, and a mind capable of denying any pull of the blood. Even so, one suspects that at times the blood threatens Poe. Pym's disquisition upon the horrors of the blood seem rather more excessive than satire upon superstition requires.

CHAPTER XXVIII

LYRICAL SELF-INDULGENCE
AND THE RAPE OF SENTIMENT

In "From Poe to Valéry" (1948) Eliot is writing of poets with whom he has had strong affinities much earlier, and with one of them an active friendship. Even so, it is a little surprising to find him this late in his career tracing so narrowly a thread from Poe to his contemporary and friend. For by the beginning of World War II, the decaying fabric of thought that we inherit from post-Renaissance gnosticism had revealed considerably more about the "dissociation of sensibility" than Eliot had understood when he established that phrase among our critical shibboleths—the separating of thought and feeling occurring at about the time of Dryden and Milton. By this time in his career Eliot knows well that the poet who concentrates for his salvation upon process in poetry is but one instance of many modern attempts to escape the threatening outer world in our "Age of Alienation." What is equally surprising is that, having concluded that Valéry carried the turning in upon the self through the poetic process as far as it can go, Eliot declines conclusion on the ground that he cannot speak as prophet of the next development in our literature. "An aesthetic which merely contradicted it would not do. To insist on the all-importance of subject-matter, to insist that the poet should be spontaneous and irreflective, that he should depend upon inspiration and neglect technique, would be a lapse from what is in any case a highly civilized attitude to a barbarous one." Eliot's is a conclusion sounding strangely like an off-echo from that poet Stephen

Dedalus. Stephen, taking refuge from the world through exile, silence, and cunning, rebukes Cranly for suggesting that he might better take refuge in becoming a Protestant since he is in revolt from the Catholic position. "I said that I had lost the faith . . . but not that I had lost self respect. What kind of liberation would that be to forsake an absurdity which is logical and coherent and to embrace one which is illogical and incoherent?" Eliot speaks as if the antithesis of a "barbarous" aesthetic were the only alternative to the surrealist dead end.

A tradition out of Whitman which, in its surface at least, is in conflict with Poe was not only well-established in our letters as Eliot was speaking but was about to enjoy a revival whose effect upon our poetry has proved considerable. William Carlos Williams was at last respectably established. The movement, to be dubbed "Beat," would declare him father and Whitman grandfather, with its object to make the poet the soul of the nation while freeing him from enslavement to ideology such as had led to the party-line conscription of literature in the 1930s. Most directly, however, the movement was in sharp reaction to the influence of Eliot and the "New Criticism," now settled comfortably into the academy. In its own conception of the science of verse, it was opposed to what Kenneth Rexroth characterized at the time as the "cornbelt metaphysicals," that literary establishment bred in writing courses such as those at the University of Iowa, which Miss O'Connor was attending at about this time.

The Beat concern with prosody was but a surface spectacle, often barbarous, of the general attack upon that literary establishment which had learned modern uses of Donne and the English metaphysical poets, and had learned them largely through Eliot's own interest in those poets. For all the weakness of formalist imitation in the cornbelt antagonists whom the Beats attacked, however, there were metaphysical undercurrents, residual forces deeper than technique. There was the latent concern for tradition such as had led Eliot toward his conversion, for instance. And Agrarian principles of a republican aspect (as opposed to the Marxian brand that had flourished in art twenty years earlier) might be discovered in Andrew Lytle teaching at Iowa. (One of his students was Mary

Flannery O'Connor from Milledgeville, Georgia.) One finds that gagging bone still gnawed by Rexroth, elected expounder of the Beats, as late as 1970. He says of the Fugitives that they were "militant defenders of the Myth of the Old South," with Ransom "their overseer" and Donald Davidson "a poetaster and professor . . . whose social tracts greatly resemble speeches given by Senator Bilbo, or a generation later, Senator Eastland, to the Annual Convention of the Mississippi Browning Society." That "the Fugitives were pure Aryans" is the kind of rhetorical fireworks passing as criticism all too common among the Beats and their associates from the beginning. It is anachronistic in Rexroth in the 1970s, revealing that he had not understood. Still, a metaphysical disparity between the early Eliot and the Fugitive-Agrarians (who battled the Eastern establishment also) is fundamental.

What must not be overlooked is that, in spite of such irresponsibility as Rexroth displays, there were some good reasons to object to Eliot's influence, even as there was reason to object to Milton's, as Eliot had done in a famous essay. (Eliot felt obliged to write again on Milton, exonerating him as responsible for weak followers, a point to be borne in mind when one considers Eliot's own bad influences upon a subsequent poetry.) At any rate, the sophisticated uses of irony flourished in academic hothouses—the toying with paradox, the clever entertainments of ingenious explication practiced upon Donne or Rilke. As viewed from New Jersey or San Francisco, the academic games appeared as a frivolous play with the poet's gift and craft, whereby the poet himself carefully protected himself from a full commitment to his calling, to his "vocation." Indeed, such an abuse was the end one might have predicted from Eliot's early dictum that the poet's personality should be excluded from his poetry. Never mind that Eliot himself had, by World War II, modified his position significantly on that point. That word of change in Eliot had not reached the American heartland, or it seemed not to have reached it; for the dissociation of the poet's personality from his poetry gives some authority from the poet himself for that academic "objectivity" with which writing was so burdensomely approached. For Eliot to have declared himself High Church Tory and Classicist was but gossip about personality, something like the rumors of Hollywood love affairs: a matter of biography quite separate from the pure concern for art. The New Criticism had, in effect, established a Neo-scholasticism in which aesthetic process was the end. The older academic disciplines were suspicious of the academic validity of writing courses anyway, and the more scientific the approach to writing, the less difficulty there was at the local level with those minions of scholarship of a Germanic or Harvardian bent. In addition, there was the objective proof of publication: these school writers were being published, particularly by the establishment in the East, and although academic "accountability" had not become an enunciated principle at the time, only the attendant publicity from publication prevented that intrusion. The conception of literature bred in the schools still dominated the New York publishing scene, in so far as New York made deferential bows to "literature." (New Directions was a conspicuous exception, one of the first houses to publish the West Coast poets.) The elitist university quarterlies fostered the movement, feeding into their pages the more promising of the school poets; certainly that was how the matter stood as viewed from Sausolito.

So above all, the Beat poet must demonstrate that he was committed at a level of personal sacrifice, giving a populist flavor to the new movement such as was particularly attractive to the young, who were already becoming politically conscious. One proof of commitment was his appearance in little magazines that faded like snowflakes on the desert's bosom, increasingly a matter of prestige as a reaction to the rival poets' support by celebrated publishing houses. There was the financially successful San Francisco City Lights series, and there were daring public performances in coffee houses from which the new poets moved onto campus, but for the most part the claim and the effect was at the grass roots level of poetic sensibilities. Then coffee houses began to be covered (as the poet was not on occasion, a cause of the effect) by the daily press, and even by *Time* and *Life*. The question that rises from this background is whether the Beat Movement, which was beginning to sweep the country and undermine the academic literary establishment on its own ground—on the campus and in the publishing houses—was in fact returning poetry to more viable roots, or whether the dead end Eliot sees Valéry reaching, out of Poe, did not leave the Beats themselves in wandering mazes lost. For the ethereal element out of the Orient, a renewed entry into Western poetry, did not replace the basic influence of those poets from Baudelaire through the Dadaists, whose antics in their own day against the establishment made them prime sources of public relations gimmicks and supplied subsequent criticism with titilating anecdotes. One somehow still prefers Nerval's leading a lobster for a stroll with a ribbon leash to a Ginsberg strip-tease.

A close look at Allen Ginsberg reveals that at the base of his assumptions about himself he is not far removed from Poe. And lest Poe's metrical mechanics seem to set the two far apart, we might remember as well that Poe's own prosody was a revolt against the popular establishment of his day, as much a revolt as Whitman's would presently be. The iambic foot was decidedly the enemy to Poe, along with the pentameter line. Even Poe's complaints against the Eastern literary establishment sound familiar; its publishing was centered in Boston rather than New York and its principal journal was the *North American Review*, over which brooded the spirit of Emerson, as Eliot's was assumed to dominate the *Sewanee* and *Kenyon* in those simplified objections to university quarterlies one meets in a Rexroth. Poe's scathing remarks about the "magazine poets," about the "clique" of writers made welcome in the pages of the *North American Review*, have ironic echo out of San Francisco a hundred years later.

For instance, one notices the tone, and even prescient details, in such as the following from Poe's *Marginalia*:

> Nicholas Ferrar, were he now living, would be not a little astonished to find thoroughly established here, by our Magazine poets, the very "perpetual chant" which he so unsuccessfully struggled to establish in the village of Little Gidding.[1]

The fundamental assumption that joins Poe with the Beats is self-

---

1. Poe says on another occasion: "It was the misfortune of Mr. Pinckney of South Carolina to have been born too far south. Had he been a New Englander, it is probable that he would have been ranked as the first of American lyricists, by the magnanimous cabal which has so long controlled the destinies of American letters, in conducting the thing called 'The North American Review.' "

sufficiency, spawned in part in each by a pragmatic necessity. *The Southern Literary Messenger* had to serve Poe's needs as best it could, as *New Directions Annuals* and, later, the *Evergreen Review*, served the scattered poets of the new movement of the 1950s. There is a difference, but it does not erase the significant similarity: the Beat Poet's indulgence of the self extends to the outer world, which Poe preferred to keep at bay. The body and its sensations are glorified as they are not to Poe, which is one reason the *Evergreen Review* seized upon the movement and for a time exploited it, profiting from the devouring outrage of residual Puritan sensibilities.

The concern of Poe's French descendants with the body and its relation to the external world is also more open than Poe's, and that too made those French poets of the surrealist movement as attractive to the disaffected poets of the post-World War II era as their interest in language had made them to Eliot and Pound much earlier. But upon this attraction there enters a new emphasis already alluded to, that of Eastern mysticism. Eliot had succumbed to Eastern thought for a while, studying Sanskrit formally for two years at Harvard. (Traces of that interest linger as late as the *Quartets*.) If Emerson had found Eastern thought congenial to his intellectually refined transcendentalism, Whitman likewise saw in it possibilities for an expansion of consciousness to inform perhaps his expansions of poetic form. Eastern thought was not a new discovery to the American poet in the 1950s. It was, however, now advanced as an alternative to the Christian foundations Eliot had come to rest upon beyond the surrealist influence, an alternative to those Western foundations upon which most of the Fugitive-Agrarians built. The devotion to Western tradition in their thought is really the point at issue in Rexroth's demagogic reference to Naziism ("the Fugitives were pure Aryans").

We suggested earlier that symbol refined out of Poe through Baudelaire into the surrealist movement proper became opaque, rather than transparent as it is to Dante. The effect of the shift is to close that outer world upon the poet; nature itself is seen increasingly as contributing to his isolation, even if it contributes to his imagery in more naturalistic ways than one finds in Poe. That is the limitation in the movement that concerns Eliot when he concludes that Valéry is the dead end of the movement. But with the revived influence of Eastern thought upon surrealist techniques, the poet seems allowed to have his cake and eat it too, with curious effects upon the resulting poetry. It is worth introducing a comment from Miss O'Connor at this point concerning the new American poets' new interest in the East. Her remark reflects her position and it allows us a perspective upon that influence. She observes, in reviewing Suzuki's *Zen and Japanese Culture* for the *Bulletin*, that Zen "is non-conceptual, non-purposive, and non-historical, and therefore admirably suited to be exploited by the non-thinker and pseudo-artist." If we apply the remark to our argument here, Zen can be seen as dispelling the dilemma the new poets encountered in the opaque symbols of surrealism. It yields a San Francisco fog in our poetry, but a fog from which the spectre of Poe has not been successfully expelled, any more than Hart Crane was able to expel it in his dank "Tunnel" under Brooklyn Bridge.

We might observe that Poe as *poeté maudit* did not find the city a suitable correlative to his own tortured, prophetic vision of the abyss to which Baudelaire gave local habitation and a name, his beloved Paris. For one thing, Poe's concern for the sole self turns him to the house and room, where Baudelaire's is a more generously agonized concern. The "hypocrite lecteur" is his brother many times multiplied, the city a collection of many rooms of selves. Poe could not see such possibilities in Boston when he was there, though Eliot was to do so—in his "Preludes," for instance. Poe's grotesquery, distilled from the eighteenth-century Sublime of Edmund Burke by those fires of determinism which removed most traces of the transcendent in eighteenth and nineteenth-century thought, becomes the ghost of despair haunting the twentieth century's Unreal City. But it is a ghost not sufficiently exorcised by Zen Buddhism, though Allen Ginsberg makes the attempt, as if he might shout life into that vague specter of isolation, J. Alfred Prufrock. (*Howl* is a response as directly to Prufrock, I should say, as to *The Waste Land*.)

We may recall Baudelaire's remark that all men have an "invincible taste for prostitution," which is the source of our "horror of solitude." The poet, he says, is different, since he wants to be alone, but then this is only "prostituting . . . in a special way." But one might better understand that special way of the poet as incest with the self, Narcissus being a kindly figure of that perversion. And Ginsberg does appear rather like Baudelaire's poet-prostitute. Yet he is more violent, for he attempts to rape the world, not waiting to be solicited. In spite of the complaint that the literary establishment prevents him, he has an appeal to a large audience grown up in the climate of mass eroticism which has moved in upon society after World War II. *Howl* had a phenomenal sale to a world in which love had been made worldly by such debauchery as obliterates the person through orgies of feeling spent in humanity's name. (The closeness of *Hair* to *Deep Throat* is obscured by one's assumption of righteousness in defending *Hair*.) There occurred a general rape of sentiment through the multitude of social and political causes which were justified by the pronouncement of a general guilt. We created for ourselves thereby a secularized version of Original Sin, allowing collectivist submergence of personal responsibility. Sin secularized has led to our fulfilling Unamuno's prophecy that in our century people would die in the streets of sentimentality. We have seen both the literal fulfillment of that prophecy and the metaphorical one, Donne's old metaphysical conceit for the sexual act having been acted out on stage and in the streets. We can *die* by love if not live by it in a way which even Enoch Emery can be made to feel, though indeed he may have been born knowing that way, like Miss O'Connor's Bible salesman.

In the interests of the obliteration of the self, a submergence in emotional movements, Ginsberg rises as the new poet of sentimentality, replacing Joyce Kilmer. (An interesting hybrid between Kilmer and Ginsberg is that poet of the confused popular spirit, Rod McKuen.) Born of surrealist visions, Ginsberg's surface disguise (abandoned metrics) does not conceal a likeness in him to that late nineteenth-century poetry of the bathetic which addresses itself (in our illustration) to God on behalf of trees. But that was a kind of sentimentality against which surrealism itself evolved in protest. Ginsberg's yoking of the concrete world to abstract concepts shocks by its dislocation. "The blond nose of truth" seems profound, but the object of such manipulation is rather to exorcise awareness than to arrive at truth, a truth that turns us to the reality of *being*. It boggles the mind, as does "Trees." Still it is not automatic writing, though it attempts to move in that direction through disjointed paradox. (We should not, of course, overlook that species of automatic writing which the rigidity of metrics allows. Most popular poetry at the turn of the century was such, leading Pound to declare the first Herculean labor in poetry's stalls to be the overthrowing of the pentameter line.)

There follows from Ginsberg's poetic strategy his interest in those mysteries of oneness to be found in Zen, through which one presumably moves toward a silence beyond the uses of language. What we actually find in his poetry, however, is that Ginsberg moves in an opposite direction: wordy repetitions, progressively louder, through which the shocking collocation becomes dulled to an incantation. ("Repeat the word 'table' twenty times over," says Polanyi, "and it becomes a mere empty sound." Or we may do the same with a phrase, or even an idea.) Ginsberg too, as Eliot says of Poe, has "the feeling for the incantatory element in poetry, of that which may, in the most nearly literal sense be called 'the magic of verse'." It is fakiry, Ginsberg encouraged by his guru-ship to suppose that any word that has passed through him onto paper is by its earlier presence in him—its medium—thereby certified poetry. Not automatic writing, but inspired Eastern holy writ, the instrument of the obliteration of awareness.[2]

If the intellect can play games with irony and paradox to reserve its commitment from the world, as some of Eliot's followers were accused of doing, the emotions imitating sensation can also pretend high poetry, a music without words. Once more we have a

---

2. Frost's description of Karma as "the only nothing that is something" is more witty than convincing of its ultimate revelation. As preparation for revelation it may be quite otherwise. Dom Aelred's *Zen Catholicism*, reviewed by Miss O'Connor in the *Bulletin*, suggests Zen as a preliminary to the revelation of our existence in God, with affinities in its exercises to the mystical offices described by St. John of the Cross, by the author of *The Cloud of Unknowing*, and even by St. Thomas. "To dispose oneself to look directly at reality is . . . what Zen is all about." In a passage scored by Miss O'Connor in the text and paraphrased in her review, Aelred says: "Once more there is unanimity among those qualified to instruct us: the Buddhist 'emptiness,' the Zen 'nomind,' the 'void' of St. John of the Cross, the 'cloud of unknowing,' are various descriptions of the same prerequisite: to see things in their 'suchness'— above all, to bring the mind into contract with the ultimate Source of all things—one must keep one's own thoughts out of the way."

version of form without substance, a manifestation of that old enemy, gnosticism, whose goal Voegelin reminds us is to gain power over being (*esse*). We are not surprised then to find Miss O'Connor's reservations extended to the San Francisco School. She remarks, in her review of *Zen and Japanese Culture*, the significant difference in the engagement of the world as reflected in the deaths of Christ and Buddha: "Christ, vertical in agony against the cross, the Buddha contentedly falling asleep on his couch." But we remember too that for the academic form of noncommitment to the world such as one may find in the writer of the writing schools, she has reservations as well. She must have had Iowa in mind when she said: "Unfortunately, there is a kind of writing that can be taught; it is the kind you then have to teach people not to read." The remark is in response to a question about the teaching of writing, published in *Four Quarters*, January 1961. She adds: "This does not mean that writing courses are not valuable, but that their value is limited to doing a few things which will help the student with talent to a greater critical awareness." The explosion of writing courses and programs since Miss O'Connor's comment has enveloped the world beyond the academy, its fallout reaching deep into the community. Innumerable courses and classes available from ghetto to evening classes for the townsfolk, most funded by Federal government and built upon the assumption that social and psychological values of "self-expression" are inevitable. But the "student of talent," for whom Miss O'Connor is concerned, still appears as rare a creature as Miss O'Connor found him to be.

CHAPTER XXIX

ADOLESCENT DOMINATION
OF ADULT SENILITY

Flannery O'Connor was a student at a small college deep in Georgia, about to set out for Iowa, when Eliot was coming to the conclusion that Poe's assault upon the kingdom of beauty had reached its dead end in Valéry. The cartoons she was drawing of and for the local community of scholars seem hardly directed toward beauty, though they show that already her eye is on the disparity between reality and what we make of reality. For the 1945 annual, *Spectrum*, she did the end papers: bedraggled coeds amid the chaos of new campus construction, stepping in rain-filled holes, as they are run off the sidewalks and even up trees by the smart ranks of WAVES in uniforms, the WAVES followed by a mangy, broken-tailed hound as her last word. She is included in the yearbook as editor of the *Corinthian*, the student quarterly whose purpose is to "search out and to encourage any talent in writing the students may have." Her senior picture is accompanied by the information that she has an "A.B. Social Science," and she appears in the collective pictures of the "International Relations Club," a club concerned with the United Nations, with "special emphasis on China and Russia." Membership in that club requires "a 'B' overall average" and "superior work in social science." She is also a member of the "Town Girl's Club" whose purpose is to "encourage cooperation and sociability between local girls and dormitory students."

The cartoons born of all this "extra-curricular" activity show her observing with amusement the antics of her peers and superiors. A sharp-nosed waif of a coed is telling another horror, "This place will never amount to anything until they get a Student Committee on Faculty Relations." A neater version of the same spokesman, with one hipped-fist and a finger under the nose of a fat town girl is explaining daylight saving time as any abstractionist might: "you don't have to get a rooster . . . all you have to do is set your clock back." A librarian is being asked, "Do you have any books the faculty doesn't particularly recommend?" Miss O'Connor is already close to that point of observation from which she speaks much later in reviewing Sister Medelva's *Conversations with Cassandra*. In the book are recorded conversations with children "who make wise comments on life, art, and the world in general." "These children," says Miss O'Connor in her *Bulletin* review, "are very hard to take." In her cartoons she was at any rate discovering a direction the poet might take: rather than the lyrical indulgence of the self, one might look with a dramatic eye upon lyrical self-indulgence, seeing it in contrast to a larger encompassing reality. In the deflation of self-importance that such a position makes inevitable, a confidence in one's own awareness of the larger reality makes comedy possible. Otherwise, a sense of futility and despair must draw the observer back into self entrapment, either into lamenting the insignificance of the self with that pathos which moves toward sentimentality, the direction so largely taken by the literature of the antihero; or in final defense, into a bitter destructive irony which plays the illusion of self-importance against the meaninglessness of existence. But neither Kafka's drift nor Thomas Hardy's is appealing to Miss O'Connor. The principal reason for the direction she takes is suggested by the fact that she was also a member of the Newman Club at Georgia State College for Women, otherwise called GSC or "Jessieville." She is Catholic, born and bred.

One wonders, seeing the position of intellectual advantage Eliot held at the end of World War II, that he could not also champion that old possibility for the poet in his own dilemma. Years before he had recognized a futility in these matters that with himself he too much discussed, too much explained, most particularly the impasse of language with reality. In that impasse his confidence in the word was shaken, and he had long since turned to the Word. Still he will predict for the poet only that

> the extreme awareness of and concern for language which we find in Valéry is something which must ultimately break down, owing to the increased strain against which the human mind and nerves will rebel; just as, it may be maintained, the indefinite elaboration of scientific discovery and invention, and of political and social machinery, may reach a point at which there will be an irresistible revulsion of humanity and a readiness to accept the most primitive hardships rather than carry any longer the burden of modern civilization.[1]

The role played in the 1960's by "Student Committees on Faculty and Government Relations" bears Eliot's prophecy out, and with an accompanying barbarism as an alternative in poetry. But adolescent domination of adult senility does not appear to be a wise solution, at least not to Miss O'Connor. Among those books not "particularly recommended" by the faculty to which she turned was the *Summa Theologie* and Maritain's *Art and Scholasticism*. Maritain's book is one Eliot had every reason to be familiar with. He had known Maritain's work for a long time, translating some of it himself for publication in the *Criterion*. Nor need one risk the hubris of future prophecy in observing the metaphysical justification of the arts by Maritain in *Art and Scholasticism*, a work which attempts a careful account of the relation of art to life, out of St. Thomas and on grounds to which Eliot is firmly committed. The work analyzes the present state of the arts as well, in passages heavily scored by Miss O'Connor. And that crusty monk of art, Eric Gill, is also professing and practicing Maritain's arguments, both Gill and his work well known to Eliot.

Maritain's book proved crucial to Flannery O'Connor in her concern for establishing clearly in her own mind the role of the artist in relation to reality, to the Church, and to an audience. It

---

1. Werner Heisenberg, in *Physics and Beyond*, makes a similar observation, seeing the direction modern physics is bent upon, where it will make its own metaphysics of abstractions toward what Maritain calls a mathematical heaven. Physics, says Heisenberg, is attempting "to construct the elementary particles, and with them the world, from alternatives in the same way as Plato tried to construct his regular bodies, and the world, from triangles. . . . It calls for thought of such abstraction as has never been used before, at least not in physics . . . We cannot exclude the possibility that after some time the themes of science and technology will be exhausted, that a younger generation will be tired of our rationalistic and pragmatic attitude."

treats the abiding problems of belief in relation to expressions of belief. It echoes the formalist concerns of poets like Eliot and Ransom, Davidson, Tate, who were anxious to distinguish between legitimate sentiment in art's relation to life and sentimentality as a distortion of both life and art. She repeatedly echoes Maritain. Art is a "habit" of the artist, to which she adds that "habits have to be rooted deep in the whole personality." In opposing the general supposition "that art must be utilitarian, that it must do something, rather than be something," she takes her stand firmly on the principles elucidated by Maritain, not with Poe. The fiction writer "writes neither for everybody, nor for the special few, but for the good of what he is writing." St. Thomas Aquinas "says that art does not require rectitude of the appetite, that it is wholly concerned with the good of that which is made. He says that a work of art is a good in itself, and this is a truth that the modern world has largely forgotten." But art is not a recreation to fill one's leisure; it is a calling, through which God is glorified to the extent of one's gift, for "what is good in itself glorifies God because it reflects God. The artist has his hands full and does his duty if he attends to his art. He can safely leave evangelizing to the evangelists." He is required to pay "strict attention to the order, proportion, and radiance" of what he is making. "The basis of art is truth, both in matter and in mode. . . . St. Thomas said that the artist is concerned with the good of that which is made."

It is from Maritain and Thomas that she advances her argument for the importance of reason to art. "If you have read the very vocal writers from San Francisco, you may have got the impression that the first thing you must do in order to be an artist is to loose yourself from the bonds of reason, and thereafter, anything that rolls off the top of your head will be of great value. Anyone's unrestrained feelings are considered worth listening to because they are unrestrained and because they are feelings. St. Thomas called art 'reason in making'. . . . a very cold and very beautiful definition . . . ." And in an allusion to Question I, Article 9 of the *Summa*, in which St. Thomas is arguing the uses of metaphor, she says, "The Lord doesn't speak to the novelist as he did to his servant Moses, mouth to mouth. He speaks to him as he did to those two com-

plainers, Aaron and Aaron's sister, Mary [Miriam]: through
dreams and visions, in fits and starts, and by all the lesser ways of
the imagination."² And a few pages later she has recourse to Question I, Article 10, in which Thomas quotes St. Gregory: "St.
Gregory wrote that every time the sacred text described a fact, it
reveals a mystery. This is what the fiction writer, on his lesser level,
hopes to do."³

What is necessary, in the intricacy of these ideas, is to disentangle the relationships of truth, beauty, and the artist's responsibility for those concepts to God and to his fellow man. To see the
relationships is to see how Miss O'Connor can at once eschew the
evangelical as a concern of fiction and at the same time hold beauty
as responsible to the good and the true, to which one is recalled by
art. Maritain makes a distinction between the responsibilities of
prudence and art, a passage carefully marked by Miss O'Connor:
"Prudence operates for the good of the worker, *ad bonum operantis*,
art operates for the good of the work done, *ad bonum operis*, and
everything which diverts it from that end adulterates and
diminishes it." "Art . . . remains outside the line of human conduct,
with an end, rules, and values, which are not those of man, but of
the work to be produced." Its primary focus is not upon salvation.
The danger to the artist lies in a failure to distinguish between
prudence and art and to see the restricted intellectual focus within
which art operates. For because the artist is, as Maritain says,
"first a man and then an artist," battles inevitably rage within him
between the claims of prudence and art. "The artist will . . . require
a measure of heroism to keep always in the direct line of action and
not sacrifice his immortal substance to the devouring idol in his

2. QI, Art. 9, Reply Obj. 2: "The ray of divine revelation is not extinguished by the sensible
imagery wherewith it is veiled, as Dionysius says: and its truth so far remains that it does not
allow the minds of those to whom the revelation has been made, to rest in the likenesses, but
raises them to the knowledge of intelligible truths; and through those to whom the revelation
has been made others also may receive instruction in these matters. Hence those things that
are taught metaphorically in one part of Scripture, in other parts are taught more openly.
The very hiding of truth in figures is useful for the exercise of thoughtful minds, and as a
defense against the ridicule of the unbelievers, according to the words, Give not that which is
holy to dogs (Matt. vii, 6)." Miss O'Connor marks the passage in her text.

3. QI, Art. 10: "Gregory says: Holy Scripture by the manner of its speech transcends every
science, because in one and the same sentence, while it describes a fact, it reveals a mystery."

soul. The truth is that such conflicts can be abolished only on condition that a deep humility make the artist as it were unconscious of his art, or if the all-powerful unction of wisdom imbue everything in him with the repose and peace of love." Otherwise, pride elevates him to god as artist. Even though he has put aside the claims of false prudence, he may lose his life when he thinks he has saved it.

In the difficulty Maritain describes here, lies the importance to Miss O'Connor of Maritain's statement out of St. Thomas that art is a habit. But it is a habit to be cultivated with the full powers of the intellect. That will allow one to avoid, perhaps, the fundamental error an artist may make who, in seeing himself as creator analogous to God, succumbs through pride to an idolatry of the creature in his soul to which he gives form. That is the danger Eric Gill speaks to, out of Maritain's book also, when he says, in *Beauty Looks After Herself*, "in so far as the idea of the artist is not formed by what he sees but is formative of what he makes, so and so far he is actually a creator—the father indeed of his works. But it is only in respect of beauty that man is a creator. The search for truth is not invention; it is the search for what *is*. . . . Only the beautiful is an end in itself and only beauty is ever new." Since truth is the necessary subject of art, and since the true is derived from good, in the creation of beauty an intrinsic good is celebrated. Art is man's active adornment of *what is* with beauty, in Gill's argument.

It is in the context of this argument that one better appreciates the limited praise Miss O'Connor makes of naturalistic art, for in so far as the naturalist builds upon what he sees as true of the good, whether or not he recognize or acknowledge the cause of the true and good, his art will reflect the glory of God. Good art, like good criticism "will reflect a Catholic view of reality," regardless of the artist, only provided that he have the habit of art, which makes the good of the made object the paramount concern. This does not mean that the artist is made a whole man by his devotion. "Without philosophy," says Gill, "man cannot know *what* he makes, without religion he cannot know *why*." "If the artist," says Maritain, "were to take for the final end of his activity, that is to say for beatitude, the end of his art or the beauty of his work, he would be, purely and simply, an idolater." He will have arrogated to himself the power of beatification. "It is therefore absolutely necessary for the artist, *qua* man, to work for something other than his work, something better beloved. God is infinitely more lovable than Art." "Do not," Maritain advises, "make the absurd attempt to sever in yourself the artist and the Christian. They are one, if you really *are* a Christian, and if your art is not isolated from your soul by some aesthetic system. But apply only the artist in you to the work in hand; precisely because they are one, the work will be as wholly of the one as of the other." That advice is clearly in Miss O'Connor's mind as she speaks of her art in relation to her Christianity from the time she first begins to speak of it. In his essay on "Art and Prudence," which draws heavily from Maritain's book, Eric Gill says the kernel of the matter: "Beauty is the splendour of Being. The beautiful thing is that which being seen pleases." And when we add Maritain's remark that "A Christian work would have the artist, as artist, free," we have the primal sources of Miss O'Connor's aesthetics spelled out. She does not simply echo them; she examines them as rigorously as her intellectual powers allow and she finds them valid. As a Christian—a realist of distances—she celebrates the beauty of Being; she is a prophet recalling us through art to known but forgotten truths, most particularly to the glory of creation.

If her approach to the beautiful is through the indirection of exaggeration, that is the concession her art must make to the almost blind and almost deaf. It is an approach which recognizes just how alien her Christian vision is, not only to the popular spirit of the age, but to the intellectual movers of that popular spirit, among whom the philosophers and poets are so entangled with the disparity between the world and its word that art and thought seem inaccessible. If comedy seems her conspicuous mode, its essence is tragedy when fully revealed—tragedy hardly available to the modern given the drift of thought for the past two hundred years. She recognizes that difficulty in Erich Heller's *Disinherited Mind: Essays in Modern German Literature and Thought*, underlining the following passage, in which Heller suggests that Goethe does not distinguish between the claims of art and of prudence:

> For tragedy presupposes the belief in an external order of things which is indeed incomplete without the conformity of the human soul, but would be still more defective without the soul's freedom to violate it. Yet Faust's

dilemma is different. His 'two souls' are merely the one soul divided in itself because it knows of no independent external reality to which it is related as a free agent. . . . Faust . . . is . . . torn between the belief in a world to which, strive as he may, he has no access whatever, and the belief in himself as the creator of his own world. Thus the spiritual extremes of his existence are not guilt and atonement, but despair and titanism. It is a situation unresolvable in tragedy.

One measures a distance traveled from Marlowe's Faustus, whose science is Baconian magic as Lewis suggests, to Goethe's Faust whose science is the magic of the imagination. In both there is a concern for power, but it is a power whose ultimate source and proper end have been lost. Nietzsche says "when Power becometh gracious and steppeth down into visibleness—Beauty I call such stepping down." Beauty is power incarnate, which expresses the matter as it may be acceptable to the Thomist position. But when power becomes the agent of man's mind, rather than seen as stepping down through the mystery of grace in the Incarnation, it becomes the substitute for spirit to intramundane thought. That is how Matthew Arnold, among others, is led to see poetry as the new religion to serve man along with the new science. The Dynamo supercedes the Virgin as the focusing symbol in which two worlds meet: the self in its control of nature replaces the Incarnation. Or perhaps the Dynamo functions through surrogate symbols in art: Mr. Shiftlet's '28 or '29 Ford or Haze's Essex or Mrs. Turpin's very modern pig parlor. Through the attractions of beauty, we worship the idols we make, whether social systems or modern conveniences. But in doing so we have made sacrifice of our "immortal substance" through the illusion that we are the cause of being from which shines forth the beauty that captivates us.

CHAPTER XXX

WORDS: RECOVERED STONES FROM THE RUBBLE

We may return now to our old theme, the old battle of language's entanglement of the mind, in a conclusion to our present volume and as prelude to our next. In that next volume we shall see the battle as it becomes a part of the American scene through the Puritan mind. That words seem to keep Being at a distance from mind is a rather spectacular part of the war waged in words in the first quarter of the present century, a war signalled by the concerns of phenomenology, psychology, and the multiplicity of new ologies of our age. Such complexities draw our thought across the ocean to Europe. The triumph of Existentialism as philosophy and of the Absurd as literature seems to mark a victory of mind over language, though at frightful expense to what Thomas or Voegelin calls *being*. In the wake of that triumph, a linguistics of a scientific cast moves in to command the field, though the multiplicity of faction in linguistic "science" reminds one of the splintering that seems inevitable to any radical reformation, whether in science, politics, or religion. The continuity of life in language, with language seen as the "home" into which being enters as guest in Heidegger's thought, seems less acceptable as a serious concern to the new science of words than is a reduction of the architecture of language toward blueprint, under the lingering shadow of Baconian philosophy.

The eagerness of potential "directors" for practical uses of such blueprints is enough to give one cautious pause. For whether it

is the advertiser or the social manipulator—in a capitalist or
socialist context—what seems missing is that reverence for being
which alone protects man from his inclination to an abuse of being,
most particularly of his own. We have considered Flannery O'Connor's use of the comic in calling us back to known but forgotten
things; her humor is used to awaken in us that hunger for being
which the natural world most immediately satisfies as it draws us
into a community of being. She speaks to a world drifting in conglomerate units of power at the mercy of the gnostic directors of
power. But even humor itself is at the moment invaded by those
powers. The first International Symposium on Humor meeting at
the University of Wales has just disbanded, after considering with a
deadly seriousness such matters as "intrahumans," "arousal fluc-
tuations," and "stimulus discrepancies." The paper in which these
terms appeared concluded that if one can't think, one won't
get the joke. To the question "Do you have any observations on the
possibility that certain persons are inherently teaseworthy?" an
American psychologist responded, "No, I believe the matter is entirely situational, teasewise." Peter DeVries makes comic use of
such absurdity to a diminishing audience. Waugh, Swift, and
Orwell combined are needed to save our sanity from the attack of
such pseudo-minds. But one cannot be content merely to laugh at
or laugh off what such a symposium aims at. One professor, studying Little League baseball jokes, is anxiously serious because
"When we learn why people laugh, we will be able to use humorous
material as a tool," presumably to control and direct society.

In the confusions of his spiritual crisis, the poet may feel
himself even more justified in his defense against the world, his
withdrawal from it into a private bubble, as he observes the
deliberate diminution of meaning in the exterior world by the new
science and new thought. For both science and philosophy seem in
conspiracy against the created world. The poet, given the apparent
entrapment of consciousness by language, especially as he uses it to
keep himself inviolate from the world, finds himself progressively
isolated from those other worlds of separate consciousnesses that
revolve like ancient women gathering fuel in vacant lots. This, says
Marcel, in *Presence and Immortality*, "is the hour of tragic pes-

simism." Remembering such an experience, "I seem to have suddenly rejected or torn up the veil of comforting illusions which masked life for me and by means of which I strove to provide for myself an endurable existence. . . . this fascinating power seems to press into its service my desire for rectitude, my desire not to let myself be deluded." Out of such moments there may emerge "a philosophy of heroism," such for instance as Hemingway builds his art upon, "but it can lead either to suicide or to the surrender of a being who breaks down when pitted against a scandalous world." That is the moment when one, as Eliot finds himself forced to do, wipes his hand across his mouth and laughs at the prospect of revolving unconstellated worlds.

But Eliot rallies at last to the poet's responsibility to purify the dialect of the tribe, in the interest of the continuity of spirit in the world. The realization that the created world is God's creature is the most significant change in Eliot between his "Preludes" and "Ash-Wednesday." At that crossroads where the reduction of meaning—the alienation of being from consciousness—by science and philosophy crosses the collapse of one's defenses against a meaningless outer world there occurs the particular crisis to the mind which Eliot dramatized for us in *The Waste Land.* And from that point he begins to purify his own conception of the poet's role, seeing in language not only its roots in the past, but its present power of communicating "presence," the Word in the desert. It is a realization which St. Thomas has in mind, in a passage from the *Summa,* underlined by Miss O'Connor:

> Natural things are midway between the knowledge of God and our knowledge: for we receive knowledge from natural things, of which God is the cause by His knowledge. Hence, just as natural things that can be known by us are prior to our knowledge, and are its measure, so the knowledge of God is prior to them, and is their measure; as, for instance, a house is midway between the knowledge of the builder who made it, and the knowledge of the one who gathers his knowledge of the house from the house already built.

And similarly, in a passage she also marked:

> . . . the knowledge of God is to all creatures what the knowledge of the artificer is to things made by art. Now the knowledge of the artificer is the cause of the things made by his art from the fact that the artificer works through his intellect. Hence the form in the intellect must be the principle of action . . . .

And the instrument of the artificer's action, if he is the poet, is words, inherited and common to intellect however much abused. The necessity of metaphor to the intellect, in its approach to God through the created world, is crucial to Thomas, as it is to Miss O'Connor. It became so to Eliot. For in that new dispensation of insight after his tragic despair, image no longer appears opaque symbol, as in Mallarmé, but a window. Eliot too became a realist of distances. The decayed house of the self which is cause of despair in "Gerontion," has yet its stairs to be negotiated with difficulty in "Ash-Wednesday" toward a prospect upon the garden of the world. Marcel in *Presence and Reality*, engages the point of Eliot's intense concern, enunciated at the opening of *The Waste Land*, the relation of *memory* to *desire*. We note that, in "Ash-Wednesday," Eliot has moved beyond that concern to confront the entanglement of hope and despair. "Desire," says Marcel, "is by definition egocentric: it tends toward possession. . . . Hope implies a prophetic assurance which is really its armor and which prevents the being from beaking down, internally first of all; but it also prevents him from giving up . . . ."

Eliot is interested in language more as Marcel is than as Heidegger. Marcel, in his late introduction to the *Metaphysical Journal* (1950), a work under way at the time of Eliot's own early struggle, says he eschewed and eschews that approach to the problem of language which leads Heidegger to a creation of neologisms, a renovation of language to attract being into "presence." "Heidegger thought it necessary to create an almost entirely new terminology. . . . [Neologisms] always seem to be barbarous. . . . May we not say that the mode of current expression, by the very fact that it has served a multitude of different cases, has become charged with a genuine potential that neologisms lack? . . . The mind . . . does not feel that it is 'at home'; it feels that it is 'nowhere,' as in certain modern edifices that lack a past and a style."

One may put the matter closer to our earlier concern for community by saying that Marcel appreciates the sense of an historical "presence" in words. It is not merely a matter of feeling oneself somewhere rather than nowhere; it is a matter of feeling that the mind is in a "somewhere" *and* accompanied by other minds in a community of anticipation. While Marcel declares himself "inclined to accept Heidegger's formula to the effect that language is the domicile (*das Haus*) of being," the house one builds is of stones from the rubble of the past, carrying in them the felt presence of a gathering of mind out of time, accompanied by a feeling of our being at home, even though we may be hungry for that larger country of our hope. The "fatal consequences of the spirit of abstraction" says Marcel, is that such a spirit "leads to fanaticism, in other words, to idolatry, . . . invariably accompanied by a paroxysm of objectivization [this applied equally to Marxist materialism and Nazi racism]." One suspects that Marcel here touches upon a cause of Heidegger's momentary alignment with Hitler, the effect of his objectivization in the attempt to approach being in which the living presence of being is denied to language as to consciousness, even when there is an expectation of a coming "presence." Marcel surely describes the course one may observe in the development of Noam Chomsky as a political activist of a decidedly fanatical bent, out of his own linquistic concerns. And in Wittgenstein's contributions to logical positivism, through a conception of words as "things" configured to "atomic facts," one similarly finds such "objectivization" in language seen as a picture of reality. Reality is here understood at that level which, for the poet, may allow what Miss O'Connor calls "a great tragic naturalism" from which is excluded the larger mystery of being itself, but the possibility is a chancy one. (It is of parallel interest that, just as Heidegger felt himself misunderstood in the applications of his thought by those who championed it, so does Wittgenstein.)

That exclusion of the larger mystery of being, as we have seen, is the cause of despair in Flannery O'Connor's protagonists from time to time. She seems rather to have intended Mr. Shiftlet as such a character, with the possibility of developing him beyond the confines of his story. (Shiftlet moves into our ken, and then we move on with him at the end.) We see him at a moment in the story which Marcel would recognize, though it is a moment seemingly comic. When he is forced to marry the idiot daughter before the Ordinary, Shiftlet emerges from the courthouse "morose and bitter, as if he had been insulted while someone held him." He insists that the civil ceremony was "just something a woman in an office did, nothing but paper work and blood tests. What do they know about my blood? . . . It didn't satisfy me at all." When Mrs. Crater rejoins that it satisfied the law, Shiftlet says, and spits at the same time, "It's the law that don't satisfy me." Shiftlet's moment of despair, from which he nevertheless recovers with alacrity, seems hardly worthy of remark by Marcel, but it is particularly interesting in the light of Marcel's illustration of his point in relation to Miss O'Connor's concern for the sacramental dimension of life. More seems implied than the comedy of a con man against whom the law may now be invoked. (Shiftlet crosses the state line beyond the law before sundown.) Marcel says that:

> Despair is a hybrid, it is a thought which is in process of becoming a representation; or perhaps it is the other way around. Here the image of the succession of generations, together with the connected ideas of place and function, play a determining role.
>
> As a concrete illustration of this I have only to recall the indescribable gloom which I see emanate from the offices of the notary public. This gloom is . . . worse than that of cemeteries, perhaps because the accumulated dossiers strike us as a ridiculous and sham substitute for perenniality.

The life we would save, if it is to have meaning, seems inextricably bound up with that sense of community that involves the succession of generations and the focus of place, through which being is encountered in its earthly fullness.

That crossroads where our thought crosses the reduction of meaning in the world, thus threatening our collapse, may (as Marcel suggests) lead to the emergence of a heroic philosophy quite other than the one which Eliot labored toward and Miss O'Connor freely inherits. Wallace Stevens, whom we called earlier a disciple of Poe, realizes at such a point that "after one has abandoned a belief in God, poetry is the essence that takes its place as life's redemption." "I ought," Stevens says in a letter," to say that it is a habit of mind with me to be thinking of some substitute for religion. . . . My trouble, and the trouble of a great many people, is the loss of belief in the sort of God in Whom we were all brought up to believe. Humanism would be the natural substitute, but the more I see of humanism—the less I like it." The alternative seems to be to establish, by the action of the imagination, a world to replace the world which now seems "set up in such a way as only to foment in us the temptation to despair." As with Poe, Stevens's procedure is not a radical one with language, not a creation of a new language, but a shifting of the old language. Eliot will come to see the lady in the garden going in Mary's color. Flannery O'Connor will use Mary's blue in crucial but traditional ways. But blue becomes for Stevens the sustaining color of the imagination upon the world, not neologism but sacerdotal heraldry of the mind's kingship over its own version of reality. One of Stevens's difficulties is that he assumes his own spiritual crisis as peculiar to our age, rather than its being what C. S. Lewis might make of Stevens's moment of crisis: the first truly spiritual experience Stevens has had. If one translate our world's *science* and *philosophy* to *empirical knowledge* and *logic*, what we recognize is the ancient dilemma, the old battle between faith and reason, which is everyman's lot within the tensional grounds of being. The substitution Stevens sometimes makes is "an expression of paganism" such as he declares his "Sunday Morning" to be. It is of some interest to recall that he, like Eliot, has second thoughts on "humanism." Had no other prospect opened, Eliot like Stevens might well have settled for paganism over the pseudo-religion, Humanism, which caused some hard feelings between him and his old teacher Irving Babbitt in the late 1920s.

It is nevertheless true that at the time Stevens was a young man we as a civilization had largely exhausted what Voegelin calls our residual religious sentiment, a sentiment whose symbols had become progressively opaque; the sense of community in and through those symbols was atrophied. The battle among the poets, and within individual poets, became largely whether one must create a new language or recover the old, a battle in which, for instance, Pound stands between Stevens and Eliot. But the poet's problem with words is not his only. One might suggest that our century's thinkers have been most concerned with the nature of religious experience, however it manifest itself and whatever they choose to call it. And perhaps C. S. Lewis's remarks in *Miracles*, to which we have already alluded, sheds some light on that problem, in so far as the problem may be said characteristic of the modern age rather than of the particular mind in any age. "Many a man, brought up in the glib profession of some shallow form of Christianity, who comes, through reading Astronomy, to realise for the first time how majestically indifferent most reality is to man, and who perhaps abandons his religion on that account, may at that moment be having his first genuinely religious experience." It is such a moment that haunts the imaginative writer most acutely in these past two centuries, breaking out in a variety of reaction— Melville, Hardy, Stephen Crane, Poe, Twain, Shelley, Arnold, Joyce. To see in what way the starting point is similar to, though the final witness of their work is quite different from, that of Hopkins or Eliot or Flannery O'Connor, we take a sentence from François Mauriac, a writer whom Miss O'Connor is particularly drawn to:

> I hear quite clearly someone calling me an old fool . . . who does not realize he is only a fleck of mold on the surface of an insignificant planet in this cosmos comprising quintillions of solar systems. . . . Yes, but that ocean of galaxies is conceived in the mind of a single being.

Mauriac's is the premise of Poe's *Eureka* at first blush, but finally it is something quite different—a part of a general affirmation of the meaning of the world, and of an inner presence in creation which gives the lie to such a reduction of being as Mauriac paraphrases. The burden of Mauriac's memoirs, as of his fiction, is an affirmation of Christ, and of a spirit in man larger than intellect. For Mauriac stands opposed, as does Maritain, to that denigration of existence which reduces even the spirit of man to a function of reason exercised upon process.

Lewis, in his "Preface" to D. E. Harding's *Hierarchy of Heaven and Earth*, gives a summary history such as Poe's:

> At the outset, the universe appears packed with will, intelligence, life and positive qualities; every tree is a nymph and every planet a god. Man himself is akin to the gods. The advance of knowledge gradually empties this rich and genial universe: first of its gods, then of its colours, smells, sounds and tastes, finally of solidity itself as solidity was originally imagined. As these items are taken from the world, they are transferred to the subjective side of the account: classified as our sensations, thoughts, images or emotions. The Subject becomes gorged, inflated, at the expense of the Object. But the matter does not end here. The same method which has emptied the world now proceeds to empty ourselves. The masters of the method soon announce that we were just as mistaken

(and mistaken in much the same way) when we attributed 'souls,' or 'selves' or 'minds' to human organisms, as when we attributed Dryads to the trees. . . . We, who have personified all other things, turn out to be ourselves mere personifications. . . . And thus we arrive at a result uncommonly like zero. While we were reducing the world to almost nothing we deceived ourselves with the fancy that all its lost qualities were being kept safe (if in a somewhat humbled condition) as 'things in our own mind.' Apparently we had no mind of the sort required. The Subject is as empty as the Object. Almost nobody has been making linguistic mistakes about almost nothing. By and large, this is the only thing that has ever happened.

When the self is discovered empty, after having emptied the world, there occurs a stronger temptation than ever to make of art a substitute reality—to propose art as a substantial object to which the restless homeless consciousness migrates as its center. In a passage in Maritain's *Creative Intuition and Poetry*, a chapter called "Poetry and Beauty," Flannery O'Connor marks a section which relates to this inclination. Maritain is concerned with a distortion of art in the modern world. It is an effect to which Poe contributes in championing the poet's and the poem's autonomous existence, though Maritain is concerned with the shift as it has origin in Rousseau. It develops, Maritain says,

> from creative emotion as intentional means or vehicle of poetic knowledge, to brute or merely subjective emotion as sheer psychological phenomenon becomes the matter of the work and a *thing* to be expressed by it. As a result modern literature, in its lower moments, has been invaded by a double disease: emotionalism (that is, search after the creativity of the intellect and the purity of poetic intuition) and, at the same time, shallow intellectualism (that is, falling back on the empty contrivances of a merely constructive or critical reason estranged from the heart, to make up for the weakening of intuitive reason and of the intellect's genuine creativity stirred by creative emotion and poetic experience).

The terms fall thick and fast here, but one knows with what care Maritain will have prepared for their use. His "creative emotion as intentional means" is quite contrary to Poe's clinical interest in the "emotional effect" of the poem. It is, indeed, rather close to Wordsworth's concern with emotion expressed in the "Preface" to *Lyrical Ballads* and by his practice. And it is worth mentioning here also that Maritain in his book makes a particular attack upon Eliot's ideas on the problem as expressed in "The Perfect Critic" and "Tradition and the Individual Talent," the latter Eliot's attack on Wordsworth. (Maritain's argument with Eliot is presented in a long footnote in his chapter on the "Nature of Poetic Knowledge.") The attack on that shallow intellectualism which falls back "on the empty contrivances of a merely constructive or critical reason estranged from the heart" is very much an attack upon the early Eliot. Eliot rejects Wordsworth and announces, in his review of *Ulysses,* that myth will now replace the old narrative method in the attempt to deal with the chaos of the modern world, a manipulative attitude toward myth very like that of Heilbroner's which we rejected earlier.[1]

What is lost, Maritain's argument indicates, is that quality of poetic intuition and appreciation of creative emotion as an intentional means of poetic knowledge, through which art finds its proper anchor in a creation larger than the privately-made world, that world on which "merely subjective emotion as sheer psychological phenomenon [has] become the matter of the work and a *thing* to be expressed by it." While it does not follow that Maritain would approve the art of Hawthorne, it is evident that he would, in the same way Miss O'Connor does, approve the center of Hawthorne's concern, for Hawthorne is not content with "a merely constructive or critical reason estranged from the heart." Hawthorne's allegory does not function as Eliot's early conception of myth would have it—as a device for structural control. It is a device, learned of Bunyan and Spenser, through which he attempts that reunification of sensibility which would bring intellect and heart into accord—which would, in our earlier terms, reunite faith and reason to their proper roles. For all his reservation about and opposition to the Puritan's deep suspicion of art, Hawthorne seems also to sense a danger to the artist which Maritain speaks of as a temptation to make art an idol, a substitute reality in which the artist presides as high priest.

---

1. We must remember, of course, that Eliot puts those early arguments behind him, as he moves on to "Ash-Wednesday," after which he speaks very highly of Wordsworth, and his late essay on Poe is a repudiation of a position very close to the one he held at least up to *The Waste Land.* I have written at some length on this shift in Eliot, in *T. S. Eliot: an Essay on the American Magus, The Reflective Journey Toward Order* and in *Eliot's Reflective Journey to the Garden.*

Maritain's "creative emotion" is a means, an instrument of the creative act, such as one finds poets testifying to. Wordsworth sees poetry as emotion recollected in tranquility. It involves a giving up of the self to the work analogous to the reader's giving of himself, the experience of which to the poet or reader is sometimes described as being "caught up." Hopkins's approach to the world through poetry, most particularly his concern for "inscape," is an attempt to be "caught up" in a vision of the created world through words. As such, it is an attempt upon experience analogous to the rapture or ecstasy in the moment of vision as represented by St. Thomas, an imaginative (as opposed to intellectual) seeing. Since, says St. Thomas, "prophecy implies a certain obscurity and remoteness from truth," we therefore "term 'prophets' . . . those who see in imaginative visions." And the poet's images are a necessity out of our remoteness from the distant reality. It is in the light of this argument that Miss O'Connor sees herself in a prophetic role as artist, in the exercise of which she presents epiphanies intended to catch one up in vision, in an experience of mystery such as that she attempts in dramatizing a descent of the Holy Ghost through the medium of a water stain on Asbury's ceiling.

Maritain does insist, and Flannery O'Connor joins the position, that a poem is an end in itself inasmuch as it is art. But it is not an instrument to be deliberately turned upon the reader by the poet for its effect, as a mirror of subjective or brute emotion. The poet, she says, must pay "strict attention to order, proportion, and radiance" in what he is making. Those aspects of the made thing make possible its beauty. And here she echoes once more St. Thomas's argument that beauty lies in the perfection, brilliance, and proportion of the made art, each of which relates ultimately to a supreme degree of those qualities in God. This means most particularly that art may not rest its end in any pragmatic or evangelical justification. Its *being* is its end. But in so far as it realizes those qualities, it must of necessity reflect upon the supreme Beauty which is God, regardless of the poet's limitations of vision—regardless of whether he is a "realist of distances" or not. For the poet may, "by his responsibility to the things he sees, . . . transcend the limitations of his narrow vision," as Miss O'Connor says. That is why the fiction writer's chief responsibility is "neither for everybody, nor for the special few, but for the good of what he is writing." She makes that point emphatically in a passage which underlines the premises of her aesthetics:

> St. Thomas Aquinas says that art does not require rectitude of the appetite, that it is wholly concerned with the good of that which is made. He says that a work of art is a good in itself, and this is a truth that the modern world has largely forgotten. . . . we want to make something that will have some utilitarian value. Yet what is good in itself glorifies God because it reflects God. The artist has his hands full and does his duty if he attends to his art. He can safely leave evangelizing to the evangelists.

It should be noted that the remarks are made to a Catholic, a baptized, audience in defense of the artist's freedom as established by St. Thomas. But it should also be noted that her defense does not set aside from art its inevitable glorification of God in that degree to which it approaches perfection as art.

A point of concern here is that, while the poem (or story) is a made thing, when its matter becomes subjective brute emotion as sheer psychological phenomenon, art has abandoned its proper role to assume the role of science. Though Poe is often cited as one of the fathers of the New Criticism, one of whose general tenets is the independence of the work of art from entrapment in the world, he is no purist in the position. He cannot resist using the poem as an instrument upon the psyche of the reader. Poe the anti-pragmatist, the violently anti-utilitarian, nevertheless understands the poem to be an instrument in the control of the poet, and for him the poet becomes to a considerable degree an empiricist of the psychological. His singlemindedness in questions of art embraces more than one contradiction. He is not only one of the fathers of the New Criticism; he is also, as we have observed, one of the fathers of the new science of propaganda, in which power is manipulated by the new directors of the popular spirit of the moment. Poe's discussions of the poem and of its effect upon the reader have the aura of the clinical about them. The uses of art he advocates make the poem's reflection of the complexity of beauty hazardous to one's spiritual health (though it carries no warning on its label) in so far as it sacrifices the primary concerns for order, proportion, and radiance to the clinical and analytic.

This change in the conception of the nature and role of art which Maritain describes is concomitant with the rise of the specialized sciences, and especially with the emergence of psychology as a "science." Novels are considered in her day, Miss O'Connor says, "to be entirely concerned with the social or economic or psychological forces that they will by necessity exhibit." But those are forces in the general flow of experience which have been separated out and raised to the level of science to the exclusion of others. The result, however intricate, when followed as restrictive laws of art, will make art an abstraction in which the resonance, the "radiance," of full being is neither sounded nor reflected. One finds, after all, a Freudian reading of *Oedipus the King* far more limited than the experience of the play itself. And the difference between two highly stylized murder mysteries, Sophocles' play and "Murders in the Rue Morgue," is the difference between the terrors of being on the one hand and a mere horror submitted to ratiocination on the other. To avoid that double disease of modern literature as reflected in its lower moments, Miss O'Connor attempts in her work a use of what Maritain calls "creative emotion," to reflect in her art that mystery upon which all existence depends, even those works imaginatively projected by the individual mind. That is why she repeatedly insists upon the creative imagination as a gift, requiring a humility in the artist in its presence. She counters the second disease, pure ratiocination, with revelation, opposing the shallow intellectualism that uses "the empty contrivances of a merely constructive or critical reason estranged from the heart"—whether it be a prose poem like *Eureka* or an imposed mythology in the manner Eliot ascribes to *Ulysses*.

We remarked earlier that Voegelin has come to see history, not as lineal events in time only, but more inclusively as revelation within the individual soul. It is, he says, "a mystery in process of revelation." His critique of the modernist revolt against that truth finds an "imaginative game of liberation" which "derives its momentum from an intensely experienced alienation and an equally intense revolt against it." Such, we have seen, has been the recourse of artists like Poe. And that modernist address to the uses of the imagination which he represents, whether manifested in art or the social realm, becomes the antagonistic spirit that Flannery O'Connor's characters engage in themselves and in others. For she shares, in this respect, Voegelin's view of the modern world, though the authority of her vision is not only history but the Church. Fiction is for her, as history for Voegelin, "a mystery in process of revelation" through the agency of the individual writer, gifted by grace. But where Voegelin uses the diverse and scattered record of man to locate a timeless presence in the flux of history through the mode of philosophy, she uses most specifically the Bible, through a mode of fiction depending quietly upon analogy and metaphor to point toward revelation. Most particularly, she casts the moment of our own history with which she deals against that moment of history between the final verses of Malachi in the Old Testament and the Crucifixion in the New. The principal figure for her dramatic purposes is John the Baptist and, as we said in the beginning, the central meaning is located by Malachi's and John's words:

> Behold I will send you Elijah the prophet before the coming of the great and dreadful day of the Lord: And he shall turn the heart of the fathers to the children, and the heart of the children to their fathers, lest I come and smite the earth with a curse.
>
> I indeed baptize you with water unto repentence: but he that cometh after me is mightier than I. . . . he shall baptize you with the Holy Ghost, and with fire.

In her copy of St. Augustine's account of his wrestling with the mystery of such Scripture, *The Confessions,* Miss O'Connor has scored a passage in which Augustine records his discovery of depths in Scripture, with the aid of an intellect few would account shallow:

> For now what things, sounding strangely in the Scripture, were wont to offend me, having heard divers of them expounded satisfactorily, I referred to the depth of the mysteries, and its authority appeared to me the more venerable, and more worthy of religious credence, in that, while it lay open to all to read, it reserved the majesty of its mysteries within its profounder meaning, stooping to all in the great plainness of its words and lowliness of its style, yet calling forth the intensest application of such as are not light of heart; that so it might receive all in its open bosom, and through narrow passages waft over towards Thee some few, yet many more than if it stood not aloft on such a height of authority, nor drew multitudes within its bosom by its holy lowliness.

If Chaucer found it necessary to defend his broad style by reference to the style of Scripture, it did not prevent his being misread in subsequent ages as a rather artless naturalist or an anthologizer of other men's art. Not many but would now grant him to be highly sophisticated and original, and even Dryden's complaint of Chaucer's limping numbers has been rather thoroughly demonstrated as a blindness in that highly perceptive seventeenth-century critic. We need not be surprised at the lesser attempts upon Miss O'Connor's fiction which, though generally granting her a respectable artistry, see her work still as either a naturalistic reflection of a segment of the South, or as a satire upon those figures who are in fact her heroes. Those Raybers among the critics however may yet come to see that in her work she is striving for an art that will answer the complicated necessity of the Scriptures as described here by Augustine.

What is required is that one be neither shallow intellecually nor averse to an application of that intellect such as is not light of heart. First appearances turn out to mask deeper realities, the deeper mysteries which are her true subject. She may often sound like Poe: "Detail has to be controlled by some overall purpose and every detail has to be put to work for you." But the overall purpose of her own fiction is not simply an effect upon the reader, but a particular homage. Her overall purpose is "founded on the theological truths of Faith, but particularly on three of them which are basic— the Fall, the Redemption, and the Judgment." She is "preoccupied" with "belief and with death and grace and the devil." Such are the mysteries that determine her larger purposes in the practice of art as art:

> St. Gregory wrote that every time the sacred text describes a fact, it reveals a mystery. This is what the fiction writer, on his lesser level, hopes to do. The danger for the writer who is spurred by the religious view of the world is that he will consider this to be two operations instead of one. He will try to enshrine the mystery without the fact, and there will follow a further set of separations which are inimical to art. Judgment will be separated from vision, nature from grace, and reason from imagination.

What she thus describes is the temptation to the artist of

Manicheanism, a danger she attempts always to guard against in her own work. It is the action of what Maritain would call a shallow intellectualism. She reflects that shallow species of thought in characters like Julian and Hulga, one of the revelations she attempts through her fiction.

> Those who believe that art proceeds from a healthy, and not from a diseased faculty of the mind will take what the good fiction writer shows them as revelation, not of what we ought to be but of what we are at a given time and under given circumstances; that is, it is limited revelation but revelation nevertheless.

Miss O'Connor says in effect that she has no necessity to write some *Eureka*: it is there before her, in the Bible and in St. Thomas, but in the world immediately about her also. Her fiction speaks to the possibilities of being and of a country toward which, in our universal experience, we long even when we cannot name it. If we make of it the Land of *Nada*, that shall be our inheritance, though even that country is not our own invention, the last prop to our pride thus denied. For Nothingness has no meaning separate from Somethingness, whereby it gains a certain existence. The choice is the choice between falling away from that Somethingness, which is God, toward the Devil, or falling toward God. The "country" we choose is our own, though we are not its cause. And so we are homesick for it. That at any rate is what Miss O'Connor believes, more deeply than figuratively, for as she says of her long experience as artist,

> I have found . . . from reading my own writing, that my subject in fiction is the action of grace in territory held largely by the devil.

From the beginning she has known this. Margaret Fuller, that vaporous transcendentalist (so the story goes) confided in Thomas Carlyle that she was now prepared to accept the universe. "By God, Madam, you'd better!" he is supposed to have replied. That is the apparent allusion Miss O'Connor makes with her dry humor to a reporter visiting her in Andalusia one afternoon, an envoy from the courts of the popular spirit of the age sent to fetch back news about her remarkable artistry,

I can accept the universe as it is—I don't have to make up my own sense of values. I can apply to a judgment higher than my own. I'm not limited to what I personally feel or think. And I have a sense of personal responsibility; I believe that a person is always valuable and always responsible.

INDEX